# A Systematic Theology of Love

## VOLUME 1:
## GOD AND CREATION

### THOMAS JAY OORD

© 2026 SacraSage Press & Thomas Jay Oord

SacraSagePress.com & ThomasJayOord.com

*All rights reserved. No part of this book may be reproduced in any form without written consent of the author or SacraSage Press. SacraSage Press provides resources that promote wisdom aligned with sacred perspectives. All rights reserved.*

*Interior Design: Nicole Sturk*
*Cover Design: Thomas Jay Oord and Nicole Sturk*

*Print (Hardback): 978-1-968136-50-5*
*Print (Paperback): 978-1-968136-43-7*
*Electronic: 978-1-968136-44-4*

*Printed in the United States of America*

---

*Library of Congress Cataloguing-in-Publication Data*

*A Systematic Theology of Love: God and Creation, Vol. 1 / Thomas Jay Oord*

# Dedications

This book is dedicated to three dead theologians and three living ones.

In the 1970s, Daniel Day Williams and Mildred Bangs Wynkoop wrote complementary theologies. Wynkoop's book, *A Theology of Love*, introduced an important perspective that differed from the legalism in the holiness communities in which I was raised. She followed John Wesley in understanding holiness through the lens of love, and she was influenced by Williams.

Daniel Day Williams's book, *The Spirit and the Forms of Love*, provided conceptual tools for me as a graduate student. He drew explicitly from process theology in thinking through love's philosophical and theological implications. Both his book and Wynkoop's influenced me in my early academic journeys in theology.

John B. Cobb, Jr., is the third dead theologian to whom I dedicate this book. John was one of my professors at Claremont Graduate University and a major source of encouragement for decades after I completed my doctoral degree. John said that the D. D. Williams book was the closest that process thought had to a systematic theology. I remember thinking, "Maybe someday I'll write a systematic theology of love."

The three living theologians to whom I dedicate this are Louise Kelley, Michael Lodahl, and Amos Yong.

Amos Yong and I are roughly the same age, and he's been a constant source of encouragement, beginning in graduate school. I have little doubt that my emphasis upon God as spirit owes a great deal to Amos's arguments.

Michael Lodahl is my biological cousin, and he has been a frequent conversation partner and trail-blazer in Wesleyan-Process thought. I'm confident my forays into creative theological reflection have been influenced positively by Michael.

Finally, Louise Kelley is my mother. She wouldn't call herself a theologian, but her influence has shaped me profoundly in the ways of love. As I finished writing this book, I expected her life to finish soon too. I see a deep continuity between my drive to live a life of love and my mother's energy, creativity, and earnestness. Thanks, Momma!

# Table of Contents

*Dedications* — v

**THE PRIMACY OF LOVE** — 1
  1. First of Its Kind — 3
  2. Reasons to Believe — 35

**THE UNIVERSAL SPIRIT OF LOVE** — 59
  3. A Loving God — 61
  4. Universal, Incorporeal Spirit — 87
  5. Becoming Spirit — 111
  6. God Is Not Omnipotent — 137
  7. Amipotent Spirit — 163
  8. The Spirit is A Relational Person Who Feels — 185
  9. One, Everlasting, All-Knowing Spirit — 211
  10. The Proper Role of Mystery — 237

**CREATION AND PROVIDENCE** — 255
  11. *Creatio Ex Nihilo* and Other Creation Theories — 257
  12. Ever Creator — 291
  13. Amipotent Providence — 319
  14. Solving the Problem of Evil — 357
  15. The Problem of Good, Miracles, and God's Will — 387

*Conclusion to Volume One* — 427
*About the Author* — 429
*Acknowledgements* — 431
*Index* — 435

# The Primacy of Love

CHAPTER ONE

# First of Its Kind

## THE BIG IDEAS

- This is the first book with the title, *A Systematic Theology of Love*.
- Given the prominence of love in religion and especially Christianity, it should surprise us that no one has written a book with the title *A Systematic Theology of Love*.
- We might imagine various reasons love has not been the orienting concern of systematic theologians.
- We have many good reasons to prioritize love when doing systematic theology.
- An adequate systematic theology of love ought to have a clear and concise definition of love.
- Love is best defined as acting intentionally, in relational response to God and others, to promote overall well-being.
- Open and Relational Theology is a natural home for a systematic theology of love.
- Open and Relational Theology says God engages in giving-and-receiving relationships with creation and moves temporally into an open future.
- This book is the first in a three-volume systematic theology that puts love at the center.

This is the first book with the title, *A Systematic Theology of Love*. I say this having scoured libraries and databases searching for books with this title. I found none. Someone may have written such a book, of course, and not published it. Or a book with this name may have been lost to history. Others may have undertaken the task described in the title but chosen a different name. Perhaps I will discover a book titled *A Systematic Theology of Love*, but to my knowledge, this is the first.[1]

Given that Christians claim love should be central to understanding God, the lack of love-based systematic theologies should surprise us. A strong case could be made for love as the central theme of Christianity.[2] The Apostle John declares, "God *is* love," and the themes of love emerge over and over in the Bible.[3] It would seem appropriate, if not expected, that Christian systematic theologians would make love their orienting concern.[4]

Christians aren't the only people of faith who care about love. Jews, Muslims, Bahai, Sikhs, Hindus, and theists from other traditions champion love in their own ways.[5] While scholars in these traditions are less likely to write systematic theologies, no one in those traditions, to my knowledge, has written a book called "A Systematic Theology of Love."

Among the books that come close is Gerald Bray's *God is Love: A Biblical and Systematic Theology*. The subtitle implies a systematic view of God and love that aligns with scripture.[6] But in reality, Bray's book isn't systematically consistent.

---

[1] This chapter is dedicated to Stephen G. Post. Stephen's encouragement of me both personally and in the "ways and power" of love have been inspirational.

[2] I explore in detail what Christian scriptures say about love in *Pluriform Love: An Open and Relational Theology of Well-Being* (Grasmere, ID: SacraSage, 2022).

[3] Although not called a systematic theology of love, the first Christian systematic theology, written by Origen, does a better job than most in emphasizing love. See *On First Principles*, John Behr, ed. and trans. (Oxford: Oxford University Press, 2018).

[4] Mildred Bangs Wynkoop is a good example of a theologian who offers a powerful theology of love but doesn't claim to offer a systematic theology. See *A Theology of Love* (Kansas City, MO: Beacon Hill, 1972).

[5] See, for instance, Henry Bayman, *The Secret of Islam* (Berkeley, CA: North Atlantic, 2003); Adis Duderija, *Essays on Critical-Progressive Islam* (Independently published); Shai Held, *Judaism is About Love* (New York: Farrar, Straus, Giroux, 2024); A. Helwa, *Secrets of Divine Love* (Naulit, 2020); Valerie Kaur, *See No Stranger* (One World, 2021); Swami Padmanabha, *Evolution in Divine Love* (Inword Publishers, 2025).

[6] The Christian Bible has many forms, versions, and translations. The ancient manuscripts from which the books that comprise contemporary Bibles derive are pluriform and fluid. In fact, there is no definitive canon. On this diversity, see Brian Felushko's writings on Substack. See also Lee Martin McDonald, *The Formation of the Biblical Canon: Volume 1 & 2* (London: Bloomsbury Academic, 2025); Jacob L. Wright, *Why the Bible Began* (Cambridge: Cambridge University Press, 2023).

Bray says God is "in control of everything that happens," for instance. But he also says creatures rebel "of their own free will."[7] How can God control everything but creatures rebel freely? Bray says this allegedly loving God permits evil that could have been prevented. But love as we know it prevents preventable evil. And Bray envisions a God who predestined some people for eternal damnation.[8] A truly loving God, by contrast, wants salvation for all.[9] These are a few among other inconsistencies in the Bray's theology.

I mention the inconsistencies in Bray's work to illustrate a difference between systematic theologies and other theological projects.[10] Systematic theologians seek to avoid contradiction and aim for internal coherence. In other words, rational consistency is the nonnegotiable hallmark of systematic theologies. The best of them also align with broad themes of scripture, fit lived experience, and inspire us to promote flourishing.

## Reasons Love Has Not Been Central

Why do systematic theologians rarely afford love preeminence? I've not conducted an official survey to answer this question. But here are my guesses based on my readings and interactions:

### Love Has Many Meanings

In English, "love" has many meanings, and this diversity leads to different languages of love and connotations. For instance, there are significant differences between loving strangers, romantic partners, ice cream, family, God, enemies, and rock-n-roll. And yet "love" is used to describe them all. The meaning of love lacks clarity.

---

[7] Gerald Bray, *God is Love: A Biblical and Systematic Theology* (Nashville, TN: Crossway, 2012), 26.

[8] Ibid., 23.

[9] Ibid., 17.

[10] For diverse ways Christians throughout the centuries have understood Christian love, see Bernard V. Brady, *Christian Love* (Washington, DC: Georgetown University Press, 2003); Carter Lindberg, *Love: A Brief History Through Christianity* (Oxford: Blackwell, 2008); and David P. Polk, *God of Empowering Love* (Anoka, MN: Process Century, 2016).

It's not just that love has multiple meanings in everyday use; love also has multiple meanings in scripture. Biblical writers don't use the Greek and Hebrew words we translate "love" consistently. And some translators consider a variety of biblical words not usually translated "love" as synonyms for the word.[11] Consequently, there are multiple biblical theologies of love, because the scriptural witness is multi-vocal.[12]

We might wonder, for instance, whether biblical writers instruct us to love the world. God "so loved the world," says the Apostle John, and many biblical writers say believers in Christ ought to love one another. But other writers reject love for the world. John's first letter says, "Don't love the world or anything in the world" (1 Jn. 2:15-17). And the writer of 2 Timothy chastises Demas because "he loved the world" (2 Tim. 4:10). So, should we love the world or not? In these cases, the meaning of "love" changes depending on the context.

We find other examples too. Sometimes biblical authors endorse love for oneself (e.g., the second greatest commandment).[13] Or they assume self-love would be natural (e.g., Eph. 5:28). But other times the biblical writers criticize self-love (e.g., 2 Tim. 3:2). So, should we love ourselves or not? We can point to many instances in which biblical writes say God wants us to forgive and love our enemies. But other biblical passages have God saying, "show them no mercy" (Deut. 7:2) and seemingly endorsing violence toward enemies (e.g., Exod. 23:27; 1 Sam. 15:1-3).[14] Does love do violence or not?[15]

---

[11] For instance, Nijay Gupta includes Greek words for desire in his exploration of love as described in scripture. Those words include *zeloo* and *epitheymeo* (*The Affections of Jesus Christ* [Grand Rapids, MI: Eerdmans, 2025], ch. 3). I think Gupta errs in this practice, however. Although desire is a component of love, it is neither love itself, nor a form thereof. He may have sidestepped this error had he clearly defined love at the outset of his book. See my criticisms of love as desire in *Pluriform Love*, chs. 5-6.

[12] Werner Jeanrond puts it well: the "Bible doesn't contain any pure or original passage on love to which we could return for any timeless and unambiguous understanding of love" (*A Theology of Love* [London: T & T Clark, 2010], 40).

[13] Love for oneself seems to be implied in Jesus' second greatest commandment. See Mk. 12:28-34; Mt. 22:36-40; Lk. 10:25-28.

[14] Several biblical scholars offer helpful ways to interpret texts of terror. See, for instance, Eric A. Seibert, *The Violence of Scripture* (Philadelphia: Fortress, 2012).

[15] Jason Tripp explores the question of divine hypocrisy in "Is God a Hypocrite?" in *Amipotence*, vol. 2, Brandon Brown, et. al., eds. (Grasmere, ID: SacraSage, 2025).

We can't solve these conflicting biblical claims by simply examining the Greek or Hebrew words for love. In fact, the word translated "love" in the conflicting New Testament passages above is *agape*.[16] *Agape* has many meanings in the Bible, and those meanings don't always agree with one another. When love has such diverse connotations, theologians will be tempted to choose an orienting concern other than love to anchor their systematic theologies.

If love is to be central in systematic theology, we need to address its meaning.

### Theologians Rarely Define Love Well

A second reason systematic theologians have not taken love as their central theme relates to the first: few theologians define love clearly.[17] Even "those who write best about love," says Jules Toner, "devote very little space to considering what love is."[18] Without a clear and coherent understanding, we can't craft a clear and coherent theology of love.

The few who *do* define it often choose definitions that undermine love's primary meaning in the Bible. Flawed definitions often lead to flawed conclusions. St. Augustine is a perfect example. Although biblical writers mostly use "love" to describe actions that promote abundant life, blessedness, or well-being, Augustine defines love as desire.[19] Countless theologians adopt his mistaken approach.[20]

---

[16] I explore the various Hebrew and Greek words translated "love" in my book *Pluriform Love*. See chapters 3-7.

[17] In his *The Four Loves*, C. S. Lewis explores types of love but never defines love. Jason Lepojarvi notes this omission (*God Is Love but Love Isn't God* [PhD thesis University of Helsinki, 2015], 68).

[18] Jules Toner, *The Experience of Love* (Washington, DC: Corpus Instrumentorum, 1968), 8. Edward Collins Vacek also complains that scholars fail to define love well. See *Love, Human and Divine* (Washington, DC: Georgetown University Press, 1994), 34.

[19] "Love is a kind of craving," says Augustine (*Eighty-Three Different Questions*, 35, 2). Augustine lays out what this means theologically in *Teaching Christianity* (De Doctrina Christiana), John E. Rotelle, ed., Edmund Hill, trans. (Hyde Park, NY: New City, 1996). See my evaluation of this in *Pluriform Love*, chs. 5-6.

[20] Many have criticized Augustine for his views of sex. My criticism of Augustine's focus on desire extends far beyond his particular issues with sex. For a sustained theological criticism of Augustine, see Werner Jeanrond, *A Theology of Love*.

In *Teaching Christianity*, Augustine poses a question: "How does [God] love us?" Because Augustine defines love as desire, he thinks God desires by either enjoying or using us. If God "enjoys us," says Augustine, "it means he is in need of some good of ours, which nobody in his right mind could possibly say."[21] We have nothing of value, according to Augustine, because God already has all values eternally. So, God can't love/desire us in the sense of needing us.

Because he defines love as desire, Augustine says God loves by desiring what's valuable.[22] Being wise, God desires only the *most* valuable. This means, says Augustine, God only desires/loves Godself. The world and its creatures aren't of highest value, so God doesn't love them, at least not for their own sakes.

The only way God can love/desire us, according to Augustine, is to use us. "He doesn't enjoy us, but makes use of us," he says. "Because if he neither enjoys us nor makes use of us, I can't find any way in which he can love us."[23] Augustine realizes his definition of love leads to a problem. Because he believes God must be entirely self-sufficient, Augustine says God "doesn't make use of us, either." At least not "in the same way as we use things." He explains: "Our making use of things is directed to the end of enjoying God's goodness." But "God's making use of us is directed to his goodness."[24] In short, God only loves Godself. By defining love as desire, therefore, Augustine is forced to conclude God doesn't love the world.

Still more problems arise for Augustine because of his unhelpful definition of love. According to him, creatures love properly when they desire what's most valuable. The most valuable is God. Consequently, proper desire doesn't involve love for neighbors, oneself, or creation, at least not for their own sakes.[25] We shouldn't *actually* love one another.

---

[21] Augustine, *Teaching Christianity*, Book 1, paragraph 31.

[22] Hannah Arendt explores this in *Love and Saint Augustine* (Chicago: University of Chicago Press, 1996).

[23] Ibid., Book 1, paragraph 32.

[24] Ibid.

[25] See my full discussion of Augustine's failed theology of love in *Pluriform Love* (Grasmere, ID: SacraSage, 2022), chs. 5-6.

Augustine tries to explain this contorted view: "Every human being, precisely as human, is to be loved on God's account," he asserts. "All things are to be loved for God's sake."[26] We should "take pity on each other," he says, "so that we may all enjoy [God], not one another."[27] This means that "when you enjoy a human being," says Augustine, "you are really enjoying God rather than the human being."[28]

With Augustine's definition of love as desire, it's difficult to make sense of even the most basic Christian themes about love for neighbors or love for ourselves. And given the confusion this definition of love has generated, it might be tempting to say defining love at all must be misguided venture. Love is *inherently* indefinable, says one argument, because words can't capture love's profundity. Consequently, only fools would attempt a systematic theology of love.

I agree with those who say words can't capture love *fully*. But words can't capture God fully either, and yet theologians write tome after tome. No definition captures all relevant truths of any subject, person, or activity. But words convey *some* truth, and they're necessary for written communication. An adequate systematic theology of love, therefore, must define love clearly and use it consistently, while admitting that words can't capture love fully.[29]

Systematic theologians often fail to define love and define it well.

## Systems Can't Capture Love

A third possible reason theologians don't write systematic theologies of love pertains to skepticism of grand belief systems. Although good systematic theologies attempt to account for God and reality, some

---

[26] Augustine, *Teaching Christianity*, Book 1, paragraph 28.

[27] Ibid., Book 1, paragraph 29.

[28] Ibid., Book 1, paragraph 37.

[29] I offer a sustained defense of my definition of love in *Pluriform Love*, ch 2 and *Defining Love* (Grand Rapids, MI: Brazos, 2010). I explore scientific dimensions of love in *The Science of Love* (Philadelphia: Templeton, 2005) and *The Altruism Reader* (Philadelphia: Templeton, 2012). On the science of love, see Stephen Post, et. al., *Altruism and Altruistic Love* (Oxford: Oxford University Press, 2001).

theologians give the impression their systems capture *all* truths. An all-inclusive system would be the Final Word.

By contrast, I doubt that any systematic theology can address everything. Some of the largest and most comprehensive—e. g., the work of Thomas Aquinas or Karl Barth—fail to account for crucial ideas. God and the world are bigger than any system. Theologians who realize systems of thought can't capture love fully, therefore, may choose not to write systematic theologies of love.

My systematic theology also isn't the final word. But systematic theologies that account for what we think important, and those that strive to be rationally consistent, should be preferred to theologies that ignore major issues. Organized knowledge is preferable to chaos. I agree with Alfred North Whitehead that "an attack upon systematic thought is treason to civilization."[30]

In this work, I aim to orient ideas about God and life systematically around love, while seeking existential fit. I seek harmony of understanding and adequacy to life.[31] But this book will likely overlook important topics, and I don't aim to provide all truth for all time. Other readers and scholars will need to add to, revise, and enhance my proposals.

Although this systematic theology isn't the full and final statement on God, love, and existence, I aim for it to be better than unsystematized theologies and those that ignore the primacy of love.

### *Love is Considered Sentimental and Not Intellectually Rigorous*

A fourth possible reason systematic theologians have not taken love as their orienting concern pertains to its perceived "fluffiness." Love isn't capable of intellectual investigation, goes this argument, because it isn't intellectually rigorous. In fact, some who champion love for theology do so to express anti-intellectualism.

Blaise Pascal gets at this issue with his pithy line, "The heart has reasons that reason knows not of." Pascal isn't opposed to reason, but he believes it can't account for crucial aspects of life. He thinks reason

---

[30] Alfred North Whitehead, *Adventures of Ideas* (New York: Free Press, 1967), 162.

[31] Alfred North Whitehead uses this nice phrase in *Science and the Modern World* (New York: Free Press, 1967), 76.

comes second to experience, for "it is the heart which experiences God," says Pascal, "and not the reason."[32] I like his emphasis upon experience, and I admit that propositional statements fail to account for love. But I don't think we should pit experience *against* reason and intellectual sophistication.

To counter the criticism that love must be fluffy, squishy, and opposed to reason, I won't shirk from intellectual sophistication or academic rigor in this systematic theology of love. While I write in accessible prose, I consult and cite leading theological, biblical, philosophical, and scientific scholars. I also draw from poets, artists, and activists. I suspect most readers will be surprised at logical consistency.

Other theologians may not regard love as systematic theology's central motif because they consider the term too sentimental, permissive, or choosing the status quo. Stanley Hauerwas has these worries, for instance. He says love is too sentimental to do the hard work needed for building character and making difficult decisions. "The ethics of love is often but a cover for what is fundamentally an assertion of ethical relativism," says Hauerwas. It is "an ethics of tolerance that makes kindness the central virtue" and "becomes a justification for our own arbitrary desires and likes." "Great immoralities are not the result of evil intentions," he says, "but a love gone crazy with its attempt to encompass all mankind within its purview."[33]

Hauerwas rightly criticizes simplistic and misguided views of love. And he rightly emphasizes the importance of communities and practices for living well. But Hauerwas's attacks on weak versions of love-based theology don't address the strong versions. Some of the greatest examples of those who champion love—including Jesus of Nazareth—do so in the face of persecution, self-doubt, the pressures of empire, and death.[34] They're not excessively sentimental or permissive. Hauerwas seems unaware that a theology that defines love well can account for

---

[32] *Pascal's Pensees* (New York: E.P. Dutton, 1958), 277-78.

[33] Stanley Hauerwas, *Vision and Virtue* (Notre Dame, IN: Notre Dame University Press, 1981), 124-25.

[34] Many New Testament scholars point to love as the heart of Jesus' and New Testament ethics. See examples of such scholars in the previous footnotes.

community, hard decisions, practices, counter-cultural activism, and virtues.

As I see it, love takes sides, and it always sides with the work of promoting flourishing, justice, beauty, and liberation.[35] To do this, it sometimes disrupts and resists; it also comforts and heals. I agree with Maria Pilar Aquino who says, "Love takes up the desires of the poor and oppressed and commits itself to the transformation of human misery."[36]

I also reject Hauerwas's claim that love goes "crazy" when it attempts to encompass all within its purview. Instead, I believe love has the common good in mind, although its focus is typically upon particular contexts and communities. Because love seeks overall well-being, it doesn't advance the good of a few at the expense of the whole. That's unjust. It joins Hauerwas in stressing the importance of developing virtue, inculcating practices, and growing in community.[37] But it seeks to promote *overall* well-being.

Love, as I understand it, consults head and heart, brain and body, knowledge and vital piety.

### *Overlooked Voices and Lived Experiences*

Theological systems sometimes exclude or marginalize the voices of women, people of color, the disabled, the queer community, and the other-than-human creatures on the planet.[38] Systematic theologians may claim to address our most pressing questions, but they sometimes ignore scientific advances, the role of emotions, climate change, gender and sexuality issues, the arts, political oppression, and so on. Theologians sometimes rely upon abstract claims that oppose the

---

[35] Gustavo Gutierrez argues similarly in *The God of Life* (Maryknoll, NY: Orbis, 1991).

[36] Maria Pilar Aquino, *Our Cry for Life* (Maryknoll, NY: Orbis, 1994), 157.

[37] Guided by the work of Pitirim Sorokin, Jeffrey Wattles expresses the importance of developing a loving character in *Living in Truth, Beauty, and Goodness* (Eugene, OR: Cascade, 2016). Sorokin's primary book of love is *The Ways and Power of Love*, Stephen G. Post, intro. (Philadelphia: Templeton, 2002 [1954]).

[38] Brandon Ambrosino expresses his disdain for theological systems that excluded him as a gay man. See his book, *Is It God's Will?* (New York: Morehouse, 2025).

practical living of diverse people.³⁹ A fifth reason no one has written a book called *A Systematic Theology of Love,* I suspect, would be that some people assume systematic theologies, by definition, neglect marginalized voices and lived experience.

In his post-colonial theology, Steve Watson argues that systematic theologies easily become univocal. They purport to have arrived at complete insights into the nature of God and existence. Systematic theologians can act as if they've "seen Revelation's heavenly city in full come down to earth through brilliant thinking or synthesis," says Watson, "usually that of a single, white man."⁴⁰ And this means, says Marcella Althaus-Reid, "discourses on power have been systemized, classified, and organized in Systematic Theology."⁴¹ Systematic theology reflects Eurocentric, patriarchal, and institutional assumptions.⁴² I believe we should take this critique seriously.

I recently asked an artificial intelligence (AI) engine to list the current thirty best-selling systematic theologies. The list generated was telling. Every top-selling systematic theology was written by a white man in the Reformed Evangelical tradition. All thirty! Systematic theologies have been written by women and people of color, of course, but they aren't top-sellers.⁴³ This lack of diversity gives the impression that

---

³⁹ Alex Forrester addresses this issue and argues for the power of amipotent love. See "The Supremacist Soteriology of Divine Omnipotence," in *Amipotence, vol. 2,* Brandon Brown, et. al., eds. (Grasmere, ID: SacraSage, 2025).

⁴⁰ See Steve Watson, *All Flesh Shalom: A Post-Colonial, Open and Relational Constructive Theology of Major Themes in the Gospels* (Doctoral Dissertation at Northwind Theological Seminary, 2025).

⁴¹ Marcella Althaus-Reid, *Indecent Theology* (London: Routledge, 2000), 23.

⁴² James Cone makes this kind of argument in *A Black Theology of Liberation* (Maryknoll, NY: Orbis, 1990). Among those who criticize theologians for being patriarchal, see Elizabeth A. Johnson, *She Who Is* (New York: Crossroad, 1992); Catherine Keller, *From a Broken Web* (Boston: Beacon, 1986); Rosemary Radford Ruether, *Sexism and God-Talk* (Boston: Beacon, 1983); Marjorie Hewitt Suchocki, *God, Christ, Church* (New York: Crossroad, 1982); Delores S. Williams, *Sisters in the Wilderness* (Maryknoll, NY: Orbis, 1993).

⁴³ See Katherine Sonderegger's work for an example of a systematic theology written by a woman (*Systematic Theology, Volume 1* [Minneapolis: Fortress, 2015]). See James Evans for a systematic theology written by a person of color (*We Have Been Believers,* 2nd ed., [Minneapolis: Fortress, 2012]). Amos Yong explores systematic theology for global Christianity in *Renewing Christian Theology* (Waco, TX: Baylor University Press, 2014). So does Veli-Matti Kärkkäinen, *Global Introductions to Systematic Theology,* 3 vols. (Grand Rapids, MI: Baker Academic, 2002–2004).

writing systematic theologies must be an activity reserved for white men benefitting from systems of power.

I'm also a white man. But I write this systematic theology influenced by many voices, including voices very different from my own. In doing so, I agree with Watson that we should be "engaging the widest variety of thinking and experience to build open-ended reflections that express our best current thinking on all things in light of God."[44] Drawing from wide varieties of experience strengthens a systematic theology of love. I'm also taking a very different perspective from the dominant Reformed tradition.

Because I'm limited, I'm sure I'll fail to include some voices. And my own experiences will undoubtedly blind me to some experiences of others. I don't have a God's-eye perspective, nor am I entirely neutral or objective. For my errors and oversights, I apologize in advance.

I also encourage criticism and suggestions from voices I've missed.[45] I join with Watson in "dialogically and ongoingly imagining and re-imagining Revelation's heavenly city in the context of our current experience of earth."[46] And I join Hanna Reichel by reading liberation and systematic theologies together, rather than assume they must be kept separate.[47]

To prioritize love, this systematic theology of love draws from many sources, and I hope to do them justice.

### Sovereignty Trumps Love

The sixth and most important reason that, until now, no book has been titled *A Systematic Theology of Love* has to do with the lure of other orienting themes. Although I've not done a survey, I suspect the most common theme orienting systematic theologies has been sovereignty.

---

[44] Watson, *All Flesh Shalom*.

[45] Along these lines, I'm grateful for the criticism of my friend Karen Baker-Fletcher. For instance, see her essay, "A Womanist Liberative Response to Oord's Theology of Amipotence," in *Amipotence*, vol. 2, Brandon Brown, et. al., eds. (Grasmere, ID: SacraSage, 2025).

[46] Watson, *All Flesh Shalom*.

[47] Hanna Reichel articulates this well in *After Method* (Louisville, KY: Westminster John Knox, 2023).

*First of Its Kind*                                                                                                     

It dominates the thirty best-selling systematic theologies I mentioned. For many theologians, organizing theology around a particular view of divine power seems more alluring than organizing around love.

Starting with omnipotence can lead to a high degree of internal consistency. But omnipotence-based theologies fail to fit lived experience or scripture well. Most systematic theologies privileging omnipotence explain away creaturely freedom, for instance, and can't solve the problem of evil. They at least implicitly endorse the status quo and institutional ways of thinking. Omnipotence-oriented theologies portray God's love in ways that bear little resemblance to love as we know it.

The idea of sovereignty closely aligns with the centrality of divine glory in Reformed systematic theologies. The Westminster Confession claims the chief purpose of humans is to glorify God, and all creation gives deity glory.[48] If giving glory ought to be our primary purpose, glory would be a reasonable central theme for the systematic theologian. And glory-based theology should, theoretically, inspire worship.

A close look at theologies oriented around glory, however, reveals that most build from a prior commitment to sovereignty.[49] When clashes between sovereignty and love arise, the inconsistencies are often brushed aside with appeals to mystery: "God's ways are not our ways." And what counts as divine love doesn't correspond with what we normally consider loving. "In glory, God predestines some for hell," theologians might say, for instance. "All glory to God!" It's hard to make sense of such reasoning and difficult to worship a deity who sends people to eternal conscious torment.

The attraction to sovereignty was evident early in Christianity, and we can see the priority of omnipotence in the major Christian creeds.[50] The Apostle's Creed, which is probably the most cited, starts with claims about an almighty God (*omnipotens*) but never mentions love.

---

[48] See *The Westminster Confession of Faith*, in *The Creeds of Christendom*, rev. ed., Philip Schaff, ed., vol. 3 (Grand Rapids, MI: Baker Academic, 2007), 596–673.

[49] For an example of a systematic theology that claims to center on divine glory but is actually more concerned with omnipotence, see Millard J. Erickson, *Christian Theology*, 2nd ed. (Grand Rapids, MI: Baker, 1998).

[50] On this, see Rita Nakashima Brock and Rebecca Ann Parker, *Saving Paradise* (Boston: Beacon, 2008).

Christian alignment with empire, among other things, tempted early theologians to imagine deity as an authoritarian emperor rather than a loving nurturer.[51]

Systematic theologies that come closest to taking love as their orienting concern typically use the language of grace.[52] The words for love are found far more frequently in scripture than words for grace, but I suspect theologians appeal to grace because "love" has so many meanings. To their credit, grace-oriented theologies typically fit lived experience better than sovereignty-oriented ones, and they usually avoid describing love in incomprehensible ways.[53] But most retain the idea of God's omnipotence and essential independence from creation.[54] And many say God punishes now and may punish the unrepentant forever in hell.[55]

Saying God must be omnipotent and essentially independent prevents theologies from answering well the atheist's chief objection: the problem of evil.[56] If grace explains the way of an all-powerful deity, why doesn't God gracefully prevent genuine evil? If love for creation remains primary, why doesn't God necessarily and everlastingly love creatures? If grace is always God's way, why would this deity punish or send some to eternal conscious torment? Failing to answer questions like these well sabotages systematic theologies, whether oriented around sovereignty, glory, grace, or something else.

It's time to put love first in systematic theology.

---

[51] John Sanders has written eloquently about authoritative vs. nurturant views of God. See his book *Embracing Prodigals* (Eugene, OR: Cascade, 2020). See also Chris Hanson, *Open and Relational Parenting* (Grasmere, ID: SacraSage, 2025).

[52] For examples of grace-centered theologies, see Barry L. Callen, *God as Loving Grace* (Nappanee IN: Evangel, 1996); H. Ray Dunning, *Grace, Faith, and Holiness* (Kansas City, MO: Beacon Hill, 1988).

[53] Randy Maddox offers an especially helpful theology of grace, and he draws from the work of John Wesley. See *Responsible Grace* (Nashville, TN: Abingdon, 1994).

[54] Stanley Grenz chooses the eschatological community as the integrative motif in his systematic theology. Happily, this choice leads him to say God is relational. Unhappily, Grenz retains traditional views of divine power and independence. See *Theology for the Community of God* (Nashville, TN: Broadman & Holman, 1994), 30.

[55] David Anzalone explores the promise of amipotence in addressing the question of hell in his essay, "Hell and Amipotence," in *Amipotence, vol. 2*, Brandon Brown, et. al., eds. (Grasmere, ID: SacraSage, 2025).

[56] For an example of this, see Kenneth J. Collins, *The Theology of John Wesley* (Nashville, TN: Abingdon, 2007).

## REASONS TO MAKE LOVE CENTRAL

I've addressed possible reasons systematic theologians have not taken love as their orienting concern. But what are the reasons love *should* be primary?

### *Love's Centrality in Scripture*

Jews and Christians find a strong argument in their scriptures for making love central to systematic thinking about God.[57] The most common description of God in the Hebrew-language portion of the Bible is this: "The Lord, the Lord, a God merciful and gracious, slow to anger, and abounding in steadfast love and faithfulness, keeping steadfast love for thousands, forgiving iniquity and transgression and sin . . ."[58] The phrases of this description differ somewhat in various books of the Bible, but their focus remains upon a loving deity.[59]

A good argument can be made that "steadfast love" (*hesed*) is the most common short description of God in the Hebrew Bible. The Psalmist repeatedly says, "the earth is full of the steadfast love of God" (Ps. 33:5) and "the steadfast love of God endures forever" (Ps. 117:2 and elsewhere). Love is so central to the Hebrew Bible's witness that, as Rabbi Shai Held puts it, "Judaism is about love."[60]

---

[57] In addition to other texts on love and scripture cited in this chapter, see the work of Patrick Mitchel, *The Message of Love* (London: Inter-Varsity, 2019).

[58] See Exod. 20:6; 34:6-7; Num. 14:18; Deut. 5:9-10; 7:9; 1 Kings 3:6; 2 Chron. 30:9; Neh. 9:17, 31 Ps. 86:15; 103:8, 17; 106:45; 111:4; 112:4; 145:8; Jer. 30:11; 32:18-19; Lam. 3:32; Dan. 9:4; Joel 2:13; Jon. 4:2; Nah. 1:3. Terence Fretheim argues this point well in *The Suffering of God: An Old Testament Perspective* (Philadelphia: Fortress, 1984), 25. See also Michael J. Chan and Brent A. Strawn, eds., *What Kind of God? Collected Essays of Terence E. Fretheim* (Winona Lake, IN: Eisenbrauns, 2015).

[59] Among the many texts that explore love in the Old Testament, see especially Chan and Strawn, eds., *What Kind of God?*; Terence Fretheim, *The Suffering of God* (Philadelphia: Fortress, 1984); Shai Held, *Judaism is About Love: Recovering the Heart of Jewish Life* (New York: Farrar, Straus and Giroux, 2024); Brad E. Kelle and Stephanie Smith Matthews, eds., *Encountering the God of Love* (Kansas City, MO: Foundery, 2021); Jon D. Levenson, *The Love of God* (Princeton: Princeton, 2016); J. Richard Middleton, *The Liberating Image* (Grand Rapids, MI: Brazos, 2005); Song-Mi Suzie Park, *Love in the Hebrew Bible* (Nashville, TN: Westminster/John Knox, 2023); John Shelby Spong, *The Sins of Scripture* (New York: HarperSanFrancisco, 2005).

[60] Shai Held makes this point in his aptly titled book *Judaism is About Love*.

In the New Testament, the letters of the Apostle John explicitly say, "God is love" (1 Jn. 4:8, 16), and the ensuing discussion suggests we should see this statement as more than metaphorical. In fact, John and other writers say love constitutes the key to knowing God (e.g., 1 Jn. 4:7-8). Love for the world, says Jesus, prompted God to make eternal life available (Jn. 3:16). Deity loves all, and sends rain to benefit everyone (Mt. 5:45). And Paul says nothing "will be able to separate us from the love of God in Christ Jesus our Lord" (Rm. 8:39).[61]

In the coming chapters, I will argue that love shouldn't *just* be central to a doctrine of God. It should be central in other facets of systematic theology too, especially ethics. Because God loves us, say biblical writers, we ought to love God, others, ourselves, and creation. The Apostle Paul calls love "the greatest" (1 Cor. 13:13) and a "more excellent way" to be followed (1 Cor. 12:31). The writer of Ephesians tells readers to "imitate God, as dearly beloved children, and live in love, as Christ loves us . . ." (Eph. 5:1). The phrase "love one another" appears often in the New Testament, prompting many to consider it the primary ethic for humans. Above all, says Paul, we should "pursue love" (1 Cor. 14:1).[62]

Love functions well as the Bible's central theme.

### *Love's Centrality to Jesus*

Christians feel the force of a second reason that theologians ought to make love central in systematic theology: Love was central to Jesus. His life, teachings, and ministry revolve around it. The primary task for humans, says Jesus, is to love God and neighbor as themselves (Mt. 22:34-40; Mk. 12:28-34; Lk. 10:25-28). These commands aren't unique to Christianity, however, because they are found in the Hebrew scriptures (e.g., Dt. 6:5; Lev. 19:18). Israel's law and prophets rest on them.

---

[61] See Paul R. Sponheim, *Love's Availing Power* (Minneapolis: Fortress, 2011).

[62] New Testament scholars that emphasize the priority of love include Richard A. Burridge, *Imitating Jesus* (Grand Rapids, MI: Eerdmans, 2007); Victor Paul Furnish, *The Love Command in the New Testament* (Nashville, TN: Abingdon, 1972); Scot McKnight, *The Jesus Creed* (Brewster, MA: Paraclete, 2007); Russell Pregeant, *Knowing Truth, Doing Good* (Minneapolis: Fortress, 2008).

Jesus understood love as not limited to the near and dear. "Love your enemies," he says, by "doing good" to them (Lk. 6:35).[63] His followers should love by doing good even to those who hate them (Mt. 5:44). This love takes many forms, including friendship, self-sacrifice, generosity, listening, helping the least, self-love, and seeking various ways to collaborate with God.

Jesus also portrayed God as loving.[64] He claims God should be addressed as an intimate Father—*Abba*—who cares for children. This Lover cares for all creatures, including common birds (Mt. 6:26). And love compels God to seek what's good for creation: salvation, blessedness, and flourishing. Jesus calls us to replace the idea that God should be feared with the idea that God is loving.[65]

Even Jesus' death points to love. The combination of an empire's desire for power, systems of injustice, and Jesus' relentless love led to him being crucified. But even this dark and seemingly god-forsaken event promotes well-being, says Paul. "We know love in this: Christ died for our benefit" (Rom. 5:8).[66] And we ought to follow his example by giving our lives for others.

The Christian gospel includes the belief that God raised Jesus from the dead. The love that resurrected Jesus also raises to life those who follow him. Paul puts it like this: "Because of his great love for us, God, who is rich in mercy, made us alive with Christ even when we were dead in transgressions—it is by grace you have been saved" (Eph. 2:4-5).

If Jesus' life, teachings, death, and resurrection point to love, an adequate Christian systematic theology must prioritize love.

---

[63] See William C. Spohn, *Go and Do Likewise* (New York: Continuum, 2000).

[64] See Gregory Boyd, *Cross Vision* (Minneapolis: Fortress, 2018); John B. Cobb, Jr., *Jesus' Abba* (Minneapolis: Fortress, 2016); Tripp Fuller, *Divine Self-Investment* (Grasmere, ID: SacraSage, 2019); Brad Jersak, *A More Christlike God* (New York: Plain Truth, 2016); Brian Zahnd, *Sinners in the Hands of a Loving God* (London: Waterbrook, 2017).

[65] Natalya Cherry explores this in *Believing INTO Christ: Relational Faith and Human Flourishing* (Waco, TX: Baylor University Press, 2021).

[66] On the role of love in Jesus' vocation in atonement, see Chris S. Baker, *The Invitation: How Open and Relational Theology Enhances N.T. Wright's Use of Vocation in Atonement* (Grasmere, ID: SacraSage Press, 2025).

## Loving Relationships Matter Most

A third reason systematic theologians should take love as their central theme relates to the first two. If God is loving and wants us to have loving relationships with God, neighbors, enemies, ourselves, and all creation, relational love ought to be central to understanding God and existence.[67] Loving relationships matter most.[68]

Healthy living isn't primarily about right doctrines. Beliefs matter, but loving relationships matter more. Right relationship with God, others, ourselves, and creation have love as their focus, because they seek to promote well-being, flourishing, and the common good.[69] Adequate systematic theologies, therefore, portray God and creation in ways that support this primary aim to live a life of love.

Nearly all cultures and religions acknowledge that healthy relationships matter for well-being.[70] One of my favorite examples is *ubuntu*, a word widely thought to represent a pan-African worldview.[71] *Ubuntu* "defines the African philosophic understanding of being as wholeness," says Mogobe Ramose, "as a perpetual and universal movement

---

[67] Among the many who argue this point, see R. T. Mullins, *Eternal in Love: A Little Book about a Big God* (Eugene, OR: Cascade, 2024).

[68] Stephen G. Post has spent a career arguing for the health benefits of love and altruism. Among his books, see Stephen G. Post, ed. *Altruism & Altruistic Love* (New York: Oxford University Press, 2002); *Altruism and Health* (Oxford: Oxford University Press, 2007): *The Hidden Gifts of Helping* (New York: Broadway, 2011); *Pure Unlimited Love* (New York: Morehouse, 2025); *Unlimited Love* (Philadelphia: Templeton, 2005).

[69] For explorations of the relationship between health, flourishing and love, see Tyler VanderWeele, *A Theology of Health: Wholeness and Human Flourishing* (Notre Dame, IN: University of Notre Dame Press, 2024); "On the Promotion of Human Flourishing." *Proceedings of the National Academy of Sciences of the United States of America* 114, no. 31 (2017): 8148–8156.

[70] Representatives from the world's religions make this case in *Altruism in World Religions*, Jacob Neusner and Bruce Chilton, eds. (Washington, DC: Georgetown University Press, 2005). It also arises often in *Open and Relational Theology and It's Social and Political Implications: Muslim and Christian Perspectives*, Jonathan Foster, et. al., eds. (Grasmere, ID: SacraSage, 2024).

[71] Augustin Kassa explores the relationship between *ubuntu*, *ma'at*, and cosmogony in "The New Catholicity Emerging from Cosmologies of Wholeness: Ubuntu, Pauline, Big Bang, and Cosmotheadrism," (Doctoral Dissertation at Villanova University, 2025).

of sharing and exchange of the forces of life."[72] *Ubuntu* says, "'I am because I belong,'" says Desmond Tutu. "I am because we are, for we are made for togetherness, for family."[73] And *ubuntu* extends to relationships with other creatures. "Humanity isn't embodied solely in the individual," says Michael Eze, "but is a quality derived through interrelatedness with other beings, creatures, and elements."[74]

Although loving relationships between God and creation and between creatures and other creatures are widely acknowledged as crucial to living well and understanding reality, relational love is rarely the centerpiece of systematic theology. Some theologians say God is essentially related to Godself in Trinity, but few say healthy God-creature relationships are essential to understanding God. Many of the most influential theologians—e.g., Thomas Aquinas—portray God in a nonrelational way, as I will show in later chapters. Rather than "God is love," their starting point becomes "God is self-sufficient."

Others theologians claim a holy God can't be in the presence of unholy creatures. Rather than love, purity is their orienting concern.[75] Some say God's "love" is reserved for the elect and the unrighteous suffer eternal conscious torment after their deaths. Words from Jonathan Edwards's famous sermon, "Sinners in the Hands of an Angry God" illustrate this:

> The God that holds you over the pit of hell, much as one holds a spider, or some loathsome insect, over the fire, abhors you, and is dreadfully provoked: his wrath towards you burns like fire; he looks upon you as worthy of nothing else, but to be cast into

---

[72] Mogobe B. Ramose, *African Philosophy Through Ubuntu*, Revised Edition (Harare, Zimbabwe: Mond, 2002), 41.

[73] Desmond Tutu, *God Isn't a Christian* (San Francisco: HarperCollins, 2011), 22.

[74] Michael Onyebuchi Eze, "Humanitatis-Eco (Eco-Humanism): An African Environmental Theory," in *The Palgrave Handbook of African Philosophy*, Adeshina Afolayan and Toyin Falola, eds. (New York: Palgrave Macmillan, 2017), 621–32. See also Alexis Kagame, *La Philosophie Bantu-Rwandaise de l'Être*, First reprinted ed. (New York: Johnson Reprint Corporation, 1966).

[75] Paul Hoard and Billie Hoard explore this in terms of disgust theology. They offer a vision of a deity who accepts and embraces those considered contaminated. See *Eucontamination: Disgust Theology and the Christian Life* (Eugene, OR: Cascade, 2025).

the fire; he is of purer eyes than to bear to have you in his sight; you are ten thousand times more abominable in his eyes, than the most hateful venomous serpent is in ours.[76]

This systematic theology of love begins with love that seeks healthy relationships. It says God essentially loves creatures and always wants positive relations with all. It assumes creatures have agency too, and they can respond well or poorly to the loving God who interacts with them. Therefore, the quality of relationships depends upon a God who, by nature, loves all and upon creatures who choose whether to love in response. Nothing—including sin—can separate us from a deity who necessarily loves and relates with all. And God sends no one to eternal conscious torment in hell.

Systematic theology ought to prioritize relational love, because it's central to how we best understand God and existence.[77]

### *Experiences of Love Supersede Religious Institutions*

Many today are suspicious of belief in God and wary of institutional religion. Once orthodox claims about divinity are now considered nonsense or irrelevant. The institutional Church has harmed saints, seekers, sages, and sinners. Faith deconstruction has become a well-trod path, and some people decide to stop talking about God altogether.[78]

---

[76] Jonathan Edwards, *"Sinners in the Hands of an Angry God,"* in *The Works of Jonathan Edwards*, Vol. 22, Harry S. Stout, Nathan O. Hatch, and Kyle P. Farley, eds. (New Haven, CT: Yale University Press, 2003), 403.

[77] Other theologies that prioritize love include those in previous footnotes and George Newlands, *Theology of the Love of God* (London: Collins, 1980); Gary Chartier, *The Analogy of Love: Divine and Human Love at the Center of Christian Theology* (Charlottesville, VA: Imprint Academic, 2007).

[78] Tripp Fuller and I have written an accessible book addressing deconstruction. See *God After Deconstruction* (Grasmere, ID: SacraSage, 2024). See also see Michael Camp, *Breaking Bad Faith* (Oak Glen, CA: Quoir, 2023); Matthew J. Distefano, *Heretic!* (Oak Glen, CA: Quoir, 2018); Martha Elias Downey, *Go Wide* (Oak Glen, CA: Quoir, 2023); Peter Enns, *Curveball* (San Francisco: HarperOne, 2023); Jonathan Foster, *The Reconstructionist* (Oak Glen, CA: Quoir, 2021); Heather Hamilton, *Returning to Eden* (Oak Glen, CA: Quoir, 2023); Dana Robert Hicks, *The Quest for Thin Places* (Grasmere, ID: SacraSage, 2024); Olivia Jackson,

Despite the trauma that institutions can cause and toxicity some theologies generate, love remains attractive to people. It's far easier to get conversations about love off the ground than conversations about God, at least productive ones.[79] Most people admit to having deep intuitions about love, although those intuitions may differ radically from what's taught about God and religion. Some have mystical experiences and feel profound peace and oneness with creation, but typical theologies don't account for those experiences well.

The language of love better accounts for the growing realization that we all should embrace inclusion, difference, and empathy. Rather than an obstacle to theological reflection, we should celebrate the rich diversity of humans and other creatures in this wild world. And we should empathize with those who are in pain, disoriented, or traumatized.[80] Love seeks the good of all.

Love provides a framework for making sense of our yearnings for flourishing. It compels the progressive to work for a better world and the conservative to preserve gains from the past. If we think of love as the center of ultimate reality, many feel compelled to align themselves with it. And love can guide everyday attempts to live in harmony with the near and dear, strangers and enemies. At its best, a systematic

---

*(Un)Certain: A Collective Memoir of Deconstructing Faith* (London: SCM, 2023); James F. McGrath, *Beyond Deconstruction* (Grand Rapids, MI: Eerdmans, 2026); Brian McLaren, *Faith after Doubt* (New York: St. Martins, 2022); Linda Mercadante, *Belief Without Borders* (Oxford: Oxford University Press, 2014); Jim Palmer, *Being Jesus in Nashville* (Grasmere, ID: SacraSage, 2024); Glenn Siepert, *(Re)Thinking Everything* (Glenn Siepert, 2022); Nat Turney, *The Seeds of De(con)struction* (Glen Oaks, CA: Quoir, 2023); Todd Vick, *The Reconstructing of Your Mind* (Glen Oaks, CA: Quoir, 2021).

[79] James McClendon starts his systematic theology with ethics, particularly ethics as understood by the church. This approach seems promising for what it might entail for a systematic theology of love. Unfortunately, McClendon doesn't prioritize love. And for those traumatized by church abuse, his appeal to ecclesiology as primary seems naive or overly optimistic. See James W. McClendon Jr., *Ethics: Systematic Theology,* Vol. 1 (Waco, TX: Baylor University Press, 2012).

[80] The exploration of theologies of trauma have increased in recent decades. Among the excellent work, see Jennifer Baldwin, *Trauma-Sensitive Theology* (Eugene, OR: Cascade, 2018); Serene Jones, *Trauma and Grace,* 2nd ed. (Louisville, KY: Westminster, 2019); Janyne McConnaughey, *Trauma in the Pews* (Glendora, CA: Berry Powell, 2022); Shelly Rambo, *Spirit and Trauma* (Louisville, KY: Westminster John Knox, 2010).

theology of love will account for these intuitions, overcome institutional obstacles to flourishing, and inspire us to live well.[81]

When people consider their experiences of love most valuable, a wise systematic theologian takes love as their orienting concern.[82]

## What Is Love?

Getting clear on love's meaning will overcome obstacles that thwart attempts to place love at the center.[83] A particular definition of love guides the constructive proposals of this systematic theology:

**To love is to act intentionally, in relational response to God and others, to promote overall well-being.**

I've explained this definition in detail in books and articles I've written.[84] So I'll briefly address the phrases of the definition here.

### *To Act Intentionally*

Love requires intentional action. Both scripture and everyday life emphasize the importance of decision-making for love. What Jesus called the first and second greatest commandments involve intentional action: "Love the Lord . . . and love your neighbor as yourself." As I use it, the word "intentional" connotes three aspects: deliberation, motive, and freedom.

---

[81] Kevin Hector emphasizes the practical and experiential benefits of good theology. This systematic theology of love assumes Hector's argument, although this first volume doesn't make the case explicitly. For Hector's argument, see *Christianity as a Way of Life: A Systematic Theology* (New Haven, CT: Yale University Press, 2023).

[82] For the systematic theology most often cited for stressing the importance of experience, see Friedrich Schleiermacher, *The Christian Faith*, ed. H. R. Mackintosh and J. S. Stewart, 2nd ed. (Edinburgh: T&T Clark, 1928). A contemporary work in this tradition is Douglas F. Ottati, *A Theology for the Twenty-First Century* (Grand Rapids, MI: Eerdmans, 2020).

[83] For an exploration of the various meanings of love, see Denis de Rougemont, *Love in the Western World* (Princeton: Princeton University Press, 1983 [1940]).

[84] I have defined and explained love in various academic books. See especially, *Defining Love* (Grand Rapids, MI: Brazos, 2010); *The Nature of Love: A Theology* (St. Louis, MO: Chalice, 2010); and *Pluriform Love*.

The deliberation aspect of love pertains to decisions. Sometimes we ponder slowly and carefully, as we deliberate on the options available. But our decisions don't usually involve extensive reflection, because we typically make spur-of-the-moment choices. Love requires a measure of deliberation, therefore, whether fleeting or prolonged.

The motive aspect of intention says love isn't accidental; it *purposely* does good. Motives matter. We should not call an action "loving," for instance, when the person meant to do harm. Put another way, ill will proves incompatible with love. The motive aspect reminds us that an action's consequences don't determine whether it was done in love.[85] Aspirations remain crucial, because love assesses prospectively what might promote flourishing among potential outcomes.[86] Love has good motives.

The freedom aspect of acting intentionally refers to self-determination, or what philosophers call "libertarian freewill." Love requires at least some freedom to choose among opportunities. This freedom doesn't mean the ability to do absolutely anything, however. Genuine freedom will always be limited, because concrete circumstances, histories, bodies, limited awareness, and more constrain what's possible.[87] Love requires decisions with good motives done with a measure of freedom.[88]

## In Relational Response to God and Others

Love requires relations. The second phrase of my definition addresses this crucial aspect. Creatures relate to a God who makes creaturely love possible, and God relates with creatures. Love is relational.

---

[85] Clarence Graham White explains why plausible ethics are not primarily oriented around consequences. See *Open and Relational Ethics* (Clarence Graham White, 2024).

[86] I discuss in detail love's motives and consequentialism in *Defining Love*, chs. 1-2.

[87] I call this "genuine but limited freedom." See my essay, "Genuine (but Limited) Freedom for Creatures and for a God of Love" in *Neuroscience and Free Will,* James Walters and Philip Clayton, eds. (Eugene, OR: Pickwick, 2020). Daniel Day Williams also makes this point in *The Spirit and Forms of Love* (New York: Harper and Row, 1968).

[88] On the importance of motives for agency, see Alfred R. Mele, *Motivation and Agency* (Oxford: Oxford University Press, 2003).

Entirely isolated individuals—if they ever existed—could not love. We are interdependent creatures and never entirely alone.[89] An act of love in one moment draws from relational influences from previous moments, and these relational bonds form part of what creates each creature. The one who loves in the present moment relates to their past selves as well, so "others" includes our past moments of existence.

As I see it, God acts in each moment to call, inspire, and empower creatures to love. We can love because God loves us (1 Jn. 4:19); the Spirit is a necessary cause for creaturely loving. God relates with creation moment by moment and enables us to act intentionally, in relations with others, to promote overall well-being.

Love is more than relationships, however.[90] To define love *only* as relational responses would mean that unhealthy, abusive, and vengeful relations could be expressions of love. That's not true. And sometimes, we must sever or at least diminish unhealthy relationships so that we flee evil and cling to what is good (2 Tim. 2:22).[91] Love constitutes more than relationship.

Love often, if not always, includes emotional elements.[92] Emotions emerge in relations, and they're key features of existence. Love should

---

[89] Catherine Keller argues eloquently for interdependence in several books. As an example, see *No Matter What* (New York: Fordham University Press, 2025).

[90] Reacting to views that ignore relationality, Vincent Brummer defines love simply "a reciprocal relation." And he says, "we should look on love as a relationship, which involves partners adopting a complex set of attitudes towards each other." Vincent Brummer, *The Model of Love* (Cambridge: Cambridge University Press, 1993), 156, 162.

[91] Love sometimes is defined as seeking union. Paul Tillich, for instance, defines love as "the drive towards the unity of the separated." See Paul Tillich, *Love, Power, and Justice: Ontological Analyses and Ethical Applications* (Oxford: Oxford University Press, 1960), 25. Love defined as seeking relational union fails to account for well-being as love's goal, however. We can unite with others but do so intending harm. In addition, "union" could be easily interpreted as losing one's individuality. Two or more become one and lose independent distinctiveness. Erich Fromm makes this second point when he says, "mature love is union under the condition of preserving one's integrity, one's individuality" *The Art of Loving* (New York: Harper, 1956), 19.

[92] Martha Nussbaum argues for the compatibility of emotions and intelligence for love and ethical reasoning in *Upheavals of Thought* (Cambridge: Cambridge University Press, 2001). Thandeka makes the argument in a more accessible way in *Love Beyond Belief: Finding the Access Point to Spiritual Awareness* (Salem, OR: Polebridge, 2018).

not be *equated* with emotions, however, even positive ones.[93] Despite betrayal, pain, anger, apathy, or resentment, love turns the other cheek and repays evil with good. Love forgives, an inherently relational activity, despite emotions that tempt us to seek revenge.[94] Love involves relations with God and others, and these relations include various emotions.[95]

### To Promote Overall Well-Being

Love aims to do what's beneficial, positive, or helpful. Love tries to promote overall well-being, and it takes millions of forms in doing so. Love always aims to do good.[96]

Saying love aims for well-being fits the general way biblical writers understand love.[97] "Love your enemies," says Jesus, by "doing good" to them (Lk. 6:35), and love does good even to those who hate (Mt. 5:44). Jesus describes the way of love by telling a story of a Samaritan who helps an injured stranger (Lk. 10:25-37). "The Lord is good to all," says the Psalmist, "and his compassion is over all that he has made" (Ps. 145:9). We should "give thanks to the Lord, for he is good, and his love endures forever" (Ps. 136:1).

Perhaps the most common biblical reference to love's aim would be "salvation." This therapeutic word is associated with health, healing,

---

[93] Some psychologists define love as one emotion among others. I think this definition is inadequate. For examples, see Barbara L. Fredrickson, *Love 2.0: Creating Happiness and Health In Moments of Connection* (New York: Plume, 2013); Susan Hendrick and Clyde Hendrick, "Love," in *Handbook of Positive Psychology*, C. R. Snyder and Shane J. Lopez, eds. (Oxford: Oxford University Press, 2002).

[94] Samuel Powell argues for a rethinking of emotion and reason in *The Impassioned Life: Reason and Emotion in the Christian Tradition* (Minneapolis: Fortress, 2016).

[95] R. T. Mullins explores issues like these in *God and Emotion* (Cambridge: Cambridge University Press, 2020).

[96] This emphasis upon well-being as love's aim differs sharply from how love is understood by Augustine. It also differs from love as depicted by James K. A. Smith in *You Are What You Love* (Grand Rapids, MI: Brazos, 2016). In Augustine and Smith, love is simply desire, and the point is to desire the appropriate things.

[97] In previous work, I have argued that biblical writers never offer a clear definition of love. See *Pluriform Love*, ch. 1. Werner Jeanrond argues similarly, saying the "Bible doesn't contain any pure or original passage on love to which we could return for any timeless and unambiguous understanding of love" (*A Theology of Love*, 40).

and wholeness.[98] I've chosen "well-being" instead of "salvation" for my definition of love, because it encompasses various words and phrases pertaining to flourishing. Well-being is a term also commonly used in contemporary health, social sciences, and philosophy.[99]

The reference to *overall* well-being addresses the role of justice. Because love aims for the common good, a loving person doesn't heap benefits upon the few to the obvious detriment of the many. Nor does the loving one heap benefits upon the many to the obvious detriment of the few. That's not just. Rather than opposing love, therefore, justice is an aspect of it. To act justly would be to seek *overall* well-being.

We typically aim to love the near and dear. This makes sense, because our awareness is limited, and we have special obligations to family, friends, and local communities. But we must also consider the good of those we know less well, and those at a distance. Loving the foreigner, the outcast, the enemy, and other creatures means promoting the common good.

In sum, I propose a definition of love as acting intentionally, in relational response to God and others, to promote overall well-being. This definition applies to divine and creaturely love, although I'll argue that God's love differs in scope, duration, mode, etc. This systematic theology aims to provide a coherent theological framework with love at the center. It addresses key issues of existence, while seeking to maintain rational consistency and fit with widespread experience, including the experience of diverse others.

## Open and Relational Theology

In addition to being the first book titled *A Systematic Theology of Love*, this work represents an expression of open and relational theology. Of course, my proposals don't constitute *the only* ways an open and relational thinker might understand systematic theology, God, or love.

---

[98] See John B. Cobb, Jr., *Salvation* (Anoka, MN: Process Century, 2020).

[99] For essays on the theology and science of love, see Matthew T. Lee and Amos Yong, eds., *The Science and Theology of Godly Love* (DeKalb, IL: Northern Illinois University Press, 2012).

The open and relational theological community is diverse and includes people of faith within various religious traditions, or none.

Because open and relational theology is for many a fairly new phenomenon, I'll offer a thumbnail sketch here.[100] This theological vision comes in *many* varieties, and some of its advocates would describe it differently than I do. But here are what I take to be ideas that open and relational thinkers share.

### Relational

The word "relational" has several meanings, but the primary one in open and relational theology pertains to God. For God to be relational means God influences creation and creation influences God. God makes a difference to existence, and existence makes a difference to God.

Saying God is relational will seem obvious to most people. The idea fits the general description of God in the Bible, and it aligns with how most people talk about God today. But many traditional theologies don't emphasize God's relationality.

Leading theologians of yesteryear and some today—in Christianity, Islam, Judaism, and other traditions—say God isn't relational. They claim God is impassible: humans and other creatures can't affect or influence deity. Because love involves relational giving and receiving, however, it's difficult to imagine non-relational or impassible love. So it makes little sense to say, "God is love" but deny God is relational.

Open and relational theology says God interacts with us and creation moment by moment. Rather than aloof, unmoved, or unaffected, God cares for and interacts with all. In fact, God and creatures literally make history together. This theology accounts for the widespread desire of many people to have a relationship with God and the widespread belief that our lives matter.

---

[100] Many ideas in open and relational theology are ancient. But I coined the label "open and relational theology" in 2001 to bring together scholars at the American Academy of Religion to explore theology under a common umbrella.

Most in the open and relational community also use "relational" to talk about interactions between us, other humans, and creation in general. We live in an interrelated universe, and our actions make a difference to others and ourselves. This means that creatures are partly determined by the way they relate to other people, creation, and God. Absolute isolation is a myth.

God is relational, in the sense of giving and receiving.

## *Open*

To say God and creation make history together leads naturally to the meaning of "open" in open and relational theology.[101] This word identifies the future as a realm of possibilities rather than a settled state of affairs. "The future" doesn't exist. This means, in part, that God neither foreordains nor foreknows what will occur. As they experience in the present, God and creatures respond to the past and face yet-to-be-realized futures.

Many systematic theologians conceive of God as outside time, nontemporal, or timeless. In some mysterious way, this deity knows what happens in the future as if it has already occurred. But open and relational thinkers argue that God could only be certain about the future if it's fixed, settled, or completed. And if the future were already decided, we couldn't make free choices among possible futures.

Open and relational theology says God experiences time. This means that God experiences sequentially, moment by moment, like creatures do. God's life is also in process. The one whom biblical writers call "the living God" experiences the adventure of becoming.[102] God

---

[101] Open Theism. Richard Rice first proposed the label, "openness of God," and the basic ideas of Open Theism in his book, *The Openness of God* (Nashville, TN: Review and Herald, 1980). Rice recounts this and related events in *The Future of Open Theism: Antecedents and Opportunities* (Downers Grove, IL: IVP Academic, 2020). The phrase rose to prominence thanks to a book co-authored by David Basinger, William Hasker, Clark Pinnock, Rice, and John Sanders called, *The Openness of God: A Biblical Challenge to the Traditional Understanding of God* (Downers Grove, IL: InterVarsity, 1994). For an accessible introduction to open theism, see Chad Bahl, *God Unbound* (Grasmere, ID: SacraSage, 2021).

[102] I have written two accessible introductions to open and relational theology. See *Open and Relational Theology: An Introduction to Life-Changing Ideas* (Grasmere, ID: SacraSage, 2022) and *A Living and Loving God: Introducing Open and Relational Theology* (San Diego: DTL, 2025).

is timefull rather than timeless, temporal rather than nontemporal, timely rather than static.

If God is fundamentally relational and the future open, open and relational theology says our awareness of making free choices makes sense. We face live options when choosing in each moment. Neither atoms, genes, neurons, environment, culture, nor God entirely determines our lives.[103] We're genuinely free, although our freedom has limits.

Perhaps most appropriate for the current project, open and relational theology provides a helpful framework for making sense of what scripture and experiences say about love. A relational God who moves with free creatures into an open future would be a Spirit whose love aligns with love as we know it. And because this deity doesn't control all that occurs, we live in genuine give-and-receive relationships with God and others.

Open and relational theology has a natural affinity with a systematic theology of *love*.[104]

## A Word About this Work's Structure

Over the centuries, theologians have addressed theological issues in a particular order when writing their systematic theologies. They usually start with methodology and then move to the doctrine of God before concluding with eschatology. With a few exceptions, the present systematic theology follows the standard order and addresses the usual issues. But the vision of love at the core of this theology leads to some atypical outcomes, unusual variations, and novel proposals.

---

[103] Shaleen Kendrick explores the importance of love for neuroscience and spirituality in "Neuro-Relational Spirituality and Religious Power Games," in *Amipotence, vol. 2*, Brandon Brown, et. al., eds. (Grasmere, ID: SacraSage, 2025).

[104] Few open and relational systematic theologies have been written. The few include David Ray Griffin, *The Christian Gospel for Americans: A Systematic Theology* (Anoka, MN: Process Century, 2019); Sharon Baker Putt, *A Nonviolent Theology of Love Peacefully Confessing the Apostles' Creed* (Minneapolis: Fortress, 2017); Jon Paul Sydnor, *The Great Open Dance: A Progressive Christian Theology* (Eugene, OR: Pickwick, 2024). Although she calls her work a "practical theology," Marjorie Hewitt Suchocki's book *God-Christ-Church* has systematic elements (New York: Crossroad, 1989).

Readers may notice I've not placed methodological issues in the usual order. Although most systematic theologians start with method, this approach can, unfortunately, direct readers away from the author's primary concerns. Those who care little about method also grow bored. For these reasons, I'm placing my discussion of methodology at the conclusion. But careful readers will notice my methodological preferences as they read the chapters.

This book represents the first of three volumes in this Systematic Theology of Love. In this first volume, I address arguments for God's existence, divine attributes, questions about mystery, the God-world relationship, God as creator, providence/miracles, the problem of evil, and more.

The second volume starts with divine communication/revelation, and explores scripture as a particular type of revelation. It then moves to incarnation, with a lengthy discussion of Jesus of Nazareth. Volume 2 also addresses trinities, sin, and the Spirit's transformation of humans and creation.

The third volume addresses issues in ethics, such as racism, feminism, LGBTQ+, and climate change. It also addresses religious pluralism and ecclesiology. I explore eschatology last, and then I turn to the method questions I delayed addressing in the first chapter.

Over and over, themes of love will be at the fore in these volumes. No major theological issue goes untouched by those themes. I encourage readers to remind themselves often of the definition of love I've offered in this chapter. It differs from how other theologians regard love, and it differs from some popular meanings of the word.

## Conclusion

To my knowledge, this is the first work explicitly titled *A Systematic Theology of Love*. For various reasons, other systematic theologians have not chosen this title or taken love as their orienting concern. This is odd, at least for Christian theologians, given the preeminence of love in the Christian scriptures. Love has likely been neglected because it has many meanings, is often undefined, and takes a backseat to divine sovereignty or some other concern.

In addition to love being the central theme of the Bible, there are other reasons to make it the centerpiece of systematic theology. To make it such, we need a clear definition of love. I suggest love is best defined as acting intentionally, in relational response to God and others, to promote overall well-being. Among other things, this definition integrates the roles of motives, freedom, relationships, justice, emotions, and the common good.

This systematic theology of love assumes the conceptual winsomeness of open and relational theology. Among other things, this theological tradition says God and creatures genuinely affect one another, the future is open rather than fixed, and deity experiences time like we do. It also offers rational consistency and experiential fit.

Love isn't the only important subject or only divine attribute, of course. But the following volumes of this systematic theology prioritize love in ways not done so previously. This project offers new ways of thinking about God and existence, overcoming conceptual confusion common in other systematic theologies.[105] And it encourages a love-based way of living that assumes real relationships between God, us, and creation.

---

[105] In being a project of reforming the doctrine of God, this systematic theology of love bears resemblances to the project of F. LeRon Shults in *Reforming the Doctrine of God* (Grand Rapids, MI: Eerdmans, 2005). Of course, the particulars of my proposals differ from those of Shults.

CHAPTER TWO

# Reasons to Believe

## THE BIG IDEAS

- Many people appeal to scripture, tradition, personal experience, and nature to argue for God's existence, but each appeal has flaws.
- The traditional arguments for God's existence have merit but are not, in themselves, finally convincing.
- We have many good reasons to doubt God exists, especially the problem of evil and problem of divine hiddenness.
- We best make sense of intuitions about love and ultimate meaning when we posit the existence of a divine Lover.
- We can make a good abductive case for God's existence, and our diverse experiences play key roles in this case.
- At stake in arguments for and against God's existence is the *kind* of deity we think might exist.
- The best arguments *against* God's existence assume omnipotence.
- We have good reasons to believe in the God in whom love comes first.

The question of God's existence lies at the heart of theology.[1] If God is an illusion, people of faith are mistaken, and theology reduces to psychology, anthropology, or sociology.[2] People in the past may have

---
[1] This chapter is dedicated to Edwin Crawford, my first philosophy professor and one who challenged me to think carefully about arguments for and against God's existence.
[2] See Richard Dawkins, *The God Delusion* (New York: Mariner, 2008).

simply assumed God exists, but most today demand evidence, experiences, and/or arguments. We want reasons to believe.[3]

The question of God's existence is intimately tied to beliefs about God's attributes and actions. When asking *whether* God exists, we implicitly wonder *what kind* of God exists. Most thoughtful people of faith reject the deity rejected by atheists. "Describe the God you don't believe in," they say, "and I probably don't believe in that divinity either." Although I explore divine attributes in later chapters, they're relevant when we consider reasons to believe or doubt.[4]

People of faith use a number of strategies to justify their faith in God. They often employ those strategies when trying to persuade nonbelievers, too. Some strategies prove weak, but others are strong, in the sense of being more plausible.[5]

## Arguments from Revelation

### Biblical Witness

One way to justify belief in God starts with the assumption that God has self-revealed in a sacred book. For most Christians, that's the Bible. For Muslims, it's the Qu'ran. But it could be another text or set of writings. Some people think multiple religious texts reveal God's existence, because God is present to, and communicating with, the writers of sacred writ.

This strategy for arguing for God's existence demands reasons to think scripture must be truthful. Some systematic theologians,

---

[3] Peter Harrison makes a strong case belief in God was assumed by most ancient people, including scholars. See *Some New World: Myths of Supernatural Belief in a Secular Age* (Cambridge: Cambridge University Press, 2024). Ronald Thiemann argues this has changed so much that contemporary people require reasons to believe. See *Revelation and Theology: The Gospel as Narrated Promise* (Notre Dame, IN: Notre Dame University Press, 1985).

[4] For a classic discussion of arguments for and against God's existence, see Hans Küng, *Does God Exist? An Answer for Today*, trans. Edward Quinn (Garden City, NY: Doubleday, 1980). For an accessible introduction to Christian views of God, see Ian S. Markham, *Understanding Christian Doctrine*, 2nd ed. (Oxford: Wiley and Sons, 2017).

[5] Charles Taylor explores these issues and more in *A Secular Age* (Cambridge, MA: Belknap Press of Harvard University Press, 2007).

therefore, feel the need to begin their projects with lengthy arguments for the Bible's trustworthiness. They might claim scripture as inerrant, clear, and sufficient for demonstrating the reality of deity. The Bible functions in this way, goes the thinking, because God is, in some way, its author or source. But this argument is circular: we know God exists because God tells us that fact in a text God guarantees to be true.

Take the influential work of Wayne Grudem as an example. To begin part one of his systematic theology, Grudem has five chapters under the heading "The Doctrine of the Word of God." In them, he argues for biblical inerrancy and says, "all the words of scripture are God's words." Because God can't speak falsely, scripture proves the existence of God. The circularity of this argument is vicious.[6]

Other theologians say we should trust what scripture says about God because those who follow its teachings bear good fruit. The Bible inspires positive transformation. While this argument has some weight, readers of scripture also have used the Bible to justify immense harm. Some have advocated slavery, genocide, sexual abuse, and intolerance, for instance. The so-called "fruit of scripture" argument prompts some readers to deny full status and dignity to women, people of color, and the LGBTQ+ community. In addition, there's the fact that some who never or seldom read scripture—and some who doubt God exists—nevertheless act in loving ways. They bear good fruit too.

This systematic theology of love doesn't claim scripture proves God's existence or even that it's God's Word. The Bible has errors; it's not clear; it's not sufficient for proving God.[7] In fact, biblical writers sometimes describe deity in contradictory ways, and various authors

---

[6] To his credit, Grudem admits his argument is circular, but he thinks the circularity warranted. See Grudem, *Systematic Theology*, 73, 78.

[7] On the problems of inerrancy, see Gregory Boyd, *Inspired Imperfection* (Minneapolis: Fortress, 2020); Gabriel Gordon, *God Speaks: A Participatory Theology of Inspiration* (Glen Oak, CA: Quoir, 2021); and essays in Thomas Jay Oord and Richard Thompson, eds., *Rethinking the Bible* (Grasmere, ID: SacraSage, 2018).

promote opposing ideas.⁸ This shouldn't surprise us, because diverse and inconsistent humans wrote the Bible.⁹ God didn't.

Despite its flaws, I'll draw from the Bible and the wisdom I find in it. Scripture doesn't have to be infallible, perfectly consistent, or "the Word" to be a valuable resource for systematic theology. But to answer well whether God exists, we can't rely solely upon a book, and we should shun circular arguments.

*Tradition*

Another strategy to establish God's existence draws from religious tradition. This argument says the witness of saints and sages—and this includes the church but extends beyond it—demonstrates the existence of God. Billions of believers can't be wrong, the thinking goes.

This strategy can expand to include widespread religious experiences across religions and outside them. The universality, variety, and persistence of religion are impressive, and this phenomenon can't be dismissed easily.¹⁰ Some even say belief in God must be innate; we know God exists if we listen to our hearts;¹¹ only fools and sinners think otherwise.¹²

Relying upon religious traditions or widespread spiritual experiences to justify belief requires demonstrating why we should trust these traditions and experiences in the first place. But the diversity of traditions, spiritual encounters, and claims about God raises questions about the veracity of any of them. The variety is staggering!

---

⁸ Edward Klink and Darian Lockett explore this diversity among various biblical theologies. See *Understanding Biblical Theology: A Comparison of Theory and Practice* (Grand Rapids, MI: Zondervan, 2012).

⁹ Chad Bahl and I address what open and relational theology can bring to biblical interpretation. See "Open and Relational Hermeneutics," in *Handbook of Postconservative Theological Interpretation*, Ronald T. Michener and Mark A. Lambert, eds. (Eugene, OR: Cascade, 2024).

¹⁰ David Ray Griffin addresses this under the category of "the holy." See *The Christian Gospel for Americans: A Systematic Theology* (Anoka, MN: Process Century, 2019), 91.

¹¹ On this, see Justin Barrett, *Born Believers: The Science of Children's Religious Beliefs* (New York: Atria, 2012).

¹² For a biblical argument for innate knowledge of God, see Paul's letter to the Romans (1:19). Paul calls those who deny this inner sense of God "wicked" (Rom 1:18).

Those in one tradition claim God wants violence, for instance, but others say deity is nonviolent. Some think God always controls creatures; others say God sometimes controls; still others say God never controls. One tradition says divinity dwells with the ancestors but not with us, another says deity is present to all of us. One tradition says God has a localized body, but others say the Spirit must be bodiless. Some believers claim God puts politicians into power, others disagree. Huge numbers of people describe God as love and light; others say deity remains indescribable.

Who's right?

We must also take seriously those who *don't* have profound, direct experiences of God. Many people say they don't sense God or have dramatic encounters with the Holy. God is hidden. Instead of dismissing the earnest but disappointed seeker as a fool or unfaithful, we should ask why they *lack* religious experiences. It doesn't seem to be their fault.

This systematic theology of love draws from various voices and traditions. Although it arises primarily from Christianity, it doesn't rely exclusively upon the Christian tradition or its members. In fact, I'll criticize some Christian theologians strongly, even prominent ones. And I don't rely upon the claims of any tradition as proof for God's existence.

Billions of believers might be wrong.

### *Personal Experience*

Instead of relying upon outside sources, some people of faith trust their own experiences to justify belief in God. Many say they've had a mystical experience that can only be explained by divine activity.[13] This approach to establishing God's existence draws from private knowledge.[14]

---

[13] Daniel Dombrowski offers a strong argument from mysticism in *Process Mysticism* (Albany, NY: SUNY, 2023). Mysticism in a Whiteheadian key is basis for Roland Faber in *Depths As Yet Unspoken* (Eugene, OR: Pickwick, 2020).

[14] For a scholarly argument for God's existence based on religious experience, see Caroline Franks Davis, *The Evidential Force of Religious Experience* (Oxford: Clarendon Press, 1999).

It's hard to argue against personal experience, but this approach to proving God has distinct disadvantages.[15] First, personal experience isn't easily, if at all, transferable to others. Unique events that assure one person of God's existence are rarely, if ever, duplicated. Many who enjoy dramatic experiences of the divine even admit they can't articulate the truth of their encounters. The utterly ineffable nature of personal experiences fails to support apologetics.

Add to this the apparent fact that personal experiences are always influenced by various factors: cultural, political, environmental, bodily, historical, racial, and more. Skeptics can easily dismiss personal experiences of the divine, therefore, by pointing to merely creaturely forces and factors that might account for them. And the self-reflective believer might second-guess their purported experience of the divine. "Did I really feel God," they might ask, "or was that warm feeling the aftereffects of the hot peppers from dinner?"

Taking private experience as proof of God faces another disadvantage. The passage of time can undermine a person's confidence in a past encounter. The person of faith may be certain in one moment but uncertain later. Doubts arise. Additional experiences (or lack thereof) affect how the person interprets what happened previously. This erosion of confidence can be especially noticeable among those exploring new ideas, fresh evidence, and receiving advanced education.

While personal experience matters, it doesn't function well as definitive proof of God's existence.[16]

---

[15] Wesley J. Wildman explores the relationship of personal religious experiences to science, especially brains, in *Religious and Spiritual Experiences* (Cambridge: Cambridge University Press, 2011).

[16] I appreciate the way Douglas Ottati builds from experience in his systematic theology. While I don't think personal experiences of Something More prove God's existence, they're essential elements in honest theological construction. See *A Theology for the Twenty-First Century* (Grand Rapids, MI: Eerdmans, 2020), part 1. Ottati is indebted to Friedrich Schleiermacher for this emphasis upon experience. On how an open and relational theology might draw from Schleiermacher's emphasis upon experience, see Chad Bahl, *The Death of Supernaturalism* (Grasmere, ID: SacraSage, 2025).

## General Revelation

I turn now to what some theologians call "general revelation" or "natural theology." They use these terms to differentiate knowledge of God based on a sacred text, tradition, or dramatic experience from knowledge derived from science and the natural world.[17]

The Apostle Paul appeals to general revelation to argue for God's existence. "What can be known about God is plain," he says in a letter to the Romans, "because God has shown it. Since the creation of the world, God's eternal power and divine nature, although invisible, have been understood and seen through the things God has made" (Rom. 1:19-20).

The animals, other creatures, and plants point to a Creator, says natural theology. So do the smallest molecules and the grandest galaxies. "The heavens declare the glory of God," writes the Psalmist, "and the firmament proclaims God's handiwork. Day to day pours forth speech, and night to night declares knowledge" (Ps. 19:1-2). In short, nonhuman creatures and wider creation might give reasons to believe.

Sharp distinctions between special and general revelation or between revealed and natural theologies can be confusing, however. Those distinctions fade when we realize that humans—their books, traditions, and experiences—are part of nature rather separate from it. Humans are animals too. Calling some books "special" undermines the significance of revelation in creation more generally. And distinguishing between "revealed" and "natural" theologies implies that nature doesn't reveal God.

As important as arguments based on creation are for God's existence, general revelation doesn't prove, but only points to, God. Natural theology doesn't prove it either. Although *all* theology is natural and *all* revelation general, neither actually proves divinity. While it's possible to infer God's existence from nature, that's not proof.

---

[17] In several books, Alister McGrath offers positive ways to embrace natural theology. See *The Open Secret: A New Vision for Natural Theology* (Oxford: Blackwell, 2008); *Re-Imagining Nature: The Promise of a Christian Natural Theology* (Oxford: Blackwell, 2017).

Scientific research and theories can be important for theology, however, and science has been at the heart of my own writings.[18] But insofar as science relies upon the five senses and insofar as deity can't be perceived by those senses, scientists can't detect God. And insofar as science aims to be value neutral, it can't adjudicate claims about a *loving* God.[19] What *is* the case scientifically doesn't determine how we *ought* to live.

## Traditional Proofs of God's Existence

People of faith have traditionally looked to various philosophical arguments to prove God's existence. Each argument has sophisticated forms and critics have offered equally insightful arguments against them. I'll not wade through details, but I encourage curious readers to explore literature on the subject.[20] I'll briefly outline the primary arguments, however, and offer my own criticisms.

### *Designer and Orderer*

One argument for God's existence arises from the profound order and intricate design we observe in ourselves, other creatures, and the universe. It seems unlikely these features arose entirely by chance or from creaturely actions alone. Our observations of order and design, therefore, provide grounds to speculate that an Orderer or Designer exists.

Examples of order and design range from the extraordinarily precise conditions at the start of our universe (fine-tuning) to the

---

[18] See *God in an Open Universe: Science, Metaphysics, and Open Theism*, Thomas Jay Oord, William Hasker, Dean Zimmerman, eds. (Eugene, OR: Pickwick, 2011); *The Polkinghorne Reader* (Philadelphia: Templeton, 2010). See also my own books, *Defining Love* (Grand Rapids, MI: Brazos, 2010); *Divine Grace and Emerging Creation* (Eugene, OR: Pickwick, 2009); *Science of Love* (Philadelphia: Templeton, 2004).

[19] An expanded science that acknowledges nonsensory perception and value offers more promise, but even this expanded account of science shouldn't claim the objectivity many think essential to science.

[20] Some of the better discussions can be found in philosophy of religion books. See, for instance, *Reason and Religious Belief*, 5th ed. Michael Peterson, et. al., (Oxford: Oxford University Press, 2012). See also *Philosophy of Religion*, Thomas Jay Oord, ed. (Kansas City, MO: Beacon Hill, 2003).

emergence of life (abiogenesis) to the beautiful creatures we encounter in our world (teleology) to the intricacy of the eye and diverse ecosystems (complexity). The more we explore our wild and wonderful world, the more it amazes us. As we gaze into galaxies with telescopes or marvel at the minuscule with microscopes, we find creation fantastic. A Designer must exist who created the conditions for our amazement, the argument goes.

Critics of this argument, however, point to ample evidence of disorder and chaos as well. While the human eye may be amazing, for instance, it can develop macular degeneration, cataracts, diabetic retinopathy, glaucoma, and amblyopia. Other parts of the human body have problems too. If a wise and omnipotent deity creates these structures, it would seem there should be fewer and less harsh natural failings and disasters.[21]

Creation's evidence for God's existence is mixed.

## *Beauty*

Closely aligned with the argument from design and order is one that says the beauty we perceive in the universe suggests the existence of an Artist. Not only does the natural world display awe-inspiring splendor that seems not to have arisen on its own, but creatures this Artist made generate amazing beauty too. It seems there's more beauty in our evolving world than what's necessary to prompt species to pass along genes to offspring.[22] According to this argument, an Artist must exist.

The criticism of this argument points, however, to the ugliness and monotony we also witness. While we delight in photos generated by deep-space cameras, the vast amounts of vacuous space might trouble us too. Most of space consists of virtual nothingness. One would think an omnipotent Artist could have done better.

It's also not hard to imagine many of the dreary environments, boring circumstances, and ugly creatures we encounter as more beautiful

---

[21] For instance, see Abby Hafer, *The Not-So-Intelligent Designer* (Eugene, OR: Cascade, 2015).

[22] Patricia Adams Farmer explores this in her beautiful book, *Embracing A Beautiful God* (Patricia Adams Farmer, 2013 [2003]).

or less boring, and so on. We might think there's not enough art to prove the existence of an Artist. And too much of life is dull.

*First Cause*

A third philosophical argument for God's existence arises from the fact that we live in a world of cause and effect. We witness chains of causation, observing previous causes leading to subsequent effects. This prompts some to wonder if this cause-and-effect sequence had an absolute beginning. A First Cause must exist, some say.

The argument for God based on a First Cause proves rather weak. We have neither logical nor empirical reasons to think the cause-and-effect chain requires an absolute beginning. The sequence could be everlasting. Besides, most who claim God as the First Cause of the universe also believe that deity had no beginning. If we allow for a beginningless Divine Cause, why not a beginningless sequence of creaturely causes?[23] To deny this seems special pleading.

I'll explore this particular argument in more detail when addressing God as Creator. But as traditionally formulated, the First Cause argument doesn't prove God's existence.

*Source of Values*

A fourth argument for God's existence builds from widespread intuitions about right and wrong, good and bad, or helpful and unhelpful. Our sense of values and morality, says the argument, arises from a Moral or Aesthetic source. This Standard for values, the claim goes, transcends personal or communal preferences, and it transcends cultural conditioning and evolutionary propensities. A Source of values exists as the basis for morality.

---

[23] Kalam Argument. The first cause argument is often called "the Kalam Cosmological Argument," after an 11th century Islamic group and a philosopher named Al-Ghazali. William Lane Craig has been a vocal proponent in recent decades; see his *The Kalām Cosmological Argument* (Eugene, OR: Wipf & Stock, 1979). In my chapters on God's creating, I'll criticize the first cause argument as usually articulated.

This argument faces significant challenges. If an omnipotent God reveals what's right and wrong, why do people have different views of morality? In some cultures, people praise polygamy, for instance, but it's immoral in others. Some believe abortion goes against God's command; other good-hearted people disagree. Some say murder is wrong but then say God also sometimes wants us to kill (e. g., Abraham and Isaac). Some say deity desires patriarchal norms to maintain the structures of society; others say God wants egalitarian norms. Moral intuitions vary.

We also don't need to believe in a personal God as a standard for morality, say critics of this argument. While transcendent standards may be necessary, we could believe in impersonal rather than personally-derived moral principles. Our need for values, therefore, doesn't establish God's existence. I'll address this when I explore the problem of good.

## Existence is Part of God's Greatness

A fifth philosophical argument for God's existence assumes God is the greatest conceivable being.[24] We can be assured this deity exists, says the argument, because it's greater for a being to exist than be a mere idea. Existing must necessarily be part of what it means for God to be the greatest being. And if we think it's greater to be personal than impersonal, we might add that a personal deity exists. If we think necessary existence is greater than contingent existence, God exists necessarily.[25] And so on.

I'm not convinced by this argument. I don't find it plausible to make the leap from having an idea of God to saying God must exist. As Immanuel Kant puts it, "existence isn't a predicate," which means existing or not isn't an aspect of something but the question of whether

---

[24] While Anselm of Canterbury is most often identified with this argument for God's existence, others have advanced it in various forms. See his *Proslogium*, Sidney N. Deane, trans. (LaSalle, IL: Open Court, 1979).

[25] Charles Hartshorne and Alvin Plantinga shift the ontological argument toward the modal claim that God necessarily exists. See Hartshorne, *Man's Vision of God* (New York: Harper and Row, 1941); Plantinga, *God, Freedom, and Necessity* (New York: Harper and Row, 1974).

it is.²⁶ Adding the idea of necessity to the mix doesn't change the equation.²⁷

Claiming God is the greatest conceivable or perfect being, however, does help as we consider what the divine might be like. If we think love an attribute of the greatest One, for instance, we then have reasons to counter those who say God doesn't love—even if those claims come from scripture. If it's greater to be omnipresent than constrained to one place, we would then have reason to think God is omnipresent—even if a theologian says God withdraws.²⁸ And so on.

Pondering the attributes of a Perfect Being can be helpful, but I reject the notion that the *idea* of deity requires God's existence.²⁹

## ARGUMENTS AGAINST GOD'S EXISTENCE

We can also find good reasons to *deny* God exists.³⁰ Some criticisms of the arguments above have pointed to them. I'll add other reasons below and offer brief responses.

### Evil

The occurrence of evil is far and away the strongest reason to doubt God exists. We best formulate this reason by asking why an omnipotent and loving deity doesn't prevent genuine evil.³¹ Those who say

---

²⁶ See Immanuel Kant, *Critique of Pure Reason,* J. M. D. Meiklejohn, trans. (London: J. M. Dent and Sons, 1950), 16.

²⁷ Joshua Rasmussen offers a strong argument for the ability of reason to bring one to belief in God. See *How Reason Can Lead to God: A Philosopher's Bridge to Faith* (Downers Grove, IL: InterVarsity, 2019).

²⁸ Jürgen Moltmann argues that God withdraws from creation in many books. See, for instance, the essay, "God's Kenosis in the Creation and Consummation of the World," in *The Work of Love*, John Polkinghorne, ed. (Grand Rapids, MI: Eerdmans, 2001) 146.

²⁹ For a good overview of these arguments and their contemporary advocates, see *Reason and Religious Belief*, Michael Peterson, et. al., eds. (Oxford: Oxford University Press, 1998).

³⁰ Friedrich Nietzsche offers some of the stronger arguments against God's existence. See, for instance, *Beyond Good and Evil* (New York: Penguin, 2003).

³¹ Genuine Evil I join David Ray Griffin in defining a genuine evil as an event that, all things considered, makes the world worse than it might have been. I'll explain and expand on this definition in later chapters of this book, but also see Griffin, *God, Power, and Evil* (Louisville, KY: Westminster John Knox, 2004). I compare genuine evil to necessary and gratuitous evil

God allows but doesn't cause evil don't escape the problem. A loving God would prevent evil, and if omnipotent, *could* prevent it.

The problem of evil takes many forms because pointless pain and harm come in many forms. Horrific evils especially challenge belief, but even mundane suffering can offer grounds to doubt a deity exists. Whether considered individually or taken together, therefore, instances of evil give reasons to reject the idea God exists.[32]

For reasons I have explicated before and will explain in future chapters, the strongest response to the problem of evil rejects the concept of divine omnipotence.[33] I will replace standard views of divine power with what I call "amipotence." Amipotence is the power of God's uncontrolling love, and it says God can't control others, including creatures and creation that cause evil.

A solution to the problem of evil also involves noting that God is a bodiless spirit. God doesn't have a localized divine body with arms, hands, wings, feet, teeth, or tail. Consequently, an incorporeal Spirit can't prevent evil that embodied creatures sometimes can. Few theologians have taken seriously the traditional claim that God is incorporeal, but doing so proves crucial to solving the problem of evil.

Some people of faith pose the problem of good as a counterargument to the problem of evil. If God doesn't exist, they ask, why is there so much *good* in the world? Things should be much worse, uglier, more chaotic, and more violent if there were no deity. And if no transcendent Standard exists by which we make value judgments, why even consider an event *evil*? Without God, good and evil become mere personal preferences.[34]

---

in *The Uncontrolling Love of God* (Downers Grove, IL: IVP Academic, 2015), ch. 3. See also *Gottes Liebe zwingt nicht*, Matthias Remenyi, Foreword; Julia Nöthling and Felix Fleckenstein, trans. (2020); *O Amor Nao Control Ador de Deus* (2020); *God kan het niet*, David van Beveren and Rik den op Bouw, trans. (2024).

[32] Grace Ji-Sun Kim and Susan M. Shaw address this question from the perspective of survivors of sexual abuse. See *Surviving God* (Minneapolis: Broadleaf, 2024).

[33] See Brandon Ambrosino, *Is It God's Will?* (New York: Morehouse, 2025); Russ Dean, *The Power of the God Who Can't* (Eugene, OR: Resource, 2023); Jason Liesendahl, *Gott Kann Auch Nicht Alles* (Stuttgart: Ruach Jetzt, 2024); Tim Reddish, *Does God Always Get What God Wants?* (Eugene, OR: Cascade, 2018).

[34] I address the problem of good in *The Uncontrolling Love of God*, ch. 3 and in a later chapter of this book.

These are important questions, and I'll address them. But the problem of good doesn't neutralize the problem of evil. The best response to both problems denies divine omnipotence and affirms God as the source and standard for good. The problem of evil and problem of good can be resolved when affirming a God of uncontrolling love.

*Ambiguous Revelation*

A second argument against God's existence addresses questions of revelation. If God exists, why doesn't deity self-reveal in clearer and less ambiguous ways? Why isn't God's existence obvious? Where's the indubitable evidence?

If we think knowing God helps us live well—which most believers claim—we would think a loving God would *want* to self-reveal in obvious ways. And if God were omnipotent, no obstacles could inhibit deity from disclosing what's necessary for our flourishing. In short, the hiddenness of God is a strong argument against belief. It's understandable, therefore, why those frustrated by their lack of religious experiences doubt God exists.[35]

Two response to the hiddenness problem can be helpful. One response denies that God is omnipotent. If God *can't* control creatures and circumstances to self-reveal in obvious ways, we shouldn't blame God for not communicating clearly. In other words, God can't.[36]

The second response pertains to claims about God's incorporeal composition. If God is a universal spirit without a localized body, we shouldn't expect to detect God with our five senses. Whatever divine revelation entails, sensory perception won't help us much when discerning divine communication. And that's not God's fault.

---

[35] Brian McLaren addresses many of these issues in his work. See, for instance, *Faith After Doubt* (New York: St. Martins, 2021). See also Mark Karris, *Religious Refugees* (Glen Oak, CA: Quoir, 2020). Tripp Fuller and I address these issues in *God After Deconstruction* (Grasmere, ID: SacraSage, 2024).

[36] On issues of divine hiddenness, see Tim Miller, *The Silence of the Lamb: Exploring the Hiddenness of Christ and God* (Grasmere, ID: SacraSage, 2025). I'll address the issue in the second volume of this systematic theology of love.

Denying divine omnipotence and saying we can't know God through sensory perception can help us counter other reasons to doubt deity exists. Take the problem that the Bible has errors, for instance. We should say an uncontrolling God can't guarantee an inerrant Bible. This deity can't guarantee 1) the authors of scripture understood God or the world properly, 2) an infallible canonization process, 3) the safe-guarding of biblical texts from errors in transmission, or 4) the perfect printing of the text. A God who isn't omnipotent also can't guarantee accurate interpretations. The fact that individuals, traditions, and religions have divergent beliefs makes sense if the Spirit can't, by its nature, reveal in crystal-clear ways.

### Other Arguments

There are other arguments against God's existence.[37] Some people say science, especially evolution and the Big Bang, make belief in God unnecessary. Others argue that a loving God would not allow political tyrants to oppress people. Some doubt a loving God would send people to hell. Others doubt a loving God would allow women, queer people, the disabled, or people of color to be persecuted.[38] And because God does so few miracles and fails to answer many prayers, some people doubt that God exists. In coming chapters, I'll address each of these objections.

Other arguments against God's existence emerge from theological inconsistencies. These inconsistencies can be identified with questions such as these: How could God be certain about the future (omniscient) and yet creatures freely choose options to alter the future? How can God be able to do anything (omnipotent) and yet not be able to tell a lie or tie a shoe? How can God be present to all creation (omnipresent)

---

[37] David Fergusson responds to potent critics of theism in *Faith and Its Critics: A Conversation* (Oxford: Oxford University Press, 2009).

[38] Among the important books to address divine action and evil toward women, see Monica A. Coleman, Nancy R. Howell, and Helene Tallon Russell, *Creation Women's Theology* (Eugene, OR: Pickwick, 2011); Monica A. Coleman, *Making a Way Out of No Way* (Minneapolis: Fortress, 2008); Grace Ji-Sun Kim and Susan M. Shaw, *Surviving God* (Minneapolis: Broadleaf, 2024).

and yet sometimes intervene from outside? How can God be unchanging and unaffected (immutable and impassible) and yet have emotions and responses as described in scripture? How can God be personal, in the sense of interacting moment by moment, and yet timeless (nontemporal)? How can God be all-forgiving (omnibenevolent) but sometimes punish? And so on.

Such questions lead some to think the very idea of God incoherent. And this questioning is justified, at least as theologians typically define God. These inconsistencies prompt other people of faith to think incoherence is a virtue, not a problem. So, they appeal to mystery. But embracing incoherence about God makes people of faith especially vulnerable to fraud, tyrants, hucksters, strongmen, and cults. Coherent theology matters.

## Meaning, Love, and More

My earliest memories involve believing God exists. Everyone I knew believed in God, and in my youngest days, I never seriously doubted. I became a teenage evangelist, in fact, engaging in fervent evangelical witnessing to people at school, on the street, at the beach, in bars, and door to door. It was difficult for me to understand why any serious thinking person would *not* believe.

In my early twenties, however, I took a philosophy of religion class. While reading the course assignments, I encountered strong arguments against God's existence. These arguments led me to doubt I had solid grounds to believe. For the sake of intellectual honesty, I became an atheist/agnostic. For some time, I didn't believe.

Two issues prompted my return to faith. First, I wanted to think my life and life in general were ultimately meaningful. I couldn't imagine how this could be true if there were no ground of ultimate meaning most people call "God." This need for meaning didn't *prove* God's existence, of course, and even today I'm not certain. But my quest for meaning led me back to belief.

The second issue arose from my deep intuitions about love. I thought I ought to be a loving person, and everyone ought to love. In some deep sense, I felt that love must answer our most important questions. These intuitions seemed to need a Source beyond, while including, influences from my body, upbringing, social settings, and evolutionary history. I surmised, therefore, that a Lover exists as the impetus for my intuitions of love. This thought process provides no proof of God's existence, however, and even today I'm not certain.

Based on my quest for meaning and need to make sense of love, I took a risk and believed in God again. I continue to risk today.[39] Since my stint as an atheist/agnostic, I've slowly reconstructed my views about God and creation. Today, my believing that God exists doesn't rely upon indubitable proof or undeniable evidence.[40] But neither is it blind, arbitrary, or uninformed.

I have reasons to believe.

### *Abductive Reasoning*

Many arguments for God's existence use deductive reasoning. They start with a truth a person can allegedly know with certainty. It may come from a book, tradition, mystical experience, science, independent reason, or some other authority. From that absolute truth, other truths are deduced, in the sense of teasing out the absolute truth's implications. Effective deduction, the idea goes, has a sure foundation from which one derives certain conclusions.

I don't find deductive reasoning helpful when pondering God's existence. I doubt there are error-free foundations from which we could start deducing immutable truths. No book, tradition, experience, rationality, or authority can be infallible, and that includes the Bible. I suspect absolute truth exists, but I doubt any human knows it absolutely.

---

[39] In this risking, I agree with what Aaron Simmons calls "risk with direction." See *Camping with Kierkegaard* (Wisdom/Work, 2023), 3.

[40] Clint Schnekloth argues for progressive Christianity in *A Guidebook to Progressive Church* (Clint Schnekloth, 2024). Randall Rauser makes a good case for progressive Christianity in response to Alisa Childers and others in *Progressive Christians Love Jesus Too* (Two Cup Press, 2022). For accessible material on this, see the Progressive Christianity organization, directed by Mark Sandlin and Caleb Jones (https://progressivechristianity.org/) and Progressive Christianity Network Britain, chaired by Simon Cross (https://www.pcnbritain.org.uk/).

I'm attracted instead to inductive reasoning when considering God's existence. And to its partner, abduction. Inductive reasoning draws together evidence to make a claim that's probably, but not certainly, true. It reasons from specific observations to form general conclusions. This way of thinking leans upon empirical evidence, scriptures, science, reason, and various experiences to speculate that God exists. But induction never provides airtight certainty.

Effective abduction is a practice that surveys as much evidence as possible and explores all the arguments available, for and against. From this, it arrives at a tentative, but plausible, explanations. Scientists call this process "inference to the best explanation." But even within science, the explanation will be fallible and always open to change. The process of revision is ongoing.

Abductive reasoning requires risk and curiosity. The verdict will always be out, so we act in light of our best speculation.[41] In terms of theology, this means the question of God's existence will never be fully resolved. But we can have reasons to think God *might* exist and that God remains part of the best available theory for understanding life, given various arguments, experiences, traditions, sacred texts, feelings, and more. The case for God's existence, while not air-tight, is more plausible than alternatives.

I don't pretend to be bias-free or completely objective when I reflect on these matters. No one can be. My interpreting will be shaped by world views, conceptual frameworks, or grand narratives. The evidence I gather, and my reasoning, fit well or poorly into these grand frameworks. Assessing which framework proves best will be an ongoing venture.

As I see it, the best overall framework for life accounts for the widest amount of experience. It will make sense rationally, and the ideas will fit together. The best framework proves adequate to the facts available and can be applied to practical living. We ought to be humble

---

[41] William James argues for risking belief in God in his essay, "The Will to Believe." Find it and other relevant writings in *The Will to Believe, Human Immortality, and Other essays in Popular Philosophy* (New York: Dover, 1960).

as we seek the best overall framework, being open to reconsidering, deconstructing, and reconstructing.[42]

My belief in God isn't an air-tight proof but a wager that love is central to life's best explanation.

## OTHER REASONS TO SPECULATE GOD EXISTS

Abductive reasoning functions within a flexible conceptual and experiential matrix. Consequently, it includes other reasons to think God exists, reasons not usually identified among the traditional proofs.

Take great sex as an example. In the ecstasy of intimacy and orgasm, we sometimes experience the Divine. We might even sigh, "Oh, God!" in a rapturous moment. This connection between God and sex explains why some religions include sex workers at their temples, as problematic as that may be. When sex is great, Something More seems at work. Sex can be a reason to believe.

Or take the birth of a newborn. Parents can feel a unique Presence in the birthing process or when holding the infant. Grandparents may feel the same. The miracle of a mother's womb and the creation of a tiny someone incline many to thank Someone. Experiences of wonder with infants can be another reason to believe.

Sporting events and athletic feats also inspire us. The thrill of victory prompts many to thank God for, in some way, helping them win. Just watch post-game interviews. More than once, I've experienced spiritual ecstasy when the team I was on, or the one I rooted for, won a championship. And I've felt the collective effervescence of an unexpected win prompting me to hug complete strangers in unrestrained joy. But the agony of defeat can also reveal the divine. Many athletes and fans feel a Comforter when they endure disappointment. Some credit the Divine for sustaining them amid letdown and loss.

One of my most profound spiritual experiences came at a U2 concert. Although I'd been listening to the band since my teens, I didn't see them live until my forties. When hearing live music that carried me

---

[42] This tentative and fallibilist take on theology fits Demian Wheeler's general approach in *Religion within the Limits of History Alone* (Albany, NY: SUNY, 2020).

through life's ups and downs, I experienced a Transcendent response. I went to a U2 concert and ended up worshiping Someone without an instrument! Music can point to a Musician alongside musicians.

The arts can woo us into states we think must be sparked by Divinity. Insights from an audio interview or the prick of our conscience from a great book may seem holy. More than once, I've sat silent in a theater after watching a film that moved me to contemplate a Mover. I felt this way after watching *Schindler's List*, for instance, and more recently *Everything Everywhere All at Once*. I feel it when Sam carries Frodo to Mount Doom in *The Lord of the Rings*.

As a nature photographer, I've had plenty of "God moments." When composing a scene, I sometimes feel a Jolt. I felt close to the Creator while photographing a moose and her calf, a grouse and chicks, and two Gopher snakes copulating. I consider these creatures my companions, and I greet them, "Hello, friend." This animal friendship, as I see it, is prompted by the Friend of all creation. But a photographic experience can be revelatory.

Speaking of friends, My wife is my closest confidante and life partner. While our marriage has its ebbs and flows and while neither of us is perfect, I feel Another in our relationship too. My wife isn't God, but I sometimes sense God profoundly when in her presence. Our enduring partnership provides one reason I speculate that the steadfast love of a divine Friend endures forever.

Moments in a religious worship service can transport me into communion with a holy Presence. I've felt Conviction when kneeling at an altar, a Glow when receiving communion, and Ecstasy when standing, arms outstretched, singing with gusto. I've also felt a Nudge in silent meditation, as I attend to the gentle caress of Love. However, boring worship and long sermons make me think a devil exists!

I could add more experiential reasons to believe.[43] Each points to the fact that in various settings and circumstances, we sometimes get the impression that Something More is active. This More includes but

---

[43] Douglas Ottati offers a list of ways we may have a sense of the divine. Those include a sense of dependence, thankfulness, obligation, remorse, limitations, grandeur, and assurance. See *A Theology for the Twenty-First Century*, 38-42.

transcends natural actors, factors, and forces.[44] Such reasons to believe won't be proofs, but they *are* evidence. They influence me to think God exists.

I personally think the More I encounter is an objective reality most call "God." But I'm not certain. So, while I don't claim to know deity with certainty or describe divinity with full accuracy, I live hoping my faltering language might signify something true.

## What Kind of God?

Reasons to believe in God vary in their persuasiveness. And the counterforce of reasons *not* to believe varies. After weighing each and considering all, I conclude it's more plausible to believe that God exists than not. Others will weigh the reasons and conclude differently.

Most arguments for belief point to subjective evidence of God's presence and love. Many people report feeling loved by God, and some interpret specific events as evidence of divine care. In various ways and at various times, many of us get the impression a compassionate Lover acts in our lives and the universe. Arguments based on love prove compelling to many.

Note that the strongest arguments *against* God's existence share something in common: they implicitly or explicitly assume God can control creatures or creation.[45] Most presuppose the all-powerful deity whom they believe in or deny can bring about outcomes singlehandedly. The best arguments for atheism assume the deity to be rejected is omnipotent.

---

[44] I have been influenced in this thinking by the classic texts of Friedrich Schleiermacher and William James. See Friedrich Schleiermacher, *The Christian Faith*, ed. H. R. Mackintosh and J. S. Stewart (New York: Harper & Row, 1963[1831]) and William James, *The Varieties of Religious Experience* (New York: Longmans, Green, and Co., 1902).

[45] Divine Control. When I use "control," I mean acting as the sufficient cause of some creature, circumstance, or event. To describe such control, I use phrases like "singlehandedly decide outcomes," "unilaterally determine events," "divine fiat," or others that depict God as the sole cause of some result. John Frame is among many theologians who claim God has "control over all things." See John Frame, "The Sovereignty of God," (https://www.thegospelcoalition.org/essay/the-sovereignty-of-god/) Accessed 1/28/2023.

Our experiences don't require this assumption. None of us experiences omnipotence or absolute sovereignty.[46] No one knows first-hand that God is all-powerful. But believing God is omnipotent is the default for billions of people, including theists, atheists, and agnostics.

For a host of reasons, this systematic theology rejects omnipotence. This rejection has numerous upsides, and I'll identify them in due time. But I'll note here that we overcome the strongest reasons for atheism/agnosticism when we affirm that a loving Spirit exists who can't control creatures or creation. God isn't all-powerful.

If God isn't omnipotent, for instance, the Lover of the universe isn't culpable for failing to prevent evil. God can't. And this is a big deal! Atheists and agnostics often cite the problem of evil as their primary reason to doubt. And rightly so. But few consider the possibility that a loving God exists who isn't omnipotent.

Rejecting omnipotence also helps account for the errors, contradictions, and inconsistencies in the Bible and other sacred texts. An all-powerful God could eliminate those problems; an uncontrolling Lover can't. The Bible could be inspired by an uncontrolling Inspirer and yet it still would reflect the worldviews, biases, and misunderstandings of the authors. An uncontrolling God also can't control interpretations of scripture.

Perhaps the best objection to the billions of people who say they experience God and receive divine revelation comes by pointing out their contradictory claims about who God is and what God wants. One person genuinely believes God wants children sacrificed, for instance, while another believes God reveals such killings as wrong. Some feel strongly that God want them to take revenge and go to war, but others strongly believe God wants forgiveness. One group thinks God has revealed that all women should serve in secondary roles, while others think God wants women as leaders. God purportedly tells the faithful that queer people need conversion therapy, while others believe God celebrates rather than rejects queerness.

---

[46] James McLachlan makes his point powerfully in "The Meaning of God is to Love and Be Loved," *Amipotence*, vol. 1, Chris S. Baker, et. al., eds. (Grasmere, ID: SacraSage, 2025).

The stakes are high in contradictory revelations like the ones outlined above. These purported experiences of who God is and what God wants aren't just unimportant debates over how many angels can dance on a pin. Rather, an *omnipotent* God could guarantee crystal-clear messages about who God is and what God wants. In fact, an all-powerful God could ensure that everyone understands what leads to flourishing and all necessary truths for salvation, without ambiguity. And yet earnest people with good motives have experiences of God with sometimes contradictory revelations. And those contradictions have real and sometimes profoundly negative impact. A loving God who can't control our interpretations of the divine, however, isn't culpable for failing to clear up contradictory revelations.

As we saw earlier, arguments for God's existence from the design, beauty, and order can be compelling. But lack of design, ugliness, and disorder present us realities with which we must reckon. If God were omnipotent, we shouldn't encounter so many flaws, ugliness, and chaos in the created order. A Spirit who influences all that exists but can't control anyone or anything, however, makes better sense given beauty *and* ugliness, design *and* randomness, order *and* chaos.

The claim that God serves as the source of our intuitions of value and the Standard of morality is strong. But there's a problem: an omnipotent God could provide clear answers to moral conundrums and solve widespread disagreement about values. And yet good and wise people disagree. We can solve this problem by saying a Moral Source and Standard exists who isn't omnipotent.

Our long and winding evolutionary process, which includes senseless death and species dead ends, makes better sense if God influences but can't control creation. The loving God who can't control neither installs nor supports political or ecclesial tyrants.[47] An uncontrolling God of love sends no one to eternal conscious torment (hell). The God who can't stop evil singlehandedly won't be culpable for failing to stop

---

[47] On the problems that come from high-control religion, see Laura Anderson, *When Religion Hurts You* (Grand Rapids, MI: Brazos, 2023). On the politics of amipotence, see Matthew Baker, "The Panarchist Politics of Amipotence," in *Amipotence, vol. 1,* Chris S. Baker, et. al., eds. (Grasmere, ID: SacraSage, 2025).

the harm done to women, queer people, the disabled, people of color, or anyone else. The uncontrolling but invisible Spirit doesn't voluntarily hide, but also can't self-reveal in a controlling way. And a noncoercive deity can't do miracles singlehandedly or answer prayer by fiat.

## Reasons Matter

To argue that God exists, people of faith appeal to scripture, tradition, personal experience, and nature. But each of these appeals has flaws. Traditionally, a set of additional arguments for God's existence have been offered. But none of them, on their own, prove convincing. We have good reasons to doubt God exists. Among the best reasons are the problem of evil and the problem of divine hiddenness.

Most of us—maybe all of us—have deep intuitions about love and meaning. While those intuitions don't provide proof of God's existence, they make sense if a divine Lover is a source for them. A good abductive case for the existence of a deity can be made from various experiences of transcendence.

Reasons for and against God's existence matter. As we've seen, the strongest and weakest of them make assumptions about divine attributes and activities. Each assumes a particular *kind* of God, and the strongest reasons to deny God's existence assume deity is or could be controlling. The strongest reasons to believe God exists affirm divine love but reject omnipotence.

Although I'm not certain, I have good reasons to think God exists. It's more plausible to me, all things considered, than a theory of existence without the divine. But I could be wrong. This systematic theology of love makes a case for what I consider the most reasonable view of reality in general and God in particular.

I turn now to describe the God of this open and relational, systematic theology of love.

# The Universal Spirit of Love

CHAPTER THREE

# A Loving God

## THE BIG IDEAS

- When wanting consistency, it helps theologians to choose an orienting concern or set of concerns.
- Love is the orienting concern of this systematic theology, and deity is the loving Spirit.
- God loves by acting intentionally, in relations with creatures, to promote overall well-being.
- God is love, but love isn't God.
- Divine love is self-giving, others-empowering, uncontrolling, and pluriform.
- God is gracious, merciful, compassionate, and just . . . but not how traditional theologies have understood these words.
- God's love is freely expressed in one sense but necessarily expressed in another.
- Biblical writers sometimes portray God's love rightly but other times wrongly.
- Love is an essential attribute of God rather than a contingent one; the Spirit must love.
- A God worthy of my worship must be a deity in whom love comes logically first.

The previous chapters identified many reasons to believe (or not) in God. While evaluating them, I noted that each reason includes assumptions about God's attributes and activities. What *kind* of God we think exists matters.[1]

---

[1] This chapter is dedicated to Brad Kent. As my graduate school professor in theology and philosophy of religion, Brad introduced me to many ideas in this book. His personal encouragement and friendship were especially important as I explored these ideas.

Some people reject belief in God because of the inconsistencies in traditional descriptions of deity. It's hard to believe in, let alone worship, an incoherent divinity. And an utterly inconceivable God, to which some appeal, can't be loved on purpose, because we'd have no idea what or who we're loving. We also couldn't have a clue if, or how, an inconceivable deity loves us. Without a clear and coherent view of the divine, we're likely to be confused about how to follow what Jesus called the greatest commands: love God and others as ourselves.

Inconsistency has consequences.

To avoid incoherence and inconsistency, wise systematic theologians will prioritize God's attributes around one or more themes. An organizational focal point becomes their orienting concern, integrative motif, or regulative idea.[2] If a theologian wants their theology to align with widespread experience and the apparent facts of existence, they will also consider their theological beliefs in light of actual living. Ethics and aesthetics also matter.[3]

Some theologians will reject the idea of prioritizing one or a few divine attributes when doing systematic theology. They attempt to treat each attribute equally. But this inevitably leads to incoherence. And careful readers still detect implicit priorities in theologies that claim to value every divine attribute or idea equally.

Whether explicitly or not, most theologians have prioritized omnipotence. We detect this priority, for instance, when theologians say God controls, or can control, creatures. It's present when they say God chooses whether to love, claim God must be essentially independent, assert that God causes or allows evil, say God voluntarily hides, claim God remains unaffected by creatures, say God must be immutable in all respects, or assert that God singlehandedly decides our fate for the afterlife. In most theologies, omnipotence obviously, or subtly, reigns.

---

[2] On this in relation to perfect being theology, see T. J. Mawson, *The Divine Attributes* (Cambridge: Cambridge University Press, 2019).

[3] Because I think views of ourselves and creation matter for systematic theology, I appeal often to personal experience, communal experiences, and the sciences. I agree with Eberhard Jüngel when he says, "God can't be thought of as God without simultaneously considering the world and its situation." See Eberhard Jüngel, *God as the Mystery of the World*, Darrell L. Guder, trans. (Grand Rapids, MI: Eerdmans, 1983), 57.

## GOD IS . . . ?

The writers of scripture, saints and sages, and everyday people alike describe God in various ways. Words can't reveal the full truth about God, of course. It's natural to think some descriptions of deity lean more symbolic or metaphorical, while others are more straightforward or univocal. Good theology embraces some types of mystery, as I'll explain in a later chapter. But even those who claim *all* language about God is mysterious typically use language about the divine that functions closer to the literal than symbolic.

For instance, biblical writers say, "God is a rock" (Ps. 18:2). Few people read this statement and think God must be a chunk of stone somewhere in the universe. They'll likely think the statement serves as a metaphor identifying God as secure, stable, or trustworthy. The words "secure, stable, and trustworthy," therefore, function as more straightforward descriptions of deity. These words can't tell us the *full* truth, and their meanings aren't timeless, but we wager they're more accurate than the more literal meaning of "God is a rock."

Take another description from scripture: The biblical writers represent God as a hen who protects her chicks.[4] Few people think God is an actual bird with wings, clucking, and safeguarding offspring.[5] Most think this language portrays God as one who loves, cares, and protects. It's closer to the truth to say "lover," "care-giver," "protector," and other words. But even more literally accurate words can't give us the full truth about God, because their meanings are slippery.[6]

Whether our words can say anything true about God is a long-standing and complex debate. I proceed in this book by assuming language about the divine provides partial but not full truth. I also believe we can know something but not everything about God, even while we should avoid claiming certainty.

---

[4] See Ps. 36:7, 57:1, 63:7, 91:4, 57:1, 63:7, 91:4; Mt. 23:37; Lk. 13:34.

[5] One exception is Mark Wallace. See *When God Was a Bird: Christianity, Animism, and the Re-Enchantment of the World* (New York: Fordham University Press, 2018).

[6] Jacques Derrida's project reveals the incessant imprecision of language. For how it affects religious language, see John C. Caputo, *The Prayers and Tears of Jacques Derrida: Religion without Religion* (Bloomington, IN: Indiana University Press, 1997).

I consider two "God is" statements the most straightforward descriptions of deity. Those are "God is love" and "God is spirit." Each requires explanation, of course,[7] and neither tells us everything we want to know. But these two statements lie at center of this systematic theology, and I often use the phrase "loving Spirit" when referring to God.

This open and relational, systematic theology of love orders the divine attributes around, and understands various divine activities as pointing to, a universal Spirit of Love. I take this as my regulative idea or orienting concern. For the remainder of this chapter, I'll explore how I interpret "God is love." I'll explore what I mean by "God is spirit" in the next chapter.

## GOD IS LOVE

Biblical writers place a special emphasis upon God and love, and many contemporary people readily connect the two. The theologian John Wesley put love's priority this way: "God is often styled holy, righteous, wise," but "he is said to *be* love: intimating that this is . . . his reigning attribute, the attribute that sheds an amiable glory on all his other perfections."[8] Timothy Jackson seems to agree when he says, "'Love' is God's proper name, in the sense that it is the most univocal identification we can make of God."[9] I agree with Wesley and Jackson.

When Wesley says God is said to *be* love, he's referring to the Apostle John's words, "God is love" (1 Jn. 4:8, 16). And this fits with Jackson saying "love" is God's proper name. On a spectrum between

---

[7] Karl Barth notes the central significance of "God is love" and "God is spirit." "The two [phrases] explain one another," Barth says. "To say 'love' in the Johannine sense is to say 'Spirit . . .' And to say 'Spirit' in the Johannine sense is to say 'love.'" Barth's interpretation of the two is intricately tied to his doctrine of the trinity, however, and not to God's essential love for creation. See *Church Dogmatics*, Vol. IV/2, edited by G. W. Bromiley and T. F. Torrance (Edinburgh: T&T Clark, 1958), 757.

[8] John Wesley, *Explanatory Notes on the New Testament* (New York: Lanes and Scott, 1850), 1 John 4:8. For a scholarly overview of Wesley's theology, see Randy L. Maddox, *Responsible Grace* (Nashville, TN: Kingswood, 1994).

[9] Timothy P. Jackson, *Christian Charity and Social Justice* (Princeton: Princeton University Press, 2003), 24.

literally and symbolically true, "God is love" sits closer to literal.[10] Being true, however, doesn't make the three-word phrase crystal clear.

Systematic theologians interpret the biblical assertion "God is love" variously. How each thinks about the other divine attributes and God's action affects their interpretations. Their understanding of time, causation, existence, freedom, relations, and well-being also influences what they think. For instance, it's common for Christian theologians to claim God necessarily loves Godself but doesn't necessarily love creation. I disagree with this, as I'll explain in due time.

Like any important claim, "God is love" needs explanation.

## Defining God's Love

I earlier defined love as acting intentionally, in relational response to God and others, to promote overall well-being. A lover's aim is flourishing. The Spirit's love fits this definition too, which means divine love isn't altogether different in kind from creaturely love. It's not an exception to the fundamental principles that apply to all lovers and their loving activity.[11]

To say, "God is love" means, in part, that the Spirit acts intentionally, in relational response to creation and past divine experiences, to promote overall well-being. Just like creaturely love, divine love seeks to enhance the flourishing of the beloved.[12] An act of the Spirit's love is an event, as God intentionally relates with others, their environments, and their own histories. And because divine love must be relational, creaturely activity plays a part.

---

[10] On this claim, see Gustavo Gutierrez, *The God of Life* (Maryknoll, NY: Orbis, 1996).

[11] Alfred North Whitehead makes this point in his thinking about God and creation. He says, "God isn't to be treated as an exception to all metaphysical principles, invoked to save their collapse. God is their chief exemplification." See *Process and Reality: An Essay in Cosmology*, Corrected edition by David Ray Griffin and Donald W. Sherburne (New York: Free, 1978 [1929]), 343. For an overview of Whitehead's view of religion, see Daniel A. Dombrowski, *Whitehead's Religious Thought* (Albany, NY: SUNY, 2017).

[12] Paul J. Schutz offers a beautiful theology of well-being in *A Theology of Flourishing: The Fullness of Life for All Creation* (Maryknoll, NY: Orbis, 2025).

To say the Spirit loves means that God is a relational person.[13] Divine love is, therefore, more than an idea, desire, relationship, force, union, or energy. These words may describe love's elements or goals, but they aren't love in themselves. Put another way, the Spirit's love is value-laden action done in response to creatures and creation with the intention of advancing what's good.[14] God gives and receives, in the sense of affecting creaturely others and being affected, and the Spirit seeks overall well-being.

My definition of divine love draws from various sources, including scripture, our moral intuitions, perfect-being theology, and creaturely experience. It breaks with classical theologies that define love exclusively as desire or union. It also breaks with contemporary definitions that focus exclusively upon relationships, energies, or affection.

As I argued earlier and have argued elsewhere, my definition of love includes the valid dimensions of these alternative perspectives.[15] When properly defined, however, love's primary focus is promoting abundant life, flourishing, blessedness, *shalom*, or well-being. This focus fits the majority of the biblical witness to love and fits with a primary way most people understand love today.

In coming sections, I'll explain how divine love differs from creaturely love in mode, duration, and extensiveness. I believe God transcends creatures in these ways, because there are unique features of the Spirit's love. But divine love doesn't differ in kind from creaturely love, so the fundamental definition of love I offer applies to both God and creatures.

Divine love isn't an exception to loving; it exemplifies loving.

---

[13] Vincent Brummer stresses the importance of relations for love in *The Model of Love* (Cambridge: Cambridge University Press, 1993).

[14] On the importance of actions for theology, see Malcolm Torry, *An Actological Theology* (Eugene, OR: Wipf and Stock, 2024).

[15] See my extensive discussion of various definitions and types of love in my books *Pluriform Love* and *Defining Love*.

## LOVE ISN'T GOD

Some claim the phrase "God is love" can be interchangeable with "love is God." We can equate the two, they say, like we might "an unmarried man is a bachelor" with "a bachelor is an unmarried man." For them, love and God mean the same thing.[16]

Equating love with God doesn't fit the context of John's letter, however, nor other biblical writings. After all, John says, "love is *from* God." If love is from God, it can't *be* God.[17] When biblical writers instruct readers to "love one another," they're not telling them to *God* one another. Love is an action, while the Spirit, I will argue, is a universal person. Persons act; acts don't person.

Equating love with God easily leads to dismissing creaturely love. The twentieth century's most influential theologian of love, Anders Nygren, made this mistake. He argued that God sovereignly determines creaturely love.[18] "All choice on man's part is excluded,"[19] says Nygren. Instead of thinking the Spirit empowers creatures to love freely, Nygren uses the domination language of master and slaves for divine action.[20] What we think to be creatures loving, he says, is *actually* God.[21]

Identifying love with God easily leads to dismissing creatures entirely. This results in either a pantheism that erases all distinctions between the divine and creation, or an affirmation of human depravity

---

[16] A number of theologians employ the trinity as a way to equate love and God. The Johannine text doesn't explicitly support this, however. And the equivocation and confusion that often ensues fails to help us gain clarity. For an example, see Karl Barth, *Church Dogmatics*.

[17] Some appeal to John 1:1 to say that just as the word was *from* God and also *is* God, so love can be from God, and is also God. I interpret the John 1 passage to be a wisdom Christology that personifies the Logos rather than claiming Jesus must literally be God. I address this issue in volume two of this systematic theology of love.

[18] See Anders Nygren, *Agape and Eros: A Study of the Christian Idea of Love*, trans. Philip S. Watson (Chicago: University of Chicago Press, 1982), 75. See also 76-81.

[19] Ibid., 213.

[20] John B. Cobb, Jr. argues that humans require divine grace in "Human Responsibility and the Primacy of Grace," *Thy Nature and Thy Name is Love*, Bryan P. Stone and Thomas Jay Oord, eds. (Nashville, TN: Abingdon, 2001).

[21] For an extensive review and criticism of Anders Nygren's theology of love, see Thomas Jay Oord, *Pluriform Love*, chs. 3-4.

that erases all creaturely value and agency. I reject both results. We are wise to differentiate love and God, but say instead the Spirit inspires creatures to express love.[22]

"If we love one another," John says, "God abides in us, and God's love is perfected in us" (4:12). This passage identifies God's presence in creaturely loving. In fact, says John, "those who abide in love abide in God, and God abides in them" (4:16). These lines point to a close connection between God and love without collapsing the two.

Love isn't God, because love is action in relation, aimed at flourishing.

## Self-Giving, Others-Empowering

I interpret the Johannine phrase "God is love" to mean, in part, that creaturely love requires the Spirit's empowering. Deity is the source, instigator, or inspiration for our loving. As John puts it, "we love, because [God] first loved us" (1 Jn. 4:19). "Whoever doesn't love doesn't know God," John also says, indicating this necessary connection (4:8). This shows us what it means for God to "abide" in those who love.

To use philosophical language, the Spirit is a necessary cause for every expression of creaturely love. Without God empowering them, creatures could do nothing (Jn 15:5). Because the Spirit necessarily and by nature loves all, however, God necessarily empowers all. Love for creation comes logically first in the divine nature, so the Spirit will not, and cannot, abandon us. God necessarily loves creation, and we are all "beloved" (Eph. 5:1; 1 Jn. 4:7).

The Spirit never turns creatures into robots. "Since God loved us so much," says John, "we also ought to love one another" (12). "Ought" in this phrase suggests free choices on our part, and scripture, in general, assumes creaturely freedom. We freely decide how to respond to God's empowering invitations. Those beloved by the Spirit—which would be everyone and everything—can choose whether to cooperate.

---

[22] Paul Fiddes argues in favor of "Love is God." For reasons I give here, I disagree. See the Fiddes essay, "God Is Love, But Is Love God? Towards a Theology of Love as Knowledge," in *Love as Common Ground: Essays on Love in Religion*, Paul S. Fiddes, ed. (New York: Lexington, 2021).

# A Loving God

In each moment of existence, the universal Spirit invites creatures to love God, others, themselves, and/or creation.[23] Put simply, a loving God calls us to love. Many theologians call God's enabling of creatures "prevenient grace."[24] The loving Spirit comes before and makes possible free creaturely responses in each moment, so creatures depend upon God's inspiring grace.[25]

God's prevenient love empowers rather than overpowers others.[26]

## Uncontrolling

A hallmark of this systematic theology is the claim that God's love is uncontrolling. Because uncontrolling love comes logically first in God, and because the Spirit self-gives and others-empowers, divine love *can't* control.[27] The Spirit loves everyone and everything and, therefore, can't control anyone or anything. God *can't*.[28]

---

[23] John Wesley expresses this well when he says God doesn't "take away your liberty, your power of choosing good or evil." And "[God] did not *force* you, but being *assisted* by [God's] grace you, like Mary, *chose* the better part." In "The General Spread of the Gospel," Sermon 63, *The Works of John Wesley*, vol. 2 (Nashville, TN: Abingdon, 1985), 281 (italics in original).

[24] For examples of theologians who employ this view of prevenient grace, see Barry L. Callen, *God as Loving Grace* (Nappanee, IN: Evangel, 1996); John B. Cobb, Jr., *Grace and Responsibility* (Nashville, TN: Abingdon, 1995); Kenneth J. Collins, *The Theology of John Wesley* (Nashville, TN: Abingdon, 2007); Gregory Crofford, *Streams of Mercy* (Lexington, KY: Emeth, 2010); Steve Harper, "Amipotence in the Wesleyan Tradition," in *Amipotence, vol. 2*, Brandon Brown, et. al., eds. (Grasmere, ID: SacraSage, 2025); Michael Lodahl, *God of Nature and of Grace* (Nashville, TN: Abingdon, 2003); Randy L. Maddox, *Responsible Grace* (Nashville, TN: Abingdon, 1994); Thomas Jay Oord and Michael Lodahl, *Relational Holiness* (Kansas City, MO: Beacon Hill Press of Kansas City, 2005); Johan Tredoux, *Mildred Bangs Wynkoop* (Kansas City, MO: Foundery, 2017); Mildred Bangs Wynkoop, *A Theology of Love* (Kansas City, MO: Beacon Hill, 1972).

[25] Risto Saarinen explores the theological nuances of giving and the gift. See *God and the Gift* (Collegeville, MN: Liturgical, 2005).

[26] Brandon Brown expresses this beautifully in "The Prevenience of Amipotence," in *Amipotence, vol. 2*, Brandon Brown, et. al., eds. (Grasmere, ID: SacraSage, 2025).

[27] Graham Adams expresses these ideas in his various books, especially in his use of anarchy language. See *Holy Anarchy* (London: SCM, 2022). See also Adams's essay, "Amipotence with Added Anarchy," in *Amipotence, vol. 2*, Brandon Brown, et. al., eds. (Grasmere, ID: SacraSage, 2025).

[28] I explain the implications of this view for thinking about evil in *God Can't: How to Believe in God and Love after Tragedy, Abuse, and Other Evils* (Grasmere, ID: SacraSage, 2015). See also *Dio No Puede*, Lemuel Sandoval, trans. (2019); *GOTT kann das nicht!* Michael Trenkel and Dirk Weisensee, trans. (2020); *Deus Nao Pode*, Ricardo Quadros Gouvea, trans. (2023).

While the Spirit of Love always serves as a necessary cause for creaturely loving, it's never a sufficient cause.[29] God's love enables and inspires but "never forces its own way," to use the language of the Apostle Paul (1 Cor. 13:5). The Spirit lovingly gives freedom, agency, self-determination, and indeterminacy to all creatures, depending on their complexity. God can't fail to provide these gifts, nor can God withdraw nor override them. They are, to use the Apostle Paul's words, "irrevocable" (Rom. 11:29).

Some people call the control of others "coercion." This word has multiple meanings, however, and most pertain to psychological threats or bodily force. A bully might coerce his victim by threatening bodily harm. A rugby player may coerce by smashing another player on the pitch. A king may coerce a neighboring country by threatening war.[30] In philosophical parlance, however, "coerce" refers not necessarily to violence or threat, but to unilateral determination, in the sense of one actor or cause entirely controlling another.[31] To coerce, philosophically speaking, would be to act as a sufficient cause by unilaterally determining others.

The Spirit doesn't coerce anyone or anything in any of these senses.[32] God doesn't bully, although the Spirit may warn us of possible dangers. God doesn't exert violent bodily impact either, because the Spirit doesn't have a divine body.[33] And God doesn't threaten war. The Spirit

---

[29] In previous writings, I have used "almighty" to describe God's uncontrolling power. I've said God is almighty, 1) in the sense of being mightier *than* any other being; 2) in the sense of exerting might *upon* all others; 3) in the sense that God is the source of might or empowerment *for* all. While I continue to think God can rightly be understood as almighty in these three ways, I now wish I had emphasized the priority of love. "Amipotence" better describes the power of God's love than "almighty," and I'll explain what I mean by amipotence in a later chapter.

[30] John H. Buchanon express this worry in his essay, "Why Can't God Do More?" in *Amipotence*, vol. 1, Chris Baker, et. al., eds. (Grasmere, ID: SacraSage, 2024).

[31] Palmyre Oomen explains this issue well in "God's Power and Almightiness in Whitehead's Thought," *Open Theology*, 1:1 (2015).

[32] Paul Sponheim reimagines divine power in light of love in *Love's Availing Power* (Minneapolis: Fortress, 2011). Brian Zahnd aims to rethink God in light of love in *Sinners in the Hands of a Loving God* (London: Waterbrook, 2017).

[33] Deanna M. Young addresses issues of divine power in relation to Old Testament stories that have been interpreted as requiring divine control. She argues otherwise. See *Unblaming God: Interpreting the Old Testament Through the Lens of Jesus Christ* (Grasmere, ID: SacraSage, 2023).

can't coerce in the sense of unilaterally determining creatures or creation, which means God can't singlehandedly decide outcomes. The implications of the Spirit's love being uncontrolling will become clearer in later chapters, and I'll explain it further when I discuss divine power.[34]

Love that controls isn't love at all.

## Pluriform

The Spirit and creatures express love in an unimaginably large number of ways. Scripture tells us that neither death, nor life, nor angels, nor rulers, nor things present, nor things to come, nor powers, nor height, nor depth, nor anything in all creation will be able to separate us from diverse expressions of God's love (Rom. 8:38-39). And yet these expressions align with the general definition of love I've offered.

Love's definition is uniform, but its expressions are pluriform. "Love is a many-splendored thing," to quote Shakespeare, because the fruit (plural) of the Spirit is love (Gal. 5:22).

Some theologians say divine love takes only one or maybe just a few forms, and many use various Greek words for love to make these arguments. Anders Nygren, for instance, argued that God's love must be *agape* not *eros*. Augustine argued that divine love is self-oriented desire, which means *eros* not *agape*.[35] Still others say God essentially loves only in Trinity, which means God necessarily loves with *philia* but not *agape*.[36]

---

[34] On God's love as uncontrolling, see Thomas Jay Oord, *The Uncontrolling Love of God* (Downers Grove, IL: IVP Academic, 2015); L. Michaels, et. al., eds., *Uncontrolling Love* (Grasmere, ID: SacraSage, 2017); Annie DeRolf, Christy Gunter, John Loppnow, and Lon Marshall, and Thomas Jay Oord, eds., *Love Does Not Control* (Grasmere, ID: SacraSage, 2023); Jeff Wells, et. al., eds., *Preaching the Uncontrolling Love of God* (Grasmere, ID: SacraSage, 2024).

[35] See my discussion of Augustine in chapter one of this book and in *Pluriform Love*, ch. 5.

[36] No Agape in Trinity. The words *philia* and *agape* (and their various forms) have various and often overlapping meaning in scripture. *Eros* also has various meanings in ancient texts. The claim that God doesn't express *agape* in Trinity assumes a definition of *agape* that involves a lover responding to actions that bring ill-being rather than well-being. Therefore, *agape* can't be expressed among perfectly loving members of the Trinity. I explain this in my exploration of Jürgen Moltmann's book, *The Trinity and the Kingdom of God*. See Thomas Jay Oord, "Jürgen Moltmann's Doctrine of the Trinity and Creatio Ex Nihilo," *Religion Online* (https://www.religion-online.org/article/Jürgen-moltmanns-trinitarian-theology-and-creatio-ex-nihilo/)

Given the biblical witness and widespread experience, it makes better sense to say God and creatures express many forms of love. Love is unlimited, in the sense that everyone is worthy of love, and loving takes a myriad of expressions.[37] These forms vary widely but include at least three archetypes: *agape, eros*, and *philia*.

God and creatures express *agape* when they act intentionally, in relational response to God and others, to promote overall well-being in response to actions that harm, destroy, or are sinful. *Agape* promotes well-being in response to ill-being.[38] It turns the other cheek, metaphorically speaking. God and creatures express love *in spite of* something negative happening.[39]

God and creatures express *eros* too.[40] This form of love involves acting intentionally, in relational response to God and others, to promote overall well-being in response to what's beautiful or valuable. *Eros* is a form of love expressed *because of* something being valuable, and it often seeks to enhance or enjoy what's good. God and creatures demonstrate *eros* in response to the value inherent in others or the future value that might arise.[41] *Eros* tries to make a value-laden world better.[42]

---

[37] Stephen G. Post explores various forms of love in his book. See, for instance, *Pure Unlimited Love* (New York: Morehouse, 2025).

[38] For diverse notions of *agape* and their implications for theologies of love, see Craig A. Boyd, *Visions of Agape: Problems and Possibilities in Human and Divine Love* (Burlington, VT: Ashgate, 2008).

[39] See my lengthy discussion of the meaning of *agape* in *Pluriform Love*, chs. 3-4. See also the work of Chris Hanson to incorporate the three archetypes in *Open and Relational Parenting: Loving Parents Reflecting a Loving God* (Grasmere, ID: SacraSage, 2025).

[40] Among those who make strong arguments for divine *eros*, see Paul Avis, *Eros and the Sacred* (Harrisburg, PA: Morehouse, 1989); Virginia Burrus and Catherine Keller, eds., *Toward a Theology of Eros* (New York: Fordham University Press, 2007); Janna Gonwa, "Eros, Agape, and Neighbour-Love as Ontological Gift," *Toronto Journal of Theology*, 31:1 (Spring 2015): 84-93; Werner Jeanrond, *A Theology of Love* (London: T & T Clark, 2010); Catherine Osborne, *Eros Unveiled* (Oxford: Clarendon, 1994).

[41] For a powerful argument that God enjoys creation, and creatures ought to enjoy in response, see Elaine Padilla, *Divine Enjoyment: A Theology of Passion and Exuberance* (New York: Fordham University Press, 2015). Rita Nakashima Brock offers an erotic theology in *Journeys By Heart: A Christology of Erotic Power* (New York: Crossroads, 1988).

[42] See my lengthy discussion of *eros* in *Pluriform Love*, chs. 5-6.

God and creatures also express *philia*. This form of love acts intentionally, in relational response to God and others, to promote overall well-being in solidarity or companionship with others. While all forms of love involve relationship, *philia* builds from relations to promote well-being. *Philia* is expressed in *koinonia*, friendship, and community.[43] Those who express it intend to promote well-being *alongside* or in collaboration with creatures and creation.[44]

While it's crucial to have a clear definition of love and to identify love's forms, actual expressions of love often matter most. Love in people's lived experience makes a concrete difference to them, and experienced love will often be more inspirational than love in theory. For instance, the Spirit of Love expresses forgiveness as a form of love by forgiving everyone. This belief is crucial theologically, but it's fairly abstract. It matters greatly that we also believe God forgives us as particular individuals for our particular sins. We *ourselves* are forgiven.[45] And we can love by forgiving those who harm us.[46]

The Spirit loves by enjoying and rejoicing in the world's value. It would be hard to treat ourselves, others, and creation with respect and admiration if we thought creatures were valueless. This general truth matters in theory. But it's also crucial to believe God finds *us* valuable as individuals, families, and communities. Children sing, "Jesus Loves Me," because of this truth. It's also crucial to believe God finds our enemies and strangers valuable so that we might also. We find these themes in worship songs such as "Love Like You" and "God of Justice."

Love is uniform in essence but pluriform in expression.

---

[43] For how theologians have understood friendship, see Liz Carmichael, *Friendship: Interpreting Christian Love* (London: T & T Clark, 2004); Mary E. Hunt, *Fierce Tenderness: A Feminist Theology of Friendship* (New York: Crossroad, 1994); Gilbert C. Meilander, *Friendship* (Notre Dame: University of Notre Dame Press, 1981).

[44] See my lengthy discussion of *philia* in *Pluriform Love*, chs. 7-8.

[45] Kevin Hector explores well themes of love and forgiveness in *Christianity as a Way of Life: A Systematic Theology* (New Haven, CT: Yale University Press, 2023), ch. 6.

[46] Matthew Ichihashi Potts argues well that forgiveness is choosing not to retaliate rather than salving the conscience of the harmer or ignoring one's pain. See *Forgiveness: An Alternative Account* (New Haven, CT: Yale University Press, 2022).

## Grace, Mercy, and Compassion

The language of love is multi-faceted, and the biblical witness reflects this diversity. We commonly find references to God's grace (χαρις), for instance, in scripture. People debate the meanings of the grace, and the meanings vary depending on the context.[47] When connected with God, the word generally refers to divine favor, blessing, or goodness toward creation. Most biblical commentators have been quick to say that grace is an active word rather than something abstract.[48] God's grace manifests as a good gift given.

Systematic theologians often add that divine grace is "unmerited." This aligns with my saying God loves necessarily, because love comes first in the divine nature. God loves creatures, no matter what.

Theologians who teach total depravity, however, often mean by "unmerited" that humans are valueless sinners. And they want to emphasize how utterly awful and worthless creatures are. Millard Erickson illustrates this when he says, "grace contemplates humans as sinful, guilty, and condemned."[49] Some call this "worm theology," in the negative sense associated with Isaac Watts's well-known lyric that God saves "such a worm as I."[50]

Grace must be reclaimed from so-called "worm" theologies. I believe we better understand grace as a way to talk about the Spirit's unconditional love for intrinsically valuable creatures. The Spirit unwaveringly loves those of inestimable worth. God's grace, therefore, represents divine love for creatures whether they promote well-being (love) or ill-being (sin). The Spirit loves valuable creatures, no matter what they do (Tit. 3:4-7).

Negatively framed references to the love word "mercy" have also arisen from unhelpful theologies. Those saying God is merciful or "has mercy" often do so in a context that points to human sin. These

---

[47] One of the better analyses of grace comes from Brent J. Schmidt in *Relational Grace: The Reciprocal and Binding Covenant of Charis* (Provo, UT: BYU Studies, 2015).

[48] See, for example, James D. G., Dunn, *Romans 1-8* (Dallas: Word Books, 1988), p. 17.

[49] Millard J. Erickson, *Christian Theology*, 2nd ed. (Grand Rapids, MI: Baker, 1998), 322.

[50] See the Watts hymn, "Alas, and Did My Savior Bleed."

theologians say God shows mercy by choosing to withhold punishment.[51] At least *sometimes*. This view fits the ancient philosopher Seneca's definition of mercy as "leniency in matters of exacting punishment."[52] The common prayer, "May God have mercy upon me," can give the impression God will punish unless persuaded otherwise!

Rather than understanding "mercy" as leniency in punishment, I believe we better understand it as the Spirit's necessary loving response to creatures.[53] God is necessarily merciful.[54] The Spirit evaluates all we do, including when we do harm, and tenderly loves us. We find no situation in which God may punish, harm, or injure creatures, so we don't need to pray for God to mercifully avert vengeance.[55] God *always* forgives, blesses, and heals; the Spirit, by nature, is never vengeful.[56] Just as grace has been wrongly linked to human sin, therefore, mercy often has been wrongly linked to divine punishment (Ps. 103:10).[57]

Finally, references to God's compassion in scripture and everyday language point to key theological claims about the Spirit. Traditional

---

[51] Paul Joseph Greene addresses the theological problems that arise when love is sidelined. See *The End of Divine Truthiness* (Eugene, OR: Wipf and Stock, 2018).

[52] Seneca, *De clementia*, Susanna Braund, trans. (Oxford: Oxford University Press, 2009), II, 3, 1.

[53] Gregory Anderson Love argues eloquently for a nonviolent God revealed in Jesus. See *Love, Violence, and the Cross: How the Nonviolent God Saves Us Through the Cross of Christ* (Eugene, OR: Cascade, 2010).

[54] Charles Atkins explores the importance of unqualified divine love for prisoners. For instance, see his essay, "Amipotence Confined," in *Amipotence, vol. 2*, Brandon Brown, et. al., eds. (Grasmere, ID: SacraSage, 2025).

[55] A number of scholars have argued against the notion that God uses violence. See Gregory A. Boyd, *Crucifixion of the Warrior God*, 2 Vols. (Minneapolis, MN: Fortress, 2017); Matthew Curtis Fleischer, *The Old Testament Case for Nonviolence* (Eugene, OR: Cascade, 2024); Gregory Anderson Love, *Love, Violence, and the Cross* (Eugene, OR: Cascade Books, 2010); Sharon L. Baker Putt, *A Nonviolent Theology of Love* (Minneapolis: Fortress, 2021); Eric A. Seibert, *Disturbing Divine Behavior* (Philadelphia: Fortress, 2009) and *The Violence of Scripture* (Philadelphia: Fortress, 2012); Deanna M. Young, *Unblaming God: Interpreting the Old Testament Through the Lens of Jesus Christ* (Grasmere, ID: SacraSage, 2023).

[56] Adis Duderija argues from an Islamic perspective for amipotence as mercy. See "From Amipotence to All-Encompassing Mercy," in *Amipotence, vol. 2*, Brandon Brown, et. al., eds. (Grasmere, ID: SacraSage, 2025).

[57] This thought is illustrated in the chapter title coined by Robert Luhn, "God isn't Mad at You." See Thomas Jay Oord and Robert Luhn, *The Best News You'll Ever Hear* (Grasmere, ID: SacraSage, 2011).

theologians deny that God empathizes with creatures. They base their denial upon the view that God isn't causally related to creatures, in the sense of being affected or influenced by them. Consequently, God as traditionally described can't be compassionate.

By contrast, this systematic theology of love champions divine compassion. God feels emotions and responds to creatures. Divine compassion is God's emotional response and action after empathizing with suffering creatures. Relational theology affirms the numerous biblical references to divine compassion.

Believing the Spirit is compassionate, necessarily merciful, and loves creatures with intrinsic value provides a firm basis for us to trust God. A God who doesn't empathize can't relate to our suffering. A God who may or may not be merciful isn't trustworthy. And a God who thought creatures valueless would be likely to neglect them.

Theologies that prize punishment over forgiveness, independence over compassion, and depravity over creaturely value misconstrue the Spirit's love.

## Distributive, Restorative (Not Retributive) Justice

The biblical witness points to a Spirit who has a particular desire to help the poor, marginalized, harmed, and least of these. In fact, God's greatest anger is reserved for those who neglect or mistreat those with fewer resources or opportunities.

Numerous biblical passages refer to a God who forgives, but some portray God as punishing. And for some theologians, punishment cashes out as an aspect of the Spirit's justice. By "justice," they mean God induces pain or loss of some kind in response to sin. In fact, it's not uncommon for traditional theologians to insist we must balance love with justice, God's mercy with divine punishment.

When Millard Erickson addresses divine justice, for instance, he advocates for "enforcement of appropriate consequences for wrong action." "God's justice requires that there be payment of the penalty of sin," he says, and "the offer of Jesus Christ as atonement" is required so that "both the justice and love of God" can be maintained.[58] "There is tension" between the two, he says, "only if one's view of love requires that God forgive sin without any payment being made. But that is to think of God as different from what he really is. Moreover, the offer of Christ as atonement shows a greater love on God's part than would simply indulgently releasing people from the consequences of sin."[59]

Erickson's argument rests on a retributive, tit-for-tat, eye-for-eye view of justice. He can't imagine God forgiving or "indulgently" releasing people from payment or punishment. To believe deity freely forgives would be, as he sees it, "to think of God as different from what he really is." For Erickson, justice means God meting out the consequences sin deserves.

This systematic theology of love views God's justice differently. God always forgives and always indulgently releases people. The Spirit of steadfast love never needs payment and never punishes. Rather than Jesus paying some price to a vengeful God for atonement, his death reveals a God who refuses to seek revenge and who repays evil with good.[60] This deity works to restore to health those broken from sin and evil.

We do better to understand divine justice as the Spirit's concern for the well-being of all, especially those most jeopardized in life, mistreated, impoverished, or threatened. A loving Spirit's justice won't ever be punitive; it's distributive and restorative. By "distributive," I mean God wants us to distribute resources among the whole rather than hoard it for the few. And God's response to sin and evil will always be a course of action aimed at rehabilitation and restoration.

It's true that there will be natural, negative consequences that come from sin and evil. And it's true that God grieves, can be angry, and laments. But the Spirit who feels negative emotions when creatures

---

[58] Nichole Torbitzky offers a much better theory of atonement in "Amipotence and Atonement," in *Amipotence, vol. 2*, Brandon Brown, et. al., eds. (Grasmere, ID: SacraSage, 2025).

[59] Erickson, *Christian Theology*, 324-25.

[60] Tripp Fuller addresses Jesus from an open and relational theology perspective in *Divine Self-Investment: An Open and Relational Constructive Christology* (Grasmere, ID: SacraSage, 2021).

harm one another or themselves always forgives and never punishes, works to heal rather than inflicting harm, and reconciles the parties involved rather than retaliating.

The Spirit isn't in the punishment business.

## The Spirit's Love as Free and Necessary

"God is love" means that love is an essential attribute of the Spirit's nature. The Spirit loves, because love is what deity does.[61] God inevitably loves, no matter the condition of creatures and creation. To put it another way, there are no circumstances in which deity exists and doesn't love creatures. And because not even the Spirit can change the divine nature—God "can't deny himself" (2 Tim. 2:13)—the Spirit of Love should be understood as essentially loving.

Theologian Jacob Arminius can be helpful in understanding how God loves by nature and, therefore, necessarily. Arminius argues that God doesn't freely decide to be good. "It is the summit of blasphemy to say that God is freely good," he says. "God is good by natural necessity, according to his entire nature and essence."[62]

God's essential goodness is at stake in this debate. "If God be freely good, that is, *not* by nature and natural necessity," Arminius argues, "[God] can be or can be made *not* good." After all, "as what anyone wills freely, [God] has it in his power not to will; and whatever anyone does freely, he can refrain from doing."[63] Therefore, God is, according to Arminius, necessarily and not freely good.

When we apply this way of thinking to God and love, it means the Spirit isn't freely loving. With Arminius, we should say that God loves by nature. If God were to decide freely *whether* to love, God could freely decide *not* to do so. Not even God could keep God from doing

---

[61] Ilia Delio writes powerfully about God's nature of love in *The Emergent Christ* (Maryknoll, NY: Orbis, 2012).

[62] See *Works of James Arminius*, William Bagnall, trans. (London: Derby, Miller, and Orton, 1853), 344, 345.

[63] Ibid., 345. Emphases added.

evil, because love would *not* have logical priority nor be the Spirit's reigning attribute.

If love doesn't come first among God's attributes, there's no reason to think God *will* always love us. Or *has* always loved us. To put it negatively, we can't trust a God whose nature isn't love. Such a deity could break bad; the divine could do dastardly deeds. Put positively: we can always trust the Spirit whose nature is love and, therefore, loves necessarily. This Spirit *always* acts for the good of creation.[64]

When I explored the definition of love earlier, I said love involves freedom. I also said various forces, factors, and actors limit a lover's freedom. So, does saying the Spirit necessarily loves mean my love definition doesn't apply to God?

No, it does apply. God loves by necessity in one respect but freely in another. By nature, the Spirit must love, because love comes before choice in God. The divine nature limits what the Spirit can do, if "limit" is the right word for this logical entailment based upon a metaphysical reality. To the question *whether* the Spirit will love, the answer is God loves necessarily.[65]

But God loves freely as an experiential free agent. As the Spirit moves moment by moment into an open future, deity freely chooses which forms and expressions of love to enact. God can't be certain which will yield the best results, because the future isn't something actual to be known, and creatures freely contribute to outcomes.[66] To the question of *how* the Spirit loves in each moment, therefore, the answer

---

[64] John Peckham addresses issues like these in *The Love of God: A Canonical Model* (Downers Grove, IL: InterVarsity, 2015). He argues that God's love for the world isn't necessary but also not arbitrary. Given that Peckham predicates God's love ultimately upon the divine will, I see no way he can overcome the charge of arbitrariness. On this, see Peckham's chapter, "The Volitional Aspect of Divine Love."

[65] Some open and relational theologians put God's free choice logically before God's nature. Or they affirm divine freedom and dismiss divine essence altogether. For reasons I note in this and future chapters, I disagree. But for examples of open and relational thinkers who prioritize freedom above all else, see Paul Fiddes, *The Creative Suffering of God* (Oxford: Clarendon, 1992).and Jon Paul Sydnor, *The Great Open Dance: A Progressive Christian Theology* (Eugene, OR: Pickwick, 2024).

[66] Ryan Patrick McLaughlin explores this in relation to my claims about amipotence. See his arguments and my response in "The Loving God Incapable of Love," originally published in *Amipotence, vol. 1*, Chris S. Baker, et. al., eds. (Grasmere, ID: SacraSage, 2025).

would be that the Spirit freely chooses among the best options in relation to creation. In this sense, God loves freely.⁶⁷

Only in God does love necessarily come before free choice. After all, God *is* love.

## Scriptural Diversity

Saying the God who *is* love also freely chooses *how* to love fits important aspects of the scriptural witness. According to scripture, God sometimes regrets and repents.⁶⁸ To regret is to wish one would have made a different choice. To repent is to make a different choice than previously or change plans about what will be done in the future. Regretting and repenting language assumes God makes free choices among possibilities, and God can't be certain which will be most fruitful.

To claim, as I have, that God necessarily loves all requires me to deal with biblical passages that portray God as unloving. For instance, the writer of Malachi has God say, "I have loved Jacob, but Esau I have hated. I have laid waste his hill country and left his heritage to jackals of the desert" (1:2-3). Because God *is* love, in the sense of necessarily loving, I interpret this passage to reflect the writer's perspective and not the truth about God.⁶⁹ This portrait of the divine comes from mistaken humans.

Or take the story of God's reaction to Israel making a golden calf to worship. The writers of the book of Exodus have God say, "I have seen these people, and they are a stiff-necked people. Now leave me alone so that my anger may burn against them and that I may destroy them"

---

⁶⁷ The helpfulness of distinguishing between God's nature and experience seems to have eluded Arminius, influenced as he was by Luis de Molina.

⁶⁸ Terrence Fretheim writes often and well about divine repentance in scripture. In addition to Fretheim's books, see "The Repentance of God: A Key to Evaluating Old Testament God-Talk," *Horizons in Biblical Theology*, 10.1 (1988), 47-70. https://doi.org/10.1163/187122088X00049

⁶⁹ John Wesley assumed problematic biblical passages could be interpreted to affirm God's love. "No scripture can mean that God isn't love, or that his mercy isn't over all his works." See "Free Grace," *The Bicentennial Edition of the Works of John Wesley*, Vol. 3 (Nashville, TN: Abingdon, 1984), 556. On Wesley's hermeneutic of love, see Rem B. Edwards, "John Wesley's Non-Literal Literalism and Hermeneutic of Love" *Wesleyan Theological Journal* 51:2 (2016):26-40; Edwards, *John Wesley's Values — And Ours* (Lexington: Emeth, 2013).

(32:9-10). But Moses says to God, "Turn from your fierce anger; relent and don't bring disaster on your people" (32:12). Moses then reminds God of the promise of ancestors and land. Exodus says, "the Lord relented and did not bring on his people the disaster he had threatened" (32:14).[70]

I don't think God needs to be reminded to do good, and I don't think God ever considers destroying or hating people.[71] I conclude these scriptures don't accurately portray God. To claim God necessarily loves, therefore, requires us to interpret some biblical passages as reflecting the misunderstandings of the writers that penned them. While the overall portrayal of God points to a Spirit of steadfast love, some passages (wrongly) portray God as unloving.

Or take the writer of Hosea as one who offers diverse biblical language about God and love. At times, God is portrayed as one who threatens humiliation upon Gomer/Israel because of her unfaithfulness. But these threats aren't genuine, because the text also says the compassionate Spirit can't abandon or destroy the beloved.

> How can I give you up, Ephraim?
>     How can I hand you over, O Israel?
> How can I make you like Admah?
>     How can I treat you like Zeboiim?
> My heart recoils within me;
>     my compassion grows warm and tender.
> I will not execute my fierce anger;
>     I will not again destroy Ephraim,
> for I am God and no mortal,
>     the Holy One in your midst,
>     and I will not come in wrath (Hosea 11:8-9).

---

[70] On this story and others like it, see Matthew Korpman, *Saying No to God: A Radical Approach to Reading the Bible Faithfully* (Glen Oak, CA: Quoir, 2019); J. Richard Middleton, *Abraham's Silence: The Binding of Isaac, The Suffering of Job, and How to Talk Back to God* (Grand Rapids, MI: Baker, 2021).

[71] Eric A. Seibert addresses divine violence well. See *Disturbing Divine Behavior: Troubling Old Testament Images of God* (Minneapolis: Fortress, 2009); *The Violence of Scripture: Overcoming the Old Testament's Troubling Legacy* (Minneapolis: Fortress, 2012).

When the writer portrays the Spirit saying, "I am God and no mortal," we find a fundamental distinction between the One who *must* love and creatures who can choose not to love. This passage suggests that God's nature is love.

All of these examples suggest that biblical writers, like us, were learning what love looks like.

## Essential and Contingent Attributes

A common way to prioritize one or some divine attributes identifies those the theologian thinks essential to God and those they think contingent. Essential attributes are necessary aspects of God's nature; but God may or may not manifest the contingent attributes. Other theologians divide the divine attributes between the absolute and the relative, the natural and the moral, or greatness and goodness. Although these labels differ, the divine attributes that theologians assign to each category usually remain the same across systematic theologies.

By definition, the essence of a thing identifies what makes it what it is. Essential divine attributes therefore make God who God is, no matter what.[72] Contingent divine attributes, by contrast, are properties that God doesn't essentially need. God can be God without those attributes; deity may or may not exhibit them.

For instance, if God exists necessarily and nothing could terminate deity, existence is an essential attribute. If God could exist without creating and relating with creatures, by contrast, creating and relating would be contingent. If God necessarily exists as Spirit, nothing and no one could destroy God's spiritness. It's essential. If God could exist without loving creatures, however, love for creatures would be contingent.

The list of essential attributes theologians typically assign God includes independence, omnipotence, omniscience, immutability, impassibility, eternality, timelessness, freedom, goodness, glory, unity,

---

[72] R. T. Mullins explains essential and contingent attributes well in *Eternal in Love: A Little Book about a Big God* (Eugene, OR: Cascade, 2024).

and holiness. Most traditional systematic theologians say these attributes would be true of God isolated from creation.

Their usual list of contingent attributes includes love, creating, providence, miracle-working, communicating with creatures, compassion, wisdom, mercy and grace, patience, forgiving, justice, anger, and empathy. These attributes and activities are optional to deity. According to most theologians, God only takes on these attributes or does these activities if creatures or creation exist. They're unnecessary to God in Godself.

Some theologians who embrace a social doctrine of the Trinity think some attributes are essential on the traditional list of contingent attributes. For instance, God may essentially and everlastingly communicate and love among triune persons. If so, internal communication and love for Godself would be necessary. But divine communication with and love for creation would remain contingent.

Notice that the usual accounts of God say love for creation isn't essential to God. Love for creatures, therefore, doesn't tell us who God essentially is. In traditional theologies, God could exist without ever loving creatures. Most systematic theologians don't think God's love for creation is "natural," "absolute," or part of God's "greatness."

The usual accounts also say God existed without creation and then, for some reason, created creaturely others from nothing. If true, this would mean creating must not be an absolute or necessary feature of what it means to be divine. Creating isn't part of what makes God great, according to theologians holding this view, and creating isn't natural for deity, nor one of God's essential activities.

This theology of love differs from traditional systematic theologies when it considers love for creation an essential divine attribute. Creating and relating with creation are also essential to deity. Loving, creating, and relating are time-related activities, which means God must be essentially time-oriented too. In these and other ways, this systematic theology reconfigures the usual lists of essential and contingent attributes. These ideas will become clearer in coming chapters as I elaborate.

God's essence isn't independence *from*, but relational love *for*, creation.

## Worship-Worthy

Incoherent descriptions of God leave me uninspired. I am not motivated to worship if deity is portrayed as exceedingly powerful or sinlessly pure, but not perfectly loving.[73] Charles Wesley describes a God worthy of worship as "Love divine, all loves excelling."[74] When it comes to worship, I believe love matters most.

Some events in the universe fill us with wonder and awe. Many are nonhuman phenomena, such as earthquakes, northern lights, solar eclipses, hurricanes, dramatic cloud formations, mountaintops, or comets and shooting stars. As a photographer, I try to capture their drama with my camera. People of faith sometimes attribute these extraordinary occurrences to the divine will or God's power, and they worship in response.

Dramatic events don't always prompt me to worship God, however. An earthquake may inspire awe, for instance, but as an action it's not, in itself, worthy of worship. When a natural event causes more harm than good, I doubt God wanted it. A volcanic eruption may generate immense terror, but when it leads to unnecessary suffering, I don't believe it was God's will.

An inconsistently loving God isn't worthy of worship. I might fear this deity, but cowering in terror isn't adoration. Rabbi Harold Kushner was right when he said, "You can fear an all-powerful God, but you can't love him."[75] Worshiping the Spirit requires positive dimensions beyond sheer power—dimensions related to love, beauty, justice, truth, compassion, and so on. A good God whose actions have inspired good outcomes would be worship worthy.[76]

---

[73] On criteria for worship worthiness, see Lina Langby, *God and the World* (Albany, NY: SUNY, 2026).

[74] Charles Hartshorne agrees. See his book *The Zero Fallacy and Other Essays in Neoclassical Philosophy*, Mohammed Valady, ed. (Peru, IL: Open Court, 1997), 167.

[75] Harold Kushner, "Would an All-Powerful God be Worthy of Worship?" in *Jewish Theology and Process Thought*, Sandra B. Lubarsky and David Ray Griffin, eds. (Albany, NY: SUNY, 1996), 90.

[76] Andrew Davis argues that neither reasonless brute fact, unrelenting power, logical necessity, nor utter mystery can present a God worthy of our worship. See his essay, "God, Value, and

If worship includes wholehearted trust and admiration, then we can't worship a God who causes or allows evil.[77] That God doesn't love consistently. Keith Ward rightly says that "a God who is worthy of worship must be so good that it could never conceivably be evil." Our natural response to the supremely loving One would be attraction, admiration, and awe.[78]

I've argued that love is the Spirit's primary attribute, and love always seeks flourishing. This means worship of the Perfect Lover won't ever be static or complete. Worship and relationship with God remains, as Alfred North Whitehead put it, an "adventure."[79] And because a loving God will be relationally affected by what we do, our worship makes a real difference to us and to God.

I feel motivated to worship consistently and without reservation the One who loves consistently and without reservation. Nothing less.

## Conclusion

The characteristics of the God we believe in makes all the difference. Some people reject faith in God because traditional depictions of deity seem inconsistent, especially when it comes to love. Some theologians portray God's love as so totally unlike love as we know it, we could have no idea what it means for the Spirit to love us.

This systematic theology places "God is love" at the center of its proposals. Rather than juggling divine attributes in incoherent tension or accepting the tension but appealing to mystery, this theology seeks a consistent account of the Spirit in whose nature love is the reigning attribute.

---

Ontological Gratitude," in *From Force to Persuasion: Process-Relational Perspectives on Power and the God of Love* (Eugene, OR: Cascade, 2024), 172-185.

[77] Doral Hayes addresses this important issue in "Uncontrolled Worship," in *Amipotence, vol. 2*, Brandon Brown, et. al., eds. (Grasmere, ID: SacraSage, 2025).

[78] See Keith Ward, *Confessions of a Recovering Fundamentalist* (Eugene, OR: Cascade, 2019), 46-47.

[79] Alfred North Whitehead, *Science and the Modern World* (New York: Free Press, 1967), 192.

To make sense of the Spirit's love, we should believe it's not entirely different from ours. God isn't an exception to metaphysical principles of love but their ultimate expression. The Spirit *necessarily* self-gives and others-empowers to promote well-being, because God *is* love. A Spirit worthy of our worship always loves, loves in diverse ways, and never controls anyone or anything.

CHAPTER FOUR

# Universal, Incorporeal Spirit

## THE BIG IDEAS

- Jesus describes God as spirit, and deity's composition or "stuff" is best understood in terms of spirit.
- The divine Spirit is like breath, wind, mind, gravity, and the spark of life.
- The classic view that says God is immaterial leads to numerous problems.
- As the living God, the Spirit has both material and mental dimensions.
- The Spirit is universal and affects all creation, but deity isn't perceptible by our five senses.
- Though an active agent, the universal Spirit doesn't have a localized divine body.
- The world isn't literally the Spirit's body, but we can act as God's metaphorical body.

*I*'m addressing three divine attributes in this chapter: God's spiritness, bodilessness, and universality. The three are closely related, so it's natural to explore them together. It's hard to imagine how God could be immediately present to every entity in every universe, for instance, if God has a localized body. But an incorporeal spirit can be omnipresent, and a universal spirit must be bodiless. Exploring what these claims mean will help us answer the questions of where, and what, God is.[1]

---

[1] This chapter is dedicated to Robert Luhn. It's hard to measure all of the positive ways "Pastor Bob" has influenced me over the years. He's also the first whom I remember hearing talk seriously about the holy spirit.

Theistic traditions speak of deity as Spirit or a spirit.[2] We find this true to varying degrees in Christianity (*pneuma, ruach, spiritus*), Judaism (*ruach* and *shekinah*), and Islam (*ruh*), although the meanings of "spirit" vary greatly in these traditions.[3] Those in Bahai, Hindu, Sikh, and Zoroastrian traditions also use spirit language to talk about deity, and many indigenous peoples and animistic traditions speak of the Great Spirit.[4] Theologian Jay McDaniel rightly concludes that "Spirit isn't reducible to Christianity."[5]

How each tradition understands "spirit" varies, of course, and this diversity increases when one looks at movements and figures within each religion.[6] But the fact that many religions think of God as spirit is highly significant for making sense of divine universality, incorporeality, and invisibility.[7] Conceiving of God as Spirit also orients us toward our experiences of the divine *within* history. A universally interactive Spirit can't be contained by any person, any tradition, any creature, or even any universe.

---

[2] For a classic exploration of God and/or ultimate reality as Spirit or spiritual, see Ninian Smart's book, *The Religious Experience of Mankind* (New York: Scribner, 1969).

[3] Grace Ji-Sun Kim explores the relation between spirit and *chi* in *The Holy Spirit, Chi, and the Other: A Model of Global and Intercultural Pneumatology* (New York: Palgrave Macmillan, 2011).

[4] See, for instance, JoJo M. Fung, "The Great Spirit in Indigenous Peoples' Lives and The Future of Pneumatology," Asia Pacific Mission Studies: Vol. 6: 1.6 (2024). Available at: https://archium.ateneo.edu/apms/vol6/iss1/6; Vine Deloria, Jr., *God Is Red: A Native View of Religion* (New York: Fulcrum, 1992); Randy Woodley, *Indigenous Theology and the Western Worldview: A Decolonialized Approach to Christian Doctrine* (Grand Rapids, MI: Baker, 2022).

[5] Jay McDaniel, *Living from the Center: Spirituality in an Age of Consumerism* (St. Louis, MO: Chalice, 2000), 5.

[6] Amos Yong has done immense work in applying pneumatology to interreligious dialogue, especially with Buddhism. See *Beyond the Impasse: Toward a Pneumatological Theology of Religions* (Grand Rapids, MI: Baker, 2003); *The Cosmic Breath: Spirit and Nature in the Christianity-Buddhism-Science Trialogue* (Leiden: Brill, 2012); *Pneumatology and the Christian-Buddhist Dialogue: Does the Spirit Blow Through the Middle Way?* (Leiden: Brill, 2014).

[7] Many Hindu and Indian religions speak of God or ultimate reality as spiritual consciousness. On this, see Eliot Deutsch, *Advaita Vedānta: A Philosophical Reconstruction* (Honolulu: University of Hawaii Press, 1969); Swami Padmanabha, *Evolution in Divine Love: The Eternal Becoming of God, Soul, and Matter* (Inword, 2025); Sarvepalli Radhakrishnan, *The Hindu View of Life* (Oxford: Oxford University Press, 1927).

Using "Spirit" as a word for God involves speculating about divine ontology or God's being. Spirit language prompts us, says Sharon V. Betcher, to think of God "within the planetary and cosmic milieu."[8] As a self-described "crip" theologian of disability, Betcher argues that emphasizing God as Spirit points us to present realities, including our suffering and embodiment.[9] This same Spirit, says Betcher, can be seen as an "ever newly emergent force for making the world go on" despite suffering, disability, empire, and more.[10] The language of God as a loving and wise Spirit supports diverse forms of flourishing here and now.

Many others speak of God's spiritness.[11] Biblical scholar Marcus Borg says divine spiritness "stresses relationship, intimacy, and belonging."[12] Feminist theologian Elizabeth Johnson says Spirit "evokes a universal perspective and signifies divine activity in its widest reaches."[13] Reformed Theologian Jürgen Moltmann says divine spiritness "means that God is present in creation and in history in the ungraspable, life-giving energy."[14] Womanist theologian Deloris Williams says, "the Spirit is the sustaining presence of God who enables survival, giving Black women energy to endure and resist."[15] And Amos Yong, the preeminent theologian of Spirit, says, "God is Spirit, and . . . the Spirit is the one who creates, renews, and empowers all cultures to respond to God in their own tongues."[16]

---

[8] Sharon V. Betcher, *Spirit and the Politics of Disablement* (Minneapolis, MN: Fortress, 2007), 2.

[9] Ibid., 3.

[10] Ibid., 24.

[11] In some ways, my work is an example of what LeRon Shults and Andrea Hollingsworth say is the 21st century task of "interpreting the experience of the Spirit of the biblical God." See *The Holy Spirit* (Grand Rapids, MI: Eerdmans, 2008), 89.

[12] Marcus Borg, *The God We Never Knew* (San Francisco: HarperSanFrancisco, 1997), 71.

[13] Elizabeth A. Johnson, *She Who Is* (New York: Crossroad, 1992), 83.

[14] Jürgen Moltmann, *The Spirit of Life*, Margaret Kohl, trans. (Minneapolis: Fortress, 1992), 9.

[15] Delores S. Williams, *Sisters in the Wilderness: The Challenge of Womanist God-Talk* (Maryknoll, NY: Orbis, 1993), 127.

[16] Amos Yong, *The Spirit Poured Out on All Flesh* (Grand Rapids, MI: Baker Academic, 2005), 18. For others who equate God and Spirit, see Ada María Isasi-Díaz, *Mujerista Theology* (Maryknoll, NY: Orbis, 1996); Kwame Bediako, *Christianity in Africa* (Maryknoll, NY: Orbis, 1995); Chung Hyun Kyung, *Struggle to Be the Sun Again: Introducing Asian Women's Theology* (Maryknoll, NY: Orbis, 1990).

In this chapter, I address these key dimensions of God as Spirit. Note I'm exploring God's composition as a universal and incorporeal spirit. I'm *not* yet addressing what some Christians call the Holy Spirit as the third member of the trinity.[17] I'll address trinitarian issues in a later chapter.[18] Here, I'm exploring the ontological "stuff" of which divinity consists: spirit.[19]

## Jesus Describes God as Spirit

Although various scriptures call God "Spirit," Jesus identifies the very stuff of the divine as spirit. The writers of John's gospel record Jesus saying, "God is spirit" (4:24). I read this not as a reference to the third person of the Trinity but apparently a statement about the composition of the divine.

This statement comes in Jesus' conversation with a woman from Samaria. The woman has come to this conversation alone, and she'd been married many times. Jesus' disciples would have considered her a foreigner and a member of a false religion. In other words, in this story this Samaritan was of the "wrong" faith, at a place not considered holy, without community—and also female, while not maintaining the primary relationship of wife that society expected.

---

[17] Blair Reynolds addresses the Holy Spirit from a process theology perspective. See Blair Reynolds, *Toward a Process Pneumatology* (Selinsgrove, PA: Susquehanna University Press, 1990).

[18] Pneumatology. I am grateful to Amos Yong for his conversations and writings on pneumatology. I consider him to be the expert on the spirit. Among his many books on pneumatology, see *Spirit of Love* (Waco, TX: Baylor University Press, 2012). Sallie McFague explores the advantages and disadvantages of calling God "Spirit." I find none of her disadvantages convincing. See *Models of God* (Philadelphia: Fortress, 1987), 169-71.

[19] Among those who have written well on the spirit, see Kenneth J. Archer, *A Pentecostal Hermeneutic: Spirit, Scripture, and Community* (Cleveland, TN: CPT, 2009); Michael Lodahl, *Shekhinah/Spirit* (Eugene, OR: Wipf and Stock, 2012); Bradley Shavit Artson, *God of Becoming and Relationship* (Woodstock, VT: Jewish Lights, 2013); Clark H. Pinnock, *Flame of Love* (Downers Grove, IL: InterVarsity, 1996); Joshua D. Reichard, *Pentecost, Process, and Power* (PhD diss., University of the Western Cape, 2010); Marjorie Hewitt Suchocki, *God-Christ-Church* (New York: Crossroad, 1982); Michael Welker, *God the Spirit* (Minneapolis: Fortress, 1994); Amos Yong, *Spirit-Word-Community* (Eugene, OR: Wipf & Stock, 2006).

Jesus tells her that worshiping God isn't confined to mountains or Jerusalem. He twice says believers "worship God in spirit and truth" (4:23, 24). Then Jesus says, "God is spirit." The point seems to be that true worship will be possible anywhere and for anyone, because God is a universal spirit rather than a localized object or regional deity. The Spirit of Love, it's implied, isn't confined to sacred spaces, groups, genders, social expectations, or religions. God is uncontainable.

## What is Spirit?

Like "love," biblical writers use the Hebrew and Greek words we translate "spirit" in diverse ways. The two most common words for spirit are *ruach* (Hebrew) and *pneuma* (Greek). Each word occurs about 400 times in scripture. Later, the Latin *spiritus* was used for both words.

Biblical writers often use "spirit'" when referring to God,[20] but sometimes they use it for air, wind, or breath.[21] Other times, "spirit" refers to a spiritual being[22] other than God, such as angels, demons, or other deities. Sometimes "spirit" refers to minds, hearts, or souls.[23] Other times, it denotes a general way of thinking, an attitude, or pattern of living.[24] The diversity of meanings can be bewildering!

Unfortunately, the context of the biblical word translated "spirit" doesn't always indicate clearly which meaning applies. Consequently, biblical translators make choices when rendering the ancient languages. Wise people can nevertheless disagree on how to interpret the

---

[20] See Gen 1:2; Exod 31:3; 2 Chr 15:1; Matt 28:19; Mk 1:8; 3:29; 12:36; Lk 1:15, 35, 41; 2:25–26; Jn 20:22; Acts 1:2, 5, 8, 16; 2:4; 1 Cor. 12:3; 1 Thess 4:8.

[21] See Gen 3:8; 6:17; 7:15; Exod 15:8, 10; Num 11:31; Job 1:19; 9:18; Ps 1:4; Prov 25:23; Eccl 1:14, 17; Isa 11:4; Ez. 37:7-10; Jn 3:8; Heb 1:7.

[22] See Mt 8:16; Mk 1:26; Lk 24:37; 4:36; Acts 19:12.

[23] See Gen 7:22; Gen 41:8; Gen 45:27; Deut 2:30; Job 7:11; Ps 51:10; 51:17; 77:6; 78:8; 143:4; Prov 15:13; 17:22; Isa 26:9; Lam 4:20; Mk 2:8; Lk 23:46; Rom 8:16; 1 Cor 2:11; 1 Cor 5:5; Col. 2:5.

[24] See Isa 29:10; Rom 8:15, 11:8; Eph 2:18; 2 Tim 1:7.

biblical passages in which we find the word for "spirit."[25] The word is slippery.

The diversity of meanings should remind us that biblical writers are grasping to give an account of themselves, the world, and God.[26] Their accounting has always been influenced by various experiences, cultures, theologies, and more. Accounts of God and reality will never be perfect—even in the Bible. We have license, therefore, to draw from ancient descriptions without being wholly constrained by them.

Although analogies and metaphors can't ever account for God fully, I turn to four analogies I believe help make sense of God as an invisible, incorporeal, and universal spirit.

### *God is like wind or breath*

We find comparing God to wind or breath typical in scripture, and this analogy has several advantages. A common word for God in the Hebrew scriptures, *yahweh*, is pronounced as if breathing in and out. Jesus compared God to the wind and said it influences us without our knowing from where it comes (Jn. 3:8). We can see the wind's effects, because we observe tiny particles whisked about, see trees swaying, or feel a gust. These effects point to the fact that wind and breath have causal force and a physical dimension.

Just as we can't directly see wind and breath, however, we can't see God. In fact, we seem unable to perceive God with any of our senses. People of faith typically say at least some events reflect divine causation. But most can't articulate well how God's causal influence works, even though they perceive themselves as affected by an unseen Friend, Comforter, Presence, or Force. The Spirit influences.

---

[25] Jack Levison notes that a theologian's presuppositions incline her toward particular pneumatologies. "With so many references to spirit in scripture, a plethora of possible starting points present themselves, each of which will lead in a distinctive direction . . . The choice of a starting point therefore determines the sort of pneumatology a reader cultivates." John (Jack) R. Levison, "The Spirit in the Christian Bible," *St Andrews Encyclopaedia of Theology*, Brendan N. Wolfe, et al., eds. (https://www.saet.ac.uk/ Christianity/TheSpiritintheChristianBible Accessed: 19 December 2024).

[26] Michael Lodahl explores Jewish and Christian understandings of Spirit in *Shekinah/Spirit* (New York: Paulist, 1992).

We can find at least two downsides to comparing God to wind or breath. First, airy entities don't typically have intentionality. We don't think of breath and wind making free choices, thinking, or acting purposively. And they don't love. I will argue that the Spirit does all of these activities and more.

Second, we don't usually think of wind and breath as universal. We inhale or exhale air in a particular place, and we feel a gust in a specific locale. Every atom comprising a rock, for instance, isn't present to air. By contrast, the universal Spirit is directly present to all.

The breadth of divine Breath is ubiquitous.

### *God is like a mind*

Greek and Hebrew words translated "spirit" sometimes refer to minds. Thinking that God might be like a mind has advantages, because minds have intentions, make decisions, plan, and learn. Minds typically have a subjective unity and are aware. To give an account of ourselves as experiencing subjects, in fact, it makes sense to say we are or have minds. Denying the reality of creaturely minds would be self-refuting; only minds are capable of the psychological activity of denying!

Talking about God as a Mind also has the advantage that minds both influence and are influenced. Creaturely minds are affected by bodies, events, and creation, and they show affect in response. We can't perceive creaturely minds with our five senses. A scientist can't cut open a human cranium and see a mind mingling amongst the brain and neurons. Likewise, we can't see the invisible Spirit.

To say God is mind-like,[27] therefore, aligns with saying the Spirit is an experiencing subject with subjective unity. The Spirit is affected by creaturely others, and it affects them. And just as we can't see minds when we cut open heads, we can't perceive the divine Mind with our five senses.

---

[27] In his writings, Keith Ward often compares God to a mind. For an example, see *Sharing in the Divine Nature* (Eugene, OR: Pickwick, 2020). See also Wm. Curtis Holtzen and Roberto Sirvent, eds., *By Faith and Reason: The Essential Keith Ward* (London: Darton, Longman & Todd, 2012).

But there's a downside to comparing God to creaturely minds: our minds aren't omnipresent. We typically think of minds as residing in a person's head. They're localized. Creaturely minds also apparently have a beginning, but, by contrast, an everlasting Spirit has no origin. To talk about the Spirit as mind-like, therefore, we have to be careful to add that God is universal and everlasting.

### *God is like gravity*

To my knowledge, nothing in scripture compares the Spirit to gravity. Neither Jesus nor the biblical authors were conscious of gravity in the modern sense, although they felt its effects. Many people today also function with no cognitive knowledge of gravity, and yet it influences them moment by moment. Most scientists consider gravity universal, although this universality can't be measured and gravity's pull varies in intensity.[28]

Similarly, an invisible Spirit influences even those not cognitively aware of its existence.[29] That includes those who deny the reality of God. Like gravity, the Spirit exerts causal or attracting influence, despite not being able to see it.[30] Like God, gravity appears to be universal.

The downsides of comparing God to gravity prove similar to the downsides of comparing the Spirit to wind and breath. Gravity as an active force doesn't have intentionality, make free choices, think, or act purposively. Gravity can't love, if one thinks love involves acting intentionally, in relational response to God and others, to promote overall well-being. Deity is like gravity in some ways, but God is unlike it in others.

---

[28] Jay McDaniel compares the Spirit of love to plasma in "Felt, Not Grasped: The Spirit as Plasmatic Love," in *Renewing Faith*, Sheri Kling, ed. (Grasmere, ID: SacraSage, 2025).

[29] Among those who compare God to gravity, see Ilia Delio, *The Unbearable Wholeness of Being* (New York: Orbis, 2014); Pierre Teilhard de Chardin, *The Divine Milieu*, Bernard Wall, trans. (New York: Harper & Row, 1960); Simone Weil, *Gravity and Grace,* Emma Craufurd, trans. (London: Routledge & Kegan Paul, 1952). Bradford McCall brings together a collection of Philip Clayton's writings under the title, *God and Gravity* (Eugene, OR: Cascade, 2018).

[30] Philip Clayton explores the action of the Spirit in a collection of essays called *Adventures in Spirit* (Philadelphia: Fortress, 2008).

## God is living

Biblical writers often say God is "living."[31] And we sometimes identify "spirit" as active life or a life-force, either when talking about creatures or Creator. According to the biblical witness, the Spirit is dynamic, animated, and organism-like.[32] Rather than dead or static, the Living Spirit affects creation, and creation affects deity. God is a dynamic actor.[33]

Combining the Spirit as living with the Spirit as breath, various biblical writers say divine breathing is a creative force in the universe. In the book of Job, for instance, Elihu says, "The Spirit of God has made me, and the breath of *Shaddai* gives me life" (33:4). The Living Spirit enlivens others; Life creates life.

We can see one disadvantage in this way of thinking in the tendency to imagine a Living God having the same limitations as creatures. Living creatures have limited influence, for instance, because they're always located in a specific place. Living creatures are also typically embodied (ghosts being a possible exception), whereas the Living Spirit is universal and doesn't have a divine body. And living creatures are born and die; God remains everlasting.

In sum, saying the Spirit can be compared to wind, breath, or air points to the causal force of an invisible deity. Saying the Spirit is like gravity acknowledges God's invisible but universal influence. Saying the Spirit lives indicates that deity is a dynamic, relational actor. And saying the Spirit is like a mind supports the intentionality and relations necessary for love. Rightly understood, these various claims and images trying to capture the universal, incorporeal, and living Spirit support the notion that God acts intentionally, in relational response, to promote overall well-being.

---

[31] E.g., Deut. 5:26; Ps. 42:2; Matt. 16:16; Acts 14:15.

[32] "When spirit is understood as pure, undifferentiated consciousness, it fails to express the personal character of God." John Macquarrie, *Principles of Christian Theology* (New York: Scribner, 1966), 152.

[33] Rory Randall makes a strong argument for the compatibility of open and relational theology with Spirit-oriented theologies. See *An Open Theist Renewal Theology* (Grasmere, ID: SacraSage, 2021).

## God Isn't an Immaterial Spirit

In affirming God's composition as an incorporeal spirit, many theologians say deity must therefore be immaterial. This leads to absolute philosophical distinctions between matter and spirit, between physical and mental entities, between the spiritual and the worldly. Charles Hodge illustrates this when he says, "Spirit isn't matter, or matter spirit . . . In revealing to us that God is a Spirit, [the Bible] reveals that no attribute of matter can be predicated of the divine essence."[34]

Claiming the Spirit as immaterial puts God in a realm with other immaterial beings, if such beings exist. People typically view creatures and creation, by contrast, as material. According to some theologians, humans represent a mix of matter and spirit: they are, or have, material bodies with immaterial souls. This way of thinking implies a mind-body dualism famously articulated by Rene Descartes, in which humans have material bodies and mental souls/minds.

Two impulses prompt theologians to say the divine Spirit must be immaterial. We have the biblical claim that God is invisible. If the Spirit were material, goes the thinking, God could be seen. Behind the other impulse lies a philosophical framework built primarily by Plato, which prioritizes abstract forms and ideas. Augustine and Aquinas united the invisible God of scripture with Plato's philosophy to argue that God is an immaterial substance who is timeless, formless, and unchanging.

Claiming God is immaterial creates numerous problems. One pertains to explaining how an immaterial deity could interact with material creation.[35] An immaterial/spiritual God would be different in kind, after all, from material/physical creatures.[36] The problem of how an immaterial God might interact with a material world mirrors the

---

[34] Charles Hodge, *Systematic Theology*, vol. 1 (Peabody, MA: Hendrickson, 1999), 378-379.

[35] John Polkinghorne puts it this way: "If God is conceived as a totally immaterial spirit acting upon matter, then one is faced with the classical interaction problem." John Polkinghorne, *Science and Providence* (Philadelphia: Templeton, 2005 [1989]), 57.

[36] Ian Barbour argues similarly: "A dualistic picture of an immaterial God intervening in a material world raises severe problems for coherent models of divine action." Ian G. Barbour, *Religion and Science: Historical and Contemporary Issues* (San Francisco: HarperSanFrancisco, 1997), 270.

mind/body problem. Traditional theologians claim to solve this by saying that because an immaterial God supernaturally created matter, divinity can act upon it. These theologians rarely explain "how" this acting happens, however, and they often employ the hand-waving phrase "in such a way."

A second problem with divine immateriality involves questions about how humans perceive the Spirit. Theologians typically regard claims about accessing God with our five senses as symbolic rather than literal. "No one has seen God," says John's gospel (Jn. 1:18), and most think biblical references to hearing God's voice are metaphorical. By the modern era, many scholars shifted from saying humans directly perceive deity to believing humans only infer God's existence from observations of the world. The question of how a creature could directly perceive God remained unresolved, although some appealed to spiritual senses.[37]

Positing an immaterial God creates a third problem of separating of reality into what is important—the spiritual—and the unimportant—the material. If people of faith believe an immaterial God is of the highest value, they will understandably be likely to reject the material world and want to unite with the immaterial One. The influential spirituality of Thomas a Kempis in *The Imitation of Christ*, for example, consistently criticizes the material world and calls readers to the spiritual.[38]

Believing God must be immaterial easily undermines the appreciation of, and care for, creation. Thinking only the spiritual is ultimately significant inclines many to neglect the material care and needs of the poor and oppressed. After all, their salvation would be thought

---

[37] Spiritual Senses As one influenced by empiricism, John Wesley spoke of a sixth sense by which we perceive God. He called this "spiritual senses," in part because we must have these sensory powers to perceive a spiritual God. I address Wesley's view of spiritual sensations in "Grace and Social Science: Nonsensory Perception of God in a Constructive Postmodern Wesleyan Philosophy," *Jnanadeepa: Pune Journal of Religious Studies*, 5.2 (July 2002): 121-135. See also Kenny Johnston, "Perceiving Wesley: An Analytical Study of Epistemological Uses of Perception in John Wesley's Theology," *The Methodist Review* 14 (2002): 78-117.

[38] See Thomas à Kempis, *The Imitation of Christ*, Aloysius Croft and Harold Bolton, trans. (Garden City, NY: Dover, 2003). I address the problems this raises for imitating God in "Imitating God," in *Exemplars, Imitation, and Character Formation: A Philosophical, Psychological, and Christian Inquiry*, Eric Yang, ed. (New York: Routledge, 2025).

spiritual and not also material. The hard spiritual/material distinction can incline us to think the climate crisis and ecological concerns are unimportant, and to denigrate the human body, gender, and sexuality in general.

When theologian strip God of materiality, problems ensue.

## The Mental-Material Spirit

This systematic theology proposes that the universal Spirit has both material and mental aspects. Rather than being entirely immaterial, the universal deity is a person with material and mental aspects who, through uncontrolling love, gives to and receives from creatures and creation who also have material and mental aspects.[39] God is a material-mental Spirit.

My claim that God has both materiality and mentality doesn't mean we find two objects in God. And we shouldn't think of these as two actual or substantial parts in the divine. The mental-material Spirit is one. These two dimensions form *logical* aspects of the Spirit, ontologically inseparable in the unity of divine life.

The mental and material aspects of the Spirit aren't also two natures. God has just one nature.[40] And while the word "material" has meant "substance" for some, I use the word material to talk about the physical dimension of becoming. I oppose idealist ontologies that claim existence consists of nothing but ideas, and conversely I oppose materialist ontologies that say only what's material is real. Both

---

[39] Material-Mental Monism The ontology from which I am drawing that says all of creation has a mental aspect is often called "panpsychism" or "panexperientialism." For various reasons, I call my version "material-mental monism." On why this general approach to ontology makes sense see Philip Goff, *Galileo's Error* (New York: Vintage, 2020); David Ray Griffin, *Unsnarling the World-Knot* (Eugene, OR: Wipf and Stock, 2008).

[40] Whitehead "Natures" of God Alfred North Whitehead postulated that God has two aspects or what he called a "primordial nature" and a "consequential nature." The primordial features God's abstract essence, and the consequential includes God's concrete experiencing. It's unfortunate that he called these two aspects "natures," however. I side with the majority of theologians who say God's unity requires God having one nature. But I retain Whitehead's intuition about two aspects in God. For Whitehead's discussion of God's primordial and consequent natures, see *Process and Reality*.

materiality and mentality are aspects of reality, and both are aspects of God.

To say God has a material dimension may lead us to ask why we can't perceive it with our five senses. But God can be invisible and yet have a material aspect. We know of creaturely entities, such as molecules, that have materiality but are unseen. The elements of the periodic table we affirm as real, but some can't be seen. And phenomena like gravity can exert real causal influence without being seen. So does dark matter. Analogously, the Spirit has material and mental aspects we can't detect with our five senses, although I'll argue in later chapters that we perceive God through nonsensory perception.

Some theologians quote Jesus to establish God's immateriality.[41] "Spirit has no flesh and bones" says Jesus in reference to his resurrected body (Lk 24:39). Most biblical translators use the term "ghost" instead of "spirit" in this passage; however, saying Jesus isn't a ghost here has nothing to do with God being immaterial. Many creaturely objects have materiality without having flesh and bones. This verse doesn't establish divine immateriality.

Each of the two aspects in the Spirit—the mental and the material—remain essential for making sense of God's actions and responses. The mental dimension is the source of the Spirit's thinking, willing, decision making, planning, and more. God's mentality also grounds the values necessary for love. The Spirit's mentality includes the realm of possibilities envisaged eternally but presented to creation when the contexts are appropriate. God's mental aspect remembers all that's occurred.

The Spirit's material aspect proves crucial for understanding God as a cause among causes. God's materiality is universal and affects all creation. But God can be a cause and yet not control outcomes. The Spirit acts as an efficient cause alongside other causes and is influenced by them. Among other things, saying a material-mental Spirit exerts efficient causation makes it easier to imagine divine action in an age of science.[42]

---

[41] As an example, Millard Erickson says God is spiritual and not composed of matter (*Christian Theology*, 2nd ed. [Grand Rapids, MI: Baker, 1988], 294).

[42] I explain what I mean by God as an efficient cause in "The Divine Spirit as Causal and Personal," *Zygon*, 48:2 (June 2013): 454-465; and in chapter four of *The Death of Omnipotence and Birth of Amipotence.*

It's also crucial to posit the Spirit's material-mental aspects for understanding how God feels. The Spirit is truly affected emotionally, and this affect involves both cognitive and physical dimensions. And because the Spirit has a material dimension, creaturely mystical experiences involve real encounters with the divine. They should not be explained away as simply human projections. Insisting on material aspects in God also importantly allows us to understand what it means for the Spirit to empower and invite creatures.

The Spirit's mentality and materiality prove important for conceptualizing divine love interacting throughout the fabric of existence.

## BIBLICAL SUPPORT FOR A MENTAL-MATERIAL GOD

Because most theologians have for so long considered God entirely immaterial, it may surprise some to discover biblical statements that support my claim that the universal Spirit has material aspects. Many scholars come to scripture with biases based on metaphysical assumptions that privilege the immaterial. But a growing number of biblical scholars criticize those assumptions.

We previously noted that a Hebrew word for spirit—*ruach*—often translates as "wind'" or "breath." Such airy phenomena have materiality we usually can't see. Analogously, God's materiality exerts causal influence similar to how wind and breath exert causal influence. And we can extend these analogies between the Spirit and gravity, minds, and living persons. In other words, we have grounds to imagine that *ruach* has a material dimension.

The New Testament word for spirit—*pneuma*—has even stronger connections to materiality. Unlike the modern tendency to think of *pneuma* as immaterial, ancient thinkers considered it to have materiality.[43] The word was central to Stoic thinking, which strongly influenced the writings of the Apostle Paul. "When a Stoic says that God's essence

---

[43] On *Pneuma* and the Apostle Paul, see Troels Engberg-Pedersen, *Cosmology and Self in the Apostle Paul: The Material Spirit* (Oxford: Oxford University Press, 2010); Matthew Thiessen, *Paul and the Gentile Problem* (Oxford: Oxford University Press, 2016). See also see Gitte Buch-Hansen, "It is the Spirit that Gives Life": A Stoic Understanding of Pneuma in John's Gospel (Berlin: de Gruyter, 2010).

is *pneuma*," says New Testament scholar Terence Paige, "he doesn't mean either that God is immaterial or that the *pneuma* is a sentient being apart from (or secondary to) God; he means that God is made of matter like everything else that is real, and the matter of which God is made is *pneuma*."[44] Gordon Fee agrees: "Paul's 'Spirit' language is personal and active; it should not be confused with philosophical notions of a disembodied spiritual essence."[45]

According to a number of Hebrew Bible scholars, what is true of *pneuma* applies to *ruach*. "Where 'spirit' is set over against the physical as a superior, immaterial reality," argues James Dunn, "the biblical sense of *ruach* is lost."[46] William Brown says that "to translate *ruach* as an immaterial 'spirit' is misleading . . . because it is something experienced, not abstracted."[47] "*Ruach* isn't some nonphysical entity," says John Walton.[48] And Terrence Fretheim says *ruach* "signals God's active, world-engaged presence—a presence that moves, energizes, and affects bodies and environments. Reading it as immaterial diminishes its theological force."[49]

I don't mean to imply that all the biblical scholars cited above explicitly endorse my material-mental monist view of the Spirit. But they do explicitly reject classic notions of God as entirely immaterial, notions present in Greek philosophy and found among leading theologians of history. Material-mental monism better characterizes the universal Spirit of love described in scripture than claims about God's alleged immateriality.

---

[44] Terence Paige, "Who Believes in 'Spirit'? Πνεῦμα in Pagan Usage and Implications for the Gentile Christian Mission," *HTR* 95 (2002): 417-36 (425). See also Paul Robertson, "Despiritualizing *Pneuma*: Modernity, Religion, and Anachronism in the Study of Paul," *MTSR* 26 (2014): 365-83.

[45] Gordon D. Fee, *God's Empowering Presence* (Peabody, MA: Hendrickson, 1994), 817. Anthony Thiselton agrees: "When *pneuma* is interpreted as an immaterial, ghost-like substance, we are no longer reading Paul but later metaphysics." Anthony C. Thiselton, *The Holy Spirit—In Biblical Teaching, through the Centuries, and Today* (Grand Rapids, MI: Eerdmans, 2013), 26.

[46] James D. G. Dunn, *The Theology of Paul the Apostle* (Grand Rapids, MI: Eerdmans, 1998), 75

[47] William P. Brown, *The Ethos of the Cosmos: The Genesis of Moral Imagination in the Bible* (Grand Rapids, MI: Eerdmans, 1999), 52.

[48] John H. Walton, *The Lost World of Genesis One* (Downers Grove, IL: IVP Academic, 2009), 26.

[49] Terrence E. Fretheim, *God and World in the Old Testament: A Relational Theology of Creation* (Nashville, TN: Abingdon, 2005), 39.

If Spirit has both material and mental dimensions, we can make sense of the numerous biblical statements about the *pneuma* and *ruach* being "in" us. This doesn't mean we're buckets into which God is poured; we don't have cavities in our bodies in which Spirit resides. Nor does the Spirit being "in" us refer to a mere abstraction or essence.

For the Spirit to be "in" us means that the material and mental God influences our experiential minds and bodies, each of which has material and mental dimensions too. God is *in* our experience, in other words, and as material creatures, our experience has materiality. Rather than a purely immaterial Being influencing purely material creation, the material/mental Spirit influences creatures with material/mental aspects.

Careful readers will notice that I rarely use the word "spiritual" when talking about God. I avoid this way of talking because many systematic theologians have conceived of God as an entirely immaterial, spiritual being with no physical dimensions. By contrast, I believe God has mental and material dimensions as a universal, loving Spirit. At least when talking about deity, I avoid saying God is "spiritual."

The biblical God of *ruach* and *pneuma* isn't an abstract phantom but a universal Lover with matter and mentality.

## A Universal Spirit

Most theologians claim God is present to all creation. The usual word they use is "omnipresent." If taken literally, that word could connote pantheism: God is everywhere because God *is* everything.[50] To avoid this connotation, we need clarity.

Instead of the word omnipresent, I typically use "universal" to say the Spirit of Love is present *to* everyone and everything in every universe.[51] The Spirit can be present *to* all without *being* all. Insofar as creatures are experientially affected by others, God is *in* all creaturely

---

[50] Pantheism comes in many forms, and its adherents aren't always consistent in saying literally everything is God. See Mary-Jane Rubenstein, *Pantheologies: Gods, Worlds, Monsters* (New York: Columbia University Press, 2021).

[51] Mark Feldmeir explains God's universality in accessible prose. See *Life after God: Finding Faith When You Can't Believe Anymore* (Louisville, KY: Westminster John Knox, 2023)

experiences, albeit with varying degrees of influence. This is a form of theoenpanism, which says God is in all of creation without being all creation.[52] I'll explore panentheism and theoenpanism in later chapters.

The biblical support for a universal God isn't as clear as one might think. Various passages support the Spirit's universality. For instance, "'I am God at hand,' says the Lord. 'Do I not fill heaven and earth?'" (Jer. 23:23-24). "Where shall I go from your Spirit? Or where shall I flee from your presence?" asks the Psalmist, as an apparently rhetorical question. "If I ascend to heaven, you are there. If I make my bed in Sheol, you are there" (Ps. 139:7-8). Jeremiah speaks of a God who is the "God of all flesh" (32:27). Paul endorses the words of poets, which seem to suggest a universal deity: "In [God] we live and move and have our being" (Acts 17:28).

But other passages suggest God isn't universally present. "Truly you are a God who has been hiding himself," says the writer of Isaiah (45:15). "Because you have defiled my sanctuary with all your detestable things and with all your abominations," says God in Ezekiel's writings, "therefore I will withdraw" (5:11). The writer of 2 Thessalonians says some people "will pay the penalty of eternal destruction, away from the presence of the Lord and from the glory of His power" (1:9). God can't be truly universal if sometimes withdrawing, hiding, or not present to some.

I interpret passages saying God isn't present as reflecting 1) the biblical author's *feeling* that God is absent or 2) a situation reflecting the lack of creaturely cooperation with God. The first interpretation suggests that some passages reflect the writer's psychological state and not the truth about the universal deity. The uncontrolling Spirit of love can be present without creatures being aware of deity. An invisible God can seem distant.

The second interpretation suggests that the manifestations of the Spirit of Love depend, in part, on how well creatures align with God's

---

[52] There are many similarities between God as universally present, theoenpanism, and what Niels Gregersen calls "deep incarnation." For an explanation of Gregersen's view, see "Deep incarnation: From deep history to post-axial religion," *Theological Studies*, 72:4 (October 2016); Gregersen, ed., *Incarnation* (Minneapolis, MN: Fortress, 2015).

call. The Spirit's activity will be more obvious when creatures align themselves with love, beauty, compassion, and justice. When creatures fail to re-present the Spirit well, God can seem hidden.[53] Situations can be dire, seem God-forsaken, and generate evil consequences because creatures failed to cooperate with deity. God is most profoundly revealed when creatures profoundly align with the Spirit.

A common phrase in the Hebrew scriptures points to the Spirit's universality: it says that God "fills heaven and earth" (e.g., Jer 23:23-24). Passages like this one indicate that biblical writers don't limit God's presence to humans. Jeremiah appeals to the "God of all flesh" (32:27), in fact, and even desolate land mourns to the Spirit present to it (12:11; 4:28; 23:10; Joel 1:10, 20). God even addresses the land (16:19; 22:29).[54]

The universal presence of the Spirit is one way in which divine loving transcends creaturely loving. While the extensiveness of the Spirit's love is universal, a creature's love will be localized.[55] God loves the *whole* world, says the Apostle John (Jn. 3:16), and nothing can "separate us from the love of God," says the Apostle Paul (Rom. 8:38). By contrast, a creature's love has a limited sphere of influence.

Not only is the Spirit universally present *to* all creation, but all people and all creatures have access to divine influence. We can realistically understand that the God always available always cares, always empathizes, and always empowers for the good. And if this Spirit is always uncontrolling, creatures possess the independence necessary for free decision-making and responsibility. To put it another way, the Spirit's love is mother-like, without smothering. And as Black theologian Theo

---

[53] Jewish writers have been especially interested in divine hiddenness. See, for instance, Irving Greenberg, *For the Sake of Heaven and Earth: The New Encounter Between Judaism and Christianity* (Philadelphia: Jewish Publication Society, 2004); Abraham Joshua Heschel, *God in Search of Man: A Philosophy of Judaism* (New York: Farrar, Straus and Giroux, 1955); Richard L. Rubenstein, *After Auschwitz: Radical Theology and Contemporary Judaism* (Indianapolis, IN: Bobbs-Merrill, 1966).

[54] On these issues, see Terrence Fretheim, *God and the World in the Old Testament*, 172.

[55] As John Wesley put it, "There is no point of space whether within or without the bounds of creation, where God isn't." See "On the Omnipresence of God," in *The Works of John Wesley, Volume 4: Sermons IV (115–151)*, ed. Albert C. Outler (Nashville, TN: Abingdon, 1987), 50 (§I.2).

Walker put is, "God's omnipresent influence is good news to the whole of creation and especially good news to the oppressed."[56]

The universal divine Presence affects all creation.

## A Universal Spirit Without a Localized Divine Body

Christian scripture gives mixed answers to the question of whether God has/is a localized divine body. Some passages suggest that God is a universal and invisible spirit without a body. "No one has ever seen God," says John (1:18), and the writer of Timothy says God is the one "whom no one has ever seen or can see" (1 Tim. 6:16). Other biblical accounts, however, portray God as an embodied being who can be seen (Gen. 3), who talks (1 Sam. 3; Mt. 3:17), who wrestles (Gen. 32), and who has a butt (Exod. 33). Like they do on most issues, biblical writers send mixed messages.

Take Psalm 34:15-20 as an example. The passage says, "The eyes of the Lord are toward the righteous and his ears toward their cry. The face of the Lord is against those who do evil, to cut off the memory of them from the earth. When the righteous cry for help, the Lord hears and delivers them out of all their troubles." This passage portrays God as having particular body parts, focusing on a divine head.

I consider biblical passages that portray God as embodied to be metaphors for God's actual activities in relation to creation. Particular encounters with deity—sometimes called "theophanies"—are real, in the sense that we actually encounter the Spirit. References to God's body, ears, eyes, or face indicate the Spirit's communication with creatures. The language used to describe these encounters, however, reflect poetic flourishes and metaphorical projections. I don't think God has a literal, localized body.

To some, the incarnation of God in Jesus of Nazareth proves that the Spirit can become embodied. Some might say that if the universal and essentially incorporeal deity occasionally becomes embodied, God can

---

[56] Theodore Walker, Jr., *Mothership Connections: A Black Atlantic Synthesis of Neoclassical Metaphysics and Black Theology* (Albany, NY: SUNY, 2004), 70. Michael Zbaraschuk addresses liberation in relation to providence in *The Purposes of God: Providence as Process-Historical Liberation* (Eugene, OR: Wipf and Stock, 2015).

be temporarily corporeal. They envision God perhaps as a shapeshifter, a universal spirit who can take on, or take over, a body. In later chapters I'll address why I don't think God shapeshifted to become Jesus.

Like most theologians in the Judeo-Christian tradition, I find arguments that affirm God's incorporeality more convincing than those saying God has a divine body or can shapeshift. Part of why I think the Spirit is incorporeal and never takes on or takes over a localized body is that the embodied God creates problems for a consistent systematic theology.[57]

For instance, the God who can temporarily become localized as a body would no longer be present to all creation. Omnipresence wouldn't, therefore, be an essential divine attribute. A temporarily localized deity couldn't relate or communicate directly with creatures not immediately present to it. The Psalmist's question, "Where shall I go from your Spirit?" (Ps. 139:8) would no longer be rhetorical; we could point to places God isn't. And the Apostle Paul's claim that "in [God] we live and move and have our being" (Acts. 17:28), would only be true of those immediately present to a temporarily localized deity.

Saying that God can take on, or take over, a body also makes the problem of evil unsolvable. If God can temporarily be embodied, deity could do activities embodied creatures can sometimes do. An embodied God could use a divine hand to pull children from the paths of speeding cars, for instance. Or grab guns from murderers. A shapeshifting God could take on, or take over, bodies or objects to prevent murder, rape, genocide, and more. This deity would be culpable for failing to stop *innumerable* evils.

The notion of God "'taking over'" a creature's body also raises problems for creaturely freedom. These problems further exacerbate the problem of genuine evil and creaturely integrity. A God who takes over is coercive rather than persuasive, overpowering rather than empowering. The problem of omnipotence raises its ugly head.

The incorporeal Spirit doesn't have a divine body that prevents evil.

---

[57] For helpful ways of talking about God as Spirit, see John B. Cobb, Jr. Bruce Epperly, and Paul Nancarrow, *The Call of the Spirit* (Anoka, MN: Process Century, 2022). See also Sheri Kling, ed., *Renewing Faith* (Grasmere, ID: SacraSage, 2025).

## Is the World God's Body?

Some say that the world/universe must be God's body.[58] This way of thinking builds from the human mind-body relationship, with God as the mind and creation the body. A position saying the world is God's body can be strengthened if one believes Creator and creatures both have material and mental aspects. A mental-material divine mind could interact with mental-material creation, analogous to how creaturely minds interact with bodies.[59]

We find several drawbacks to saying the world is God's body, however. One important one: minds and bodies are creaturely. Saying the world is God's body could easily be interpreted as pantheism, thereby destroying Creator-creature distinctions.[60] I think we should affirm real differences between the creaturely universe and divine Spirit, and I'll take many opportunities in later chapters to describe those. I'll proffer a version of panentheism that maintains distinctions between God and creation, although I think the two also have similarities and are relationally entangled.

Many people of faith say humans are God's "hands and feet," and the Apostle Paul talks about believers as the "body of Christ" (1 Cor. 12:27; Eph. 4:15–16).[61] Insofar as creatures cooperate with the Spirit's leading, we can rightly consider them God's *metaphorical* hands and

---

[58] See, for instance, Nancy R. Howell, *A Feminist Cosmology: Ecology, Solidarity, and Metaphysics* (New York: Humanity Books, 2000); Grace Jantzen, *God's World, God's Body* (Philadelphia: Westminster, 1984); Sallie McFague, *The Body of God: An Ecological Theology* (Minneapolis: Fortress, 1993).

[59] There's an immense literature on whether the world is God's body. See, for instance, Daniel Dombrowski, *Analytic Theism, Hartshorne, and the Concept of God* (Albany, NY: SUNY, 1984); Charles Hartshorne, *Omnipotence and Other Theological Mistakes* (Albany, NY: SUNY, 1984); Grace Jantzen, *God's World, God's Body* (Philadelphia, PA: Westminster, 1084); Sallie McFague, *Life Abundant* (Minneapolis: Fortress, 2001).

[60] Baruch Spinoza, perhaps the best-known pantheist, believed the world was God's body. See Will Durant, *The Story of Philosophy* (New York: Simon and Schuster, 1967), ch. 4. I'm grateful to Robert Edward Reich for alerting me to this anecdote.

[61] Although the Apostle Paul advances the idea that people are the body of Christ, St. Teresa of Avila is typically cited as the originator of the specific claim that people can be God's hands and feet. Teresa of Ávila, attributed. *Prayer of St. Teresa of Ávila*. 16th century.

feet. They function as God's body, in this sense.⁶² But creatures can also fail to cooperate and, thereby, cause evil. When doing evil, they are *not* acting as God's body. To avoid attributing harm, sin, and evil to the Spirit, we should say creatures *can be* God's metaphorical body, but they aren't *literally* so.

I've presented a view of God as a universal spirit without a localized divine body.⁶³ The Spirit has mental and material aspects, but we can't perceive those aspects with our five senses. We have direct access to God through nonsensory perception, however, as I'll explain in later chapters. The Spirit is present to all creatures and all creation, but the world isn't literally God's body, and we aren't literally divine appendages. But creatures can be rightly considered God's metaphorical hands, feet, body, and so on, when they cooperate with the Spirit's call to act justly, create beauty, and express love.

The world isn't God's literal body, but when we love, we enact divine desires.

## Conclusion

The divine Lover is an incorporeal Spirit influencing all creation. As universally active and accessible, the Spirit transcends geography, social status, gender expectations, religion, and ritual. References to God as wind, breath, mind, and even gravity offer insights into divinity's invisible composition and influential activities. They point to a universal, living Actor who responds to, and is affected by, creation.

The universal Spirit of love doesn't have a localized divine body: God is incorporeal. The Spirit also can't take over bodies or shape shift, because a loving deity works persuasively rather than exerting control by singlehandedly determining others. Creatures can metaphorically become divine hands and feet and act as God's body when they

---

⁶² Lina Langby explores the revelation of divine love in the world in "The Holy Spirit is Amipotence Manifested," in *Amipotence, vol. 2,* Brandon Brown, et. al., eds. (Grasmere, ID: SacraSage, 2025).

⁶³ Matthew Segall uses the ancient notion of God as "World-Soul" in *Physics of the World-Soul* (Grasmere, ID: SacraSage, 2021 [2013]).

cooperate with divine love.[64] But this involves creaturely choosing, not deity momentarily replacing or eclipsing creatures.

Challenging traditional notions of immateriality, this systematic theology of love sees the universal Spirit as having material and mental dimensions. This view avoids the problems arising when people think God entirely immaterial. And it overcomes problems that arise when people think God entirely spiritual, in the sense of having no physical dimension. In positing that creatures have material and mental aspects, this theology of love offers a framework to make sense of interactions between the Spirit and creation.

My constant reference to divine activity and interactions between God and creation imply dynamism in the universe. This dynamism requires us to probe basic philosophical questions about the nature of existence, creaturely and divine. We turn now to address those concerns.

---

[64] Darren Iammarino address similar questions in "The Force and Forms of Love and God's Cosmic Body," in *Amipotence, vol. 1*, Chris S. Baker, et. al., eds. (Grasmere, ID: SacraSage, 2025).

CHAPTER FIVE

# Becoming Spirit

## THE BIG IDEAS

- Christian scripture portrays God as a personal being among other beings.
- Saying God is a personal being puts limits on deity, and many assume a personal deity must have a localized body.
- Rather than a being among beings, some theologians say God is being-itself.
- God as being-itself creates numerous problems for a theology that says God loves.
- Other theologians say God is beyond the category of being.
- God as beyond being creates numerous problems for a theology that says God loves.
- The biggest problem with equating God with being is the static connotations of the word "being."
- Rather than "being," we should say the dynamic Spirit is always "becoming."
- The becoming God is an everlasting series of divine occasions of experience.
- Rather than onto-theology, we ought to embrace gino-theology.

More must be said about the "stuff" or composition of the universal Spirit who loves. In particular, I want to address whether God is *a* being, or something else. Questions about *how* God exists—as an agent, force, idea, energy, ground, etc.—have led theologians into complex philosophical discussions.[1] Some even say they believe in a God who doesn't exist, because deity transcends the category "exist."

---

[1] This chapter is dedicated to Catherine Keller. Her encouragement and own theological work have been inspirational to me as I ponder the becoming, divine one.

In what follows, I aim to be clear and concise, and I'll add technical issues in footnotes. Some of what I say will seem radical to those familiar with discussions of the nature of God and being.² To others, what I advocate will seem to align with the general way biblical writers describe God. I believe my proposal also coheres with much of contemporary science and fits with the nature of love. My overall goal will be to portray well the universal Spirit who loves.

## Is God a Personal Being among Beings?

Saying God exists as a universal Spirit, as I did in the previous chapter, makes claims about what it *means* to exist. The domain of ontology ponders what existing entails; it asks about the elements of existence. Ontology speculates on what it means to *be* or *become*.

The question of God's being has sometimes been called "onto-theology." Addressing it has been difficult, and theologians and philosophers have routinely challenged it in the contemporary era.³ Exploring the nature of God's existing remains crucial, however, if we are to address 1) what it means to be a Spirit who loves and 2) whether God shares commonalities with other existents.⁴ Getting clear on these issues affects the language we use about the Spirit's love.

---

[2] Radical Theology. A group of theologians emerged in the 1960s who sought to rethink basic theological categories largely in opposition to traditional or confession theologies. This movement continues in the present in widely diverse forms. Most forms reject ideas some think orthodox and critique what many view as normative in theology. Radical Theology encompasses a variety of intersections of secular theology, death of god theologies, political theologies, cultural theologies, and constructive theologies.

[3] The philosopher Martin Heidegger is most often associated with criticizing what he called "ontotheology." His criticisms apply to a classical metaphysics of being found in theologians like Augustine and Aquinas (see Heidegger, *Identity and Difference*, trans. J. Stambaugh [New York: Harper and Row, 1969]). See also Heidegger's comments on being and God in *Seminaire de Zurch*, D. Saatdjian and F. Fedier, trans. *Poesie*, 13 (Paris, 1980), 60-61.

[4] Analogy of Being. This chapter is an explicit affirmation of analogy of being or, as I will offer as an alternative, an analogy of becoming. Karl Barth rightly rejected *analogia entis*, when "being" was understood in the Greek philosophical tradition that informed Aquinas's understanding of being. And Barth would be right to emphasize an analogy of relations between God and creatures, although I'll argue that these relations between Creator and creation are everlasting. I believe Barth went too far, however, in his early claims that God is wholly other, insofar as "wholly other" means there are absolutely no similarities between God and creatures. He should have realized that the affirmation of the human Jesus required analogies

Most biblical writers describe God as a personal Being relating with other beings or as a Subject engaging subjects and objects. In the Bible's opening pages, for instance, *Yahweh/Elohim* interacts with the deep when creating. Deity engages Adam and Eve as a being among beings (Gen 3:8), and such interaction continues in various biblical accounts. The Spirit creates, communicates, responds, and loves, all of which are activities that subjects do. God serves as a dialogue partner whom others can persuade, as encounters with Abraham suggest (e.g., Gen 18:17-33). In scripture, the Spirit also interacts as a being with Sarah, Rebekah, Moses, Jesus, Paul, Satan, slaves, kings, nations, families, rebels, and others.

The writers of scripture attribute relational roles to the Spirit. God as Friend, for instance, suggests God is a being who befriends others. God as King suggests a being with subjects; God as Mother/Father interacts with children; God as Governor or Judge is a being who governs or judges others; God as Lord leads hosts of other beings; God as Listener assumes actively receiving communication from others; and so on.

Some descriptions of the Spirit present personifications of divine attributes (e. g., Lady Wisdom), but most portray God as an actual person.[5] To love creatures, as we often say God does, implies that a divine Subject acts for the flourishing of others. This Being is affected by creatures, according to biblical authors, and responds emotionally. God can be angry (Ps. 7:11), sad (Ps. 78:40), delighted (Ps. 2:4), blessed (Ps. 145), jealous (Ex. 20:5-6), and more. These activities, responses, and emotions are typical of a being in relation to beings, a subject engaging other subjects.

---

between creation and Creator. On some readings of his corpus, he did realize this later in life. For a criticism of Barth and affirmation of analogy, see Eberhard Jüngel, *God as the Mystery of the World,* Darrel L. Guder, trans. (Grand Rapids, MI: Eerdmans, 1983 [German edition: 1977]), ch. 4. For a systematic theology that follows a Barthian emphasis upon Christ, see Thomas A. Noble, *Christian Theology,* vol. 1 (Kansas City, MO: Foundery, 2023).

[5] Several Russian theologians have developed Sophia-based theologies. See Nikolai Berdyaev, *Freedom and Spirit* (New York: Harper & Row, 1950); Sergei Bulgakov, *Sophia: The Wisdom of God* (Hudson, NY: Lindisfarne, 1993); Pavel Florensky, *The Pillar and Ground of Truth* (Princeton, NJ: Princeton University Press, 1997); Vladimir Solovyov, *Lectures on Godmanhood* (Crestwood, NY: St. Vladimir's Seminary Press, 1995).

But God isn't just *any* being, according to biblical writers. The Spirit is higher, wiser, stronger, universal, more accessible, or somehow better than others. *Yahweh* "has no equal" among creatures or deities (Isa. 40:25), and no superior counselor exists to direct or instruct the Spirit (Isa. 40:13). These superlatives distinguish deity without making God *entirely* unlike creatures, angels, and other gods. The claim that humans (at least) are made in God's image (Gen. 1:26-27) also suggests similarities between the Spirit and creatures.[6] To say that we can partake in the divine nature (2 Pet. 1:4) suggests similarities too.

In sum, the biblical witness portrays God as *a* being among other beings.

The biblical writers aren't consistent with the details of this Being, however. At times, writers describe God as not in some places (e.g., Isa. 59:1–2); other times, they describe deity as universal (e.g., Ps. 139:7–10; Jer. 23:23–24). Sometimes God is embodied (e.g., Gen. 3:8); other times, incorporeal (e.g., Deut. 4:15–16). Sometimes the Spirit forgets (e.g., Jer. 31:34); other times, deity never forgets (Ps. 105:8–10). Sometimes God is described as loving everlastingly; other times, deity must be reminded to love (e.g., Gen. 18:25; Exod. 32:11–14). Some biblical writers describe God as unchanging (Mal. 3:6), while others say the Spirit repents (Gen. 6:6–7; Jonah 3:10). Some describe deity as ignorant (Exod. 16:4, Jer. 19:5), while others say God knows all things (e.g., Isa. 46:9–10; Heb. 4:13).

To be consistent, systematic theologians must decide which scriptural descriptions seem more appropriate than others. No one can incorporate *all* biblical portrayals of God and also presents a coherent theology, let alone a coherent theology of love. Whether consciously or not, theologians employ strategies when deciding among contrary biblical notions. These strategies will be informed by other scripture passages, logic, experiences, culture, science, traditions, aesthetics, and more.

---

[6] For a strong argument that the image of God was not destroyed by sin, see John F. Kilner, *Dignity and Destiny: Humanity in the Image of God* (Grand Rapids, MI: Eerdmans, 2015). For my argument that relational love is the heart of the *imago dei*, see "The Imago Dei as Relational Love," in *Finding Ourselves After Darwin*, Stanley P. Rosenberg, ed. (Grand Rapids, MI: Baker, 2018).

## Criticizing a Personal Being among Beings

Critics of the idea that God is a being say that the idea limits deity. If God is a being, for instance, the divine would need to have a localized body. Paul Tillich is one of the more influential critics of the idea, and he says, "The being of God can't be understood as the existence of a being alongside others or above others."[7] He goes on, "Ordinary theism has made God a heavenly, completely perfect person who resides above the World and mankind (sic). The protest of atheism against such a highest person is correct."[8]

A deity who is *a* being can't be the source of other beings, say other critics.[9] We must think of God as in a class or genus outside the creaturely classes and genera the Spirit makes, because deity transcends them. God was not born, will not die, isn't limited to one place, and doesn't have attributes common to finite beings. Saying God is *a* being among beings commits the error of anthropomorphism, some claim, by transferring creaturely traits to God.

Rejecting the idea that God is a being has some startling consequences; however, Tillich embraces them. He says, for instance, that God did *not* "bring the universe into being at a certain moment." And God doesn't "govern [the universe] according to a plan, direct it toward an end, interfere with its ordinary processes in order to overcome

---

[7] Paul Tillich, *Systematic Theology*, Vol. 1 (Chicago: University of Chicago Press, 1955), 261. The idea that God isn't a being alongside other beings is widely embraced, although I reject it. John Macquarrie is another influential systematic theologian who identifies God and being. See his *Principles of Christian Theology*, 2nd ed. (New York: Scribner's, 1977).

[8] Ibid, 271.

[9] Hidden Metaphysical Assumptions One primary argument often given for why God must be the "first cause" and not an everlasting chain of divine becomings hinges on the unchallenged assumption that God must be *entirely* different from what God creates. But there's no *a priori* reason to think that beings can't share some similarities with the Being who created them. After all, creatures who give birth to other creatures share some similarities with their offspring. Another assumption says beings can't in any way explain themselves, so their existence must be wholly explained by something Else. But there's no *a priori* reason to say creaturely beings don't contribute to their own existing. And God can be an everlasting being and a necessary cause in the creation of other beings without being their sufficient cause or the first in a finite series. Self-causation can be a factor in the existence of both creatures and the Creator. Had Heidegger realized these assumptions aren't necessary, he wouldn't have needed to criticize *all* onto-theologies.

resistance and to fulfill his purpose, and bring it to consummation in a final catastrophe."[10] God doesn't do these activities, Tillich says, because doing them would reduce God to a finite cause.[11]

Tillich explains his reasoning: "If God is a being, he is subject to the categories of finitude, especially to space and substance." And "even if [God] is called the 'highest being' in the sense of the 'most perfect' and the 'most powerful,'" Tillich says, the "superlatives become diminutives. They place [God] on the level of other beings."[12] Saying that God creates, governs, directs, interferes, or even exists projects creaturely categories upon deity. The Creator isn't like creatures.

We should say instead, says Tillich, that God remains infinitely beyond us. "That which is the true ultimate transcends the realm of finite reality infinitely," he says. "Therefore, no finite reality can express it directly and properly."[13] Tillich's argument, then, concludes that God isn't a being, and divinity remains beyond, or eludes, all categories of being.

## Is God Being-Itself?

I believe Tillich's arguments against understanding God as a being are partly wrong and partly right.[14] Before addressing them, however, I

---

[10] Paul Tillich, *Systematic Theology*, vol. 2 (Chicago: University of Chicago Press, 1957), 6.

[11] Anthropomorphism The practice of projecting human bodily forms onto God is the precise meaning of anthropomorphism. But theologians also use the word to describe those who also say God feels, acts, communicates, or loves like creatures. I reject the claim that God has a localized body or a form like creatures. But I accept that God feels, acts, communicates, loves, and more analogous to how creatures do these things.

[12] Tillich, *Systematic Theology*, vol. 1, 261. Tillich argues similarly in Volume 2 of his systematic theology. "God would not be God," he says, "if he were not the creative ground of everything that has being, that, in fact, he is the infinite and unconditional power of being, or in the most radical abstraction, that he is being-itself. In this respect God is neither alongside things nor even 'above' them; he is nearer to them than they are to themselves. He is their creative ground, here and now, always and everywhere." Tillich, *Systematic Theology*, vol. 2, 8.

[13] Paul Tillich, *Dynamics of Faith* (New York: Harper and Row, 1957), 44-45.

[14] In fact, Tillich says God doesn't exist . . . in the normal way we think of existing. "The question of the existence of God can be neither asked nor answered," he argues. "It is a question about that which by its very nature is above existence, and therefore the answer—whether negative or affirmative—implicitly denies the nature of God." Tillich, *Systematic Theology*, vol. 1, 261.

want to explore what Tillich thinks to be a better alternative: God as being-itself. "The being of God is being-itself," he famously claims,[15] and Tillich thinks this is the only non-symbolic statement humans can make about the divine.[16]

Tillich isn't always clear what it means to say God is being-itself.[17] The phrase seems to be his way of saying God is the source and structure of existence. He also uses phrases like "ground of being" and "power of being" to describe the divine, which also suggest that God is the source and structure of existence.[18] When Tillich calls God being-itself, one sometimes gets the impression be believes God simply *is* existence. Yet he wants to avoid pantheism.

Creaturely persons and other beings, says Tillich, participate in being-itself. But it's not clear what "participating" means.[19] Does this mean creatures influence or change God, which would mean denying divine immutability and impassibility? Or are creatures participating in an abstract structure that constitutes God's nature? Although he doesn't answer questions like these, Tillich *is* clear that deity doesn't reside as an example of the structure of being. Rather, God *is* that structure.[20]

Tillich's discussion of God as person is puzzling. "The ultimate concern of a [human] person can't be less than a person," he says.[21] But

---

[15] Ibid.,

[16] Ibid., 265.

[17] John Macquarrie follows Tillich's reasoning about being, but I see Macquarrie as clearer. He says Being isn't an object that is but "the act or state or condition of being." *Principles of Christian Theology* (London: SCM, 1966), 98. My objections to Tillich's theology of Being-itself also apply to Macquarrie.

[18] Although Tillich sometimes describes God as the "power of being," this description aligns with God as source but not with seeing God as a powerful actor. See Paul Tillich, *The Courage to Be* (New York: Yale University Press, 1952), 173-176.

[19] Despite referring hundreds of times to creatures "participating" in God, Tillich never tells us what "participation" means. On this problem, see Ryan McAnnally-Linz, "The Multivalence of Participation in Paul Tillich's Systematic Theology," *The Journal of Religion*, 92:3 (July 2012), 373-391.

[20] Another possible interpretation of Tillich's "Being-itself" is that he's pointing to pure power or what Aristotle calls a material cause and Whitehead calls "creativity." But pure power isn't an actor and therefore not a lover, creator, redeemer, etc.

[21] Tillich, *Systematic Theology*, I, 156.

then Tillich says, "(God) isn't a person," because the category of "person" would place limits upon the divine. Rather than personal, God is the "ground" of all personality.[22] Tillich even argues that "God can't be called a self, because the concept of 'self' implies separation from and contrast to everything which isn't self."[23] Tillich doesn't explain, however, how it is God could be personal without being a person or self.

The claim that God is being-itself ends up being in tension with scriptural passages that say God is a living Being. Tillich recognizes this problem and admits that "few things about God are more emphasized in the Bible, especially in the Old Testament, than the truth that God is a living God." But he argues that "we can't speak of God as living in the proper or nonsymbolic sense." Instead, he says, "we must speak of God as living in symbolic terms."[24]

The activities and attributes that theologians typically associate with God, says Tillich, should be seen as symbols rather than straightforward descriptions. "Anything one knows about a finite thing," says Tillich, "can't be applied to God."[25] Consequently, even the statement "God is good" remains, for him, symbolic. "God is good" applied literally to God must be denied.[26]

Far more could be said about God as being-itself. We could make a good argument that Tillich is extending the claims of Thomas Aquinas and others that we should understand God as pure act. As David Bentley Hart puts it, "The God of classical theism isn't a being, not even the highest being, but Being itself—pure act, absolute simplicity, the source of all that is."[27] What I've outlined here, however, will be sufficient to articulate my evaluations of it.[28]

---

[22] Ibid.

[23] Ibid., 244.

[24] Ibid., 241.

[25] Ibid., II, 9.

[26] Ibid., II, 10.

[27] David Bentley Hart, *The Experience of God: Being, Consciousness, Bliss* (New Haven: Yale University Press, 2013), 122.

[28] Benjamin Chicka also defends a general Tillichian view of being. See his *God the Created: Pragmatic Constructive Realism and Theology* (Albany, NY: SUNY, 2022).

## Criticizing Being-Itself

I join Tillich when he says God isn't an embodied heavenly being who occasionally intervenes on Earth.[29] I also reject the spatial separation between God and creation implied by the word "intervene." God doesn't come "over here" from "out there." As universal, the Spirit remains immediately present to all. And although ontologically distinct, I believe God and creation are relationally entangled.

If "being-itself" simply means God is, as Tillich puts it, "the creative ground of everything,"[30] I affirm that. I don't think God is the *only* source of what exists, as I'll explain when I talk about creaturely co-creating. I also prefer the more common description of God as "Creator." Tillich doesn't like such words, because they imply that a Being acts alongside beings.

Despite these affirmations of Tillich's insights, I find "God is being-itself" unhelpful. So I reject it. Tillich uses this language to deny God is a person, self, or actor in the ways we understand persons, selves, and actors. According to him, God can't be a person, because "person" carries with it the limits involved in two-way relations.

Let's look a bit more at my rejection of God as ground of being or being-itself. While scholars have debated the essentials of what it means to be, we normally think of persons are agents who think, act, and respond. Ken Perzsyk describes what this means for God. "The basic or minimal idea . . . seems to be that God is a person or personal agent at least in the sense that he freely and intentionally acts and interacts with us in the light of knowledge or beliefs."[31]

But these characteristics of a person—freedom, intentionality, action, interactions, thinking—must entail limits of some sort. At the very least, a relational person can't simultaneously be the other being in the relationship. The Spirit must also be limited in the sense that

---

[29] Robert John Russell argues for non-interventionist divine action in *Cosmology From Alpha to Omega* (Minneapolis: Fortress, 2008).

[30] Tillich, *Systematic Theology*, II, 7.

[31] Ken Perzsyk, "Divine Infinity and Personhood," in *Divine Infinity*, Benedikt Paul Gocke and Christian Tapp, eds. (Notre Dame, IN: Notre Dame University Press, 2019) 323.

God can't be both free and not free, act and not act, be thinking and not thinking . . . at least not in the same ways. These are logical limits, so saying the Spirit is limited in these ways shouldn't worry people of faith who want consistent theologies.

Not only is Tillich's God not a person, "being-itself" sounds like we're talking about an impersonal structure or abstract principle. His deity isn't a living Spirit who loves, at least not in any straightforward sense. "Being-itself," "ground of being," and "power of being" don't describe a purposeful Lover who intentionally gives to and receives from the beloved.[32] Tillich's phrases portray God more like an abstract "It" than a divine "Thou," to use the language of Martin Buber.[33]

The problems that arise when we don't think of God as a subject or agent come out when Tillich discusses love. "If we speak of God as loving or, more emphatically, of God as being love, we use our experience of love and our analysis of life as the material which alone we can use," says Tillich. But divine love "doesn't mean that a higher being has in a fuller sense what we call love," he continues; "it does mean that our love is rooted in the divine life . . ."[34] In this and other instances, Tillich fails to say that "God loves the world" or other phrases common in scripture about the loving Spirit. For Tillich, divine love is an aspect of the structure of being itself; God isn't an agent who loves creatures in intentional, giving-and-receiving relationships.

Tillich responds to charges that being-itself isn't personal by citing a biblical passage that says God knows the hairs on our heads (Lk. 12:7). He adds that God knows the number of atoms and electrons in the universe too.[35] But I would respond that knowing the number of hairs, atoms, or electrons isn't the same as intentionally giving and receiving in loving relations. A computer can account for facts; the personal Spirit who loves would know facts *and* engage in intentional relationship.

---

[32] Keith Ward puts it this way: "The Christian God must be thought of as a God of love, and, if that is the case, it isn't enough to simply say that god is 'Being-itself.' Love is a personal property, and 'Being' doesn't seem to be personal at all." *Sharing the Divine Nature: A Personalist Metaphysics* (Eugene, OR: Cascade, 2020), 87.

[33] Martin Buber, *I and Thou*, Ronald Gregor Smith, trans. (Martino, [1937] 2010).

[34] Paul Tillich, *Love, Power, and Justice* (London: Oxford University Press, 1954), 109-110.

[35] Tillich, *Systematic Theology*, II, 12.

A major factor in Tillich's denial that God is a being among other beings comes down to his claim that God "transcends the realm of finite reality infinitely." We can't put finite categories upon God, he says, because divine infinity isn't an extension of such categories.[36] In these ways and more, the concept of the "infinite" plays a major role in Tillich's philosophical theology.

Although the word "infinite" can be interpreted in various ways, its basic meaning is "not finite."[37] And to be infinite in all respects equates, apparently, with being unlimited in all respects.[38] Here's the problem: if God is infinite in all respects, God must be infinitely good and infinitely evil, infinitely present and infinitely absent, infinitely wise and infinitely foolish.[39] And so on.[40]

Furthermore, if God infinitely transcends the realm of finite reality, finite language just doesn't apply to God. A deity infinite in all respects, therefore, would be absolutely incomprehensible. But anything absolutely incomprehensible would be utterly unbelievable. After all, beliefs must have content that's at least partly understandable. We can't have a concept of a deity who remains beyond all concepts. Therefore, we *literally* can't believe in a God who we think infinite in all respects, or who transcends finite reality infinitely. *All* constructive claims about the one who infinitely transcends the finite become impossible.[41]

---

[36] Ibid., 6.

[37] Infinity The meaning of the word "infinite" varies across disciplines. The complex discussion of the idea in mathematics differs drastically from how we understand infinity in physics or theology. Some theologians consider "infinity" one divine attribute among other attributes. Other theologians use the word as a modifier for particular attributes, such as that God has infinite knowledge. Tillich seems to use it in a third sense, which involves the negation of finite categories; this is the sense most common in Augustine as well. On these issues, see Benedikt Paul Gocke and Christian Tapp, eds., *Divine Infinity* (Notre Dame, IN: Notre Dame University Press, 2019).

[38] Many theologians and philosophers say that if God is in all respects infinite, we can't formulate any intelligible statements about God. On this, see Franz Krainer, "The Concept of the Infinity of God in Ancient Greek Thought," in *Divine Infinity*, Benedikt Paul Gocke and Christian Tapp, eds., (Notre Dame, IN: Notre Dame University Press, 2019).

[39] Philip Clayton wishes to overcome the problems with infinity by qualifying it with "perfect." See *The Problem of God in Modern Thought* (Grand Rapids, MI: Eerdmans, 2000).

[40] Tillich admits to being highly influenced by Augustine. Their views on God's infinity seem to match. After all, Augustine says God is "infinite in every possible respect." Book 7 5.7 p. 119

[41] As William Beardslee puts it, "if God is infinite in power and glory, nothing can stand in God's way." See William Beardslee, *Margins of Belonging* (Atlanta: Scholars, 1991), 102.

Rather than "being-itself" as the only nonsymbolic phrase for God, I propose we use "Universal Lover" as a better description of the Spirit. Language can't fully describe love or the Spirit, of course, but we need personal categories to talk about a universal Spirit who lovingly gives to, and receives from, creatures. Conceiving of the Spirit as a relational person better fits descriptions of God in scripture and in everyday life. And God must be a person if we are to imitate this Lover (Eph. 5:1).

## Is God Beyond Being?

Given misunderstandings bound to arise when we conceive of God as a being among beings or as being-itself, it's little wonder some theologians reject onto-theology altogether.[42] Some retreat into philosophical language games and claim to avoid metaphysical statements.[43] Others point to ontology itself as the problem and try to do theology without it. Some theologians think God is *beyond* being.

Jean-Luc Marion offers a sophisticated argument for this approach, and in doing so, he aims to criticize the onto-theology Thomas Aquinas advocates. Marion dismisses all talk about similarities between creatures and a divine being, including the idea that God must be a subject or person.[44] The Spirit and creatures share nothing in common, he says, because "God doesn't fall within the domain of being."[45] Instead, for Marion, we should understand God as excess, a pure givenness.

To support his claim that God is beyond being, Marion argues for "the absolute freedom of God with regard to all determinations." This includes exempting God from "the basic condition that renders all

---

[42] Jason Alvis explores this in his essay, "The Ontotheological Idolatry of Love," in *Amipotence*, vol. 1, Chris S. Baker, et. al., eds. (Grasmere, ID: SacraSage, 2025).

[43] See, for instance, George Lindbeck, *The Nature of Doctrine: Religion and Theology in a Postliberal Age* (Nashville, TN: Westminster John Knox, 1984).

[44] One sees the influence of Emmanuel Levinas's radical otherness in Marion's thought. See for instance Levinas's *Otherwise than Being*, Alphonso Lingis, trans. (Pittsburgh: Duquesne University Press, 1981). David Perrin's explores Levinas and St. John of the Cross as each speak of God beyond being. See Perrin, "John of the Cross and Emmanuel Lévinas: The Quest for God beyond Being," *Acta Theologica* 2022 (33):104-120.

[45] Jean-Luc Marion, *God Without Being,* Thomas A. Carlson, trans. (Chicago: University of Chicago Press, 1991), 3.

other conditions possible and even necessary . . . the fact of Being."⁴⁶ A deity free from all conditions and determinations, goes the argument, would be beyond being. We would have theology without ontology.

Marion interprets the biblical phrases "God is love" and "I am who I am" to indicate that the divine is beyond being. The "radical reversal of the relations between Being and loving, between the name revealed by the Old Testament (Exod. 3:14) and the name revealed, more profoundly though not inconsistently, by the New Testament (1 Jn 4:8)," Marion says, "presupposes taking a stand that is at once theological and philosophical.⁴⁷"

"God is love," according to Marion, means something other than a commonsense interpretation. It means God loves before being. "To begin with," he says, "if 'God is love,' then God loves before being."⁴⁸ Creatures exist and then decide whether to love, but God loves before existing. Only a God beyond being can love before existing.

God "comes to us in and as a gift,"⁴⁹ Marion says to explain his view. God is *agape*, a gift of love. "God gives Himself to be known insofar as He gives Himself," he says. This means that "the gift gives only itself, but in this way it gives absolutely every-thing."⁵⁰ The gift of love, therefore, according to Marion is given by no being; it is given by the One beyond being.

## Criticizing Beyond Being

I find little helpful in Marion's claim that God is beyond being. But I do agree that God's relation to love differs in some ways from creaturely relations to it. As I argued earlier, I believe God loves by necessity, and creatures love contingently. Love comes logically first in the divine nature, but not first in creatures. Rather than "God is love" meaning deity

---

[46] Ibid., xx. Marion develops these ideas most fully in the third chapter of *God Without Being*, which he calls "The Crossing of Being."

[47] Ibid.

[48] Ibid.

[49] Ibid., 3.

[50] Ibid., xxiv.

is beyond being, though, the phrase should prompt us to rethink the Spirit's *mode* of loving. "God is love" means the Spirit loves necessarily.

I find incomprehensible the notion that God can act without first existing. Or that God can love without being a subject. Only beings act; only subjects love. Loving requires existing persons. If to love means to act intentionally, the Spirit must be an intentional subject. If love requires relationships between beings, a loving God must not be beyond being or relations.

Marion seems so enamored with divine freedom that he prioritizes it over what we know about love. We see this when he claims God's freely choosing to love must be prior to God existing. Marion means his arguments to justify the temporal priority of freedom, but they result in an incomprehensible theology in which divine love doesn't require a lover. This contradicts an essential thing we know of about loving; every expression of love requires the existence of an actor.

Some of my criticisms leveled against Tillich also apply to Marion. "God as gift," for instance, sounds a lot like God as static or abstract object rather than a living, loving Spirit. A "gift" can't act intentionally nor relate in giving *and* receiving love. Being-less gifts don't have the agency to give themselves. A gift implies the prior existence of a Giver—and the Giver described in scripture has various expectations of those given the gift. Although the gift is unconditional in the sense of being unearned, it's not pure excess. It's part of real, covenantal relations.

Marion appeals to Exodus to support his view that God is beyond being. In this passage, God self-identifies as "I am who I am," at least as some translators render the Hebrew. We naturally interpret this statement as something a subject might make, however, not a speaker beyond being. Jesus also says, "I am" (Jn. 8:56-59), and many interpreters think he's referring to the Exodus passage. But he's clearly a being among beings. Besides, a number of Hebrew scholars say the Exodus passage would be better translated, "I will be whom I will be."[51] This

---

[51] See Brevard Childs, *Book of Exodus: A Critical Theological Commentary* (Louisville, KY: Westminster John Knox, 2004), 47-89; Franz Rosenweig, "Der Ewige," in *Kleinere Schriften* (Berlin: Schoken, 1937), 185; Richard Kearney, *The God Who May Be* (Bloomington, IN: Indiana University Press, 2001). See also Steven J. Bruening, "We Are Action People; We Can't Stand Still." Bruening notes that in Biblical Hebrew, the tense of "to be," as ehyeh (היהא), is incomplete.

*Becoming Spirit* 125

translation portrays God as a dynamic subject rather than a gift without being.[52]

Marion's work reminds us that to make sense of life and God, we need to ponder ontology and metaphysics.[53] We can't ignore or abandon them. We all assume theories about what it means to be, even if we do so unconsciously or inconsistently.[54] In fact, to make sense of what Marion means when he says God is *free*, a *gift*, or *comes* to us, we must assume an ontology that accounts for freedom, giving, and coming to us.[55] No adequate theology escapes metaphysics.

Love assumes ontology. We see this in the vast majority of instances in which biblical writers and everyday people talk about love. Love is something an existing subject would express in relation to others. Consequently, saying God is beyond being or being-itself just doesn't fit the vast majority of scripture, nor does it align with the way we understand love—and it doesn't support the call to imitate the loving Spirit.

## Other Ways to Talk about God

Theologians and people of faith have used other language and images to talk about God. Some people call the divine Consciousness, for instance. Other times, they say deity is the Future. Some use the language of Depth, Absence, the Universe, Womb, the Absolute, Life-Force, Intelligence, Light, Energy, Disruption, Spark, Presence, or something

---

[52] Oliver Davies offers an ontology of compassion as an alternative to an ontology of static being. See *A Theology of Compassion: Metaphysics of Difference and the Renewal of Tradition* (Grand Rapids, MI: Eerdmans, 2001).

[53] Metaphysics Is Perennially Relevant George Pattison makes this point nicely when he says, "Anyone who imagines that either Heidegger or Derrida overcame metaphysics, or that overcoming metaphysics is some sort of project that a group of sufficiently dedicated researchers might accomplish in the near future, just isn't taking this kind of philosophical thinking seriously. Metaphysical ideas don't go away just become someone gave a lecture criticizing them." See *God and Being: An Inquiry* (Oxford: Oxford University Press, 2011), 3.

[54] The early philosopher Plotinus also thought God was without being. But like many who make this claim, Plotinus often also used "being" language when talking about God. See *The Enneads*, A. H. Armstrong, trans. 7 vols. (Cambridge, MA: Harvard University Press, 1984).

[55] Emmanuel Levinas not only rejects ontology as fundamental (as Marion does) but also rejects love as a primary category to account for the face of the other.

else. Each label offers something attractive when accounting for ultimate reality. Most don't imply that God is constrained to a localized divine body, is tribal or parochial, or intervenes from outside.

The foregoing names and images for God also carry various liabilities, however, especially if we intend to put love at the center of systematic theology. Many don't account well for the intentional acting that loving requires, and others don't convey the give-and-receive inherent in loving relations. Some labels don't describe love's aim to promote well-being. Many don't align with the personal agency typical of biblical descriptions of God as creator, friend, evaluator, leader, parent, respondent, comforter, or guide.

Because the words I've listed have serious limitations when it comes to prioritizing love, they function best as secondary descriptors of the divine. No words *fully* describe deity, of course, not even my preferred words "Lover" and "Spirit." Wise theologians will paint from a rich and diverse word palette. But when we think of love as God's primary attribute, some words and images will better express the activities, receptivity, and aim for well-being characteristic of a loving Spirit.

## The Real Problem with Onto-Theology

If love is a systematic theologian's orienting concern, theologians should heed at least one major criticism of God as a being among beings. In fact, this criticism prompts me to change my language. Before I address it, let me for clarity's sake recap what I've concluded in this chapter thus far.

I've noted that most biblical authors assume God is a being among other beings, an actor among actors, a person among persons. The Spirit seems to be a subject who acts and responds in relation to others. Many divine names in the Bible suggest that God is an agent involved in creation and active with creatures. I said there are good reasons to think the living Spirit is incorporeal and universal, which means biblical passages describing God as embodied should be taken as metaphorical. I've argued that God doesn't reside in heaven and occasionally intervene on Earth. Instead, it makes better sense to say a universal Spirit is always present to, and relationally entangled with, creation. I've also insisted that "God is love" means, in part, that a personal Spirit necessarily loves others. The best language to talk about a loving Spirit, therefore, portrays deity as active, relational, intentional, and desiring well-being. And I've said God is one subject among other subjects.

Now to address the appropriate criticism that God is a being. It arises, in part, from connotations of the word "being." This word can sound static, inert, and inactive. Philosophers have historically equated "Being" with unchanging substance.[56] This term doesn't describe well the acting, dynamism, or relations essential to loving persons. It's flat.

It's not just that "being" sounds static, nonrelational, and inactive.[57] The word also ties to a profoundly misguided theological statement from Thomas Aquinas, perhaps the most influential of all systematic theologians.[58] Aquinas says God is *ipsum esse subsistens*.[59] This Latin phrase literally means "subsistent being itself," but it's commonly interpreted as meaning "God's being *is* God's essence." The phrase has two unhelpful implications, and one becomes relevant here. (I'll address the other when I explore divine simplicity.)

If God's essence is unchanging (which most theologians believe, including me), and if the divine essence is identical with God's being (which I don't believe), God must be unchanging. That's precisely how Augustine interprets the phrase. According to him, God is in all respects immutable. "God can't be modified in any way," says Augustine, "and therefore the substance or essence which is God is alone unchangeable. Therefore, it pertains to it most truly and supremely to be (*ipsum esse*)." He concludes: "that which ... can't at all be changed,

---

[56] Augustine describes God in this way: "There is at least no doubt that God is substance, or perhaps a better word would be being; at any rate what the Greeks call *ousia*." See *The Trinity*, E. Hill, trans. (Brooklyn, NY: New City, 1991), 189.

[57] The classic exposition on ontology is Aristotle's *Metaphysics*. See *The Basic Works of Aristotle*, Richard McKeon, ed. (New York: Random House, 1941).

[58] Thomistic Theology as Final In various books, John Milbank argues that Thomistic theology overcomes the problems of modern metaphysics. He advocates a return to Radical Orthodoxy. I find Milbank's claims about the sufficiency of Thomistic theology and metaphysics unconvincing. For his view, see his essay, "Only Theology Overcomes Metaphysics," in *The Word Made Strange* (Oxford: Blackwell, 1997).

[59] Thomas Aquinas, *Summa Theologiae*, 2-3, Q. 1a.2.3.

alone falls most truly, without difficulty or hesitation, under the category of being."[60]

Here's the problem: if love involves giving and receiving in dynamic relationships, the One who can't change or relate with others also can't love. If God's being is God's essence, as Augustine and Aquinas claim, the Spirit can't be a living Lover. Saying deity must be an unchanging being also doesn't fit the general drift of scripture, which portrays the Spirit as a dynamic person whose experience changes when affected by creatures. And it doesn't align with the witness of countless people who experience the Spirit as a dynamic presence.

The idea that God's being must be unchanging and entirely unlike creatures is the reason many scholars—most notably Blaise Pascal and Martin Heidegger—distinguish the God of Abraham, Isaac, and Jacob from the God of the philosophers.[61] An immutable Being doesn't sound anything like the living and loving Spirit of scripture.

We don't need to pit the Bible against philosophy, however. We need only admit that onto-theologies informed by philosophies of unchanging substance oppose much of scripture, as well as our intuitions about the dynamism of love. And we should feel free to seek a different ontology.[62] If no systematic theologian escapes metaphysics, in fact, we *should* seek a different ontology, one that makes better sense of love, in general, and the loving Spirit, in particular.

## THE EVERLASTINGLY *BECOMING* SPIRIT

I propose that rather than imagining God as "being," we should embrace "becoming" as the primary ontological category to describe the Spirit of love. Becoming is event-oriented rather than static or substantive.

---

[60] Augustine, *The Trinity*, 4.2.

[61] Heidegger makes his criticism in light of the idea that God is a first cause entirely unlike other beings. "The god-less thinking which must abandon the god of philosophy, god as *causa sui*, is thus perhaps close to the divine God." See *Identity and Difference*, J. Strambaugh, trans. (New York: Harper and Row, 1969), 72.

[62] A number of 20th century philosophers sought to rethink ontology from existentialist perspectives. Among the more influential were Martin Heidegger, *Being and Time*, John Macquarrie and Edward Robinson, trans. (New York: Harper, 2008 [1927]); Jean-Paul Sartre, *Being and Nothingness: An Essay in Phenomenological Ontology*, Hazel E. Barnes, trans. (London: Routledge, 2007 [1943]).

Saying existence involves events *becoming* fits contemporary ways of thinking about history, creativity, and science, especially biology, psychology, and quantum physics. It better fits our self-awareness as experiencers living moment by moment. An ontology of becoming prioritizes process over substance and experience over objects.[63]

To date, philosopher Alfred North Whitehead has worked out the best overall philosophy of becoming.[64] His dynamic ontology uses phrases like "actual occasions of experience" to describe living creatures. "*How* an actual entity *becomes* constitutes *what* the actual entity *is*," he says.[65] This means that we can consider every person, creature, or thing—from gluons to gophers to God—as an event or ordered series of events. Rather than comprised of inert bits of unchanging stuff, existence is comprised of events, experiences, and subjectivity.

To put it simply: to "be" is actually, first, to become.

Theologians of love should embrace divine *becoming* rather than think God is in all respects an unchanging being. By "becoming," I mean the Spirit is an experiencing, dynamic Person who engages in moment-by-moment relations with creatures and creation.[66] A becoming Spirit is *really*, not symbolically, a living deity, in the sense of moving relationally through time and enjoying new experiences.[67]

---

[63] Among the major philosophers of "becoming" we might also list Henri Bergson, Borden Parker Bowne, F. H. Bradley, Teilhard de Chardin, Charles Hartshorne, G. W. F. Hegel, Heraclitus, W. E. Hocking, William James, Charles Sanders Peirce, and Josiah Royce.

[64] For accessible introductions to Whitehead and process thought, see Andrew M. Davis, *Whitehead's Universe: A Prismatic Introduction* (Maryknoll, NY: Orbis, 2026); Julia Enxing, *Gott bewegt: Prozesstheologische Denkanstösse* (Karl Alber: Baden-Baden, 2026); Jay McDaniel, *What is Process Thought? Seven Answers to Seven Questions* (Anoka, MN: Process Century Press, 2021); Robert C. Mesle, *Introduction to Process-Relational Philosophy* (Eugene, OR: Cascade, 2017).

[65] Alfred North Whitehead, *Process and Reality: An Essay in Cosmology*, ed. David Ray Griffin and Donald W. Sherburne, corrected ed. (New York: Free Press, 1978), 34-35.

[66] Andre Rabe describes this well in *Processing Mimetic Reality: Harmonizing Alfred North Whitehead and Rene Girard* (Grasmere, ID: SacraSage, 2023).

[67] A significant philosophical tradition that emphasizes becoming over being provides metaphysical support for my claims. That tradition includes philosophers such as Henri Bergson, Charles Hartshorne, William James, C. S. Peirce, and Alfred North Whitehead. I regard Whitehead's metaphysics the most compelling, but Hartshorne's particular views about God that I find most helpful. Robert Neville challenges this tradition in *Creativity and God* (New York: Seabury, 1980). David Ray Griffin responds to Neville in *Whitehead's Radically Different Postmodern Philosophy* (Albany, NY: SUNY, 2007).

The Spirit experiences, has emotions, makes decisions, and relates.[68] And the becoming God loves.

The biblical practice of calling God "Spirit" fits well the idea of God as a becoming Experiencer whose living is dynamic.[69] Scripture writers don't regard the Spirit as a static thing, the structure of existence, or an abstract idea. Jürgen Moltmann puts it well: Spirit "means something living compared with something dead, something moving over against what is rigid and petrified."[70]

By "becoming," I don't mean God isn't yet present. The Spirit is always present. And I don't mean God only exists at some later time.[71] God exists now. Nor do I mean God could be half-baked, partly alive, or less than fully divine. I don't believe the becoming Spirit resides in the future rather than the present, or that God voluntarily hides. God's "godness" is complete, in the sense that the divine essence is

---

[68] Among the theologians making these divine becoming arguments in the process theological perspective, see Bradley Artson, *God of Becoming and Relationship* (Woodstock, VT: Jewish Lights, 2016); Timothy Burnette, *The Adventure of Becoming* (2020); Monica Coleman, *Making a Way Out of Now Way* (Philadelphia: Fortress, 2008); Julia Enxing, *Gott bewegt: Prozesstheologische Denkanstösse* (Karl Alber: Baden-Baden, 2026); Bruce Epperly, *Process Theology* (London: T&T Clark, 2011); Roland Faber, *The Becoming of God* (Eugene, OR: Cascade, 2017); Catherine Keller, *The Face of the Deep* (New York: Routledge, 2002); Jay McDaniel and Donna Bowman, eds., *Handbook of Process Theology* (St. Louis, MO: Chalice, 2006).

[69] God, Genus, and Third Man. One of the many insights of Alfred North Whitehead was his distinction between God as a being (an ever concrescing actual entity) and eternal objects. While the eternal objects as forms are in God's primordial nature, he says, they are neither created nor controlled by God. This move allows one to say God has attributes unique to a divine being while also saying the abstract categories of being—for both creatures and Creator—are neither created by God nor outside God. God is the unique instance of a divine genus. To put it another way, the "3rd man" argument in philosophical theology is misplaced because it assumes that abstractions and categories are created. I join Alvin Plantinga and the majority of philosophical theologians in saying forms, abstractions, and eternal objects such as numbers, colors, and categories are not created but eternally in the divine mind. I'm grateful to Aaron Berkowitz and Eric Manchester and his correspondence on these matters, because they helped me realize the importance of this metaphysical move.

[70] Moltmann, *The Spirit of Life*, 41.

[71] God as Future I reject theologies that portray God as future or the future. While I think God knows all possibilities for what the future might be, because these possibilities are everlastingly in the divine mind, I don't think the future is a place from which God can come.

unchanging. But "becoming" describes God's eventful and experiential living as a divine Subject in relation with creatures and creation.[72]

Technically put, the becoming Spirit is an everlasting series of divine occasions of experience. Each moment of the divine life comes into and goes out of existence, analogous to moment-by-moment creaturely living.[73] And each moment will be shaped by characteristics and traits passed along from previous moments.[74] This concept of a living God "runs through the Bible from beginning to end," says Elizabeth Johnson, "to identify the Source of life as dynamic, bounteous and full of surprises."[75]

Some of God's characteristics and traits pass along, moment-by-moment, and make up the Spirit's unchanging attributes and essence.[76] The universal Spirit who loves is an everlasting series with continuity that derives from the unchanging divine nature. The Spirit's experience is always becoming, while the divine essence is immutably eternal.

We can also talk about becoming using the language of successive "selves." We know from personal experience that our present selves differ from past selves. Our lives comprise an ongoing successions of selves as moments of experience. Selves are social, drawing from

---

[72] See Charlene Burns, *Divine Becoming* (Minneapolis: Augsburg, 2002); Roland Faber, *The Becoming of God*; Arthur Peacocke, *Theology for a Scientific Age* (Minneapolis: Fortress, 1993).

[73] John B. Cobb, Jr. puts it succinctly: "God is a being, indeed the supreme being, but not being itself." See *A Christian Natural Theology* (Philadelphia: Westminster, 1965), 133. Charles Hartshorne also argues for God as the supreme individual who exists everlastingly rather than being itself. See *The Divine Relativity* (New Haven, CT: Yale University Press, 1948), 71.

[74] We would better understand the abstract structures of existence that Tillich identifies as God/being-itself instead as ideas in God's nature. These ideas or forms shape creaturely and divine becoming. Furthermore, it isn't idolatrous to say God's life is shaped and constrained by the structures of what it means to be. Those structures or ideas are eternally in the divine nature, and God is constrained only by the essence of what it means to be divine. David Ray Griffin employs Whitehead's eternal objects well in *Reenchantment without Supernaturalism: A Process Philosophy of Religion* (Ithaca, NY: Cornell University Press, 2001).

[75] Elizabeth Johnson, *Quest for the Living God* (New York: Continuum, 2008), 4. Jürgen Moltmann writes accessibly about the living God in *The Living God and the Fullness of Life* (Louisville, KY: Westminster, 2015).

[76] Charles Hartshorne originated of the philosophical description of this idea. See "The Dipolar Conception of Deity," *The Review of Metaphysics* 31/2 (1967): 287. For a summary of Hartshorne's views, see Donald Wayne Viney and George W. Shields, *The Mind of Charles Hartshorne* (Anoka, MN: Process Century, 2020).

relations with past others. While each self differs from previous ones, we maintain some continuity in identity, because some characteristics carry over moment-by-moment.

Likewise, the dynamic Spirit of love is a series of divine selves with continuity. Unlike a creaturely series, however, the divine series is everlasting. No actual units or bits of divine substance persist moment to moment, but the divine essence persists. The divine Self has an ontology of becoming and an eternal nature of continuity. This way of thinking of God's becoming reorients how we think about the Spirit.

"Being" identifies what's unmoved; "becoming" names what moves; the moving God lovingly becomes.

## Gino-theology

I adopt an ontology of becoming, because existing is best understood as experiential, relational, and dynamic. I also adopt an ontology of becoming to ground language about God in categories that apply also to creatures. The Spirit and creatures must share at least the categories pertaining to acting, relating, perceiving, and valuing if what we say about divine loving can make sense.

To distinguish the philosophy of becoming I advocate from onto-theologies I reject, I propose a new label for theologies that see God as dynamic: "gino-theology." This term draws from the Greek word for "becoming"—*ginomai* (γινομαι)—which describes a happening, an event, occurrence, or a coming to be. (The "G" in the word is hard rather than soft, the 'I' is short, and 'no' sounds like 'know'.) The word may be new, but the ideas are not.

Gino-theology describes God's becoming.

Gino-theology points to categories of becoming to account for the dynamism of God. The becoming Spirit who loves is an everlasting series of personally-ordered divine occasions. Divine becoming is like creaturely becoming, insofar as we understand both Creator and creatures as eventful actors, feelers, thinkers, and relaters.[77] God is a divine

---

[77] Paul Tillich doesn't provide a theology of becoming. "God's participation isn't a spatial or temporal presence," he argues. His theology "includes a rejection of a nonsymbolic,

cause among creaturely causes.⁷⁸ Divine becoming differs, however, insofar as the Spirit is *all*-pervading, *ever*lasting, *perfectly* wise, *all*-feeling, and so on. God can be the only one of a genus (*sui generis*), while nevertheless sharing similarities with other genera.⁷⁹

Various theological movements fit the gino-theology framework. Those movements include open and relational theologies of various types, including process, relational, openness, and similar theologies. Such traditions argue that God is relational and changes in some ways. They're known for emphasizing God as experiential, time-oriented, personal, emotional, receptive, dynamic, and loving. But other theologians and theological movements also align with what I'm calling gino-theology.

Christians influenced by the Eastern church, for instance, have helpful language to talk about God as relational becoming. Many refer to the Spirit's activity as the "divine energies" (*energia*), which conveys the dynamism appropriate for love. When "energies" describe divine actions, Eastern Orthodox theology can distinguish between God's essence and activities. But unfortunately, the term "energies" could be easily interpreted as substantive power units rather than the Spirit's becoming. "Ginomai," I submit, might better account for God's active becoming than "energies."

The gino-theology family also includes most personalist theologies. Personalists such as Borden Parker Bowne, Edgar Brightman, Georgia Harkness, and Martin Luther King, Jr., build from the primary claim that God is a divine person relating with creaturely persons.⁸⁰ Keith Ward is an excellent contemporary example of a theistic

---

ontological doctrine of God as becoming," he says. In fact, "to speak of a 'becoming' God disrupts the balance between dynamics and form and subjects God to a process which has the character of a fate or which is completely open to the future and has the character of an absolute accident," argues Tillich. "In both cases, the divinity of God is undercut." See *Systematic Theology*, vol. 1, 245, 247.

⁷⁸ It is rare for theologians to say, as I do, that God is a cause among causes. For another who agrees with me, see Simon Kittle, "God is (probably) a cause among causes," *Theology and Science* 22:2 (2022): 247-262.

⁷⁹ Keith Ward makes a similar argument in *Sharing in the Divine Nature* (Eugene, OR: Cascade, 2020), 95.

⁸⁰ For a critical introduction to personalism, see Rufus Burrow, Jr., *Personalism* (St. Louis: Chalice, 1999).

personalist who affirms divine becoming.[81] God has intelligence, acts, relates, responds, learns, and more, all as a dynamic agent. While personalists may not use the word "becoming," their theology assumes it.

Some of what Karl Barth says aligns with gino-theology. Barth argued for divine becoming to emphasize the dynamism of the Word. "We speak of an action, of a deed, when we speak of the being of God as a happening," Barth says.[82] "God's being proceeds," he says, by actively self-revealing in history. His claim that "God's being is event" mirrors gino-theology,[83] and Eberhard Jüngel concludes that in Barth's theology, "God's being is in becoming."[84]

In his radical theology, John Caputo also embraces the gino-theological notion of God as event. This way of talking fits the movement of *differance* articulated by Jacques Derrida. Caputo refers to the Spirit as event partly because it undermines onto-theology. But to my knowledge, he doesn't explore the notion of God as a *series* of events. The dynamism Caputo rightly sees in *differance* could be understood as the Spirit's ongoing, eventful becoming.[85]

In sum, the becoming Spirit loves moment by moment in ongoing living. Rather than an unchanging being, being itself, or without being, the Spirit is best understood as always becoming. Gino-theology should replace onto-theology, because a theology of the becoming Spirit better reflects the scriptural witness, aligns with lived experience, and better supports the primacy of love.

---

[81] See Ward, *Sharing in the Divine Nature*, ch. 4.

[82] Karl Barth, *Church Dogmatics, Volume II: The Doctrine of God, Part 1*, G. W. Bromiley and T. F. Torrance, trans. T. H. L. Parker et al. (Edinburgh: T&T Clark, 1957), 267.

[83] Ibid., 271.

[84] Eberhard Jüngel, *The Doctrine of the Trinity* (Grand Rapids, MI: Eerdmans, 1976).

[85] Among Caputo's book that discuss God as event, see *The Weakness of God* (Bloomington, IN: Indiana University Press, 2006); *In Search of Radical Theology* (New York: Fordham University Press, 2020). For an exploration of Caputo's radical theology and amipotence theology, see Joshua G. Patterson, "Amipotence (Perhaps)," in *Amipotence, vol. 2*, Brandon Brown, et. al., eds. (Grasmere, ID: SacraSage, 2025).

## Conclusion

Traditional theologies portray God as a being, or being-itself. Being-itself renders the Spirit abstract, impersonal, and disconnected from the dynamic nature of love. Saying God is a being, however, can easily be interpreted to mean God could be a locally-embodied individual who intervenes from time to time. Those who think God's being is the divine essence envision deity as timeless, changeless, or beyond all finite categories. But I've pointed out that an entirely infinite God would be utterly inconceivable.

Other theologians say God is beyond being and metaphysics. But when describing this allegedly being-less deity, they slip into language that requires metaphysics. We've seen that no one who wants to talk intelligibly, consistently, and biblically can do without metaphysics.

I propose a shift from static onto-theology to dynamic gino-theology. This approach says we best understand God not as unchanging *being* but as an ever-*becoming* Spirit of Love. Gino-theology better fits the broad biblical witness, which overwhelmingly depicts the Spirit as a living, personal agent who feels, responds, and relates with others. And it better fits the way we think about our own experience of the divine.

A systematic theology that prioritizes love requires a vision of the divine that aligns with love's dynamism. We do well, then, to describe the Spirit as relational rather than aloof, an agent not an abstraction, and one whose giving and receiving is timely rather than timeless. A vision of a becoming Spirit who acts as a subject enjoys strong biblical support and experiential resonances with what we know of love.

CHAPTER SIX

# God Is Not Omnipotent

## THE BIG IDEAS

- "Omnipotent" is typically thought to mean that God exerts all power, can do anything, or can control creatures and circumstances.
- The word omnipotent and its synonyms aren't in the original languages of scripture.
- The typical meanings of omnipotence aren't in the Bible.
- God can do the "mighty deeds" described in scripture without being omnipotent.
- To make any sense, the concept of omnipotence must be qualified excessively.
- Qualifying omnipotence excessively leads to its collapse.
- Belief in omnipotence leads to various harms, including justifying evil, injustice, and oppression.
- A coherent systematic theology of love will reject omnipotence.

Saying God is omnipotent has been the default for most theists, agnostics, and even atheists.[1] But positing deity as all-powerful, "in control," or able singlehandedly to produce outcomes leads to unsolvable moral and philosophical problems.[2] In fact, the best arguments *against* God's existence assume an omnipotent deity.

---

[1] This chapter is dedicated to Donald Wayne Viney. Don has thought deeply about these ideas, and his writings and our conversations have helped me think deeply.

[2] Few theological monographs are entirely devoted to exploring omnipotence. Among the books that do, see David Basinger, *Divine Power in Process Theism* (Albany, NY: SUNY, 1988); Anna Case-Winters, *God's Power* (Louisville, KY: Westminster/John Knox, 1990), David Ray Griffin, *God, Power, and Evil* (Philadelphia: Westminster Press, 1976), Thomas Jay Oord, *The Death of Omnipotence and Birth of Amipotence* (Grasmere, ID: SacraSage, 2023), Gijsbert van den Brink, *Almighty God* (Netherlands: Kok Pharos, 1993).

If we think God is omnipotent, the problem of evil presents us with obvious questions about God's goodness. The problem presents the most severe objection to belief in God and, therefore, the biggest obstacle for a systematic theology of love. We rightly ask, "Why doesn't an all-powerful and all-loving deity *prevent* genuine evil?" The issue of divine hiddenness also presents a problem. We wonder, "Why doesn't an all-powerful and all-loving God reveal in crystal-clear ways?" Omnipotence creates other problems too.

Most believers in God—scholars and laity alike—assume the Bible supports omnipotence. But it doesn't. The word doesn't appear in biblical texts, and references to God as "almighty" are mistranslations of Hebrew and Greek words. The meanings of omnipotence also aren't found in Scripture, at least not without contradiction. And we can affirm God's mighty deeds described in sacred writ without appealing to notions of divine control. Scripture doesn't support omnipotence.

Both conservative and progressive theologians try to get around these problems by qualifying omnipotence. These qualifications take so many forms the results no longer fit the common meaning of the word. Qualified omnipotence says the Spirit can't do what's logically, mathematically, ontologically, and metaphysically impossible.[3] Further, God can't contradict the divine nature, and deity has no body parts with which to stop evil. When we make proper qualifications, saying God "can do all things," as Augustine puts it, makes no sense.

Vast harm occurs as a result of belief in omnipotence. People not only deny God exists when they witness evil or when God seems hidden, but belief in omnipotence presents us with other reasons to reject theism. Despite these problems, some retain the word "omnipotence" but redefine it radically. I think people of faith should abandon the concept and language of omnipotence and find better words to describe the power of the loving Spirit.

---

[3] Chris Lilley explores this issue concisely in "An Apology for Qualified Omnipotence," in *Amipotence, vol. 1*, Chris S. Baker, et. al., eds. (Grasmere, ID: SacraSage, 2025).

## Typical Understandings of Omnipotence

Those who affirm a doctrine of omnipotence rarely define it. Some, like Arthur Pink, resort to tautologies: "To say that God is sovereign is to declare that God is *God*."[4] Such statements don't help. A look at how most people speak—scholars and laity alike—reveals that divine omnipotence typically has one the following meanings:

1. God exerts all power.
2. God can do anything.
3. God can control creatures or circumstances.

Theologians who believe God exerts all power should say outright that deity controls everything, and some do so. In this way of thinking, deity is the omnicause of everything that happens.[5] All history plays out exactly as God wants it, because deity makes it so. Most who believe in an all-determining deity try to claim creatures somehow exert some power, simultaneous with God exerting *all* power.[6] It's a mystery, they say, how God can do everything, yet creatures also have a measure of power. I think this so-called "compatibilist" view ends up being nonsense.

Other believers say God can do anything . . . but then they qualify what they mean by "anything."[7] Augustine, for instance, says God is "He who can do all things," which sounds like deity has unlimited

---

[4] Arthur W. Pink, *The Sovereignty of God* (Grand Rapids, MI: Baker, 1984 [1930]), 19. Pink adds a number of other claims to this one, but none are clear.

[5] For a representative of the omnicause view, see Paul Kjoss Helseth, "God Causes All Things," in *Four Views on Divine Providence*, ed. Dennis W. Jowers (Grand Rapids, MI: Zondervan, 2011), 52. For a philosophical defense of theological determinism, see J. A. Crabtree, *The Most Real Being* (Eugene, OR: Wipf and Stock, 2004).

[6] Olav Bryant Smith explains concisely the problems with saying God has all power in his essay, "The Metaphysics of Love," in *Amipotence, vol. 1,* Chris S. Baker, et. al., eds. (Grasmere, ID: SacraSage, 2025).

[7] As an example of a conservative theologian who qualifies divine omnipotence, see Stephen Charnock, *The Existence and Attributes of God,* 2 vols. (Grand Rapids, MI: Baker Book, reprint 1996 [1853]).

abilities.[8] But then he also says God can't die, can't sin, can't lie, and can't be deceived. If God *could* do such activities, he adds, "He would not be omnipotent."[9]

I agree that God's power needs to be qualified in the ways Augustine lists and even many more. But I think divine power should be chiefly qualified by what we know about love. Augustine doesn't think well about love: he makes no sense, for instance, when he says the inability to do some things must be essential to omnipotence. Would the inability to know a fact be essential to omniscience or the inability to love someone be essential to being all-loving? Does the same logic apply?

Many advocates of omnipotence say or imply that God *could* control creatures or creation, but usually doesn't. They think the Spirit may control a particular state of affairs or a specific individual but mostly allows creatures to exert freedom and/or power. The deity so conceived remains essentially omnipotent but voluntarily self-limits.

It's hard to believe a voluntarily self-limited God can be consistently loving when genuine evils occur. A self-limited deity could un-self-limit and prevent them. And you'd think an omnipotent God who voluntarily self-limits could self-reveal in more unambiguous ways. If, as many theists claim, divine self-revealing is essential to salvation, wouldn't an all-loving God *want* to be known by everyone? And yet God is often hidden.

This systematic theology of love rejects omnipotence understood in each of these ways.[10] It says God doesn't and can't exert all power. There are many things the Spirit can't do. And the uncontrolling Lover can't control anyone, anything, or any circumstances.

---

[8] Augustine, *De Trinitate*, IV 20, 27 (CChr.SL), 50, 197. Despite this claim, Augustine also notes a number of things God can't do.

[9] Augustine, *Sermo de symbolo ad catechumenos* 2 (CChr.SL 46, 185-6, ), 40. Augustine's claim that God wouldn't be omnipotent if God were to lie or be deceived makes no sense. Creatures can do those things, but we don't think them omnipotent. What he must mean is that God's nature places constraints on what God can do. For my discussion of qualifications theologians make to the concept of omnipotence, see *The Death of Omnipotence and Birth of Amipotence*, ch. 2

[10] Libby Tedder Hugus agrees in her concise essay, "Good Riddance, Omnipotence," in *Amipotence, vol. 1*, Chris S. Baker, et. al., eds. (Grasmere, ID: SacraSage, 2025).

## OMNIPOTENCE ISN'T FOUND IN SCRIPTURE

The words "omnipotent" and "omnipotence," surprisingly, aren't found in the Bible. Biblical writers also don't express the three primary meanings of omnipotence I've noted, at least not consistently. Readers of scripture occasionally encounter the word "almighty" in the text, however. Translators have rendered two Hebrew words and one Greek word as "almighty," and many people of faith have equated almightiness with omnipotence.[11] But "almighty" is actually a mistranslation of the biblical languages.

One of the Hebrew words mistranslated "almighty" is *shaddai*.[12] The word appears in various books of the Bible, and scholars consider it one of the oldest names for God.[13] In Exodus, the Lord says, "I appeared to Abraham, Isaac, and Jacob as *el shaddai*" (6:3), a passage that predates the Mosaic age.[14]

Rather than meaning "almighty" or "omnipotent," however, biblical scholars say the oldest and most likely meaning of *shaddai* is "breasts."[15] This aligns with the Hebrew emphasis upon divine fertility

---

[11] Almighty? In previous writings, I've said we could rightly call God almighty in three senses. God 1) is mightier than all others, 2) exerts might upon all that exists, and 3) is the source of might for all. After discovering that biblical authors never call God almighty, I've stopped using "almighty" to describe divine power. Gijsbert Van Den Brink argues for "almightiness" over omnipotent in *Almighty God*.

[12] See William Albright, "The Names Shaddai and Abram," *Journal of Biblical Literature* 54 (1935): 180-93; E. L. Abel, "The Nature of the Patriarchal God 'El Sadday,'" *Numen* 20 (1973): 49-59; Lloyd Bailey, "Israelite 'El Shadday and Amorite Bl Shade," *Journal of Biblical Literature* 87 (1968): 434-38; Frank Moore Cross, "Yahweh and the God of the Patriarchs," *Harvard Theological Review* 55 (1962): 244-50; *Canaanite Myth and Hebrew Epic* (Cambridge, MA: Harvard University Press, 1973), 52-60; William G. Dever, *Does God Have a Wife?* (Grand Rapids, MI: Eerdmans, 2005); Jean Ouellette, "More on 'El Shadday and Bel Shade," *Journal of Biblical Literature* 88 (1969): 470-71.

[13] Nahum M. Sarna argues that "the overwhelming appearance [of *el Shaddai*] in poetic contexts points a priori to a venerable tradition, for Hebrew poetry tends to preserve or consciously to employ early forms of speech" ("El Shaddai," *Exodus Commentary* [Jewish Publication Society, 1991], 269). See also Robert Alter, *The Hebrew Bible*, 3 Vols. (New York: W. W. Norton & Company, 2019); G. Steins's summary, "Sadday," in *Theological Dictionary of the Old Testament*, Vol. 14 (Grand Rapids, MI: Eerdmans, 2004), 418-446.

[14] On this, see Sarna, *Exodus Commentary*, 269. *Shaddai* is used in the blessings promised Jacob as well (Gen. 28:1-4; 35:9) and figures into the Joseph story as blessing (Gen. 49: 22-26).

[15] Most scholarly assessments of the meaning of *shaddai* note diverse meanings but suggest "breast" and "mountain" as most likely. In addition to the sources cited in other footnotes, see *NET Bible* (Biblical Studies Press, 2005).

and fecundity.[16] *Yahweh* provides, sustains, and gives life. Rather than enshrining omnipotence, therefore, *el shaddai* describes a breasted God who nourishes and nurtures.[17] *Shaddai* isn't almighty.[18]

The second Hebrew word sometimes translated "almighty" is *sabaoth*.[19] Rather than omnipotent, the word means "armies," "hosts," "ranks," "congregation," or "council."[20] When *yahweh* or *elohim* precedes it, the word would be better translated "lord of hosts," "leader of armies," or "head of the council."[21] *Sabaoth* refers to the deity who leads; it doesn't mean "almighty."

Why are *shaddai* and *sabaoth* mistranslated "almighty" in English bibles? The answer comes from the Septuagint (*LXX*), the Greek translation of Hebrew scriptures appearing before the New Testament was written. People of faith read the Septuagint during Jesus' lifetime, and New Testament writers quote from it more than Hebrew-language biblical texts.

The authors of the Septuagint translated *shaddai* and *sabaoth* with the one Greek word *pantokrator*. The prefix *panto* means "all;" the root

---

[16] See David Biale, "The God with Breasts: El Shaddai in the Bible," *History of Religions* (1982), 252. The connection between God and breasts apparently derives from Amorite and Canaanite cultures. See also F. M. Cross, *Canaanite Myth and Hebrew Epic* (Cambridge, MA: Harvard University Press, 1973), 52-60. See also J. Gerald Janzen's extensive analysis of *el shaddai* in relation to a personal God in *At the Scent of Water* (Grand Rapids, MI: Eerdmans, 2009).

[17] *Shaddai* appears in later biblical texts, and it has other meanings. But when *shaddai* doesn't likely mean "breasts" or "mountains," a Hebrew word for God never precedes these words. I explain these issues and cite dozens of biblical scholars in *The Death of Omnipotence and Birth of Amipotence*, ch. 2.

[18] *Shaddai* occurs several times in the book of Job, but it's never preceded by *El* or another name for God. I address this use of the word and others in chapter two of *The Death of Omnipotence and Birth of Amipotence*.

[19] The term is translated "Almighty" in the NIV in many instances. As examples, see 1 Sam 1:3, 11; 4:4; 15:2; 17:45; 2 Sam 5:10; 6:2, 18; 7:8, 26, 27; 1 Kgs 18:15; 19:10, 14; 2 Kgs 3:14; 17:7, 24; 19:31; Ps 24:10; 46:7, 11; 48:8; 59:5; 69:6; 80:4, 7, 14, 19; 84:1, 3, 8, 12; 89:8.

[20] See Walther Eichrodt, *Theology of the Old Testament*, I (Philadelphia: Westminster, 1961); Otto Eissfeldt, "Jahwe Zebaoth," *Kleine Schriften*, 3 (Tubingen: J. C. B. Mohr Paul Siebeck, 1966); John E. Hartley, "Hosts," in *Theological Wordbook of the Old Testament* (Chicago: Moody Press, 1999), 750-751; W. H. McClellan, "Dominus Deus Sabaoth," *CBQ* 2:300–307; Patrick D. Miller, *The Divine Warrior in Early Israel* (Cambridge, MA: Harvard University, 1973); J. P. Ross, "Jahweh Seba'ot in Sam and Ps," *VT* 17:76–92.

[21] *Sabaoth* can be preceded by many words for deity, including *Yahweh*, *Elohim*, and *Adonai*. The Septuagint occasionally uses "Lord of powers" (*kyrios (ho) theós tōn dynámeōn*) for what in Hebrew would be "Lord of hosts."

*krater* or *krateo* has various meanings, including "hold" or "attain." For instance, God holds (*krateo*) the stars in divine hands, according to John's Revelation (1:16). But *pantokrator* literally means "all-holding" or "all-sustaining;" it doesn't mean omnipotent or almighty.[22]

The Septuagint's rendering of *shaddai* and *sabaoth* as *pantokrator* has had massive repercussions.[23] *Pantokrator* appears in the New Testament, although only ten times, nine of those in the book of Revelation. In each occurrence, we have the mistranslation "almighty," rather than "all-holding," "all-sustaining," or a related word.[24]

If New Testament writers had wanted to describe God as omnipotent, another Greek word was available. *Pantodunamis* literally means "all power" or "all-powerful." We find this word in The Book of Wisdom (11:17), a noncanonical testament written prior to the books comprising the New Testament. Biblical writers likely knew of the word *pantodunamis* but chose not to use it when describing divine power. *Pantodunamis* never appears in the Christian canon.

Centuries after the Jewish and Christian scriptures were written, Jerome translated the Hebrew and Greek texts into Latin. For *pantokrator*, he chose the Latin word *omnipotens*, which in English is "omnipotent." Jerome's decision depended largely upon *pantokrater* in the Septuagint, although he had access to Hebrew manuscripts.[25]

---

[22] Ian Robert Richardson notes that "when considering God's power as providentially sustaining the universe, *kratein* was followed by the accusative case because that was used to express 'holding' rather than 'reigning.'" See Richardson, "Meister Eckhart's Parisian Question of 'Whether the omnipotence of God should be considered as potentia ordinata or potentia absoluta?'" (King's College London, 2002), 17. The 2$^{nd}$ century bishop Theophilus, for instance, says God "is called *Pantokrator* because He Himself holds (*kratei*) and embraces (*emperiechei*) all things (*ta panta*)." *Ad Autolycum* 1, 4. Dwight Swanson criticizes my commentary and use of biblical scholarship on the word. See Dwight Swanson, "Thomas Oord on *The Death of Omnipotence*: 'Not Born of Scripture,'" *The Asbury Theological Journal*, Vol. 80: No. 1 (2025): 270-284.

[23] See G. Steins, "Sadday," 447. On this matter, see Wilhelm Michaelis, "Κράτος (θεοκρατία), Κρατέω, Κραταιός, Κραταιόω, Κοσμοκράτωρ, Παντοκράτωρ," *Theological Dictionary of the New Testament*, Vol. 3 (Grand Rapids, MI: Eerdmans, 1964), 914-15.

[24] I explore New Testament notions of God's power and cite dozens of biblical scholars in *The Death of Omnipotence and Birth of Amipotence*, ch. 2.

[25] Manfred Weippert, "Sadday," *Theological Lexicon of the Old Testament*, Vol. 3, Claus Westermann, ed. Mark E. Biddle, Trans. (1997), 1621.

Biblical scholar Karen Winslow speculates that Jerome knew *pantokrator* meant all-sustaining rather than all-powerful. His choice to use the Latin *omnipotens*, she says, likely "represents his own Platonic theological leanings."[26] Had Jerome followed the oldest meanings of *shaddai* and *sabaoth*, generations thereafter would likely not said God is omnipotent. Perhaps love, instead of control, would have become the center of systematic theological reflection.

Translations of *shaddai* and *sabaoth* misrepresent God as omnipotent.

## The Meaning of Omnipotence Is Not Found in Scripture

One might respond to these mistranslations by arguing that although the words "omnipotent" or "almighty" aren't in scripture, biblical passages assume or require their meaning. But this just isn't so.

The claim that God must be omnipotent—in the sense of literally exerting all power—doesn't fit the biblical witness.[27] We find scripture replete with claims about creaturely actions, including sinful actions God didn't want. *Sabaoth* passages identify God working alongside or against others, with their own abilities and power. Sometimes, creatures do other than what *Yahweh* wants.

New Testament writers also speak of creaturely power alongside divine power. Creatures can cooperate as God's fellow-workers (*synergoi*), says Paul (1 Cor. 3:9-10), or they can use their wills to disobey. It's impossible to make good sense of the numerous biblical references to sin if creatures don't have their own ability to act contrary to the Spirit's desires.

Some theologians claim scripture says God exerts all power, but creatures some. "Events are fully (100%) caused by God and fully

---

[26] Karen Winslow, "The All-Nurturing, All-Sustaining God of Scripture," in *Amipotence*, vol. 1, Chris Baker, et. al., eds. (Grasmere, ID: SacraSage, 2025), 244.

[27] Scholars debate whether Ecclesiastes (Qohelet) identifies God as omnipotent. The book doesn't explicitly say so. See Jacobus Gericke, "Qohelet's Concept of Deity: A Comparative-Philosophical Perspective," *Verbum et Ecclesia* 34:1, Art. #743 (2013) and Michael V. Fox, *A Time to Tear Down & A Time to Build Up* (Grand Rapids, MI: Eerdmans, 1999).

(100%) caused by the creature,"[28] says Wayne Grudem. Not only is this bad math, but it also makes God the cause of evil. So-called "compatibilism" makes no logical sense nor fits reality as we know it. "When God is seen as totally in control," says Anna Case-Winters, "any credible concept of freedom and autonomy for human beings is relinquished, and human actions lose their significance."[29] When biblical writers say God acts, we should *not* think they mean God exerts all power whatsoever, and we should not think creatures exert no power.

Some biblical passages imply God is omnipotent in the second sense I've identified. They seem to say God can do absolutely anything. "Oh Lord God," says Jeremiah, "nothing is too hard for you" (32:17). And in the New Testament, we read, "with humans this is impossible, but with God all things are possible" (Mt. 19:26; Mk. 14:36; Lk. 1:37).

But biblical writers also identify activities that are impossible for God. We find it's impossible for God to lie (Heb. 6:18; Tit. 1:2); deny God's self (2 Tim. 2:13); be tempted (Jas. 1:13b); grow tired or weary (Is. 40:28a); revoke the gifts and call given (Rom. 11:29); change God's nature (Mal. 3:6; James 1:17); break covenant (Lev. 26:44); alter what God says (Ps. 89:34); give up on Israel (Hos. 11:8a); and more examples. So, some things *are* too hard or impossible for God, according to scripture.

Following both the broad witness of scripture and logic, conservative and progressive theologians alike interpret passages that say "nothing is impossible for God" or "God can do all things" as not literally true. They see these statements as being made in light of specific actions God does in relation to creation; they're not broad statements about unlimited divine abilities.[30] The vast majority of theologians in history have admitted omnipotence must be qualified. I'll address this later in more detail.

The third common meaning of omnipotence pertains to divine control. Some theologians insist that although the biblical writers never *say* God controls, we must affirm omnipotence to make sense of

---

[28] Wayne Grudem, *Systematic Theology* 2nd ed. (Grand Rapids, MI: Zondervan, 2020), 319.

[29] Case-Winters, *God's Power*, 9.

[30] On this issue, Gijsbert van den Brink notes a difference between "abstract philosophical reasons" and "the living communication between God and man." See *Almighty God*, pp. 64-65.

scripture. By "control," I mean the idea that God entirely determines a person, creature, or circumstance to bring about some state of affairs singlehandedly. To control is to act as the sole and sufficient cause of some outcome. A controlling God could produce results in creation without help from creaturely actors or factors.

Good biblical evidence of God's omnipotent control would *explicitly* say that no creaturely actors, factors, or forces exert power alongside, or in addition to, God. To control, God would need to bring about an outcome singlehandedly. Deity would determine results for creatures by absolute fiat, and biblical passages indicating this—if they existed—would indicate that no creaturely actors or factors contributed.

Given these criteria, we find no examples of omnipotent control in the Bible. None. No passage says God forced creatures or creation, in the sense of being the only cause.[31] Biblical writers don't describe God as controlling when creating the world,[32] nor controlling when hardening Pharaoh's heart or in other Old Testament stories,[33] nor do we find God controlling in the New Testament when Mary became pregnant with Jesus, nor controlling when Jesus performed miracles, nor controlling when God raised Jesus from the dead,[34] nor controlling

---

[31] Janet Warren explores these issues in light of evil and concludes similarly to what I propose. See *All Things Wise and Wonderful* (Eugene, OR: Wipf and Stock, 2021) and *Cleansing the Cosmos* (Eugene, OR: Pickwick, 2012).

[32] For those who affirm *creatio ex nihilo*, there was nothing for God to control when initially creating. Those who reject *creation ex nihilo* usually say God worked with creaturely elements God previously created. I explain this view later in this book and in *Pluriform Love: An Open and Relational Theology of Well-Being* (Grasmere, ID: SacraSage, 2022), ch. 8.

[33] Pharaoh's Hardened Heart. Biblical writers say God hardened Pharaoh's heart *and* Pharaoh hardened his own heart (Ex 7:13; 8:11,15,32; 9:34). I agree with Terence Fretheim that "an act of hardening doesn't make one totally or permanently impervious to outside influence; it doesn't turn the heart off and on like a faucet," and "divine hardening did not override Pharaoh's decision-making powers" (Fretheim, *Exodus: Interpretation* [Philadelphia: Westminster John Knox, 2004], 97, 99). In other words, those who interpret "hardening" as "control" impose a view of omnipotence not required by the text.

[34] On Mary's cooperation with the Spirit, Jesus' miracles, and God raising Jesus from the dead—none of which control—see Thomas Jay Oord, "Essential Kenosis Christology," in *Methodist Christology,* Jason Vicker and Jerome Van Kuiken, eds. (Indianapolis, IN: Wesley's Foundery Books, 2020). Many come to these stories assuming God controls and wrongly read them as examples of omnipotence. I'll explain in later chapters how God raises Jesus in an uncontrolling way.

in the eschaton.[35] No biblical passage explicitly says God caused a state of affairs such that no creaturely factors, actors, or forces played a role. This third meaning of omnipotence isn't in the Bible.

The meaning of omnipotence isn't on the pages of scripture.

## God's Mighty Deeds?

Over the centuries, theologians have pointed to particular events in scripture as God's "mighty deeds." Many think these events—such as the exodus of Israel—require divine omnipotence. Gijsbert van den Brink appeals to this logic: "God's omnipotence appears from His *actions.*"[36] God has "unlimited power or ability to bring things about by acting in the world," van den Brink insists. "From their experience of God's mighty acts, people [in scripture] came to the conclusion that nothing could be impossible for this God."[37]

But Van den Brink and other theologians make claims about God's power that the Bible doesn't require. Although scripture writers often say deity as powerful (e.g., Ps 147:5) and they say God does mighty deeds (e.g., Ps. 98), the powerful Spirit can do mighty deeds without being omnipotent. Deity can be maximally influential without singlehandedly determining outcomes.[38] Biblical writers never say God acted alone when doing mighty deeds.

Admittedly, not every biblical text explicitly points to creaturely actors and factors contributing to God's mighty deeds. Most do, but some just say God acted. Given the overwhelming number of times biblical writers point to creaturely actions and the absence of times they say God singlehandedly brings about outcomes, we have grounds

---

[35] In various writings, I address God's relentless love, which doesn't control now or at the eschaton. See, for example, "God's Glory as Relentless Love" in *Deconstructing Hell*, Chad Bahl, ed. (Grasmere, ID: SacraSage, 2023). For an eschatology based on the renewal of the heavens and earth, see Richard Middleton, *A New Heaven and a New Earth* (Grand Rapids, MI: Eerdmans, 2014).

[36] Van den Brink, *Almighty God*, 166. The emphasis on "actions" is the author's.

[37] Ibid., 176, 177.

[38] James Travis Young agrees with my view in his fine essay, "It's the End of the World as We Know It (and I Feel Fine)," in *Amipotence, vol. 1*, Chris S. Baker, et. al., eds. (Grasmere, ID: SacraSage, 2025).

to assume God does mighty deeds—including miracles—alongside and with creaturely cooperation. Many of the miracle stories of Jesus, for instance, say explicitly the person's faith made them whole. While we rightly claim God's power as matchless—in the sense of having no equal—we don't need to also say it's unlimited.

Mighty deeds don't require an omnipotent Actor.

Even the Evangelical theologian Wayne Grudem admits the Bible points to creaturely factors, forces, and actors working alongside God. If we define divine action as "God working without means," says Grudem, this "leaves us with very few if any miracles in the Bible, for it is hard to think of a miracle that came about with no means at all." Even in biblical accounts of healing, says Grudem, "some of the physical properties of the sick person's body were doubtless involved as part of the healing." And "when Jesus multiplied the loaves and fish, he at least used the original five loaves and two fishes that were there. When he changed water to wine, he used water and made it become wine."[39]

I agree with Grudem that biblical accounts always point to, or imply, creaturely actors, factors, and forces alongside God. But as we saw earlier, Grudem thinks all events are 100% done by God and simultaneously 100% done by creatures. His statements are contradictory, so I reject them. In the name of logic, scripture, and love, we shouldn't say God does 100% or creatures do 100%. We should appeal instead to divine-creature collaboration.

If relational love is inherently uncontrolling, a loving God *requires* creaturely cooperation or conducive conditions for mighty deeds to occur. If the Spirit's love is always relational, both amazing and mundane moments shouldn't be seen as the outcome of solitary divine action. A loving deity inspires and empowers creatures or creation to collaborate.[40] As a result, mighty deeds, signs, and wonders sometimes occur. But they're not the products of omnipotence.

---

[39] Grudem, *Systematic Theology*, 355-56.

[40] Divine-Creature Synergy in the Old Testament. Judith Krawelitzki joins Fretheim and other biblical scholars in noting that Old Testament writers repeatedly describe God working *with* creatures. "*Yahweh* is my strength," says Krawelitzki, "because he enables my rescue by letting me participate in his power." God's "mighty deeds are not demonstrations of [God's] power for his own sake," she continues. "Rather, they are salvific and rescuing

An adequate assessment of scripture also requires us to account for when God did *not* do mighty deeds. God sometimes failed to rescue Israel, for instance, or failed to deliver creatures from suffering and death. The people lamented when God didn't liberate them, and they cried out in pain. The Psalms and other books attest to this. An adequate description of divine power, therefore, has to account for what a loving Spirit does and doesn't do, for what God can and can't do. It must explain the mighty acts of salvation history *and* the history of unnecessary suffering. Omnipotence fails to do both.

Christians typically think of Jesus as the clearest revelation of God's power. In this Nazarene's witness, we glimpse a God who doesn't control or dominate (*astheneias*). Jesus' servant-like life reveals God to be self-giving and others-empowering (*kenosis*) rather than omnipotent in any of the ways theologians and people of faith have typically talked about God's power.[41] Jesus not only preached a gospel of uncontrolling love, but his crucifixion also suggests that deity suffers with us, rather than dominates creatures. The cross reveals divine weakness, says the Apostle Paul, and not omnipotence (1 Cor. 1; 2 Cor. 13:4).

In sum, Christian scripture does *not* support omnipotence. It doesn't say God has all power; it claims God can't do certain things; and no passage says God singlehandedly determines outcomes. Biblical authors talk about the Spirit's dynamic action, and they say God's power is immense. But they also acknowledge limits to what God can do and point to the role creatures play in causing outcomes.

---

deeds. God bestows his power in creation and history in order that his people can participate in his power by his deeds." See Judith Krawelitzki, "God the Almighty?: Observations in the Psalms," *Vetus Testamentum* 64, no. 3 (2014): 441-42. Walter Brueggeman argues similarly: "the theological substance of Hebrew Scripture is essentially a theological process of vexed, open-ended interaction and dialogue between the Holy One and all those other than the Holy One." "Biblical Theology Appropriately Postmodern," in *Jews, Christians, and the Theology of the Hebrew Scriptures*, Alis Ogden Bellis and Joel S. Kaminsky, eds. (Society of Biblical Literature, 200), 100.

[41] John D. Caputo explores this theme in *The Weakness of God* (Bloomington, IN: Indiana University Press, 2006). We find it also in Martin Luther's theology of the cross. See Alister McGrath, *Luther's Theology of the Cross* (London: Blackwell, 1990) and Paul Fiddes, *The Creative Suffering of God* (Oxford: Clarendon, 1992). Daniel L. Migliore, *The Power of God and the gods of Power* (Louisville, KY: Westminster/John Knox, 2008), 41. John Wesley Dally explores essential kenosis in light of the Wesleyan Quadrilateral in *Putting Essential Kenosis to the Test* (Grasmere, ID: SacraSage, 2024)

And if Jesus provides our best clues to the nature of divine power, we shouldn't think of the Spirit as omnipotent.

Omnipotence—both the word and its typical meanings—isn't found in scripture.

## QUALIFYING OMNIPOTENCE TO ITS COLLAPSE

The idea that God must be omnipotent confuses even the most philosophically-minded theologians. In his influential systematic theology, Thomas Aquinas admits to being perplexed about "the precise meaning of the word 'all' when we say that God can do all things." Consequently, he says, it's "difficult to explain in what omnipotence precisely consists."[42] Alvin Plantinga surveys the work of major theologians and concludes, "I very much doubt that there *is* any one view of omnipotence clearly accepted by most classical theists."[43]

Our confusion may arise when pondering classic questions like this one: "Can God make a rock so big even God can't lift it?" The standard answer among theologians says the Spirit *can't* make this rock. Doing so would involve an ontological contradiction, and contradictions limit everyone. Creating an unliftable rock is, by definition, inherently undoable—even God can't.[44]

In addition to ontological limits, most scholars qualify the concept of omnipotence by saying God can't do the mathematically impossible. The Spirit can't make $2 + 2 = 1$, for instance. And deity can't break the laws of geometry: God can't make a round square or a four-sided triangle. Deity also can't break the logical laws of noncontradiction. The Spirit can't make a married bachelor nor make something both "A" and "Not A." In fact, God can't do millions of activities that entail

---

[42] Thomas Aquinas, *Summa Theologica*, I (Westminster, Md: Christian Classics, 1981), 1a, Q. 25, A. 3.

[43] See Alvin Plantinga, "Reply to the Basingers on Divine Omnipotence," *Process Studies* 11 (1981), 28.

[44] The literature exploring contradictions to omnipotence is immense. For a recent discussion, see Michael Wreen, "The Contradiction Approach to Solving Problems about Omnipotence," *International Journal for Philosophy of Religion and Philosophical Theology* (2022): 259-70.

ontological, mathematical, geometric, or logical contradictions.[45] God can't.

Further, many theologians qualify omnipotence by saying God can't contradict the divine nature.[46] When biblical writers say it's impossible for God to lie (Heb. 6:18; Tit. 1:2), for instance, they're pointing to qualifications on the Spirit abilities that derive from Godself. The claim in 2 Timothy that "God can't deny himself" (2:13) offers a general statement about limits derived from the divine nature.

The Spirit can't contradict the essential divine attributes. The deity who exists necessarily, for instance, can't decide to stop existing. The universal deity present to all can't be absent someplace; an omniscient divinity can't be ignorant of some fact. And perhaps most importantly, the Spirit who by nature loves everyone and everything can't fail to love someone or something.[47] In all these ways, God can't.

The Spirit's incorporeality provides one of the most important, but often overlooked, qualifications to divine power. "If God is nonphysical," says Charles Taliaferro, then "God can't do certain actions that require a body."[48] The universal Spirit has no legs, no mouth, no wings, no fins, no teeth, and so on. But many creatures have these bodily parts. Consequently, creatures can do billions of activities that an incorporeal Spirit can't. God can't.[49]

---

[45] Nick Trakakis summarizes my point when he says, "No matter how much controversy and debate may currently surround the extraordinary attribute of divine omnipotence, there is a virtually complete consensus amongst philosophers and theologians that Aquinas is correct in saying that 'anything that implies a contradiction doesn't fall under God's omnipotence...'" Nick Trakakis, "An epistemically distant God? A critique of John Hick's response to the problem of divine hiddenness," *Heythrop Journal* 48 (2007), 55.

[46] Among important books exploring the meaning of God's nature, see Alvin Plantinga, *Does God Have a Nature?* (Milwaukee, WI: Marquette University Press, 1980).

[47] Wes Morriston ably defends the claim that a morally perfect God can't be omnipotent. See Morriston, "Omnipotence and necessary moral perfection: are they compatible?" *Religious Studies* 37 (2001), 143–160.

[48] Charles Taliaferro, *A Contemporary Philosophy of Religion* (Cambridge, MA: Blackwell, 1998), 71.

[49] Some will wonder if the incarnation of God in Jesus Christ is an exception to what I've written here. It isn't an exception if one believes Jesus had the freedom to cooperate (or not) with God. For a spirit-Christology that says Jesus freely cooperated with the divine Spirit, see Thomas Jay Oord, "Essential Kenosis Christology," in *Methodist Christology*.

## Creation Qualifies Omnipotence

The Spirit's relationship with creation also implies limits on divine abilities. If creatures of varying sizes and complexity exert *some* power of their own, God simply can't exert *all* power. Power is social, in the sense of agents with power influencing other agents with power.[50] Consequently, God must be "one power among others," says Charles Hartshorne, "not the only power."[51] Saying a powerful divine agent relates with less powerful creaturely agents fits the biblical witness and our own experience of power relations. So, when it comes to exerting all power, God can't.

Other limits to divine power arise when we consider time. Major theologians say God can't change past events, for instance. Thomas Aquinas says, "that the past should not have been doesn't come under the scope of divine power."[52] John Wesley applies this to past divine actions: God "can't . . . undo what he has done."[53] Jonathan Edwards puts it this way: "In explaining the nature of necessity, in things which are past, their past existence is now necessary."[54] Again, God can't.

Fewer theologians have considered whether God could change the future. Those who think a timeless God predestined all future events should logically claim deity can't change it.[55] It's been settled. Theologians who believe God experiences time like we do should say there is no actual future to change. It's a realm of possibilities. In either

---

[50] See Simon Kittle's work on this, including "The Incompatibility of Universal, Determinate Divine Causation with Human Free Will," In Vicens, L. and Furlong, P. *Theological Determinism: New Perspectives* (Cambridge University Press, 2022), 100-118.

[51] Charles Hartshorne, *The Divine Relativity*, 138. See also Simon Kittle, "God is (probably) a cause among causes," *Theology and Science* 22:2 (2022): 247-262.

[52] Thomas Aquinas, *Summa Theologica*, 1a, Q. 25, A. 4.

[53] John Wesley, "On Divine Providence," Sermon 67, §§ 15, *Works*, 2: 541.

[54] Jonathan Edwards, *Freedom of the Will*, s.12 (New York: Leavitt & Allen, 1857), 10. On why most scholars say God can't change the past, see Ronald H. Nash, *The Concept of God* (Grand Rapids, MI: Eerdmans, 1983); Alvin Plantinga, "On Ockham's Way Out," *Faith and Philosophy*, 3.3 (July 1986): 235-269; Roger Olson, "Can God Change the Past?" https://www.patheos.com/blogs/rogereolson/2021/06/can-god-change-the-past-2/ (Accessed 12/6/21)

[55] William Hasker argues that simple foreknowledge provides no providential advantage in "Why Simple Foreknowledge is Still Useless," *Journal of the Evangelical Theological Society* 52:3 (2007).

case, theologians who consider the nature of the future say God can't change it.

For obvious reasons, ancient theologians didn't account for the scientific discoveries of recent centuries. The slow evolutionary emergence of complex life forms from less complex, as well as the old age of the universe, are two recent discoveries.[56] Each should prompt us to ask questions about the credibility of omnipotence. For instance, we might wonder, if God wanted companions capable of love, why wait billions of years to create complex lovers? And why use an agonizingly slow evolutionary process if God could instantaneously make them?

The vast amount and long extent of creaturely suffering also raises questions about omnipotence. If God could have created the world without subjecting creatures to unnecessary suffering in evolutionary history, wouldn't a loving God skip this lengthy process? Doesn't God care about other-than-human animals?[57]

And then there's the issue of creaturely freedom. A growing number of theologians say that God can't control free creatures. Leigh Vicens and Simon Kittle put it succinctly: "It must *not* be possible for God to determine what a created person freely chooses."[58] This freedom seems vital for moral decision-making among creatures. "God can create a world containing moral good," says Plantinga, "only by creating significantly free persons."[59] Once again we find limits on divine power: the Spirit can't control free creatures if they are to make moral choices.[60] God can't.

---

[56] A number of excellent books on God and evolution have been written. See, for instance, Ilia Delio, *Christ in Evolution* (New Jersey: Orbis, 2011); John Haught, *God After Darwin* (New York: Routledge, 2007); Matthew Hill, *Evolution and Holiness* (Downers Grove, IL: IVP Academic, 2016).

[57] Some of the more influential attempts to answer this question come from Richard Swinburne and John Hick. See Swinburne, *Providence and the Problem of Evil* (Oxford: Clarendon, 1998); Hick, *Evil and the God of Love*, rev. ed. (New York: Harper and Row, 1978).

[58] Leigh C. Vicens and Simon Kittle, *God and Human Freedom* (Cambridge University Press, 2019), 40. On the ultimacy of freedom, see Jeffery F. Keuss, *Freedom of the Self: Kenosis, Cultural Identity, and Mission at the Crossroads* (Eugene, OR: Pickwick, 2010); Christian J. Barrigar, *Freedom All the Way Up* (Victoria, BC: Friesen, 2017).

[59] Plantinga, *God, Freedom, and Evil*, 235.

[60] On this, see Patrick Todd, "Does God Have the Moral Standing to Blame?" *Faith and Philosophy*, 35:1 (2018), 33–55.

## God Being God?

Some theists dismiss these claims about limits to divine power, seeing them as unproblematic.[61] They say, "Qualifications to omnipotence simply tell us what it means for God to be God."

This response fails to account for significant theological diversity. Theologians differ among themselves about what can be said that's true of God, and those differences entail qualifications on divine power. Traditional theologians add limitations to God that I wouldn't, for instance.[62] Many say God can't be affected by creatures, can't change, can't experience the succession of time, and can't feel emotion in response to creaturely suffering. Even those who deny limits to God's power end up saying God can't.

Because people of faith have such diverse views of God, we should avoid saying that *all* limitations to divine power merely represent logical problems. Views of the Spirit carry ontological and metaphysical implications, and those implications vary widely. A theologian who thinks God is temporal, for instance, thinks it's simply logical that God can't know the future. But a theologian who thinks God is timeless thinks it's simply logical that God *does* know the future. At stake isn't just a logical conundrum, but competing claims about God's relation to time.

Some theologians respond to the many qualifications I've listed by saying, "An omnipotent God can do whatever He wants to do." Augustine puts it this way: "God does whatsoever He will: that is omnipotence."[63] An advocate of this position might even appeal to the

---

[61] Among those who wonder if qualified omnipotence is really dead, see Christopher Lilley, "An Apology for Qualified Omnipotence," in *Amipotence, vol. 1*, Chris S. Baker, et. al., eds. (Grasmere, ID: SacraSage, 2025); R. T. Mullins, "Omnipotence Has No Qualifications," in *Amipotence, vol. 1*, Chris S. Baker, et. al., eds. (Grasmere, ID: SacraSage, 2025); Austin Pounds, "Must Omnipotence Die So that Amipotence May Live?" in *Amipotence, vol. 1*, Chris S. Baker, et. al., eds. (Grasmere, ID: SacraSage, 2025).

[62] R.T. Mullins offers a concise and well-defended explanation of classical theism in "Classical Theism," *T & T Clark Handbook of Analytic Theology*, James M. Arcadi and James T. Turner, Jr., eds. (London: Bloomsbury, 2021). See my exploration of classical theism in relation to love in *Pluriform Love*, "Classical Theism and *Because of* Love," ch. 6.

[63] Augustine, *Sermo de symbolo ad catechumenos* 2 (CChr.SL 46, 185-6, PL), 40.

Psalms for justification: "Our God is in the heavens; he does whatever he pleases" (115:3; 135:6). If an omnipotent God wants to do something, they say, deity can do it.

But the blanket claim "God can do whatever He wants" isn't impressive once we examine it. After all, a perfectly wise God would never want to do what deity knows can't be done. A perfectly wise Spirit would never *want* to make 2 + 2 = 1, for instance, because God knows it's impossible. Nor would this God *want* to control free-will creatures, because the Spirit knows that controlling free beings is impossible. The Spirit would never want to pick up a rock, because deity has no appendages necessary for this.

"God can do whatever God wants" is an empty claim.

## *Salvaging Omnipotence?*

After we've made all the necessary qualifications, the very idea of omnipotence collapses into either meaninglessness or confusion. It makes no sense, at least if understood in the ways most people use the word.[64]

Of course, it's possible to retain the word "omnipotent" but redefine it radically. This can lead to some mind-boggling mental gymnastics. Take philosopher Richard Swinburne's attempt as an example:

> S is omnipotent during some period of time if and only if S knows all metaphysically necessary propositions and all metaphysically contingent true propositions about every event at any time earlier than the beginning of his action and all propositions that those propositions entail; he isn't moved by any nonrational influences, and is able to cause by an act beginning at any instant t and ending at any instant t2, both during that period, any metaphysically contingent event M beginning at any instant t1 later than t and ending at t2 which doesn't require

---

[64] Gijsbert van den Brink criticizes my claim that omnipotence is dead or has been killed as too violent. Here, I replace the death metaphor with collapse language. For van den Brink's criticism, see "I Believe in God the Father Almighty," in *Amipotence, vol. 1*, Chris S. Baker, et. al., eds. (Grasmere, ID: SacraSage, 2025).

him to be influenced by nonrational influences in order to do that act.⁶⁵

I suspect that 99.99% of people will see little connection between Swinburne's definition and what the word has traditionally meant or means to them.⁶⁶ Such sophisticated statements lead another philosopher Wes Morriston to say that careful "definitions of omnipotence ... frequently employ so much technical apparatus and contain so many subordinate clauses and qualifications, that it is natural to wonder whether they have much to do with what an ordinary person might mean by saying that God is all-powerful."⁶⁷ I'd add they have little to do with what even leading theologians in history have meant by the word.

Or we can change the word: theologians like Yujin Nagasawa and R. T. Mullins use the alternative label "maximal power" to describe God's influence. This strategy requires additional work, however, to explain the nature of divine power and abilities in a way that would distinguish them. This work would make better sense if those who did it explicitly renounce the concept of omnipotence in the ways the word is traditionally used. Otherwise, "maximal power" remains too vague as a moniker.⁶⁸

Anna Case-Winters offers a more promising proposal: rethink the meaning of "potence" in omnipotence. This proposal retains the word but rejects what it means to the vast majority of theologians and ordinary people of faith. As I see it, redefining "potence" requires more work than it's worth. And given that "omnipotent" and its synonyms aren't found in scripture and their common meanings are also absent

---

⁶⁵ Richard Swinburne, *The Coherence of Theism*, 2nd ed. (Oxford University Press, 2016), chap. 9.

⁶⁶ Analytic theologians often qualify omnipotence with highly sophisticated definitions. For example, see his essay, "God's Omnipotence," in *Divine Infinity*, Benedikt Paul Gocke and Christian Tapp, eds., (Notre Dame, IN: Notre Dame University Press, 2019), 222.

⁶⁷ Wes Morriston, "Omnipotence and the Power to Choose: A Reply to Wielenberg," *Faith and Philosophy* (2002), 363.

⁶⁸ See Ryan Mullins, "Omnipotence Has No Qualifications," in *Amipotence*, vol. 1, Chris S. Baker, et. al., ed. (Grasmere, ID: SacraSage, 2025); Yujin Nagasawa, *Maximal God* (Oxford: Oxford University Press, 2017).

in sacred writ, I believe the word not worth salvaging.[69] We're better off to find another word.

The practice of qualifying omnipotence—which just about every serious theologian and theistic philosopher does—ultimately leads to confusion and dead ends. The sheer number of modifications, restrictions, and limits required becomes massive. Those who undertake the task end up with highly technical definitions of omnipotence that fail to gain traction.[70] It's better to abandon the word itself.

## THE HARM OF OMNIPOTENCE

The problem with omnipotence isn't merely that the word, its synonyms, and its meanings aren't found in scripture. It's not just that omnipotence has to be qualified so drastically its meaning collapses. There are also psychological and spiritual costs to using this word.[71]

People of faith who embrace omnipotence rightly expect God to control when circumstances warrant it. Then they're disappointed and confused, even betrayed, when that doesn't happen. They rightly assume an all-powerful and all-loving deity would prevent pointless pain and unnecessary suffering, for instance. When people experience genuine evil, they understandably conclude that an omnipotent divinity could have stopped it. So when evil isn't stopped, they surmise that deity must have caused or allowed the evil.[72]

If God always loves, the Spirit will *want* to prevent genuine evil. If God is omnipotent, the Spirit *could* prevent it singlehandedly. And yet unnecessary suffering, horrific harm, and vast amounts of senseless pain occur. Genuine evil makes the world worse than it otherwise

---

[69] See Anna Case-Winters, "Love Without Qualification," in *Amipotence*, vol. 1, Chris S. Baker, et. al., ed. (Grasmere, ID: SacraSage, 2025).

[70] I argue in detail all the points in this section in *The Death of Omnipotence and Birth of Amipotence*, ch. 2.

[71] Michael Camp addresses some harms of omnipotence in "Omnipotence: The Ghostbuster of Harmful Doctrines," in *Amipotence, vol. 2*, Brandon Brown, et. al., eds. (Grasmere, ID: SacraSage, 2025).

[72] Jonathan Foster portrays controlling divine power as "Omnipotence" with a capital O. See his *Theology of Consent* (Grasmere, ID: SacraSage, 2022).

might have been.[73] The problem of evil remains, understandably, the primary reason many people don't believe in God.[74] It also drives people of faith to bewilderment and, sometimes, complacency, or even a sense of fatalism.

Belief in omnipotence undermines our confidence in God's love.

Unfortunately, belief in omnipotence can also justify colonization, injustice, and racism. "The sheer brutality of colonial conquest," says James H. Evans, Jr., "rendered the idea of God problematic."[75] After all, a *loving* God would want to rescue the oppressed, and an omnipotent deity could do so singlehandedly. The doctrine of omnipotence leads William R. Jones to ask, right in his book's title, *Is God a White Racist?* It makes no sense to say from a liberationist point of view that an omnipotent God sides with the oppressed and maintains a preferential option for the poor if this deity also allows colonization, injustice, and racism.[76] Or if these injustice are part of God's "plan."

Belief in omnipotence leads to other obstacles.[77] For instance, a loving Spirit, one would think, would provide a crystal-clear and unambiguous revelation needed for salvation, if salvation were so important. An omnipotent God could guarantee this revelation be error-free and free from misunderstanding. And this deity could make unmistakable revelation available to all. But we have no error-free, unmistakable, or perfectly-clear revelation, and billions of people never encounter the revelatory texts of good news.

---

[73] What is Evil? In later chapters, I explore definitions of evil. I define a genuine evil as an event that, all things considered, makes the world worse than it otherwise could have been had some other possible event occurred instead.

[74] Tracy Tucker addresses this issue in terms of hospice care and death. See *Can We Talk about Death?* (Grasmere, ID: SacraSage, 2025). Beth Hayward also addresses it in "All Loving Death Practices," in *Amipotence, vol. 2*, Brandon Brown, et. al., eds. (Grasmere, ID: SacraSage, 2025).

[75] James H. Evans, Jr., *We Have Been Believers* (Minneapolis: Fortress, 2012), 63.

[76] For more arguments of this sort from the perspective of the colonized and oppressed, see Ekaputra Tupamahu, "A Decolonial View of God," in *Uncontrolling Love*, Lisa Michaels, et. al., eds (Grasmere, ID: SacraSage, 2017); Randy S. Woodley, *Indigenous Theology and the Western Worldview* (Grand Rapids, MI: Baker, 2022).

[77] Among those who explore these issues, see Atle Ottesen Sovik, *The Problem of Evil and the Power of God* (Unipub AS, 2009).

The problem of divine hiddenness also presents a conundrum. It asks why an allegedly omnipotent and loving God doesn't clearly self-reveal to those wanting dynamic encounters with the divine. Many good-faith seekers desire dramatic experiences of God but don't get them. One would think a loving deity would want to self-disclose to those honestly desiring relationship. And yet countless people who seek God fail to experience the close relationship they desire, which has led many theologians to conclude that an omnipotent God voluntarily hides.[78]

Hiding doesn't express transparent love.

Other problems arise. If God is supposedly omnipotent and loves every citizen, why do wicked politicians take power? An omnipotent God could erase tyranny singlehandedly.[79] If God were always good and all-powerful, why did life evolve in a slow and painful way—including evolutionary dead-ends, ineffective mutations, unnecessary animal suffering, mass extinctions, and species who engage in surplus killing?[80] An instant and flawless creation better aligns with omnipotence. Some might ask, if God is omnipotent and all-loving, why doesn't deity stop the persecution of LGBTQ+ people? A loving Spirit would want queer people safe, and, if truly omnipotent, could provide that safety.[81] And what about the subjugation and sex-trafficking of

---

[78] On divine hiddenness, see the work of J. L. Schellenberg, *The Hiddenness Argument* (Oxford: Oxford University Press, 2015); Paul K. Moser, *The Elusive God* (Cambridge: Cambridge University Press, 2008); Tim Miller, *The Silence of the Lamb* (Grasmere, ID: SacraSage, 2025); Michael Rea, *Hiddenness and the Problem of Divine Silence* in *Divine Hiddenness* (Cambridge: Cambridge University Press, 2002); Chad Bahl, "Amipotence as a Solution to the Problem of Divine Hiddenness," in *Amipotence, vol. 2*, Brandon Brown, et. al., eds. (Grasmere, ID: SacraSage, 2025).

[79] Roger Haydon Mitchell explores this in *Church, Gospel, & Empire* (Eugene, OR: Wipf and Stock, 2011).

[80] Bethany Sollereder explores this in *God, Evolution, and Animal Suffering* (New York: Routledge, 2019).

[81] On this issue, see Michael Joseph Brennan, *Flourish: An Open and Relational Queer Theology* (Grasmere, ID: SacraSage, 2025); Garrard Conley, *Boy Erased* (New York: Riverhead Books, 2017); Jonathan Foster, *Questions about Sexuality that Got Me Uninvited from My Denomination* (Kansas City, MO: Verde Group, 2019); David P Gushee, *Changing Our Mind* (Canton, MI: Read the Spirit, 2017); Steve Harper, *Holy Love* (Nashville, TN: Abingdon, 2019); Pamela R. Lightsey, *Our Lives Matter* (Eugene, OR: Pickwick, 2015).

women? An all-powerful God could overturn structures that subjugate and rescue trafficked victims.[82]

Theologians typically give these questions and others like them unsatisfying answers.[83] Many appeal to mystery.[84] Others claim evil is actually good from God's perspective. Some say our pain reflects divine punishment, and others think deity causes or allows suffering to build our characters. Some appeal to world-building schemes in which an allegedly omnipotent God must make choices between goods. Along the way, many theologians describe divine love in ways that simply make it inconceivable.

Perhaps the best reason some theologians have for wanting to retain an idea of omnipotence stems from their conviction that, without it, they'll have to deny important claims about God's activities. For instance, some think abandoning omnipotence means abandoning the idea that God created the universe. Others think they must retain omnipotence to believe in miracles, the resurrection of Jesus, life after death, or an eschatological victory. Fortunately, people of faith can reject omnipotence but retain key beliefs about God, and I will explain how this can be in coming chapters and volumes.[85] But note that those who retain omnipotence and appeal to mystery privilege power when

---

[82] On the negative consequences that arise through the church misuses of power, see David E. Fitch, *Reckoning with Power* (Grand Rapids, MI: Brazos, 2024). Fitch addresses amipotence in "If Love is Power, 'I Want to Know What Love Is,'" in *Amipotence, vol. 1*, Chris S. Baker, et. al., eds. (Grasmere, ID: SacraSage, 2025).

[83] Kenneth L. Pearce summarizes the state of omnipotence in analytic philosophical theology by saying "every attempt so far to analyze omnipotence by saying *which powers an omnipotent being must have* has either required of an omnipotent being that it have the power to do things which is impossible that God should do or has classified unimpressive beings as omnipotent." See his essay, "Infinite Power and Finite Powers," in *Divine Infinity*, Benedikt Paul Gocke and Christian Tapp, eds., (Notre Dame, IN: Notre Dame University Press, 2019), 235.

[84] Skeptical Theism. The most sophisticated appeals to mystery are found in the skeptical theism literature. I find these appeals unsatisfactory and unhelpful. For a concise presentation of the view, see Stephen Wykstra, "A Skeptical Theist View," in *God and the Problem of Evil: Five Views*, Chad Meister and James K. Dew, Jr., eds. (Downers Grove, IL: InterVarsity, 2017). See my response to Wykstra in the same book.

[85] The strongest objections to amipotence are found in volume one of *Amipotence* (see full citation in footnotes above). I address these objections online, in this chapter, and in other chapters of this systematic theology of love. On God's uncontrolling action in miracles, including raising Jesus from the dead, see Thomas Jay Oord, "Essential Kenosis Christology," in *Methodist Christology*.

it conflicts with love. This privileging is the norm in systematic theology, not the exception.

## Conclusion

Believing God to be omnipotent remains the default position for most people. But as we've seen, this belief generates profound intellectual and existential problems. A close look at scripture shows that omnipotence isn't actually a biblical word or concept. Biblical authors describe God as powerful but not as the sole cause of events, not as capable of doing literally anything, and not as controlling creatures or circumstances. The primary meanings of omnipotence don't appear in scripture.

Scholars have long recognized that omnipotence must be qualified: God can't perform logical, mathematical, ontological, metaphysical, or moral contradictions, for instance. God's incorporeality imposes further limitations, because a Spirit without a localized body can't do certain actions. Creation, time, creaturely freedom, and other factors further constrain divine power. To make any sense, the concept of omnipotence must be qualified so radically it no longer resembles the common idea of an all-powerful deity. Omnipotence collapses.

Omnipotence as traditionally defined also leads to harmful consequences. The problem of evil and the problem of divine hiddenness remain two of the biggest, but other obstacles arise when we think deity is all-powerful. Believing God is omnipotent inclines the harmed and hurting to doubt the Spirit loves them. It has justified injustice, oppression, and inequality at the hands of those who harm, because people assume such evils must be either caused or allowed by God.[86] For a host of reasons, omnipotence harms.

For reasons I've identified in this chapter and previous ones, I deny God is omnipotent. Viewing deity as all-powerful creates insurmountable problems for a systematic theology that champions love.

I turn now to offer an alternative view of divine power. I call it "amipotence."

---

[86] Nancy Howell addresses the relationship between justice and God's uncontrolling love in "Justice Seeking Amipotence," in *Amipotence, vol. 2,* Brandon Brown, et. al., eds. (Grasmere, ID: SacraSage, 2025).

# CHAPTER SEVEN

# Amipotent Spirit

## THE BIG IDEAS

- Rather than omnipotent or impotent, the Spirit is amipotent: God's power is uncontrolling love.
- Instead of being weak, the amipotent Spirit is the most influential force we can plausibly imagine, given existence as we know it.
- Rather than think of power in terms of discrete units or as slices of a pie, we should think of it in terms of abilities and influence.
- The breadth and duration of divine influence, along with the Spirit's ability to elicit creaturely cooperation, render God most powerful.
- The Spirit isn't voluntarily or externally limited; instead, we best understand divine power in light of God's nature of uncontrolling love.
- Divine incorporeality explains why we can sometimes prevent evil that God can't.
- The logical priority of love in God's nature shapes divine freedom, which means God is free in some respects but not in others.

This chapter offers a new view of God's power. I call it "amipotence." It puts love first among the divine attributes, reframing and redefining divine power and freedom. Amipotence says the Spirit's love is necessarily and everlastingly uncontrolling. It portrays deity as strong not weak; interactive rather than inert; loving rather than aloof; and supremely influential.[1]

---

[1] This chapter is dedicated to Bruce Epperly. Bruce's creative thinking and prolific mind have been inspirational to me. And his encouragement sustains me.

When it comes to God's power, it's not all or nothing; the Spirit exerts neither all power, nor none of it. Instead of thinking of God's power in terms of units or a percentage of a power pie, I propose we should think of it in terms of abilities and influence. The Spirit's power is immense because of God's particular abilities and the extent, duration, and effectiveness of the Spirit's influence to persuade creatures to join in common cause.

Claims about the Spirit's power are intimately tied to beliefs about divine freedom. Most theologians say God must be radically free, in the sense of being neither externally nor internally constrained. Many systematic theologians portray God as essentially independent, and they insist that deity freely chooses whether to create and love others. Consequently, the God most people envision ends up being essentially free *from* loving creation rather than essentially committed *to* loving creation. I argue otherwise: God essentially relates to others.

The loving Spirit is neither omnipotent nor impotent but amipotent.

## The Spirit as Amipotent

"Amipotence" as a coinage combines two Latin words, *ami* and *potens*. (The word is pronounced "am" [as in amity], "i" [the short i sounds like "it"], and "potence.") The first part of the word means love, and the second means power, ability, or influence. Amipotence interprets John's phrase "God is love" (1 Jn. 4:8, 16) to mean we should begin with love when considering God's attributes, especially divine power. Although the loving Spirit is immensely powerful, God can't be omnipotent, because love "doesn't force its own way" (1 Cor. 13:5).[2]

Amipotence is God's uncontrolling love for everyone and everything.[3]

It's impossible for an amipotent God to be all-powerful—in the sense of having all power—because love is inherently relational. Love requires relationship with others who have power. An amipotent God

---

[2] Eric Sentell expresses this truth in a number of writings. For instance, see "God Can't Because God Cares," in *Amipotence, vol. 1*, Chris S. Baker, et. al., eds. (Grasmere, ID: SacraSage, 2025).

[3] For arguments for and against amipotence and essays expanding and developing it, see *Amipotence* vols. 1-2, Brandon Brown, et. al., eds. (Grasmere, ID: SacraSage 2025).

can't do absolutely anything imaginable, because we can easily imagine a being who doesn't love. An amipotent God also can't sin; can't be isolated; can't make 2 + 2 = 1; can't change the past; can't do what is illogical; can't grow tired; and more. Importantly, this deity can't control creatures or circumstances, because divine love *never* controls. The universal Spirit exerts maximally loving power but—thank goodness!—isn't omnipotent.[4]

An amipotent deity is immensely more powerful than any creature or any other power. The Spirit is most powerful, in part, because this universal Lover directly influences all that exists. Amipotence also says God is the most powerful because the Spirit loves everlastingly. This power is inexhaustible.[5]

The amipotent deity receives from creatures and their influence, which is a receptive power necessary for maximal effectiveness.[6] And an amipotent Spirit convinces creatures to join the work of love. Truly powerful actors persuade others to collaborate in multi-dimensional, multi-input, and multi-resourced endeavors. They force no one.

Put another way, the Spirit's amipotence is active and receptive, empowering and empathetic, wooing but persistent, relentless and inspiring. Amipotence is not weak, but is the most effective power possible in a universe of an unfathomable number of entities. Although uncontrolling, the amipotent God remains literally the most powerful force in the universe.[7]

---

[4] In addition to those in the process theological and philosophical tradition who argue similarly, see Eric Funkhouser, "On Privileging God's Moral Goodness," *Faith and Philosophy: Journal of the Society of Christian Philosophers* 23:4 (2006): 409-422; Wes Morriston, "Omnipotence and necessary moral perfection: are they compatible?" *Religious Studies* 37:2 (2001): 143-160.

[5] William Hasker argues for divine power as inexhaustible in "Infinite God, Open Future," *Divine Infinity*, Benedikt Paul Gocke and Christian Tapp, eds., (Notre Dame, IN: Notre Dame University Press, 2019), 269.

[6] Daniel Dombrowski expresses this well in his essay, "Perfect Passivity," in *Amipotence, vol. 2*, Brandon Brown, et. al., eds. (Grasmere, ID: SacraSage, 2025).

[7] Bradford McCall offers an alternative to omnipotence he calls "amorepotent." See *Macroevolution, Contingency, and Divine Activity* (Eugene, OR: Pickwick, 2023). Roger Wolsey argues for "omniamo" in *Kissing Fish: Christianity for People Who Don't Like Christianity* (Bloomington, IN: Xlibris, 2011).

Another way to speak of amipotence equates it with relational power.⁸ Relations require at least two actors, so no one person can exert all power. Affirming relational love has led some to say wrongly, I believe, that God can't act unilaterally. This sounds like a relational deity must wait or rely upon creatures before acting. That's not true. The more accurate way to describe amipotence says a loving God can't determine outcomes unilaterally. This places the emphasis not upon the acting, but upon the consequences of God's relational love and creaturely responses.

Let me illustrate the difference between acting unilaterally and determining outcomes unilaterally. Let's say I asked my girlfriend to marry me. In doing so, I act unilaterally, in the sense that I decide to pop the question by saying, "Will you marry me?" I alone don't determine the outcome, however, I can't. My girlfriend's cooperative response remains necessary for what I want—her accepting my request. Relational love involves real agents who act but never an agent who brings about outcomes singlehandedly.

## Amipotence as Maximal Power in the Service of Love

At first glance, saying God's power is love—that is, amipotence—might not seem radical. Most systematic theologians say God loves, after all, and some affirm divine love as powerful.⁹ Few theologians

---

⁸ On God's empowering and relational love, see Bernard Loomer, "Two Conceptions of Power," *Process Studies*, 6:1 (Spring 1976), 5-32; David Polk, *God of Empowering Love;* and Joshua D. Reichard, "Relational Empowerment: A Process-Relational Theology of the Spirit-filled Life," *Pneuma: The Journal of the Society for Pentecostal Studies* 36, no. 2 (2014): 1-20.

⁹ Many refer to God's power as "omnipotent love" or something similar. Examples include Gustaf Aulen, *The Faith of the Christian Church* (Eugene, OR: Wipf and Stock, 2003 [1960]); Leonardo Boff, *Church: Charism and Power*, John W. Diercksmeier, trans. (New York: Crossroad, 1986); Vincent Brümmer, *The Model of Love: A Study in Philosophical Theology* (New York: Cambridge Univ. Press, 1993); Ilia Delio, *The Unbearable Wholeness of Being: God, Evolution, and the Power of Love* (Maryknoll, NY: Orbis, 2013); Austin Farrer, *Love Almighty and Ills Unlimited* (Garden City, NY: Doubleday, 1961); Nels F. S. Ferré, *The Christian Understanding of God* (New York: Harper, 1951); Daniel Migliore, *The Power of God and the Gods of Power* (Louisville, KY: John Knox, 2008); George M. Newlands, *God in Christian Perspective* (Edinburgh: T&T Clark, 1994); LeRon Shults, *Reforming the Doctrine of God* (Grand Rapids, MI: Eerdmans, 2005); Kathryn Tanner, "The Power of Love," in *Renegotiating Power, Theology, and Politics*, J. Daniel and R. Elgendy, eds. (New York: Palgrave Macmillan, 2015); Hans Urs Von Balthasar, *Credo* (San Francisco: Ignatius, 1989). Paul Sponheim explores Soren Kierkegaard's view of omnipotent love in *Love's Availing Power* (Minneapolis: Fortress, 2011).

define love carefully, however, as I have done: saying it involves acting intentionally, in relational response to God and others, to promote overall well-being.[10] And few allow love to characterize divine power in a way that entails rejecting omnipotence. This means that few theologians can successfully overcome the problem of evil, the problem of divine hiddenness, and other conundrums.

Amipotence rejects what some theologians call "omnipotent love." In most theologies that combine omnipotence and love, love comes second to controlling power. Amipotence, by contrast, puts love first, and it regards love as *always* uncontrolling. Instead of being sporadic or weak, the amipotent Spirit is the most influential force we can plausibly imagine, given existence as we know it.[11]

Because most theologians fail to conceive of the Spirit's power in the light of uncontrolling love, they portray divine love as radically different from creaturely love. Love as we commonly know it, for instance, involves relational giving and receiving. But as we've seen earlier, theologians such as Augustine and David Bentley Hart say God's love must be nonrelational or impassible.[12] Love as we know it is expressed moment by moment, but theologians such as Thomas Aquinas and Paul Helm say deity is timeless.[13] While our love often, if not always, includes emotion, theologians such as Anselm and James Dolezal say divine love includes no emotional response.[14] Love as we know it would prevent evil that's preventable, but theologians such as Jacob Arminius and Jack Cottrell say an omnipotent God permits evil that deity could prevent.[15]

---

[10] Although I reject Tillich's view of God as being itself, he seems to agree with my claim that divine love doesn't control others. "Since God is love and His love is one with His power," he writes, "He has not the power to force somebody into his salvation. He would contradict himself. And this God can't do." (*Love, Power, and Justice* [London: Oxford University Press, 1954], 114).

[11] Kelly James Clark address this well in his essay, "The Power of Love," in *Amipotence, vol. 1*, Chris S. Baker, et. al., eds. (Grasmere, ID: SacraSage, 2025).

[12] For Hart's view, see *The Hidden and the Manifest* (Grand Rapids, MI: Eerdmans, 2017).

[13] For Helm's view, see *Eternal God* (Oxford: Oxford University Press, 1988).

[14] For Dolezal's view, see *All that Is in God* (Grand Rapids, MI: Reformation Heritage, 2017).

[15] For Cottrell's view, see Jack W. Cottrell, "The Nature of the Divine Sovereignty," in *The Grace of God and the Will of Man*, ed. Clark H. Pinnock (Bloomington, MN: Bethany House, 1995).

The concept of amipotence helps us make sense of the Apostle Paul's witness to divine power. Paul reports the Lord saying, "my grace is sufficient for you, for my power is made perfect in weakness" (2 Cor. 12:9). This passage, unfortunately, has been interpreted to mean that the weaker the creature, the more perfect God's power. We're wise to interpret it, instead, in terms of amipotence. The Spirit's graceful power requires cooperation from comparatively weaker creatures to bring about God's perfect goals. Put another way, it's the Spirit's graceful way to work with others. That's the way of love.

Rather than seeking self-sufficiency, Paul boasts in his need for "Christ's power to rest" on him. That's the beauty of cooperative relationship. Paul sees value in insults, hardship, persecution, and other difficulties, but not because he's a masochist who enjoys abuse. Instead, these problems reveal our inability to thrive alone. We must cooperate with God's symbiosis-seeking grace (1 Cor. 12:10).

Amipotence is maximal divine power in the service of uncontrolling love.

## Amipotence Puts Love First

Although some theologians blatantly privilege controlling power over uncontrolling love, most consider omnipotence co-equal with love. This would seem laudable. But in reality, *every* coherent theology privileges one or more divine attribute above others. Discerning readers can detect the attributes theologians consider primary. And, usually, that attribute is omnipotence.

For instance, many theologians talk about God's omnipotent freedom to do whatever deity decides. God can love creation or not, they say. God could have chosen not to create and remain everlastingly in solitude. A sovereign God can even freely withdraw from creation, some claim. And an omnipotent deity can control creatures. Each of these claims privileges God's omnipotent freedom *from* or *over* creation above God's love *for* it. In each, power comes before love as the most important attribute in the divine nature.

Eberhard Jüngel identifies the problem. When we understand God as "the almighty Lord," says Jüngel, "love and mercy appear to be fundamentally secondary and subsidiary to his claim to lordship. This is the earthly way of thinking of a lord: first he has all power and then perhaps he can be merciful—but then again, perhaps not. God's lordliness and lordship are thought of in the same general way. He is mighty, able, and free to love or not to love . . . the love of God becomes a secondary attribute."[16]

In amipotence, divine love comes logically prior to sovereign power and choice. Consequently, God *has* to love creatures and creation; it's God's eternal nature to do so. When we take love for creation as an eternal and essential attribute, God everlastingly creates and loves creatures. It's a metaphysical impossibility that God could love in absolute isolation. When love for creation comes before power over it, the Spirit can't withdraw from the world or abandon creation.

Theologies that put power before divine love start with God's self-sufficient omnipotence. They conceive of God as solitary from creation. Then they marvel at the fact that God chose to create, wondering why there's something rather than nothing. According to them, God could remain eternally alone, self-engaged but never creating or loving creaturely others.[17]

Amipotence, by contrast, starts with God's love for creatures and creation. It says God necessarily and everlastingly creates others to love. When conceptual tensions arise among divine attributes, the theologian of amipotence reconfigures the attributes to suit what uncontrolling love requires.

Amipotence isn't God's *only* attribute, of course. Amipotence theologies don't dismiss God's omnipresence, omniscience, everlastingness,

---

[16] Eberhard Jüngel, *God as the Mystery of the World*, Darrell L. Guder, trans. (Grand Rapids, MI: Eerdmans, 1983), 21. Paul Sponheim reimagines divine power in light of love in *Love's Availing Power* and Brian Zahnd aims to rethink God in light of love in *Sinners in the Hands of a Loving God* (London: Waterbrook, 2017).

[17] My amipotent theology is neutral on the question of intratrinitarian love. Social trinitarians attracted to the intratrinitarian love proposal can accept amipotence, because there's no contradiction between God everlastingly loving within Trinity and everlastingly loving creatures. But those who reject the Trinity should also find amipotence amenable. They can affirm the Spirit's everlasting love of creation.

wisdom, covenantal faithfulness, divine power, and so on. But they look at each attribute through the lens of love. Love prevails.[18]

The logical priority of love over power makes a difference in how we think about God.

## Power Units or Pies

An amipotent Spirit who can't control may seem to have less power than the God of traditional theologies. This deity may even seem to have less power than some creatures or creation as a whole. Neither of these claims is true, however. The amipotent Spirit has the maximal power possible given that love comes first in the divine nature and given existence as we know it. The Spirit is stronger than any creature or creation.

To say the amipotent God has "less" or "more" power implies power can be measured. To measure it, however, it seems we would need to assess power in terms of what Thomas McCall calls "units of power."[19] If cashing the concepts out in this way, we might think of God as having 1) all units; 2) more units than creatures/creation; 3) fewer units than creatures/creation; or 4) no units.

A God who exerted all power units would unilaterally determine everyone and everything. Creatures would do nothing, because they would have no power to act. This represents the "God exerts all power" form of omnipotence I identified earlier. By contrast, a God with no power units would do nothing; creatures would do everything. This view disempowers deity entirely, rendering God unable to act.

Options two and three divide power units between God and creation. Ted Peters thinks of this dividing as like cutting different slices in a power pie. "The larger the slice of pie God has," says Peters, "the

---

[18] Amipotence agrees with Martin Luther King, Jr. when he says, "Power without love is reckless and abusive, and love without power is sentimental and anemic." It agrees with King that "Power at its best is love implementing the demands of justice, and justice at its best is power correcting everything that stands against love." Amipotence adds that in God, love enjoys conceptual primacy. Although powerful, God can't overpower when implementing justice.

[19] McCall also uses "torques" as an apparent synonym for power units. See Thomas H. McCall, "'Amipotence' Isn't a 'Solution' to the Problem of Evil," *Wesleyan Theological Journal*, 59:1 (Spring 2024), 37.

smaller the power slice we creatures have." So "by metaphysically reducing God's power, [the theologian] increases creaturely power."[20] Peters opposes this way of thinking, in part, because the pie approach to power amounts to a zero-sum view.

Dividing divine and creaturely power up like this makes no sense if God and creation are always *already* interrelated and mutually influencing. The analogy also fails to clarify whether God *essentially* has all power but voluntarily gives some to creatures. Many theologians say God "shares" power with creatures, but they don't clarify whether God could choose not to share power and, therefore, control them.[21] To put it another way, God might sometimes give slices of pie, but other times eat the whole thing.

The power units and pie analogies prompt a series of questions: *where* are these power units located? Does the most powerful person have bigger units in their body (arms, brain, etc.)? If God has no body, where can we find the divine power units? Would God carry a pack with all the power, which could then be dispensed or retained at the divine whim? And if we think of power as a fixed amount divided between God and creation, what would be the amount of power necessary for the Spirit to get good results? How many units of power would God need to secure an eschatological victory? And does whatever amount of power creatures have *really* matter if God can secure the results God wants?

Probing these questions has led me to be skeptical of the concept of power units or slices of a power pie. Zero-sum views discount mutual influence and collaboration. Saying God has all power and creatures have none would make creatures divinely determined robots. But saying "God has 100% of the power" but creatures "also have 100%," which Wayne Grudem does, is bad math. It would also mean that creaturely power must somehow be equal to God's. I doubt Grudem wants to say creaturely power is equal to divine power. Unless we appeal to absolute

---

[20] Ted Peters, "Oord and Peters on Free Will, *Substack*, accessed (11/14/2025)

[21] For instance, Clark Pinnock says that "in creating Adam, God showed himself willing to share power. He doesn't insist on being the only power." Clark H. Pinnock, *Most Moved Mover* (Grand Rapids, MI: Brazos, 2001), 42.

mystery (which some theologians do), these contortions of thought just emphasize that we need language to talk about what God does, or can do, compared with what creatures do, or can do.

## POWER AS ABILITY

We start to make progress in understanding power when we consider differences among agents. Some power differences are directly related to body types. A worm can tunnel into dirt using its body alone and remain entirely submerged up to eight years. I can't remain alive underground for more than a couple of minutes. Do worms have more power than I do? Consider a sparrow. It can fly to the top of a tree in a matter of seconds. I can't. Are sparrows more powerful? Beetles can lift many times their body weight, but I can't. Who has more power?

If we compare creatures with similar body types, we'll find other power differences. Bill Gates and I have human bodies, for instance, but I can bench press more weight than he can. Do I have more power? I can hike further distances than Jane Goodall. Am I more powerful? I can bench press more weight and walk further than God, in fact, assuming deity has no body. Does this mean I'm more powerful? Clearly, the word "power" means different things in these examples.

I believe it makes better sense to talk about divine and creaturely power primarily in terms of abilities and influence. Particular agents have abilities that others don't. Worms can do things I can't; I can do things worms can't. Bill Gates and Jane Goodall influence in ways far beyond what I can, but I'm more capable in other ways. God and creatures have differing abilities.

Focusing on abilities helps us make progress in discussions of divine power vis-a-vis creaturely power. We can admit that creatures have abilities that God doesn't. We can sin and lick ice cream cones, for instance, but God can't do either.[22] God has abilities that creatures don't.

---

[22] Abilities vs. Liabilities. Some theologians distinguish between power as ability to do some task and a liability to do a task. God doesn't have the power to sin, for instance, but this is a liability (a weakness) rather than ability that God lacks. So, goes the argument, it's no diminishment of divine power. Distinguishing between abilities and liabilities when it comes to God presupposes various models of God, of course, because what some would call an

The Spirit is omnipresent and exerts influence upon all that exists, for instance, whereas creatures are localized and influence some. God exerts influence forever, knows all that's possible for an individual to know, is universally creative, and so on. God's abilities are impressive!

Emphasizing differing abilities also provides conceptual grounds for affirming differently-abled/disabled people.[23] Instead of thinking in terms of having more or less power, affirming differing *abilities* reveal unique values, activities, and possibilities. In fact, differently-abled humans influence in ways not available to others. The visually impaired often acquire hearing abilities that far exceed what's present in others, for instance, a powerful ability. The hearing-impaired can develop amazing abilities of sight. Those unable to move as freely as others often develop the ability to focus intently and rest patiently. And so on.

Accounting for differently-abled creatures helps us make sense of a differently-abled God.

## Power as Influence

We also make progress if we think of power in terms of influence. A one-minute Super Bowl advertisement, for instance, will be more influential, all things considered, than a text I send my wife. A politician who meets people in multiple cities and uses social media will likely be

---

ability—e.g., the power to not love creatures or the ability to be timeless—I would call a liability. But the unhelpfulness of the ability/liability scheme is most obvious when it comes to the abilities that embodied creatures have when compared to an incorporeal Spirit. I regard licking chocolate ice cream cones as a positive ability not a liability or weakness. But an incorporeal Spirit doesn't have a tongue to use for licking. According to the ability/liability scheme, licking ice cream is a liability for an incorporeal Spirit. This subtly privileges immaterial/spiritual activities over material/embodied ones, which has numerous negative consequences theologically and ethically. I recommend talking about abilities and inabilities rather than abilities and liabilities.

[23] For examples of disability theology, see Sharon V. Betcher, *Spirit and the Politics of Disablement* (Minneapolis, MN: Fortress, 2007); Nancy L. Eiesland, *The Disabled God* (Nashville, TN: Abingdon, 1994); Preston McDaniel Hill, *Disability Theology and Eschatology* (Lanham, MD: Lexington Books/Fortress Academic, 2024); Amy Jacober, *Redefining Perfect* (Eugene, OR: Wipf and Stock, 2017); John Swinton. *Becoming Friends of Time: Disability, Timefullness, and Gentle Discipleship* (Waco, TX: Baylor University Press, 2018); Kevin Timpe, *Embodiment, Dependence, and God* (Cambridge: Cambridge University Press, 2024); Amos Yong, *The Bible, Disability, and the Church* (Grand Rapids, MI: Eerdmans, 2011).

more influential than a local one limited to one city and who ignores social media. When we think about power as influence, therefore, we realize that breadth or span will be crucial. In terms of God and creatures, a *universal* Spirit will exert more influence than localized creatures and, therefore, be more powerful.

An exploration of power as influence also considers duration. Long-term advertisements or political campaigns will typically be more powerful than a one-off ad or brief campaigns. It's not just breadth of influence that matters, therefore, but also duration. An *everlasting* deity will have more influence, therefore, than any temporary creature and be more powerful. Aspects of God's power include divine tenacity and longevity.

As an agent in the world, a person's influence also depends upon their ability to persuade others to work to attain that person's goals. A well-funded and widespread "Get Out the Vote" campaign, for instance, may garner attention but only really convince a few. So, it wouldn't be very influential. A more influential campaign would convince many other people, who are also agents, to act. Influence is also about eliciting cooperation, therefore. We find this aspect of divine power expressed in the line, "the pen is mightier than the sword."

When we consider this aspect of influence, we find God far more powerful than any creature or creation. The Spirit is the most effective agent of all, because trillions and trillions of creatures of various sizes and abilities cooperate with divine aims to promote life, flourishing, beauty, justice, creativity, consistency, and love.

Some theologians imply that the God they envision isn't exerting 100% effort. They say God voluntarily self-limits, which implies deity could be doing more. It stands to reason, of course, that a deity exerting total effort but not controlling would be more influential than a deity only exerting partial influence, assuming the two have identical abilities.

The amipotence view says God exerts *as much influence as possible in every moment*, given uncontrolling love. As Russ Dean puts it, the amipotent "God always does everything God can do."[24] A deity

---

[24] See Russ Dean, *The Power of the God Who Can't* (Eugene, OR: Resource, 2023).

doing the utmost to persuade others will be more effective than one who chooses to do less. The amipotent Spirit is more powerful than a self-limited deity, therefore, because amipotence exerts the most influence that full-throttled loving entails.[25]

Claims about who has how much influence lead some to argue for a middle way between (1) saying God controls all and (2) saying God controls none. This middle way (3) says that God doesn't *usually* control but can and does so on occasion. We might call it the "God sometimes controls" option. This fails to help us, however, because the God it envisions could control creation to prevent genuine evil. If love doesn't control, this third option portrays God as sometimes unloving. This middle way is not viable.

Given all this, I believe we should think of power—creaturely and divine—in terms of abilities, extent and duration of influence, and effectiveness in fulfilling goals. A deity who influences as fully as possible but never controls would be more powerful than one who influences less than fully. The most powerful agents persuade others with power to join in common cause. This means that the universal Spirit of love has abilities, influence, and effectiveness that far transcend our own, or creation's in general.[26] The Spirit's superior abilities and immense influence generate unsurpassed power.

Instead of power units and zero-sum power pies, God's grandeur is uncontrolling love.

## Neither Externally Nor Voluntarily Limited

The amipotence view stands between two adjacent concepts of divine power. One view says God's power must be limited by external forces, laws, or actors. On this view, something or someone outside

---

[25] More Persuasive? John H. Buchanan wonders if an amipotent God can be more persuasive at some moments. As this paragraph indicates, I believe the amipotent Spirit always exerts the most influence possible in any moment. The effectiveness of amipotence depends, in part, on creaturely cooperation. For Buchanan's essay, see "Why Can't God Do More?" in *Amipotence*, Vol. 1, Chris S. Baker, et. al., eds. (Grasmere, ID: SacraSage, 2025), 285-290.

[26] Eleanor O'Donnell explores the relation between divine and human power. She opts for a non-omnipotent God, at least when "omnipotent" is understood in the classical sense. See her excellent book, *The Relational Power of God* (Eugene, OR: Pickwick, 2023).

deity limits divine abilities, influence, and effectiveness. Those limits may be the laws of nature, Satan, principalities and powers, systems, or impersonal forces. Whatever the reason, this view says God ends up externally constrained.

Some have interpreted Charles Hartshorne and Alfred North Whitehead as saying factors external to God limit what deity can do.[27] For instance, Whitehead says God is "in the grip of the ultimate metaphysical ground, which is the creative advance into novelty."[28] Although he doesn't consider creativity an object, many theologians interpret Whitehead as placing external limits upon deity.[29]

Charles Hartshorne says God shares power with creation.[30] This involves "a division of power," he says, that "permits distribution of powers among a plurality of beings."[31] This seems to imply that creatures limit what God can do. It's not clear whether Hartshorne thinks creaturely power arises independent of God's creating, sustaining, or loving, but some of his writings suggest this.[32]

Theologian David Ray Griffin points to metaphysical laws as the fundamental reason God's power is limited. "There are metaphysical principles which are beyond even divine decision," says Griffin.[33] This leads theologian and scientist John Polkinghorne to reject Griffin's and "process theology's conception of an external metaphysical constraint upon the power of deity." A superior vision, says Polkinghorne,

---

[27] See, for instance, Alan Rhoda, *Open Theism* (Cambridge: Cambridge University Press, 2024), 17.

[28] Whitehead, *Process and Reality*, 349.

[29] The fact that Whitehead says creatures are also in the grip of creativity leads some to believe that means that some nondivine reality or another limits what God can do. It's crucial to note that Whitehead doesn't describe creativity as an object or entity; it's the fundamental force empowering all actual entities.

[30] Donald Wayne Viney explores this in his concise essay, "Catching Up with Charles Hartshorne," in *Amipotence, vol. 1*, Chris S. Baker, et. al., eds. (Grasmere, ID: SacraSage, 2025).

[31] Charles Hartshorne, "Is Whitehead's God the God of Religion?" *International Journal for Philosophy of Religion* 1, no. 1 (Spring 1970): 41–52. Julia Enxing explores Hartshorne's view of God and world in *Gott im Werden: Die Prozesstheologie Charles Hartshornes* (Pustet, Friedrich GmbH, 2013).

[32] John B. Cobb, Jr. makes a similar argument. See "Amipotence vs. Omnipotence," in *Amipotence*, vol. 1. (Grasmere, ID: SacraSage, 2025).

[33] David Ray Griffin, *God, Power, and Evil*, 298.

should maintain "that nothing imposes conditions on God from the outside."[34]

The second view adjacent to amipotence says God voluntarily self-limits. On this view, God remains essentially omnipotent but freely chooses to self-restrain, withdraw, or allow creatures space and agency.[35] Most who affirm voluntary divine self-limitation say God occasionally controls when events seem important enough to warrant it.[36] This might mean intervening to do miracles, punish, rescue, or bring about an eschatological victory. But even if the self-limited God never chose to control creatures, this deity could, in theory, do so.

Polkinghorne explains what voluntary divine self-limitation entails. God's "act of creation involves a voluntary limitation," he says, "in allowing the other to be."[37] This means, "God doesn't will the act of a murderer or the destructive force of an earthquake but allows both to happen in a world in which divine power is deliberately self-limited to allow causal space for creatures."[38]

The voluntary self-limitation view of divine power fails in many ways. It doesn't solve the problem of evil, the problem of hiddenness, and other problems derived from omnipotence. Saying God doesn't *will* evil but *allows* it is a distinction without a real difference. An omnipotent God must want the evil allowed more than some other outcome this deity could secure through singlehanded control. But a God

---

[34] John Polkinghorne, "Kenotic Creation and Divine Action," in *The Work of Love*, John Polkinghorne, ed. (Grand Rapids, MI: Eerdmans, 2001), 96.

[35] John Peckham is a representative of this view. See *Theodicy of Love* (Grand Rapids, MI: Baker, 2018). In this and other books, Peckham claims his view is "canonical." But the Christian canon doesn't require his view and, where we differ, scripture fits just as well with the views I propose.

[36] Not Even Once/Non-Interventionist God. Philip Clayton is an exception to the view that God occasionally intervenes. Clayton believes God created the universe out of nothing, but God never intervenes nor controls—"not even once"—thereafter. I address Clayton's view in various writings. My primary criticism would be that Clayton seems to assume as necessary attributes in God's nature related to divine love for creation that the doctrine of *creatio ex nihilo* deems contingent. For my criticism, see Thomas Jay Oord, "Eternal Creation and Essential Love," in *T&T Handbook on Suffering and the Problem of Evil*, Johannes Grossel and Matthias Grebe, eds. (London: T&T Clark, 2022).

[37] John C. Polkinghorne, "Chaos Theory and Divine Action," in *Religion and Science*, W. Mark Richardson and Wesley J. Wildman, eds. (New York: Routledge, 1996), 249.

[38] John Polkinghorne, "Kenotic Creation and Divine Action," 102.

who can determine events by Fiat is ultimately responsible for what occurs. There's no ultimate difference, therefore, between an *omnipotent* God allowing evil and this deity willing it. A voluntarily self-limited God who permits evil is culpable for failing to prevent it.

Rather than portraying God as externally or voluntarily limited, amipotence says God's inability to control derives from the divine nature itself.[39] Because uncontrolling love comes logically first among divine attributes, and because the Spirit loves everyone and everything at every moment, God can't control anyone or anything at any moment. The Spirit can't control, because love doesn't control, and love comes first in the divine nature.[40] It's as simple as that.

Systematic theologies embracing voluntary self-limitation ask *whether* God will give power, agency, and/or freedom to creatures. An omnipotent but self-limited God could exert all power, if God chose. By contrast, amipotence assumes the Spirit always and necessarily loves by providing agency and freedom to creatures and creation. Amipotence, by necessity, respects the otherness of creatures, because the Spirit loves all.

Theologies of voluntary divine self-limitation ponder *whether* God will choose to control creatures from time to time. The deity of these theologies occasionally overrides creatures, or He (and people usually think of this kind of God as a "He") chooses not to give them agency. This deity might also interrupt the law-like regularities of the universe. An amipotent Spirit, by contrast, necessarily gives agency and, therefore, can't control others.[41] A loving God can't control.

---

[39] The Given. Amipotence differs from Edgar Sheffield Brightman's notion of The Given in God's nature. While Brightman helpfully says divine limitations are neither external nor voluntary, he hypotheses the Given as a "passive element" in God's nature. See *The Problem of God* (New York: Harper and Row, 1930), 113.

[40] Sarah Heaner Lancaster addresses this concisely in her essay, "Why It Matters that Love Is First," in *Amipotence, vol. 1*, Chris S. Baker, et. al., eds. (Grasmere, ID: SacraSage, 2025).

[41] Martin Luther King, Jr. Amipotence agrees with Martin Luther King, Jr. when he says, "Power without love is reckless and abusive, and love without power is sentimental and anemic." It agrees with King that "Power at its best is love implementing the demands of justice, and justice at its best is power correcting everything that stands against love." Amipotence adds that in God, love enjoys conceptual primacy. Although powerful, God can't overpower creatures when implementing justice.

Amipotence retains the theodicy advantages found in Whitehead, Hartshorne, and Griffin. Each of them says God can't stop evil singlehandedly. But instead of saying, like them, that God's inability to prevent evil derives primarily from creativity, pluralities of power, or metaphysical laws, amipotence says the Spirit's inability to control derives primarily from God's nature of love. To put it another way, God's *identity* as uncontrolling love determines God's *abilities* in relation to creation.[42]

When uncontrolling love is the Spirit's primary attribute, God can't control anyone or anything at any time.

## The Amipotent Spirit without a Localized Body

When amipotence replaces omnipotence, many feel a sense of cognitive peace. Saying God can't control anyone or anything answers the most difficult questions of suffering and evil. And it solves other problems. Putting uncontrolling love first among divine attributes seems intuitively right to many people.[43] After all, God *is* love, says scripture; not, God *is* power.

Others have wondered whether love sometimes controls. Some people reflect on occasions in which they may have stopped others from being harmed. Perhaps a parent picks up a child just before it steps on a rattlesnake. Or an alert friend stops a colleague before she drinks poison. Or another grabs the arm of a bully about to strike his victim. In these instances, it may seem that someone thwarts another person's freedom to rescue them from harm. If it's sometimes loving for us to suppress freedom, wouldn't it be loving for God to do the same?

These examples and others like them point to a difference between the universal Spirit of love and creatures with localized bodies. We explored this difference earlier, but it bears repeating. When creatures find themselves in the right place at the right time, they can sometimes

---

[42] I'm grateful to Ezrica Bennett for suggesting this language in our Claremont class conversations.

[43] For a collection of essays on preaching the uncontrolling love of God, see *Preaching the Uncontrolling Love of God*, Jeff Wells, Vikki Randall, Nicole Torbitzky, and Thomas Jay Oord, eds, (Grasmere, ID: SacraSage, 2024).

use their hands, feet, bodies, wings, claws, and so on to prevent evil. Although they don't take away freedom from others entirely, bodies can curtail or redirect the bodily freedom of others. And doing so can be an act of love.

The universal and incorporeal Spirit, by contrast, doesn't have a localized divine body in order to pick up children, grab arms, or do the other activities embodied creatures sometimes do to prevent evil. God as a universal spirit without a localized divine body has abilities and inabilities. In this case, the universal Spirit can affect all and be affected by all, but deity doesn't have a localized body with which to impact others. The Spirit calls upon and encourages creatures to use their bodies to do good and prevent evil, of course, but an uncontrolling deity can't force others to help.[44] Collaboration remains the creature's choice.

Saying that the universal Spirit of love can't control others and doesn't have a localized divine body can sound like we're placing limits on God. And this worries some people of faith. But the language of "limitation" seems appropriate only if we assume God has unlimited abilities. "Instead of saying that God's power is limited, suggesting that it is less than some conceivable power," says Charles Hartshorne, "we should rather say [God's] power is absolutely maximal, the greatest possible, but even the greatest possible power is still one power among others, it isn't the only power."[45]

"Unlimited power" and "infinite ability" make no sense if we factor in the Spirit's necessary love for creation and bodilessness.[46] Saying

---

[44] A number of scholars explore the practical dimensions of amipotence. See, for instance, Chris S. Baker addresses the practical dimensions of amipotence for people in his fine essay, "Practicing Amipotence," in *Amipotence, vol. 2,* Brandon Brown, et. al., eds. (Grasmere, ID: SacraSage, 2025); Mark Umstot, "Amipotence for Everyday Life," in *Amipotence, vol. 2,* Brandon Brown, et. al., eds. (Grasmere, ID: SacraSage, 2025); Vikki Randall also addresses practical implications of amipotence in "Living Out Amipotence," in *Amipotence, vol. 2,* Brandon Brown, et. al., eds. (Grasmere, ID: SacraSage, 2025); Deanna M. Young, "What the World Needs Now . . ." in *Amipotence, vol. 2,* Brandon Brown, et. al., eds. (Grasmere, ID: SacraSage, 2025).

[45] Charles Hartshorne, *The Divine Relativity* (New Haven, CT: Yale University Press, 1964), 138.

[46] Richard Rice explores problems with saying God is limited in *The Future of Open Theism* (Downers Grove, IL: IVP Academic, 2020). See my review of Rice's book and the topic of limits in "Open Theism and Divine Limitations" http://thomasjayoord.com/index.php/blog/archives/open-theism-and-the-question-of-divine-limitations (Accessed 12/6/21).

"God can't exert bodily impact" is just another way of saying deity must be an incorporeal and universal Spirit.[47] And if God's love is essentially uncontrolling, saying "God can't control creatures" is another way of saying "for God so loved the world." Uncontrolling love and universal incorporeality are simply divine attributes. It's who the Spirit is.

The incorporeal Spirit always expresses uncontrolling love.

## The Spirit's Sovereign Freedom

Theologians often link their view of divine power with their view of God's freedom. They cite Psalm 115:3: "Our God is in the heavens ... he does whatever pleases him." But as we have seen, just about every theologian says God can't do some activities. Doing "whatever pleases him," therefore, doesn't include God doing what's self-contradictory, illogical, ontologically impossible, contrary to the divine nature, and so on.

However, few theologians consider God's love for creatures an essential divine attribute. This deficiency derives from their commitment to omnipotence and/or their view that God creates from nothing. Consequently, most theologians explicitly or implicitly say the Spirit is free to love creatures or not, depending on whether creatures exist and/or God chooses to love them. In fact, many proclaim—as if it's admirable—that the Spirit is independently free *from* creation rather than necessarily loving it. For them, "freedom from" trumps "love for."

Karl Barth's position on these issues is noteworthy. Barth often says we should see God as "the One who loves in freedom,"[48] and he wants love and freedom to be equally primary in God. But Barth's view of God's contingent relation to creation means that divine freedom actually comes logically first when it comes to God and the universe. "God

---

[47] Donna Bowman expresses this well in her essay, "Even God Can't Have It All," in *Amipotence, vol. 1*, Chris S. Baker, et. al., eds. (Grasmere, ID: SacraSage, 2025).

[48] Karl Barth, Church Dogmatics, II/1, G. W. Bromiley and T. F. Torrance, eds. (Edinburgh: T & T Clark, 1957), 283–84. Although he speaks often of love, Barth unhelpfully says that the mystery of divine love transcends all thought and is different from all other loves. (See especially chapters 28, 29).

is sufficient in Himself as object and therefore as object of His love," Barth says. "[God] is no less the One who loves if He loves no object different from Himself."[49] This risks making God out to be self-absorbed and narcissistic—only if it's God, that's supposed to be a virtue.

These comments (and others) suggest that when it comes to God's relationship with creatures, Barth prioritizes freedom over love. According to him, God loves Godself by necessity but loves creatures contingently. As Triune and "sufficient in Himself," says Barth, God doesn't need to love creatures. "The freedom of God is the freedom which consists and fulfills itself in his Son Jesus Christ," he says. "In [Jesus], God has loved himself throughout all eternity. In Him, He has loved the world."[50] Notice that Barth doesn't say God loves creatures through all eternity. Rather, God only loves Godself throughout all eternity. God necessarily loves Godself and contingently loves creation.

Like so many theologians before and after him, Barth privileges God's self-love over love *for* creatures.[51] Barth's essentially independent God freely decides whether to create and whether to love what has been created. For Barth, God's love for the world is capricious rather than necessary. By "capricious," I mean there's nothing about creation or the divine nature that requires deity to love creatures. And when nothing requires God to love creatures, "love for creatures" becomes arbitrary and capricious.[52]

This systematic theology of love sees God's love and freedom differently. It considers love for creatures as logically primary among the

---

[49] Ibid., 280.

[50] Ibid., 321.

[51] Hermann Cremer attempts to put love first among divine attributes when he considers God. But Cremer also thinks love is free in all respects and therefore opposed to necessity. And yet he confusingly says God's actions are determined by God's essence. See his book *The Christian Doctrine of the Divine Attributes*, Robert B. Price, trans. (Eugene, OR: Pickwick, 2016).

[52] One possible move for a Barthian is to say God everlastingly loves creation through the everlasting love of the Father for the Son. This would entail that some creation would be everlastingly present for God to love. This move would overcome the problem with God's necessary self-love but contingent love for creation. It would say the Father's necessary love for the Son entails God's necessary love for creation. Because Barth affirms the doctrine of creation from nothing, however, he doesn't take the option I outline here. Some of what Eberhard Jüngel proposes comes close to the move I'm outlining, however. See *The Doctrine of the Trinity* (Grand Rapids, MI: Eerdmans, 1976).

Spirit's attributes.[53] Just as God isn't free to stop existing, not free to withdraw and be absent, not free to sin, and so on, God isn't free to stop loving creatures. The Spirit *must* love creation, because it's actually the divine nature to love others. As I will lay out in future discussions of God's creating, the Spirit *everlastingly* creates and *everlastingly* loves creatures.

Some theologians counter my argument and say God's free choosing whether to love creation is what's great about divine love. "Isn't it amazing that God has chosen to love us?" they might ask. However, if we then ask such people *why* they think deity chooses to love, most appeal to God's "heart," nature, or character. They'll say, "That's just who God is."

These responses indicate that beyond their valuing sheer choosing, most people have a more basic (if unacknowledged) belief that God is love or that loving is the Spirit's way. They don't realize this basic belief implies that the Spirit's love for creation must be necessary rather than freely chosen.

God's amipotence for creation comes logically before divine freedom.

## Conclusion

Amipotence combines the Latin words *ami* (love) and *potens* (power) to say divine power is uncontrolling love. The amipotent Spirit can't do everything imaginable or singlehandedly determine outcomes, because divine love is logical, requires relationality, and never controls. Amipotence is maximal yet non-controlling divine power directed at promoting overall well-being.

By rejecting divine control, amipotence solves the problems of evil and divine hiddenness. The universal Spirit loves every creature and all creation without ever controlling any. The Spirit who loves is neither omnipotent nor impotent but amipotent.

Discussions of power often default to zero-sum equations or imagine divine power as something like discrete power units or a slice of

---

[53] Donna Bowman works on this issue in her exploration of Karl Barth and Alfred North Whitehead. See *The Divine Decision* (Louisville, KY: Westminster John Knox, 2002).

a pie. These views treat power as a fixed quantity and ignore the relational nature of existence. A more fruitful way understands power in terms of abilities and influence. God has abilities creatures don't have, and vice versa. The breadth and duration of divine influence makes God maximally powerful. The amipotent Spirit also exerts maximal influence by persuading creatures to join the work of love. The amipotent God is the most powerful force in the universe, despite never controlling anyone or anything.

Rather than being externally limited or voluntarily self-limited, the constraints of an amipotent Spirit derive from the divine nature. God's love expands and limits what God can do. The deity in whose nature love comes first *must* love and isn't free to do otherwise. The Spirit's amipotence for creation comes logically before divine freedom.

A coherent systematic theology of love considers the Spirit amipotent.

CHAPTER EIGHT

# The Spirit is A Relational Person Who Feels

## THE BIG IDEAS

- Most major theologians say God is impassible and never receives from us.
- The biblical witness strongly supports the notion that God is relational, in the sense of giving to and receiving from creatures.
- Saying God is relational is important for understanding and affirming God as loving and personal.
- God can be a person without having a localized divine body.
- As nonbinary, the Spirit has no gender, genitalia, or sexuality.
- The dynamic Spirit changes in some respects but not in others.
- The Spirit feels emotions, including negative ones. But negative emotions don't lead God to do evil.
- God has an essence-experience binate. The divine essence never changes, but the divine experience does.
- We have many reasons to worship the God with an essence-experience binate.
- The Spirit is essentially and everlastingly related to creaturely others.

Many people of faith believe God is personal, relational, and experiences emotions.[1] Christian, Jewish, and Muslim scriptures routinely describe deity in this way.[2] These abilities and attributes

---

[1] This chapter is dedicated to Keith Ward. His work on God as a person and personal has given me courage to formulate my own, very similar, views. And his writings and friendship have been a great resource.

[2] For an example of a Jewish scholar affirming divine passibility, see Shai Held, *Abraham Joshua Heschel* (Bloomington, IN: Indiana University Press, 2013). For an example of

also seem logically required if the Spirit is loving, because lovers are personal subjects who act and feel in relationships. It makes sense, therefore, for this systematic theology of love to claim the Spirit is a relational and personal Lover who feels.

Many people are surprised to learn that leading theologians of yesteryear *denied* God has the attributes or abilities writers of scripture describe. Some contemporary theologians also deny them. These scholars, worry that imagining God in these relational ways leads to projecting human features and foibles onto the divine. It's little surprise, therefore, that these theologians don't write books, as I do, called *A Systematic Theology of Love*. They make other attributes primary in their descriptions of God.

In this chapter, I defend claims about God that are obvious to most people of faith, but have been rejected by leading theologians. I also propose a novel idea: that God has an essence-experience binate. I mean by this that the living Spirit's experience changes moment by moment in relations with creatures, but the divine nature remains unchanging. Because of this binate, the Living Lover of all relates, feels, and acts as a changing person. But unlike creatures, the Spirit has an eternally unchanging nature of love—and that's why the Spirit can't be tempted and never does evil when feeling negative emotions.

## Non-Relational Theologians

Let's look briefly at a few theologians who oppose the idea God is a person who relates and feels emotions. The great medieval theologian Thomas Aquinas, for one, rejects the idea that God is relational, if "relational" is understood as creatures and/or creation influencing God. "A relation of God to creatures isn't a reality in God," says Aquinas bluntly.[3] Instead, we should ascribe relations to God "only in our un-

---

Muslim scholars, see Mouhanad Khorchide, *Islam is Mercy* (Freiburg im Breisgau: Herder Verlag, 2014); Farhan A. Shah, "Toward a Process-Humanistic Interpretation of Islam: An Examination of Muhammed Iqbal's God Concept" (Master's Thesis, University of Oslo, 2016).

[3] Thomas Aquinas, *Summa Theologica*, I (Westminster, MD: Christian Classics, 1981), q. 6, a.2, ad 1.

derstanding."⁴ In other words, we perceive the Spirit as relational, but God *actually* isn't.

But if Aquinas were right, numerous biblical statements would be false. People can't bless God, for instance, if this means affecting the divine well-being positively. And yet the Psalmist repeatedly urges people to do this blessing activity (e.g., Ps. 103). A non-relational God can't respond to us by forgiving sin, although this idea seems central to scripture and Christian piety (e.g., 1 Jn. 1:9). If Aquinas were right, the covenants God makes with creation and the Spirit's reactions when humans break them become illusions.⁵ And so on.⁶

Another medieval theologian, Anselm, takes a similar approach. He rejects divine relations and feelings when he explores God's compassion. "How are you a compassionate God and, at the same time, passionless?" he asks in prayer. "If you are passionless, you don't feel sympathy. And if you don't feel sympathy, your heart isn't retched from sympathy for the wretched. But this is to be compassionate." In these lines, Anselm admits that compassion requires feelings and relational influence. "But you don't have either passion or sympathy," he concludes, "so how can we call you compassionate?"

Anselm answers his own question: "When you behold us in our wretchedness, God, we experience the effect of compassion. But you don't experience the feeling of compassion. Therefore, you are both compassionate because you do save the wretched and spare those who sin against you, and also not compassionate, because you are affected by no sympathies for wretchedness."⁷ Anselm believes, in other words, creatures can't affect God, and the Spirit can't feel emotional responses. We may *think* God is compassionate, says Anselm, but that's not the truth of the matter.

---

⁴ Thomas Aquinas, *Summa Contra Gentiles* II (Notre Dame, IN: University of Notre Dame Press, 1981), 13-14.

⁵ Gen. 9:11; Ex. 19:5; Deut. 7:9, 31:8; 2 Chron. 7:14; Is. 54:10; Ps. 103:17-18; Heb. 9:15

⁶ Aquinas affirms a logical relation between God and creation (like the number 2 coming logically before 3). But he rejects the witness of biblical writers that God engages in give-and-receive relations with creatures.

⁷ St. Anselm, *Proslogium*, Sidney Norton Deane, trans. (La Salle, IL, 1951), 13-14.

The Jewish medieval theologian Maimonides agrees with Aquinas and Anselm. He applies these ideas to feelings. "[God] isn't affected by external influences, and therefore doesn't possess any quality resulting from emotion," says Maimonides. He asks rhetorically, "How could a relation be imagined between a creature and God, who has nothing in common with any other being? . . . Consequently, there is no relation between Him and any other being."[8]

Notice that Maimonides assumes the Creator must be entirely unlike creatures. God can't relate with them or feel responses, thinks Maimonides, because God must be immaterial, unaffected, and timeless.[9] But none of what Maimonides says here fits the common view of God in Hebrew and Greek scriptures. And despite their influence, these ideas oppose the fundamental elements of love.

## The Spirit *is* Relational

The claims of Aquinas, Anselm, and Maimonides point to what's at stake when we say the Spirit is a relational person who feels. These theologians believe creatures can't affect God. Creatures can't influence the Spirit's emotions, actions, or beliefs. Regarding love, these three say divine love is only outgoing benevolence, with no mutual relationship influencing deity. God gives to creatures but never receives from them.

By contrast, the systematic theology I offer says that the fundamental elements required for love includes giving and receiving in real relations. This applies to both creatures and Creator. For the Spirit to relate with creatures, therefore, means deity influences them, and they in turn influence the divine.[10] To use the classic term, God is "passible."

---

[8] Moses Maimonides, "The Guide for the Perplexed," reprinted in *Medieval Philosophy*, Forrest E. Baird and Walter Kaufmann, eds. (Upper Saddle River, NJ: Prentice Hall, 2000), 560-61.

[9] Ibid.

[10] Among those who affirm God's relationality, see Michael Berra, *Towards a Theology of Relationship* (Eugene, OR: Pickwick Publications, 2022); H. Ray Dunning, *Grace, Faith, and Holiness* (Kansas City, MO: Beacon Hill, 1988); Paul Fiddes, *The Creative Suffering of God* (Oxford: Oxford University Press, 1988); Karen Baker-Fletcher, *Dancing with God* (St. Louis, Mo: Chalice, 2006); Catherine Keller, *From a Broken Web* (Boston: Beacon, 1986); Brint

The Spirit is affected, receives, suffers, responds, feels, rejoices, is vulnerable, reconciles, and emotes in relations with others.

The Spirit's love is outgoing benevolence *and* receptive empathy.[11] These dimensions of the divine life (also represented in scripture) only make sense if we believe the Spirit engages in *real* relations with creation, in the sense of mutual influence.[12] A Spirit both empathetic and benevolent can *actually* be compassionate.[13] This deity feels and reacts to creatures—including those who suffer—to promote their well-being.

To say the Spirit relates with creatures is to make claims about causation. God exerts causal influence upon others, and others exert causal influence upon God. By "causation," I don't mean creatures control God or that God controls them. Instead, I mean causation in the sense of having a real effect: in the sense of influence. The Spirit who loves exerts efficient causation, to use Aristotelean categories, not just formal or final causation.[14] But God never exerts sufficient causation, which means to be the full and only cause of some outcome.

---

Montgomery, Thomas Jay Oord, and Karen Winslow, *Introducing Relational Theology* (San Diego: Point Loma University Press, 2008).

[11] R. T. Mullins argues that even the impassiblist view of love can't account for its own claim that love seeks union with the beloved. "The Spirit's desire for unity with the beloved," Mullins says, "can't be satisfied without empathy." See "Impassibility, Omnisubjectivity, and the Problem of Unity in Love," in *Love, Divine and Human*, Oliver Crisp, et. al., eds. (London: T&T Clark, 2020).

[12] Among the many theologians who argue that God is passible, see especially Dietrich Bonhoeffer, *The Cost of Discipleship* (New York: Macmillan, 1949); John B. Cobb, Jr., *God and the World* (Philadelphia: Westminster, 1969); Isaak August Dorner, "The History of the Doctrine of the Immutability of God," in *Divine Immutability*, Robert R. Williams and Claude Welch, trans. (Minneapolis: Fortress, 1994), 82–130; Jung Young Lee, *God Suffers for Us* (Netherlands: Martinus Nijhoff, The Hague, 1974); Jürgen Moltmann, *The Crucified God* (1974), Clark Pinnock, *Most Moved Mover* (Grand Rapids, MI: Baker Academic, 2001); Jeff Pool, *God's Wounds*, Vol. 1 (Cambridge, UK: James Clarke and Co., 2009), John Sanders, *The God Who Risks* (Downers Grove, IL: IVP Academic, 2007); Daniel Day Williams, "Suffering and Being in Empirical Theology," in B. L. Meland ed., *The Future of Empirical Theology* (Chicago: University of Chicago Press, 1969), 175-94, Nicholas Wolterstorff, "Suffering Love," in *Philosophy and the Christian Faith*, Thomas V. Morris, ed. (Notre Dame: University of Notre Dame Press, 1990).

[13] Kelly James Clark addresses these issues in accessible ways in *God and the Problems of Love* (Cambridge: Cambridge University Press, 2023).

[14] Divine Causation. Aristotle argued for four modes of causation: efficient, final, formal and material. Because God has been thought immaterial and divine action that can't be perceived with our five senses, contemporary theologians have typically denied that God exerts efficient causation. I affirm efficient causation for God, however. And I argue this causal influence is possible because God has both mental and material aspects, and we perceive God nonsensorily. But divine causal influence never singlehandedly brings about outcomes.

The Bible is *packed* with passages depicting God as relational. And the Spirit who loves often responds emotionally.[15] Here's a small sample of the many passages one could cite:

- The Lord regrets that he made humans, and "his heart was deeply troubled" (Gen. 6:6).
- God "hears" the cries of Israel and is "concerned about their suffering" (Ex. 3:7).
- God "hears the groaning of the sons of Israel" and remembers the covenant (Ex. 6:5).
- God self-identifies as a "jealous God" and "unswervingly loyal" (Ex. 20:5, 6).
- God encounters a stiff-necked people, and has anger that "burns." But God "relents" and doesn't bring disaster (Ex. 32:9-14).
- Being "a compassionate God," God will "not forget the covenant with your fathers" (Dt. 4:31).
- God "remembers his covenant" and "relents according to the greatness of his lovingkindness" (Ps. 106:45).
- "My lovingkindness will not be removed from you, and my covenant of peace will not be shaken," says the Lord of compassion (Is. 54:10).
- God feels sorrow about the disaster brought on Judah (Jer. 42:10).
- God is "jealous" and "takes pity" on the people (Joel 2:18).
- God "has compassion" for Israel (Hosea 11:8-9).
- God takes "great delight" and "rejoices" (Zeph. 3:17).
- God gets "extremely angry" when the nations make disasters worse (Zech. 1:15).

---

[15] A host of Old Testament scholars argue in favor of divine passibility. For examples, see Walter Brueggemann, *Theology of the Old Testament* (Minneapolis: Fortress, 1997); Terence Fretheim, *God and the World in the Old Testament*; *The Suffering of God* (Philadelphia: Fortress, 1984); *What Kind of God?* Michael J. Chan and Brent A Strawn, eds. (Winona Lake, IN: Eisenbrauns, 2015); John Goldingay, *Old Testament Theology*, vol. 1 (Downers Grove, IL: InterVarsity, 1993); Abraham Heschel, *The Prophets* (New York: Harper and Row, 1962).

- Paul warns readers to "not grieve the Holy Spirit of God" (Eph. 4:30), which implies that creaturely action can sadden God.[16]
- James says, "The Lord is full of compassion and is merciful" (5:11).

The covenants described in scripture represent primary examples of divine relationality. God initiates them, but they require ongoing commitments and responses from creatures. When Israel fails to live up to its part of the covenants, the Spirit cries out, "O that my people would listen to me, that Israel would walk in my ways!" (Ps. 81:13). "To the extent that the covenant depends on the human partners meeting its conditions," says Jon Levenson, "covenant is exceedingly fragile. To the extent that it depends on God's reliability, it is rock-solid."[17]

Jesus envisions the Spirit as relational too. He call God an Abba (Father) who responds to children, and sees Abba's responding as intimately relational (Mk 14:36). In a story about a wayward son, Jesus describes God as a forgiving father who "felt compassion" for a lost son (Lk. 15:20).[18] In the Sermon on the Mount, Jesus encourages his listeners to imitate the Spirit's relational love: "be compassionate as God is compassionate" (Lk. 6:36).[19] And Jesus draws from images in the Hebrew Bible of a relational God when he laments, "Jerusalem, Jerusalem... how often I have longed to gather your children together, as a hen gathers her chicks under her wings, and you were not willing" (Mt 23:37).

---

[16] Paul Moser highlights the Pauline emphasis upon divine suffering in "Paul's Suffering God: Frustration in Divine Compassion," *Theology Today* (2025): 1-9.

[17] Jon D. Levenson, *The Love of God: Divine Gift, Human Gratitude, and Mutual Faithfulness in Judaism* (Princeton: Princeton University Press, 2016), 121.

[18] F. Scott Spencer explores Jesus' emotions in *Passions of the Christ: The Emotional Life of Jesus in the Gospels* (Grand Rapids, MI: Baker, 2021). See also Kurt Willems, *Echoing Hope* (London: Waterbrook, 2021).

[19] On Jesus' revelation of God as love, see Bradley Jersak, *A More Christ-Like God* (Pasadena, CA: Plain Truth Ministries, 2016); Keith Ward, *Love is His Meaning: Understanding the Teaching of Jesus* (London: SPCK, 2017).

These passages and others indicate that the Spirit's giving-and-receiving love takes many forms. Let me describe three briefly, using the Greek words commonly translated "love": *agape*, *philia*, and *eros*. First, the Spirit expresses *agape* by responding to sin with forgiveness and healing. These activities assume interactive relationship. Often, God is angry or disappointed when creatures hurt one another or creation more generally. The Spirit experiences negative emotions and yet responds with *agape*. Deity repays evil with good, and we should do the same.[20]

God also expresses giving-and-receiving *philia* love with creatures.[21] Because the Spirit who loves is relational, God enjoys friendships and engages in covenant. As the Psalmist puts it, "The friendship of the Lord is for those who honor him, and he makes his covenant known to them" (Ps. 25:14). And this friendship includes warm feelings of divine affection and fellowship (Dt. 10:15).

We find the Spirit's relationality evident in divine *eros* too—in the sense of God evaluating and valuing creatures—even if we have the word *agape* used in the text.[22, 23] God sees creation is good (Gen. 1), for instance, and responds with what seems to be feelings of pleasure. *Yahweh* delights in those who respect him (Ps. 147:10-11) and *Elohim* delights in Israel (Is. 62:4–5). In numerous biblical passages, notes Terence Fretheim, "God is happy."[24] God loves the world so much that the Spirit gives Jesus so that those who believe might have eternal life (Jn. 3:16). This loving the world sounds like valuing. I consider these valuing kinds of love examples of *eros*. *Eros*, as I will argue in future chapters, is also a major force in God's creating.

---

[20] Lk. 6:27-31; Rm. 12:21; 1 Thess. 5:15; 1 Pt. 3:9

[21] Ex. 33:12; 2 Chr. 20:7; Is. 41:8; Jas. 2:2; Js. 2:23; Tit. 3:4

[22] On God enjoying, see Elaine Padilla, *Divine Enjoyment: A Theology of Passion and Exuberance* (New York: Fordham University Press, 2015).

[23] 2 Tm. 4:8; Jn. 12:43; Hb. 1:9

[24] Terence E. Fretheim, "God, Creation, and the Pursuit of Happiness," in *The Bible and the Pursuit of Happiness*, Brent Strawn, ed. (Oxford: Oxford University Press, 2012), 34.

## The Spirit as a Person

Various scriptures assume God is a Person who makes decisions and responds to creatures, especially humans.[25] Because personhood only makes sense in relation to others, divine relationality must be essential to saying the Spirit is a Person.[26] But some theologians deny, obscure, or radically redefine God's personal dimension. Paul Tillich, as we've seen, denies that God is a person.[27]

Persons act intentionally in relationships in the sense of being free, purposive, and deliberate. They have interiority and are aware of themselves as rational agents.[28] But they're also relational agents who find themselves affected by others and environments.[29] Although universal and incorporeal, God is a person in these senses.

Divine universality or omnipresence is the biggest obstacle to thinking of God as a person. When someone says God is "personal" or is a "Person," many immediately imagine a divine body located somewhere. Many of the biblical writers have that image, in fact, at least they sometimes write as if God is an embodied person. I think the universal Spirit is an incorporeal or bodiless person.

In an earlier chapter, I described God as an agent who becomes rather than exists as a static being. The becoming Spirit is an everlasting

---

[25] For various proposals for what it means to cooperate with God, see Timothy Reddish, et. al., eds. *Partnering with God: Exploring Collaboration in Open and Relational Theology* (Grasmere, ID: SacraSage, 2021).

[26] In this section, I set aside the question of whether to think of God as three persons in Trinity.

[27] Ben Page explores from an analytic theology perspective key questions about divine personhood. See "Wherein lies the debate? Concerning whether God is a person," *International Journal for Philosophy of Religion* (2019) 85:297–317 https://doi.org/10.1007/s11153-018-9694-x

[28] Can Nonhuman Animals be Persons? I suspect nonhuman creatures can also be persons. We have good reasons to think that complex creatures think, have self-awareness, and make intentional decisions. These capacities vary in degree from that typical of humans, however. I doubt that cells would be persons, although I think they have an iota of mentality. For these reasons, I reserve the category of "person" to describe creatures with complex mentality and suspect that the less complex have mentality without the requisite sophistication necessary for personhood.

[29] Edgar Brightman and others claim that limitations are inherent in personhood. If God is a person, therefore, God must be limited in some ways. See Edgar Sheffield Brightman, *A Philosophy of Religion* (New York: Prentice-Hall, 1940).

series of divine occasions, to use Whitehead's terms. This way of talking fits nicely with saying God is a person, so long as we 1) think personhood involves relational agency, 2) think of the divine person as universal, and 3) say that God's characteristics pass from one divine occasion to the next. God is a person, but with the transcendent qualifications I have noted earlier.[30]

The "Spirit who loves" model of divine personhood sits between two other views of God. One alternative conceives of deity as utterly relational but *without* rationality, mentality, intentionality, purposiveness, etc. Call this the "relational but not rational" deity. Proponents often think God entirely material, but without the reflective abilities necessary for decisions, self-awareness, or goals.

Among the problems with the "relational but not rational" model is that this deity seems incapable of love. Without the ability to reflect, make decisions, or have aims, this God can't evaluate and intentionally choose to promote well-being. The "relational but not rational" God can't be a lover, therefore, if love involves acting intentionally and appreciating values.[31]

The second alternative view is a God with rationality but without relationality. Call this the "rational but not relational" deity. This God makes decisions (or a single decision) without taking into account creaturely influence. And this deity experiences no emotions, at least not in response to creatures. Proponents usually think the rational but not relational God is entirely immaterial, not engaging as a cause among causes. Many traditional theologians justify their models of God by starting with statements about whether deity has rational reasons to do some action, rather than justifying their model with statements about how a relational Spirit loves.

Among the problems with the "rational but not relational" view: this deity fails to engage in the responsive receiving love requires. Without real relations, this God can't be influenced by creatures nor

---

[30] Bruce Epperly argues for a "truly personal God" in *Process Theology: A Guide for the Perplexed* (London: T&T Clark, 2011).

[31] Simon Hewitt makes a similar argument that pantheism can't support the notion of a personal deity. See "God isn't a person (an argument via pantheism)," *International Journal of Philosophy of Religion*, 85 (2019): 281–296. https://doi.org/10.1007/s11153-018-9678-x

feel the emotions that accompany love. The rational but not relational deity doesn't love in any way that we could understand.

The Spirit who loves, by contrast, is relational *and* rational. The divine lover is a rational agent who acts intentionally, and who relationally responds to others to promote well-being.[32] This universal Person appreciates values and aims to enhance the beloved in ongoing relations.[33] African-American theologian Major J. Jones puts it well: "A usable concept of God must be the affirmation that the God who is, who is personal . . . is also an ultimately responsive being."[34]

## How Can Incorporeal Agents Be Persons?

Comparing the divine Person to creaturely persons raises an important issue. Creaturely persons love as agents with localized bodies. But I've argued that the divine Person should be considered a universal and incorporeal Spirit. Although being a person requires relations, does personhood require a localized body?

I say no. At least in God's case, a Person can be both bodiless and relational. Thomas Aquinas would agree, at least with the claim that God can be incorporeal and a rational Person. But he also thought God was entirely immaterial and impassible.[35] We're better off to imagine God as incorporeal and material, rational and relational, bodiless and emotional. God is both universal and personal.

---

[32] On God as a personal agent, see Philip Clayton, Philip and Steven Knapp, *The Predicament of Belief: Science, Philosophy, and Faith* (New York: Oxford University Press, 2011).

[33] Personal Idealism. The claims in this section align well with the personal idealism of theologians such as Edgar Brightman, Martin Luther King, Jr., and Keith Ward. Personal idealists claim that mind proves fundamental to reality, and mind is personal in the sense of knowing, feeling, and willing. This tradition grounds values in mind, which makes it congenial to theologies of love. This systematic theology of love incorporates the insights of personal idealism with the insights of materialism to propose a version of panpsychism I call "material-mental monism."

[34] Major J. Jones, *The Color of God: The Concept of God in Afro-American Thought* (Macon, GA: Mercer University Press, 1987), 48.

[35] At one point, Aquinas says God is a person. "Whatsoever is most excellent in creatures should be attributed to God, it is fitting that the word person should be attributed to God." (De Potentia Dei, q.9, a.3, co.) Unfortunately, Aquinas doesn't use this reasoning to posit the relationality of God.

As I argued in previous chapters, the universal Spirit has mental and material aspects. The material aspect accounts for elements necessary for efficient causation and emotional relations associated with love. Without a material dimension, God couldn't influence material creation. God's mental aspect accounts for the rational decision-making and evaluation crucial for love. The Spirit can manifest materiality and mentality without having a localized divine body.[36]

In my earlier discussion of God as Spirit, I noted various ways in which deity can be said to be mind-like, wind-like, gravity-like, and living. Each of these analogies have aspects that suggest mental and material dimensions in divinity. The analogy of God with a mind, for instance, expresses well the mental dimensions (with qualifications), especially decision making, freedom, and intentionality. The analogy of God with wind and gravity expresses well (with qualifications) the material dimensions, especially as causal powers that can't be seen. The Spirit as living incorporates both the material and mental.

A material-mental Lover can exert efficient causation upon, and receive from, creatures. This Lover can have the aims for well-being associated with final causation too. Consequently, theologies that embrace material-mental monism have a satisfactory framework to describe God as rational *and* relational, incorporeal *and* material, influencing *and* influenced.

The Spirit is a universal, incorporeal Person without a local body.

## The Nonbinary God

Historically, most people have assumed persons must be gendered as either male or female. Although we find multiple biblical descriptions of God as female or gender-neutral, most people of faith use masculine language for deity. According to this language, God must be He/Him.

Consciously or not, references to God as He/Him incline people of faith to privilege stereotypical male qualities. For instance, men

---

[36] Brittany E. Wilson explores these issues in "God's Body and the Material Turn: Divine (Im)Materiality in Biblical Theophanies," *Harvard Theological Review* 117:3 (2024): 607–30.

tend, on average, to be physically stronger than women. And many regard women, on average, as more emotionally invested than men. Of course, we can find many exceptions to these averages. But as a consequence, many theologians who conceive of God as male attribute immense power to deity, and have either rejected or minimized divine emotions such as empathy.

Just as problematic, many in religions circles have historically thought men suited for leadership, and they afforded men privileges accordingly. Women often have been, and still are, denied leadership roles. Theologians who imagine God as male justify this injustice. A significant number of people of faith have claimed God created specific hierarchies in creation, and these hierarchies place men at the top of the chain of command. Put simply: A male God gave male humans authority over females and the rest of creation.[37]

Not only have a growing number of people seen the fallacies inherent in thinking God must be male or wants men in charge, but they also realize that personhood isn't linked to gender and genitalia. Many now readily acknowledge the personhood of nonbinary people, whatever their gender preferences. Intersex people give us ready examples of why personhood doesn't require typical genitalia, reproductive capacity, or clear biological sex categories. In fact, intersex issues help us deconstruct strict sex categories in general. And nonbinary people help us deconstruct strict gender categories.

The incorporeal God of this systematic theology of love doesn't have a penis, vagina, gonads, hormones, chromosomes, or other gender or sexually-oriented body parts, codes, and functions. But we could say a non-binary God exhibits the positive qualities we find in

---

[37] A number of important books have been written on this subject. Among them are Beth Allison Barr, *The Making of Biblical Womanhood* (Brazos, 2021); Katie G. Cannon, *Black Womanist Ethics* (Louisville, KY: Westminster John Knox, 1988); Monica A. Coleman, Nancy R. Howell, and Helene Tallon Russell, *Creating Women's Theology: A Movement Engaging Process Thought* (Eugene, OR: Pickwick, 2011); Mary Daly, *Beyond God the Father* (Boston: Beacon, 1973); Sarah Heaner Lancaster, *Women and the Authority of Scripture* (Chicago: Trinity, 2002); Janel Apps Ramsey and Thomas Jay Oord, eds., *Women Experiencing Faith* (Grasmere, ID: SacraSage, 2018); Rosemary Radford Ruether, *Sexism and God-Talk* (Boston: Beacon, 1983); Phyllis Trible, *Texts of Terror* (Minneapolis: Fortress, 1984); Karen Winslow, *Imagining Equity: The Gifts of Christian Feminist Theology* (Nashville, TN: Wesley's Foundery, 2021).

creatures; qualities such as love, empathy, deliberation, wisdom, creating, rationality, and more.[38] And if we think of God as non-binary, we aren't required to call deity "He" or "Her." Some call God "they" to account for this, but others seek alternative labels.[39] To emphasize divine subjectivity and love, we will be wise, though, to use personal language for the Spirit.

Given the Spirit's unique personhood, we can rightly say God is queer. That is, deity presents unusually when it comes to gender, sexuality, identity, and orientation. In fact, divine queerness puts God in a category of one, without making the divine Person entirely unlike us as persons in various ways.

The Spirit is a universal, bodiless, and non-binary Person who lovingly relates with others.

## A Relational Spirit Changes

To say the Spirit is a Person who loves leads naturally to saying God changes. The Spirit is "mutable," to use classic language, rather than immutable, is dynamic rather than static. Because God receives from creatures moment by moment, creatures change the state of the Spirit's moment-by-moment experience. As the "most moved mover," to use the language of theologians Abraham Heschel and Clark Pinnock, God moves when moving others and being moved by them.[40]

Large numbers of biblical passages portray God as experiencing a change in response to creatures. The Spirit's feelings might change from tranquility to anger, from delight to disappointment, from desire

---

[38] On the queer implications for thinking God is nonbinary, see Tara K. Soughers, *Beyond a Binary God: A Theology for Trans Allies* (New York: Church, 2018).

[39] As an example of a theologian who uses "they" for God, see Jon Paul Sydnor, *The Great Open Dance*. Sydnor's use of "they" has the double advantage of referring to God as multiplicity in trinity.

[40] Most Moved Mover. Abraham Heschel and Clark H. Pinnock both championed the argument that a relational God isn't an unmoved mover, as Aristotle said, but the most moved mover. "If we put aside the categories and logic of Greek philosophy and try to understand biblical religion in its own terms," says Heschel, "we will soon discover that the God of the Bible isn't Aristotle's impassive, unmoved mover at all; he can only be described as 'the Most Moved Mover'" (Abraham Joshua Heschel, *The Prophets* [New York: Harper & Row, 1962], 25). See also Clark H. Pinnock, *Most Moved Mover* (Grand Rapids, MI: Baker, 2001).

to satisfaction, or from neglect to being blessed. These changes point to "before" and "after" moments in the divine living experience. In fact, in scripture we discover that what creatures do sometimes leads God to have a change of mind and to act differently. More than forty biblical passages say the Spirit "repents" (*niham*), which means God changes plans.[41]

Key claims about God as Creator, Redeemer, Savior, and Forgiver only make sense if God's experience changes.[42] Creating our universe, for instance, suggests a before and after that involves change.[43] Redeemer and Savior language suggests a change in the divine experience from times before redeeming and saving to times after they occur. Forgiving a particular sin involves a change: at one moment, the sin had not yet been committed and did not need forgiving. Later, the sin has occurred, and the Spirit forgives. The experience of the becoming Spirit changes moment by moment in relations with creatures and creation.

One argument for denying that God changes builds from a particular view of perfection. The perfect One *must* be immutable, say some theologians, because a changing God could only change from perfection to imperfection, from the optimal to suboptimal. Evangelical theologian Carl F. H. Henry puts it this way: "God is perfect and, if imperfect, can only change for the worse."[44]

Henry fails to account for the possibility that divine perfection could involve perfect change. Charles Hartshorne notes this possibility when he says God as a living person can have perfect experience in one moment, but it can be surpassed by a perfect experience in the next.

---

[41] On statements in the Hebrew Bible about God repenting, see Terence Fretheim's work, *The Suffering of God* and Michael J. Chan and Brent A. Strawn, eds., *What Kind of God? Collected Essays of Terence E. Fretheim* (Winona Lake, IN: Eisenbrauns, 2015), ch. 2. See also R. W. L. Moberly, *Old Testament Theology* (Grand Rapids, MI: Baker Academic, 2013), ch. 4.

[42] R. T. Mullins makes this point strongly as a criticism of the "timeless God." He also describes problems in thinking God must be in all ways impassible. See *The End of the Timeless God* (Oxford: Oxford University Press, 2016).

[43] This statement would be true whether one affirms creation from nothing or denies it.

[44] Carl F. H. Henry, *God, Revelation, and Authority: The God who Stands and Stays, Part One*, vol. 5 (Waco: Word, 1982), 304. For another who endorses the argument that God can't change in any sense, see Stephen Charnock in, eds. Samuel Renihan, *God Without Passions* (Palmdale: Reformed Baptist Academic, 2015), 144-154.

"The numerically distinct God-tomorrow will also be perfect," says Hartshorne, "though He will exhibit perfection in an enriched state of actuality."[45] This explains how the Spirit's experience changes, but perfectly.

It's not just that God's experience changes; love also requires change, at least in some respects. The Psalmist points to divine change and its motivation when he says God "repents according to the abundance of his steadfast love" (Ps. 106:45). To "repent" means to change; "steadfast" means *not* to change. God's love involves both forms of perfection: perfect flexibility and perfect stability. We saw this in our earlier discussion of divine love as necessary in one respect but contingently free in another.

A God who is immutable in all respects can't respond to creatures. An immutable One can't empathetically feel creaturely suffering nor compassionately respond in a timely way. Consequently, an unchanging deity can't relate in giving-and-receiving love. Put another way: the immutable God of traditional theology can't act in the ways love requires.[46]

A relational Spirit who loves must change experientially.

## The Spirit Who Feels

According to biblical writers, God feels emotions. Emotions can be defined as felt evaluations of an event, person, or situation, and the loving Spirit experiences them.[47] Emotions have cognitive and affective aspects, in varying degrees and types. And although emotions should *not* be equated with love, they typically accompany it.

---

[45] Charles Hartshorne, *The Logic of Perfection*, (LaSalle, IL: Open Court, 1962), 66. Hartshorne should be given credit for being the first thinker to articulate this expanded view of divine perfection. In addition to *The Logic of Perfection*, see *Man's Vision of God and the Logic of Theism* (Chicago and New York: Willett, Clark, and Co., 1941); *The Divine Relativity* (New Haven: Yale University Press, 1948).

[46] Carol P. Christ offers a strong argument against divine immutability in *She Who Changes: Re-Imagining the Divine in the World* (New York: Palgrave, 2003).

[47] For a concise introduction to divine emotion, see R. T. Mullins, *God and Emotion* (Cambridge: Cambridge University Press, 2020).

The Bible describes God as having a wide array of emotions, from anger to delight.[48] Sometimes the text says God is pleased, and at other times God feels jealous. References to divine "wrath" usually appear coupled with statements about anger, and these give us important clues about feelings in God's assessment of values and disvalues.

Biblical writers describe the Spirit empathizing with those who suffer. God cares, consoles, and has compassion for the hurting.[49] The Apostle Paul describes it this way: "Praise be to the God and Father of our Lord Jesus Christ, the Father of compassion and the God of all comfort, who comforts us in all our troubles, so that we can comfort those in any trouble with the comfort we ourselves receive from God. For just as we share abundantly in the sufferings of Christ, so also our comfort abounds through Christ" (2 Cor. 1:3-5).

The cognitive dimension of empathy often entails taking the perspective of another by imagining how they feel. The emotional element of empathy shares in the feelings of another. Both cognitive and emotional elements are crucial to expressing compassion, because an act of compassion involves a volitional element in which the empathizer works for the good of the hurting.[50] Although the empathizer doesn't have the *exact* experience of the other, they feel emotions in response and then ponder how best to react. Compassion, therefore, has both feeling and cognitive dimensions.

Despite the biblical witness, many theologians say God has no emotions or, to use the ancient word, no "passions." The Council of Chalcedon (451), for instance, declared as heresy the idea that God can be affected by anything or has emotions.[51] Council members said

---

[48] e.g., Exod. 4:14; Judg. 2:12; Isa. 62:4-5; Jer. 9:10, 9:24, 48:32

[49] Dave Andrews expresses the importance of compassion in his writings, including *Christi-Anarchy* (Eugene, OR: Wipf and Stock, 1999) and *Not Religion but Love* (Eugene, OR: Wipf and Stock, 1999).

[50] See Martha Nussbaum's excellent analysis of compassion in "Compassion: The Basic Social Emotion," *Social Philosophy and Policy* 13.1 (Winter 1996): 27-58). Anne Runehov addresses compassion in *The Human Being, the World, and God* (Switzerland: Springer, 2016). Oliver Davies offers a theology of compassion in his book of the same title.

[51] I agree with K. Steve McCormick when he affirms love-based doctrines, even if some theologians or councils call those doctrines heretical. See McCormick's essay, "The Heresies of Love: Toward a Spirit-Christ Ecclesiology of Triune Love," *Wesleyan Theological Journal* 37, no. 1 (Spring 2002), 35-47.

they would "repel from the sacred assembly those who dare to say that the God-head of the only-begotten is capable of suffering." On their view, only embodied beings could feel emotion: an incorporeal God can't. "Every passion of the appetite takes place through some bodily change," Aquinas would later say. "None of this can take place in God, since He isn't a body."[52]

We can understand somewhat why early people of faith didn't want to attribute emotions to God. We sometimes observe humans who let emotions undermine their reasoning or incline them to act immorally. Greek gods frequently engaged in emotional outbursts that led to their harmful behavior. These gods were "overwhelmed" or "blinded" by their emotions. Many Christians, Muslims, and Jews, therefore, have said the true God is devoid of emotion (*apatheia*), which distinguished their deity from emotionally volatile ones.

This systematic theology of love accepts at face value the broad biblical witness to divine emotions. God feels but always acts lovingly in response. The Spirit acts compassionately, for instance, and experiences pity, sympathy, or empathy.[53] God gets angry when we harm one another, ourselves, or creation, but the Spirit forgives and calls us to promote flourishing.

God experiences a wide range of emotions without doing evil.

## God's Anger, Hate, and Negative Emotions

The Spirit feels positive emotions like happiness, comfort, affection, and sympathy. But God also feels negative emotions like anger, jealousy, and hate. Some theologians claim these negative emotions would lead God to destroy or punish. Biblical authors even describe God acting in harsh and vindictive ways (e. g., Gen. 6:5–6; Gen. 19:24; Num.

---

[52] Aquinas, *Summa Contra Gentiles*, I, 89, 3.

[53] Among those who address divine empathy well, see Anna Case-Winters, *God Will Be All in All* (Louisville, KY: Westminster John Knox, 2021); Edward Farley, *Divine Empathy* (Philadelphia: Fortress, 1996); Paul Fiddes, *The Creative Suffering of God* (Oxford: Oxford University Press, 1988); Jürgen Moltmann, *The Crucified God* (London: SCM, 1974); Terryl and Fiona Givens, *The God Who Weeps* (Ensign Peak, 2012); Jeff B. Pool, *God's Wounds* (Cambridge: James Clarke & Co., 2009); Roberto Sirvent, *Embracing Vulnerability* (Eugene, OR: Pickwick, 2014).

16:32). Because I deny that the Spirit ever harms, punishes, or destroys, I need to clarify how the universal Spirit can always love, yet sometimes feel anger, disappointment, hatred, and other negative emotions.

The Spirit feels negative emotions when creatures harm themselves, others, and/or creation. God hates creaturely actions that cause evil, harm, or trauma.[54] The Lover of us all experiences anger when we fail to do justice and neglect mercy. Just as we are to "hate evil but cling to what is good" (Rom. 12:9), the Spirit also hates evil and desires the good.

To understand what it means for God to know all things, we must differentiate between first-person and third-person emotions. The anger God feels when we sin is a first-person feeling. It's *God's* feeling. But even in this experience, God doesn't feel exactly what it's like for the sinner to commit sin, because the Spirit never sins. Deity feels the pain of the harmed creatures as third-person emotions. This means that the Spirit genuinely empathizes with others but doesn't feel the exact pain that the victim feels in first-person.

We need this important distinction especially for talking about how God can feel the third-person feelings of the sinner. As morally perfect, the Spirit can't experience first-hand the emotions of, for example, a rapist. God never rapes, or desires to rape.[55] Therefore, God doesn't know those emotions first-hand. But because God remains directly present in each moment, God feels the emotional force of the victim's feelings—*and* the rapist's—in the third-person. Just as we sympathize with others experiencing harm, the Spirit sympathizes as fully as possible with both victims and perpetrators.

Some emotions that creatures feel may be particular to their unique bodily characteristics. If God doesn't have the chemical and physical makeup of creatures, we wouldn't expect God to ever feel horny,

---

[54] Helene Russell addresses the relation of love, trauma, and healing in "Can Empowering Love Heal Trauma?" in *Amipotence, vol. 2*, Brandon Brown, et. al., eds. (Grasmere, ID: SacraSage, 2025).

[55] Janel Apps Ramsey addresses the promise amipotence has for understanding God and rape in her essay, "Man, Bear, or Amipotent God," in *Amipotence, vol. 2*, Brandon Brown, et. al., eds. (Grasmere, ID: SacraSage, 2025).

for instance.⁵⁶ The desire for intercourse would not be a first-person feeling for God, but the Spirit would feel this passionate desire from a third-person perspective. God also wouldn't know from the first person perspective what it feels like to vomit. The Spirit has no stomach and throat, after all. But God can feel the emotions of vomiters as a third-person empathizer.

It's important that we believe the Spirit feels empathy in order for us to experience intimacy with God. We have difficulty feeling close to and comforted by those who have not suffered. An unaffected person can't relate to what we're feeling. A non-suffering and impassible God, therefore, just couldn't empathize with our pain. Or with our joys! By contrast, the relational Spirit who feels emotions is a fellow-sufferer who empathetically understands our pain.⁵⁷ Oppressed people can therefore feel rightly comforted by "the God of all comfort."⁵⁸ And this God rejoices with us when we have reason to rejoice.

It seems likely that any person, creaturely or divine, would need to have material and mental dimensions to feel emotions. But a localized body doesn't seem necessary. The universal and incorporeal Spirit with mental and material dimensions, therefore, can feel sad, angry, happy, blessed, and more without having any divine eyes, ears, face, or body. And God's emotions can be real, while biblical references to divine bodies and parts can be metaphorical.⁵⁹

---

⁵⁶ R. T. Mullins addresses this intriguing topic in *God and Emotion* (Cambridge: Cambridge University Press, 2020).

⁵⁷ Alfred North Whitehead famously called God the "fellow sufferer who understands" in *Process and Reality*, Corrected edition by David Ray Griffin and Donald W. Sherburne (New York: Free Press, 1978 [1929]), 351.

⁵⁸ Among the *numerous* books arguing that the oppressed can find comfort in a passible God, see James Cone, *God of the Oppressed* (London: SPCK, 1977).

⁵⁹ Body Parts and Emotions. Perhaps Aquinas and others deny divine emotions because they associate emotional expressions with bodily parts. Some creatures have eyes that fill with water when they are sad, for instance. Their faces may turn red when angry. A surprise might lead a creature to squawk or jump back. By contrast, an incorporeal God would not have a body to register such emotions. I join Aquinas and others in thinking biblical references to God's eyes, face, hands, and body are metaphors rather than literal descriptions. But instead of saying only embodied beings feel emotions, I think the incorporeal Spirit with mental and material dimensions can feel emotions.

## THE SPIRIT'S ESSENCE-EXPERIENCE BINATE

I earlier claimed that God changes in one respect but doesn't change in another. This idea proves crucial for describing the Spirit's steadfast but flexible love. God's essence of love is unchanging ("God is love") but the Spirit's experiential giving and receiving love changes ("God loves"). I call this God's "essence-experience binate."

Those who say God must be impassible and immutable are right in one respect: God's *essence* or nature is impassible and immutable. When Malachi and James quote God saying, "I am the Lord who doesn't change" (Mal. 3:6; James 1:17), we would best interpret them as referring to God's immutable essence. God's essence is unchanging and unaffected by creation.

In another respect, however, God is relational and changes. The Spirit's *experience* is passible and mutates. As the Living Lord of history, the divine experience becomes altered moment by moment as creatures and creation affect deity in ongoing relations. A personal God lovingly relates to others.

Saying the divine essence never changes but the divine experience does helps us make sense of otherwise puzzling and seemingly contradictory biblical passages. In 1 Samuel, for instance, the author says the Lord "isn't a man that he should repent." This statement points to the Spirit's immutable nature. But soon after, the author also says, "the Lord repented that he had made Saul king over Israel" (15:11, 29, 35). The second statement highlights the Spirit's changing experience. God perceives what occurred and, in the name of love, changes course. In these passages, the Spirit repents in one sense but not in another.

Or take a biblical passage often sung in worship: "The steadfast love of the Lord never ceases; his mercies never come to an end; they are new every morning; great is your faithfulness" (Lam. 3:22-23). This passage emphasizes God's essence of love as unchangingly steadfast. But it also says God's loving expressions change: they are new every moment. The two can work together.

What I call God's essence-experience binate others label "dipolar theism."[60] Alfred North Whitehead, for instance, says God has two "natures:" primordial and consequential.[61] I find it confusing to say God has two natures, however, because, as I see it, God has just one nature or essence. While no language will be perfect, I prefer to say the Spirit's essence is unchanging but deity's experience changes.

Saying the Spirit has an eternally unchanging essence but an everlastingly changing experience points to ways in which God is both transcendent and immanent.[62] Deity transcends creatures by having a timeless, unchanging, and unaffected nature; the Spirit differs from creatures in these ways. But God's experience is analogous to creaturely experience, because it's timefull, emotional, changing, and involves direct, giving-and-receiving relationships. Rather than being entirely like creatures or entirely unlike them, the Spirit shares similarities and differences with creatures.

It's hard to overestimate the importance of the Spirit's essence-experience binate. Embracing it allows us to affirm valuable insights in theologies that say God is immutable, impassible, and timeless. These attributes apply to the divine essence. But the experiential aspect of the binate allows us also to say the Spirit enjoys experiences, time, and is affected by creatures. The essence-experience binate affirms

---

[60] I am especially indebted to Charles Hartshorne for inspiring my ideas about God's essence-experience binate. Hartshorne appealed to a tripartate view, however, which distinguished between God's existence, essence, and actuality. See Hartshorne's writings in John B. Cobb, Jr. and Franklin L. Gamwell, eds. *Existence and Actuality* (Chicago: Chicago University Press, 1984), 75.

[61] Charles Hartshorne raised the phrase "dipolar theism" to prominence. See his essay "The Dipolar Conception of Deity," *Review of Metaphysics* 21:2 [1967], 273-89) and Donald Viney's explanation in "Hartshorne's Dipolar Theism and the Mystery of God" *Philosophia*, 35 (2007), 341-350. For good explorations of Hartshorne's theological views, see Daniel Dombrowski, *Analytic Theism, Hartshorne, and the Concept of God*; Donald Wayne Viney and George W. Shields, *The Mind of Charles Hartshorne* (Anoka, MN: Process Century, 2020).

[62] Transcendence Not Spatial. In many discussions of God's transcendence and immanence, the words are understood in spatial senses. A transcendent God is "out there," and an immanent deity is "right here." I find this way of speaking unhelpful, not the least because nearly every theologian thinks of God as omnipresent. It's better to think of transcendence and immanence as the differences and similarities between God and creatures. I address this in more detail in a later chapter on mystery.

the unchanging love of God's essence and divine love that changes moment-by-moment in relational experiences with others.[63]

## Worshiping an Impersonal and Unchanging Deity

Describing the universal Spirit as a relational, changing, experiential, and emotional Lover constitutes one of my primary aims and motivations for writing this systematic theology of love. These divine attributes and activities have often been overlooked or outright denied in other theologies. But they're essential for making love central to systematic theology. Furthermore, love and relationality are an important reason we would feel attracted to worship God. Many worship experiences emphasize this.

But God's essence-experience binate indicates we are also rightly attracted to the impersonal aspects of the divine. It makes sense to worship a deity whose character remains steadfast, for instance. In awe, we can praise the God with immutable character, especially when the creatures we know prove unreliable. In a world of change, we rightly worship the incorruptible One: we need the rock-solid security of God's necessary love in a world of anxiety and chaos.[64]

Fortunately, the Spirit's essence-experience binate accounts for both the motivation to worship a relational God of becoming, *and* an impersonal God of immutability. The Spirit's essence is steadfast, unaffected, secure, absolute, unchanging, and reliable. Praise be to God! But the Spirit is also an Experiencer with relational and changing dimensions that come from being an interactive Lover. Praise be to God![65]

Some religions also identify or worship nondivine Ultimates, such as Creativity, Platonic Forms, Nature, Oneness, Possibilities, the

---

[63] Or as the biblical scholar Richard Middleton puts it, "God's character . . . doesn't change, God's *modus operandi* or way of relating certainly does" ("How and Why Does God Change? Exploring the Logic of the Divine Shift after the Golden Calf," *Hebrew Studies* 66 [2025]: 8).

[64] I'm grateful to John Thatamanil for his conversations that prompted me to see the importance of diverse inclinations to worship. Thatamanil explores this in *Circling the Elephant* (New York: Fordham University Press, 2020).

[65] Brent Peterson explores what worship might look like from a Christian perspective. See *Created to Worship* (Kansas City, MO: Beacon Hill, 2012).

Pluralistic Universe, etc.⁶⁶ I'll address these Ultimates in the third volume of this systematic theology. But here I acknowledge and validate the urge to worship a deity who remains impersonal and unchanging in essence but relational and dynamic in experience.

The Spirit's essence-experience binate accounts for our urge to worship.

## THE SPIRIT'S ESSENTIAL RELATIONS WITH CREATION

I have criticized theologians who say God doesn't relate lovingly with creatures. I also criticized theologians who say God once existed alone and freely chose to relate with creation. A God who necessarily loves creatures seems more trustworthy than a God who may or may not love creation, and more worthy of praise. A deity who freely chooses whether to love creatures might intentionally choose to harm them. We can't trust that God.

I believe relational love for creation is a *necessary* attribute of the divine essence. God doesn't voluntarily choose to be affected by creatures; the Spirit is necessarily influenced. The divine One is essentially relational, or what might be called "strong divine passibility."⁶⁷

As I interpret it, "God *is* love" means that love is a necessary divine attribute. God *must* love, because it's the Spirit's nature to do so. I add that God has been loving everlasting; the steadfast love of the Lord for creation literally endures forever. If God is essentially loving, and love always involves relational giving and receiving, God must be essentially relational. To put it another way, the Spirit is necessarily and everlastingly passible.

Note that my claim God is "essentially loving" isn't primarily a claim about divine love in Trinity. That's what some theologians say and where they locate divine relationality; I'll address that idea in due time. My claim remains primarily about God's necessary and everlasting loving relations with creatures and creation. The Spirit loves

---

⁶⁶ Darren Iammarino explores these ultimates and others in *Religion and Reality* (Eugene, OR: Pickwick, 2013).

⁶⁷ See my writings on strong passibility, including "Strong Passibility," and "My Response," in *Four Views of Divine Impassibility*, Robert Matz, ed. (Downers Grove, IL: InterVarsity, 2019).

creation no matter what, because love for creaturely others is an *essential* aspect of God's everlasting becoming. To affirm unambiguously God's steadfast love for us, therefore, we should say the Spirit essentially relates with and loves creatures.

If God necessarily relates with creatures, it's *necessarily* true that the Spirit will "never leave you or forsake you" (Dt. 31:6; Heb. 13:5). And it's *necessarily* true that "the steadfast love of the Lord endures forever" (e. g., Ps. 136:1–26). To be consistent, those who say God chooses to relate with creatures should admit that the voluntarist God *could* choose to leave us and forsake us. There's nothing to prevent a contingently-related deity from abandoning creatures or annihilating them. The voluntarist God could give up on the creation project. But the Spirit who essentially and everlastingly relates with creation will *always* and *necessarily* be with, and love, us.

Saying God is essentially relational relieves us from forced attempts at apophatic gymnastics when speaking of eternal divine love. We don't have to appeal unnecessarily to mystery. It doesn't demand that God only necessarily love Godself in Trinity, as so many theologians have argued. Nor does it require us to claim God is beyond being, changeless being, or being-itself, as others have suggested. The God who essentially relates with creation can necessarily and everlastingly love creaturely others in a dynamic way that makes sense.

I'll explore in a later chapter the idea that God everlastingly creates. My point here focuses on love: an attractive metaphysics of love says God essentially relates with and everlastingly loves creation. "God is love" points to the Spirit's everlasting and necessarily relational love for creaturely others.

## Conclusion

The heart of this systematic theology offers a vision of the Spirit who lovingly relates with creation in real, emotional relationships. The Spirit isn't an abstract force or static being; instead, God is a universal, personal presence whose love is both rational and relational. Against theological traditions that consider God in all respects impassible, immutable, and untouched by creatures, this theology of love proposes a Spirit who responds, changes, and is affected by creation.

This Spirit feels with us, expressing emotions such as joy, compassion, anger, and sorrow in response to creatures. Emotions are not imperfections or anthropopathic projections; they're expressions of a God whose essence is steadfast love and whose experience simultaneously becomes shaped by ongoing giving-and-receiving relationship with creatures. I also suggested the Spirit necessarily and everlastingly relates with creation.

The Spirit's essence-experience binate affirms both God's unchanging nature and changing experiences. In a world comprising relational creatures both simple and complex, this systematic theology of love offers a vision of a God always with us, always acting for well-being, and always becoming in relationship.

God is a universal Spirit who expresses giving-and-receiving love.

CHAPTER NINE

# One, Everlasting, All-Knowing Spirit

## THE BIG IDEAS

- Loving is a time-oriented activity for God and creatures.
- Augustine's view that God is timeless has negatively shaped theology.
- God loves everlastingly, which means the Spirit loves in an unending series of moments.
- The Spirit is all-knowing, but the future is open and unknowable.
- To affirm biblical claims about God being wise, we should say God is in time rather than outside it.
- The Spirit's primary mode of knowing is feeling, not seeing.
- The Spirit feels, risks, trusts, and engages in other temporal activities.
- A timely and loving Spirit is free in some respects but not in others.
- God is one despite having various attributes and being an everlasting series of occasions.
- We should reject the classic view of divine simplicity, because the Spirit cannot be simple and also love in ongoing relations with creation.

Theologians have long debated God's relation to time, and what I have proposed in previous chapters bears directly on this discussion. In particular, I've sometimes explicitly, but often implicitly, championed divine loving as time-conditioned activity. Love needs time.

If love requires time, a timeless God can't love, at least not in a way we could understand. An adequate systematic theology of love, therefore, affirms that the Spirit's love is time-dependent rather than timeless. God engages in loving relations with others in chronologically successive moments.[1]

To make sense of God's ongoing love, we are wise to think of the Spirit as an *everlasting* series of divine occasions of experience. That's a precise way of saying the becoming Lover is "in" time rather than "outside" it. God's life consists of an endless succession of relational experiences. The theory that the living Spirit loves moment-by-moment overcomes a host of conceptual problems associated with divine timelessness.

God is also omniscient and wise. The universal Spirit knows all that can be known and sagaciously acts in relation to creation. The Spirit knows perfectly, in part, by directly feeling all that occurs. But God can't be certain what will happen tomorrow, because the future is open, creatures are free, and randomness is real. The Spirit knows what's possible, but deity doesn't foreknow what will occur, because there are no future occurrences that can be known in the present.

Exploring the loving Spirit's relation to time proves important for addressing God's unity. Most theologians believe God has no body parts or divided personality, but some also affirm divine simplicity. This classic view claims there are no conceptual distinctions *at all* in God's nature, nor experiential moments in the divine life. So understood, the doctrine of simplicity is as much at odds with a coherent theology of love as divine timelessness, impassibility, immutability, and controlling omnipotence.

In this chapter, I explore God's relation to time, divine knowing, and unity. I also address divine wisdom, risk, and trust. I argue that the Spirit's pluriform and time-conditioned loving is compatible with the unity of the divine nature and experience. Love requires time, but God's got plenty.

---

[1] This chapter is dedicated to John Sanders. John's important theological work on God and time have greatly influenced me, and I appreciate his courage in standing for his theological convictions.

## Augustine's Views of God and Time

Augustine's beliefs about God and time have highly influenced Western civilization, especially Christians. Scholars often cite his beliefs about divine immutability and impassibility. But Augustine's belief in a timeless God and his waffling about the reality of time powerfully shaped the history of theology.

*The Confessions* may be the most influential book from the most influential theologian whose writings aren't in the Bible. In it, Augustine describes key moments in his Christian conversion and his intellectual development. He wrote the book as a conversational prayer, as Augustine asks God to help him make sense of life, reality, and the divine.

In a major section, Augustine reflects upon time. "Is there anything to which we refer in conversation with more familiarity, any matter of more common experience, than time?"[2] he asks rhetorically. "We know perfectly well what we mean when we speak of [time], and understand just as well when we hear someone else refer to it."[3]

Despite the fact that he affirms we all experience and know time, Augustine says he's unable to explain what it is.[4] Past time is no more, he observes, and future time hasn't happened yet. In a real sense, he argues, neither past nor future exist.[5] We experience time in the present, although it quickly becomes the past. "We can't really say that time exists," Augustine concludes, "except that it tends toward non-being."[6]

Augustine divides time conceptually into units: years, weeks, days, instants. The present moment, he says, can be "reduced to a vanishing

---

[2] Augustine, *The Confessions*, Maria Boulding, trans. (New York: New York City Press, 2023), Book 11 14. 17.

[3] Ibid.

[4] What is time? Defining time is notoriously difficult. Most definitions end in circularity, because they use time language to define time. I assume time can't be defined by something more basic. So defining time as a succession of moments, while circular, is acceptable. As I see it, time is a metaphysical ultimate and, therefore, an experiential nonnegotiable for actual entities. On the difficulty in defining time, see R. T. Mullins, *From Divine Timemaker to Divine Watchmaker: An Exploration of God's Temporality* (New York: Routledge, 2024).

[5] Augustine, *The Confessions*, Book 11, 18. 24; Book 11, 19. 25.

[6] Ibid., Book 11 14. 17.

point."⁷ Measuring time precisely proves difficult, because we only see changes in the phenomena of the universe.⁸ Time itself can't be seen.⁹

What began with Augustine saying we all experience time ends in him claiming that time is only an aspect of our subjectivity. It's just in our heads. Past, present, and future are not objectively real, he says, but "three realities in the mind."¹⁰ The past is in our memory, the present has our attention, and the future represents our expectation.¹¹ "Time is nothing other than tension," says Augustine, "and I would be very surprised if it isn't tension of consciousness itself."¹²

Why would Augustine give up believing in the objective reality of time? A major part of the answer seems to be his view that the unchanging is better than the changing. "I saw quite plainly and with full conviction that anything perishable is inferior to what is imperishable," he says, "and what is constant and unchanging [is] better than what can be changed."¹³ Augustine's convictions reveal influence from Neo-Platonic philosophy's preference for the changeless and timeless.

Augustine's conclusion that time isn't real and that the best is imperishable aligns with him thinking God must be timeless. God is "before all things past and transcends all things future in the sublimity of an eternity which is always in the present," he says.¹⁴ In God's "eternity nothing passes but all is present." "Nothing can happen to you," he says to God, "in your unchangeable eternity."¹⁵ For God resides "above

---

[7] Ibid., Book 11 16. 20.

[8] Ibid., Book 11 27. 36.

[9] Ibid., Book 11 26. 33.

[10] Ibid., Book 11 20. 26.

[11] John Morison comes to the same conclusion. "In Augustine's The Confessions . . . he apparently viewed time as subjective in nature, that is, time was bound up in the soul of man, and being thus bound, time could not exist apart from presence of the soul." John L. Morison, "Augustine's Two Theories of Time," *New Scholasticism*, 45 (1971): 600.

[12] Augustine, *The Confessions*, Book 11 26. 33.

[13] Ibid., Book 7, 1. 1.

[14] Ibid., Book 11, 11. 13.

[15] Ibid., book 11 31. 41. Augustine makes similar claims in his other work. For instance, he says "there isn't anything past as if it has already transpired, nor anything future as if it doesn't yet exist, but whatever is simply is." And "in God's sight, [nothing exists] as past or future, but

all temporal change."[16] And deity "knows all at once," says Augustine, "without any succession of time."[17]

In fact, Augustine believes God made time.[18] "You made all eras of time, and you are before all time," he says to God, "and there was never a 'time' when time did not exist."[19] In other writings, Augustine says time is a "creature."[20] However, he never explains how God creates time and yet time isn't objectively real.

The claim that a timeless God created time leads to numerous problems. A critic might ask, for instance, what God was doing "before" creating time. We sense a problem, because "doing" is a time-oriented word. Augustine responds to this worry by calling it nonsense. There was no time before God created it, he says, so God wasn't "doing" anything.[21]

Augustine's response doesn't solve problems that arise from thinking God is timeless.[22] After all, creating is also a timely activity. To say God created before time was created makes no sense, because "timeless creating" is oxymoronic. Augustine admits to having no solution to this problem.[23]

God's creating also implies a change in God: from not creating; to then creating. But Augustine believes God can't change in any way. He

---

everything is now" (*Eighty-Three Different Questions*, trans. David l. Mosher {Washington DC: Catholic University of America Press, 1982], q. 19). And "God *comprehends* all these in a stable and eternal present . . . Nor is there any difference between his present, past, and future knowledge. His knowledge isn't like ours which has three tenses . . . God's knowledge has no change or variation" (*The City of God Against the Pagans*, trans. and ed. Robert Dyson [Cambridge: Cambridge University Press, 1998], XI, 21).

[16] Ibid., Book 12, 14.

[17] Ibid., Book 12, 13. 16.

[18] Ibid., Book 11, 11.13; 14. 17; 30. 40.

[19] Ibid., Book 11, 13. 16.

[20] Augustine, *On Genesis*, John E. Rotelle, ed. (Hyde Park: New City Press, 2002), 282.

[21] Augustine, *The Confessions*, Book 11, 13. 15.

[22] Brendan Case addresses this in "Augustine's Dilemma: Divine Eternity and the Reality of Temporal Passage," in *Augustine and Time*, Sean Hannan, John Doody, & Kim Paffenroth, eds.(Lanham, MD: Lexington, 2021).

[23] I agree with R. T. Mullins when he says, "no one has been able to explain how a timeless being can be responsible for the existence of time without immediately running into serious philosophical and theological problems, or punting to ineffable mysteries." R. T. Mullins, *Eternal in Love* (Eugene, OR: Cascade, 2024), 43.

acknowledges this problem, but has no answer. "What I don't know," Augustine says, "I don't know."[24] We can appreciate him admitting ignorance but, as I will argue, still reject his views about God and time.

## Criticizing Augustine's Ideas about God and Time

Had Augustine accepted the truth of his own experience, he might have seen the virtue of thinking time must be an experiential non-negotiable. By "experiential non-negotiable," I mean a truth about reality we inevitably live out in practice, even if some people deny it with their words. Rather than thinking time merely in our minds, we're better off believing it an essential element of existence. I call living temporally an experiential non-negotiable, because we all experience the reality of time.[25] And as Alfred North Whitehead puts it, "we must bow to those presumptions, which, in despite of criticism, we still employ for the regulation of our lives."[26]

Second, Augustine mistakenly thinks time is a creature. But without much reflection we'll conclude that time can't be an object existing in the universe or a substance inside our bodies. It's not something in addition to what exists but a constituent factor *in* or *of* all that exists. Physicists speak of "space-time" to describe existing entities, partly for this reason. Anything actually existing is in process.[27]

Third, we are wise to think time is a factor in God's experience too. The becoming Spirit of love is inherently time-oriented. God has a

---

[24] Augustine, *The Confessions*, Book 11, 11. 13.

[25] I explain this in greater detail in "Genuine (but Limited) Freedom for Creatures and for a God of Love," *What's with Free Will?* Philip Clayton and James W. Walters, eds. (Eugene, OR: Cascade, 2020), 51-66.

[26] Alfred North Whitehead, *Process and Reality: An Essay in Cosmology*, Critical edition by D. R. Griffin and D. W. Sherbourne (New York: Macmillan, 1929), 151.

[27] The most eloquent arguments that time is a constitutive of existing entities come from process philosophy. See, for instance, Timothy Eastman, *Untying the Gordian Knot* (New York: Lexington Books, 2020); David Ray Griffin, et. al., *Founders of Constructive Postmodern Philosophy* (Albany: SUNY Press, 1993); Charles Hartshorne, *The Divine Relativity* (New Haven, CT: Yale University Press, 1948); George R. Lucas, *The Genesis of Modern Process Thought* (Metuchen, NJ: Scarecrow, 1983); Nicholas Rescher, *Process Philosophy* (Pittsburgh: University of Pittsburgh Press, 2000); Alfred North Whitehead, *Process and Reality*.

history, in the sense that deity has a past.[28] God experiences in the present moment, because time is a necessary feature of the Spirit's ongoing becoming. God's experiencing is temporal and sequential.

Had Augustine paid closer attention to the ways biblical writers describe God, he might have abandoned his Neo-Platonic belief that God must be timeless. The overwhelming majority of writers in scripture describe God as timefull rather than timeless, as temporal rather than nontemporal, as a personal Experiencer rather than changeless. The God of scripture isn't timeless.[29]

Fourth, saying that God always experiences time allows one to say God existed before our universe began. A timeless God can't exist before creating, because there would be no "before" for a timeless God. "If there is no time prior to creation," explains R. T. Mullins, "then one can't make the biblical affirmation that God exists *before* creation."[30] Both those who embrace the doctrine of *creatio ex nihilo* and those who reject it should say the Spirit acts timefully—in the sense of a succession of moments—rather than timelessly.

Fifth, Augustine's preference for the immutable and timeless leads him to think a time-oriented and changing creation isn't worthy of love. As we saw in earlier chapters, Augustine believed that only the most valuable deserves love. For him, that's God. We shouldn't love creatures for their own sake, he says, and God doesn't love creation for its own sake. This world-devaluing perspective has negatively influenced countless people of faith.[31]

---

[28] I could cite many theologians who agree with Augustine's view of God and time. But I would be remiss if I didn't mention John Calvin, given Calvin's influence upon Christianity. Calvin says, "to [God's] knowledge there is no past or future" (*Institutes of the Christian Religion*, H. Beveridge, trans. [Grand Rapid, MI: Eerdmans, 1989]), 206.

[29] See, for instance, Oscar Cullmann, *Christ and Time*, F. V. Filson, trans. (London: SCM, 1951[rev. ed. 1962]); Terence E. Fretheim, *God and the World in the Old Testament* (Nashville, TN: Abingdon, 2005); John Goldingay, *Israel's Gospel*, Vol. 1 of *Old Testament Theology* (Downers Grove, IL: InterVarsity, 2003); Eldon G. Ladd, *A Theology of the New Testament* (Grand Rapids, MI: Eerdmans, 1974); C.R. Schoonhoven, "Eternity" *International Standard Bible Encyclopedia*, vol. 2, ed. G. W. Bromiley (Grand Rapids, MI: Eerdmans, 1982), 162-164.

[30] Mullins, *Eternal in Love*, 37.

[31] One of the most influential spiritual writings in history comes from Thomas A Kempis's *The Imitation of Christ*. Thomas was heavily influenced by Augustine's theology, and his spirituality is strongly world denying. For my criticism of it, see "Imitating God," in *Exemplars, Imitation, and Character Formation*, Eric Yang, ed. (New York: Routledge, 2025).

Finally, *The Confessions* has a recurring internal inconsistency. Over and over in the book, Augustine prays in conversation. He famously says to God, for instance, "Give me what I love, for I love, indeed, and this love you have given me."[32] And he says, "You, Lord ... have taken pity on us who are earth and ashes, and so it was pleasing in your sight to give new form to my deformity."[33] And so on.

Here's the internal inconsistency: it makes no sense to ask God to "give" something or "have pity" if we also think God is unchanging and unemotional. An immutable, impassible, and timeless deity can't respond to a creature's request, and it can't have pity. Furthermore, we can't even please a God who feels no emotion. Augustine's God can't change from not giving to giving, from not having pity to pity, or from not being pleased to pleased. *The Confessions* is a contradiction.

## The Everlasting Spirit

From what we know of love, it's time-conditioned activity. Love only makes sense if we think time is real for the lover and beloved. The Spirit who loves, therefore, must be timefull rather than timeless, temporal rather than nontemporal. A consistent systematic theology of love affirms time's reality by saying the Spirit of love enjoys temporal experiences rather than rests timelessly.

As my definition of love indicates, love involves action in response to the past, aimed at well-being in the future. Lovers express their actions as they feel and decide in relation to what has come before. They anticipate what might be, in the sense of how their actions might contribute to the good of God, others, self, and/or creation.

The Spirit is also a lover who acts each moment, and divine love responds to creatures and creation. Like creaturely lovers, the Spirit aims to promote well-being in future moments. God feels what has

---

[32] Augustine, *The Confessions*, 22. 28.
[33] Ibid., Book 7, 8. 12.

come before and decides what might best establish flourishing, beauty, justice, and overall well-being. Lovers experience moments in succession.[34]

The biblical authors repeatedly assume love as time-oriented—for both creatures and Creator.[35] Take divine compassion as a prime example. "I have seen the misery of my people in Egypt," Yahweh says in response to Israel being enslaved. "I have heard them crying out because of their slave drivers, and I am concerned about their suffering" (Exod 3:7-8). In compassion, God timefully works to liberate Israel from Pharaoh and lead the people to a land of milk and honey.

The Psalmist uses the language of an empathetic father to talk about God's timely love. "As a father has compassion on his children," he says, "so the Lord has compassion on those who honor him" (Ps. 103:13). The Psalmist also declares, "You, O Lord, are a God full of compassion, and gracious, long suffering and abundant in mercy and truth" (Ps. 86:15; cf Ps. 145:8-9; Is. 49:13). Divine "long suffering" would make no sense if God were timeless.

Jesus shows us a Father who, "filled with compassion," runs to meet his prodigal son and reunite him to the family (Lk. 15:11-31). Compassion is an inherently time-oriented activity, and the compassionate one empathizes with the suffering of others. In response, the lover acts for the good of those suffering. Here we have action in the present, aimed at a better future. "Timeless compassion" is an oxymoron.

This way of thinking of God, love, and time fits scripture and our own experience. African theologian John S. Mbiti points to a similar view when he says, "According to traditional concepts, time is a two-dimensional phenomenon, with a long past, a present, and virtually no future." In fact, he says, the future is absent, "because events

---

[34] Thomas Aquinas denies that God experiences the successive moments of time and calls God "eternal." He explains his view by saying, "Eternity differs from time in this way: time has its being in a sort of succession, whereas the being of eternity is entirely simultaneous." See Aquinas, *Summa Contra Gentiles,* III.I 61, 2.

[35] Richard Holland rightly notes that much of the philosophical debate about God and time occur with little to no influence from Christian scripture. If scripture were to influence the debate, it provides strong evidence for divine temporality. See *God, Time and the Incarnation* (Eugene, OR: Wipf and Stock, 2012).

which lie in it have not taken place, they have not been realized and can't, therefore, constitute time."[36] An open and relational approach comports with traditional African views of time.

If God loves essentially and everlastingly, as I've proposed, time should be seen as an essential dimension of the divine life.[37] Consequently, an essentially loving Spirit can't be eternally timeless. As the biblical writers say often, "The steadfast love of the Lord endures forever."[38] God experiences a succession of moments in the everlasting divine life.

To say "the Spirit is everlasting" means that God always exists, having never begun to be and never ceasing. God is immortal. The divine life is comprised of an unending sequence of occasions of experience. No future moments already exist in God, because the future isn't actual. No past moments exist, although the Spirit remembers what has happened. Like us, the Spirit lives in successive, present moments.[39] Put philosophically, the view called "presentism" expresses the truth of temporal existing.[40]

Some theologians say that God existed timelessly and then entered time after creating. This means the period of God's timelessness must have been a phase or span. But we understand phases and spans as

---

[36] John S. Mbiti, *African Religions and Philosophy* (Garden City, NY: Doubleday, 1969), 21.

[37] A number of theologians and philosophers make this argument. For instance, see R. T. Mullins, *From Divine Timemaker to Divine Watchmaker*; Schubert Ogden, "The Temporality of God," in *The Reality of God and Other Essays* (London: SCM, 1960); Nicholas Wolterstorff, "God Everlasting," in *Philosophical Perspectives on Eternity*, Linda Martin Alcoff and John D. Caputo, eds. (New York: Fordham University Press, 2001), 111–132.

[38] Eternal vs Everlasting. These two words are often used interchangeably in everyday speaking and in biblical translations. But I use "eternal" to mean timeless and "everlasting" to mean a beginningless and endless succession of moments of time.

[39] Presentism. The philosophical view of time I embrace is often called "presentism." It says the present moment becomes actual. The future isn't actual, and the past was once actual. All that actually exists, exists now.

[40] For defenses of presentism, see William Lane Craig, *God, Time, and Eternity: The Coherence of Theism II* (Dordrecht, NL: Kluwer Academic Publishers, 2001); R. T. Mullins, *The End of the Timeless God* (Oxford: Oxford University Press, 2016); Alan G. Padgett, *God, Eternity, and the Nature of Time* (Downers Grove, IL: InterVarsity, 2000); Richard Swinburne, *Space and Time*, 2nd ed. (Oxford: Oxford University Press, 1981); Dean Zimmerman, "The Privileged Present: Defending an 'A-Theory' of Time," in *Oxford Studies in Metaphysics, Vol. 5*, David Manley, David J. Chalmers, and Ryan Wasserman, eds. (Oxford: Oxford University Press, 2009), 211-249.

temporal rather than timeless, so a God with phases and spans can't be without time. Instead of saying a timeless God created and entered time, it's better to say deity everlastingly becomes, moment by moment, as a universal Spirit of love.

In sum, God doesn't stand outside time and see past, present, and future as a settled block. Instead, the living Spirit experiences ongoing time like creatures do, chronologically.[41] The Bible knows nothing of timeless existing, because a living Spirit who loves moment by moment isn't timeless. Divine love has an ongoing history as an everlasting series of moments.

## All-Knowing

The positive implications of believing God experiences time are wide ranging. Divine love makes better sense, as I've pointed out, when it's understood as involving experiential moments. Perhaps the best-known reason to say God resides "in" time or temporally, however, is that this view makes better sense of the Spirit's knowing in relation to creaturely freedom.

Humans (and perhaps other creatures) act with a measure of freedom. This is another experiential nonnegotiable: we all act freely even if some people deny this freedom with their words.[42] We each choose moment by moment in light of a limited number of options, and a host of factors influence our choosing. Our freedom is genuine but always limited. To choose freely involves exerting self-causation in response

---

[41] Fortunately, this view of God is also present outside the Christian tradition. Find it, for instance, in the Bhakti tradition, as articulated by Swami Padmanabha, *Evolution in Divine Love* (Mill Spring, NC: Inword, 2025); in Islam, as articulated by Saida Mirsadri, "Iqbal's Process Worldview: Toward a New Islamic Understanding of the Divine Action" in *Divine Action*, John Sanders and Klaus von Stosch, eds. (Leiden: Brill, 2022), Michael Lodahl, "The (brief) openness debate in Islamic theology," *Creation Made Free: Open Theology Engaging Science*, Thomas Jay Oord, ed. (Eugene, OR: Pickwick, 2009), 53–68; in Judaism, as articulated by Toba Spitzer, *God is Here* (New York: St. Martins, 2022).

[42] David Ray Griffin calls experiential nonnegotiables "hard-core commonsense notions." See his *Unsnarling the World-Knot: Consciousness, Freedom, and the Mind-Body Problem* (Berkeley: University of California Press, 1998), 34, 210. Jürgen Habermas calls them "performative contradictions." See his "Discourse Ethics: Notes on a Program of Philosophical Justification," in *Moral Consciousness and Communicative Action*, trans. C. Lenhardt and S.W. Nicholsen (Cambridge, MA: MIT Press, 1990).

to past influences in light of live options. A free person could have done otherwise than what she did.

Theologians who say God predestines are obviously at odds with creaturely freedom. We can't be free if God entirely determines us. Some theologians reject predestination, therefore, but still say God foreknows all that will happen. Open and relational scholars disagree, and they argue God can't foreknow all that will occur if creatures are free choosers.[43]

Take Thomas Aquinas as an example of one who thinks God foreknows all that will happen. God "has knowledge even of things that are not," says Aquinas, and "the present glance of God extends over all time, and to all things which exist in any time, as to objects present to Him."[44] This means God knows the future with certainty, because it's already "present to Him." To put it another way, Aquinas thinks a timeless God knows past, present, and future all at once, as if it were a single block of completed actions.

Other theologians say God knows what will happen, because God chose to create the best of all possible worlds. Before creating, God could foresee all possible occurrences in all possible histories, so God foreknew what any creature would do in any circumstance. And because deity is good, God chose the best possible history: ours. Theologians who make this claim typically say God's knowing is error-free, in the sense of knowing past, present, and future as necessarily true.[45]

If God knows with certainty what a person will choose and deity can't be wrong, it stands to reason that people can't choose other than what God knows to be true. They have no *live* options; there's only one path. What will occur has, in some way, been settled, and God could only be certain what will occur if the future were already decided.

---

[43] Christopher Fisher argues this point upon examining key biblical texts. See *God is Open: Examining the Open Theism of the Biblical Authors* (Christopher Fisher, 2017).

[44] Thomas Aquinas, *Summa Theologica*, I, q. 14, art 9.

[45] Richard Swinburne argues that God can't know future contingent statements before they have happened. See *The Coherence of Theism* (Oxford: Clarendon, 1977), ch. 10.

Saying God knows the decided future undermines the idea that creatures freely choose among live options. A settled future is incompatible with free choice. What's settled is no longer live.

A common response to this problem says God's foreknowing doesn't *cause* the future to be settled, fixed, or decided. Knowledge doesn't determine outcomes, goes the argument, so foreknowing can't contradict freedom. For argument's sake, it doesn't matter. God can only be certain what will happen if the future is *already* settled, no matter who or what did the settling. And a settled future is irreconcilable with choosing among live options.

Some people of faith assume a consistent free-will theology has to deny that God knows everything. But we don't have to say this. We can believe God knows all that's knowable—past, present, and what's possible—without saying God knows the future.[46] In other words, the loving Spirit knowing *possible* futures is compatible with creatures freely choosing among multiple options.[47]

This systematic theology of love embraces the view that God is omniscient. The Spirit knows all facts about what has already happened, all that's publicly knowable in the present,[48] and all possibilities about the future. The Spirit also innately knows all truths of mathematics, logic, the forms, and so on; these are ideas, abstractions, information, or eternal objects in the divine mind.[49] The Spirit who loves has

---

[46] Open theists often rightly point out biblical passages that portray God as not being certain about what will happen in the future. As an example, see Eric Sentell, "Bible Verses that Show God is Not Omniscient," *Saving Faith* (Substack), Jan. 7, 2026, https://ericsentell.substack.com/p/bible-verses-that-show-god-is-not

[47] Alan Rhoda lays out a variety of open theist options in *Open Theism* (Cambridge: Cambridge University Press, 2024).

[48] Public Knowledge. I use the word "public" here to distinguish between first-person knowledge of what occurs in the moment and third-person knowledge of what has occurred. A creature experiences in the moment and has first-hand knowledge of this experiencing. But it isn't public (third-person) yet. God comes to know *all* these creaturely experiences as a third-person knower. Some call this *de se* knowledge. We can't expect God or anyone else to know first-person experiencing, however, but it isn't yet knowledge that is publicly available. On this issue, see Patrick Grim, "Problems of Omniscience," in *Debating Christian Theism*, J. P. Moreland, et. al., eds. (Oxford: Oxford University Press, 2013), 176-78.

[49] On the doctrine of divine ideas, see Thomas Ward, *Divine Ideas* (Cambridge: Cambridge University Press, 2020).

maximal cognitive excellency without being certain what will happen in the future.[50]

## God as Wise

"Wise" is one of the more prominent but underappreciated biblical descriptions of the Spirit. According to several authors of scripture, God creates using wisdom, through wisdom, or with wisdom (e. g., Prov. 3:19-20; Ps. 104:24). The Spirit's understanding and prudence derive from wise decision-making in relation to creation (e. g., Prov. 2:2, 8:5, 12). The Psalms, the book of Job, and Proverbs even personify divine wisdom as female, and biblical scholars refer to this personification as "Lady Wisdom" or "Woman Wisdom."[51] In this image, we have a poetic personification of God's intimate activity for personal summons.[52]

In the New Testament, the Gospel writers present Jesus as the personification of divine wisdom. We find this especially pronounced in the Gospel of John, but the theme is present in Mark, Matthew and Luke too. Jesus is God's wisdom incarnate.[53] The Pauline epistles also speak of God/Christ being wise and Jesus as incarnating divine wisdom.[54]

The Spirit's wisdom prompts the writers of John's gospel to say simply, "God is light." This isn't a reference to photons or visual brilliance but to living wisdom. The passage says that "if we say that we have fellowship with [the Word] while we are walking in darkness, we lie and don't do what is true. But if we walk in the light as he himself is in the light, we have fellowship with one another, and blood of Jesus his Son

---

[50] R. T. Mullins uses "maximal cognitive excellency" in *Eternal in Love*, ch. 2.

[51] The theme appears prominently in the intertestamental scriptures of Sirach, Baruch, and Wisdom of Solomon. For an exploration of these, see Dustin L. Smith, *Wisdom Christology in the Gospel of John* (Eugene, OR: Wipf and Stock, 2024).

[52] On this, see Burton L. Mack and Roland E. Murphy, "Wisdom Literature," in *Early Judaism and Its Modern Interpreters*, Robert A Kraft and George W. E. Nickelsburg, eds. (Atlanta: Scholars Press, 1986), 377.

[53] See Dustin L. Smith's arguments in his book, *Wisdom Christology in the Gospel of John*.

[54] e.g., Rom 8:3; 1 Cor. 1:24; 8:6; Gal. 4:4-6; Eph. 1:6; Col. 1:15-20; Heb. 1:2

cleanses us from all sin" (1:5-7). In other words, "walking" with a wise God leads to fellowship and spiritual health, because these intimately link with wisdom.

Traditional systematic theologians tend to focus upon the content of divine knowledge and underappreciate God's wise decision-making. This lack of appreciation reflects their assumption that God is timeless. Wisdom as we know it, after all, involves temporal mental activity that draws from the past, evaluates the present, and discerns what may be beneficial. Wisdom must be time-oriented, therefore, rather than timeless.

To put it negatively, a timeless God can't engage in a process of being wise. The foreknowing God would be certain what will occur. But there's no need for a deity who knows the future to discern, ponder, or act prudently in the present. Those who want to take biblical passages about God's wise decision-making seriously, therefore, should reject theologies that say a timeless God has exhaustive foreknowledge.[55]

Part of what it means to love, as I have argued, is to aim to promote overall well-being. That involves wisdom. A wise lover promotes well-being more effectively, because she draws from the past and present when aiming for future flourishing. A wise lover discerns. The wise and universal Spirit discerns while experiencing the flow of time and will be, consequently, the most effective Lover. The everlasting One who always acts wisely is omnisophic, or all-wise.[56]

Wisdom assumes the reality of time, so a timeless God can't act wisely.

## Feeling, Risk, and Trust

A cluster of issues arise pertaining to God's knowing and relation to time. First, it matters *how* God knows. Just about every theologian believes God innately knows necessary truths about math, abstractions,

---

[55] Although acknowledging the biblical support for open theism, Manuel Schmid criticizes some open theists for making grand claims that the text doesn't always support. See *God in Motion* (Waco, TX: Baylor University Press, 2021).

[56] I'm grateful to Wm. Curtis Holtzen for suggesting omnisophic.

definitions, the divine nature, and so on. When it comes to how God knows concrete facts about creatures and creation, however, we should say the Spirit's mode of knowing is experiential.

Most who say God stands outside time think deity knows history by timelessly seeing it. The God "over there" watches what's happening "over here." From this distance, the argument goes, God knows past, present, and future by looking at it, all at once. To cite Aquinas again: "the present glance of God extends over all time."[57] Although Aquinas would also say God is omnipresent, his "seeing" way of knowing depicts God as a detached voyeur.

By contrast, this systematic theology of love says God's knowing comes through feeling. The universal and relational Spirit of love knows what's happening because all creatures and creation influence the Spirit. An omnipresent and relational God knows through immediate feeling rather than by watching from afar. We should think of God as a feeler, not a voyeur.

Our experience also tells us that empathy is crucial for loving well. Compassion, caring, celebrating, and other forms of love require feeling with the beloved. And the more direct the feeling, the better. The universal Spirit feels directly by empathy when rejoicing with those who rejoice and mourning with those who mourn (Rom. 12:15). As John Wesley puts it, God "is present in every part of the universe, [so] he can't but know whatever is, or is done there."[58] The Spirit's empathy plays a key role in judging the value of creaturely actions, and this evaluating involves obtaining information that comes by feeling.

Divine empathy aligns well with saying a loving Spirit takes risks. In *The God Who Risks*, John Sanders proposes a "risk model" of theology.[59] God's covenant with creation, says Sanders, "isn't a detailed script but a broad intention that allows for a variety of options regarding

---

[57] Thomas Aquinas, *Summa Theologica*, I, q. 14, art 9.

[58] John Wesley, "The Unity of the Divine Being," in *The Works of John Wesley, Volume 4: Sermons IV (115–151)*, ed. Albert C. Outler (Nashville, TN: Abingdon, 1987), 62.

[59] John Sanders, *The God Who Risks: A Theology of Providence*, rev. ed. (Downers Grove, IL: InterVarsity, 2007 [1998]), 16.

precisely how it may be reached."[60] The risk-taking God "grants humans genuine freedom to participate in this project, and he doesn't force them to comply."[61] But this means, says Sanders, that God "doesn't get everything he desires."[62]

If we begin with empathetic love and believe the future is open, divine risk-taking makes sense. After all, "love takes risks," says Sanders, "and is willing to wait and try again if need be."[63] Success in love isn't guaranteed. And risking only makes sense if the Spirit is everlasting through time not timelessly eternal.

In fact, Jesus reveals God's risk taking. His life, death, and resurrection reveal that "God isn't the all-determining power," says Sanders, but seeks to "win our hearts through the weakness of the cross and the power of the resurrection." The God who risks makes sense when "love doesn't force its own way."[64]

If God takes risks, however, deity won't be certain what will occur.[65] A risking Spirit doesn't foreknow. And this uncertainty demands a measure of trust.

Wm. Curtis Holtzen argues in favor of a God who trusts, and Holtzen uses the logic of love for his argument. "Any person who genuinely loves another must have faith in the other or, minimally, desire to have faith." So "trust is a willingness to risk something of value to

---

[60] Ibid., 244. See also Anne Dufourmantelle, *In Praise of Risk* (New York: Fordham University Press, 2016).

[61] Ibid., 174.

[62] Ibid., 207.

[63] Ibid., 179.

[64] Ibid., 193. Some of Sanders's language in *The God Who Risks* suggests he believes God is voluntarily self-limited. This means divine risk-taking in his scheme differs in some ways from the risk taking of an amipotent God who can't control others. But both open and relational models point to a God who risks.

[65] Divine Risk Models. One can question the degree of risk present in various open and relational models of God. Models that retain belief in divine omnipotence seem be less risky, insofar as God could omnipotently bring about particular states of affairs. Models that say God has pre-planned contingency plans for all free creaturely choices seem even less risky. Models such as the one I propose say divine risks pertain to how well the choices God makes will bring well-being, should creatures cooperate.

the care of another person."⁶⁶ Because God loves and risks something valuable, the Spirit trusts.

If God were wholly self-sufficient and had the power to control, says Holtzen, God would not need to trust. But if the Spirit is relational and uncontrolling, deity depends upon creation to achieve the goals of love. "As creative relational love," says Holtzen, "God's very nature moves God to trust humanity, especially those proven trustworthy, but also to take a risk on those who have not."⁶⁷

Holtzen's arguments fit nicely with biblical passages that identify the covenants God enters into with creatures. These covenants may be with individuals (Abraham), nations (Israel), communities (the church), humans in general (Adamic), or all creation (Noah story). "While it is an open future that allows covenants to be authentic," says Holtzen, "God trusts bravely but not blindly . . . Even when the risk is too great to partner and trust," he says, God's "hope that situations will change always remains."⁶⁸

The living Spirit is wise, feels, takes risks, and trusts in covenant.⁶⁹

## Is a Timely and Loving Spirit Free?

Claims about the Spirit's relation to time and knowing have implications for how we think about divine freedom. Saying God must love creatures might lead some people to think the amipotent Spirit isn't free. If deity, by nature, must love, God isn't free to do otherwise. An amipotent God, therefore, must be bound, although this binding isn't by external forces.⁷⁰ An essentially loving Spirit, it may seem, has no options from which to choose freely.

---

[66] Wm. Curtis Holtzen, *The God Who Trusts: A Relational Theology of Divine Faith, Hope, and Love* (Downers Grove, IL: IVP Academic, 2019), 28.

[67] Ibid., 128-29.

[68] Ibid., 143-45.

[69] Ann Pederson expresses this as improvisation in *God, Creation, and All That Jazz* (St. Louis, MO: Chalice, 2001).

[70] On the idea that open and relational theologies portray God as bound, see Douglas Wilson, ed., *Bound Only Once* (Moscow, ID: Canon, 2001).

Traditional theologies that consider God in all respects timeless and necessarily loving *do* present a deity who isn't free. The deity outside time foreknows with certainty what creatures will do, and a necessarily loving God would only do what's best. Consequently, a timeless God who foreknows and necessarily loves *must* bring about optimal flourishing in pre-decided ways.[71] A necessarily loving and timeless deity isn't free to do otherwise.

We seem caught in a dilemma. On one hand, a God who doesn't necessarily love creation can freely stop loving it and create evil worlds. This is the implication of traditional theologies that deny God necessarily loves creation. For them, the Spirit's love is an arbitrary choice. But I say we shouldn't trust a deity who can freely stop loving. Nothing—not even God's nature—prevents this deity from being a moral monster.

On the other hand, a timeless God who loves creation necessarily also would foreknow all that will occur. This timeless deity would apparently know precisely what brings the most good and act necessarily in light of it. This deity isn't free to do other than what God foreknows to be best, from all eternity. This God is bound.

A theology that rejects divine timelessness offers a third, and better, model of God's necessary love for creation. It assumes God moves through time as creatures do, and there is no knowable future. The living Spirit loves in the present and faces an open future comprised of real possibilities. Not even God knows with absolutely certainty what will occur.

The loving Spirit who faces an open future can't be certain what free creatures will do. Consequently, deity can't be sure which possibilities, if chosen by God or by creatures, will best promote flourishing. Some options certainly won't be good, of course, and others are unlikely to promote well-being. Committing murder, incest, and genocide will not promote flourishing, so God doesn't call creatures to choose them. But God can't be certain which among the many *good* possibilities will best establish love, beauty, and justice, especially in the distant future.

---

[71] On God's freedom to create a less than best world, see William L. Rowe, *Can God Be Free?* (Oxford: Oxford University Press, 2004).

The Spirit can't be certain, because time is real, creatures make free choices, and random events occur.

So... the Spirit woos, invites, or calls creatures to choose among the best options in each moment, without being certain of the outcomes. *How* the Spirit loves each moment is something the Spirit freely decides.[72] That's contingent. Because the future is open and love comes first in God, the Spirit freely urges creation toward optimal outcomes.[73]

Consequently, the amipotent and time-oriented Spirit is free in one sense but not free in another. If we think freedom includes the ability to make intentional choices moment-by-moment amid real possibilities and not be entirely determined by external forces and factors, the amipotent Spirit is free.[74] God freely woos us toward some forms of love over others, depending on the creature and circumstance. But the Spirit *must* love, because love comes first in the divine nature. When it comes to *whether* God loves, God must.

## One But Not Simple

The Spirit who loves is one. To make this claim may seem uncontroversial, because divine oneness seems inherent to monotheism. But for various reasons, God's oneness *is* controversial.

We can find strong biblical support for believing in multiple deities. Although monotheists like me cite the phrase "Hear O, Israel, the Lord is one" (Dt. 6:4), other passages identify many gods and a council of gods. The Psalmist says, "there is none like you among the gods, O Lord" (86:8), and "for great is the Lord, and greatly to be praised; he is to be revered above all gods" (96:4). In Exodus, Yahweh plans to

---

[72] Ryan Patrick McLaughlin has challenged my view of divine freedom. His challenge has helped me to be clearer that God's lack of knowledge about how immediate actions will benefit distant events is one key to affirming God's freedom in choosing how to love. For McLaughlin's essay, see "The Loving God Incapable of Love," in *Amipotence*, vol. 1, Chris. S. Baker, et. al., eds. (Grasmere, ID: SacraSage, 2025).

[73] Chad Bahl offers an accessible defense of an open and relational God in his book, *God Unbound: An Evangelical Reconsiders Tradition in Search of Truth* (Grasmere, ID: SacraSage, 2021).

[74] See Tim Mawson's discussion of this and other attributes of God in *The Divine Attributes* (Cambridge: Cambridge University Press, 2018).

execute judgment "on all the gods of Egypt" (12:12), and Numbers says, "Yahweh executed judgments against their gods" (33:4).

In fact, an early commandment in the Decalogue assumes many deities: "You shall have no other gods before me" (Ex. 20:3). The biblical authors often describe God instructing Israel to worship and obey only their deity, and this suggests they assumed henotheism (one God for each group) rather than monotheism. Even New Testament writers speak of multiple deities (e.g., 1 Cor. 8:5).

We can make a strong biblical argument that Israel gradually transitioned from polytheism and henotheism to monotheism.[75] This process was eventually solidified with monotheism becoming the majority view in Christian theology.[76] But the fact that scripture writers sometimes refer to multiple deities and other times say there is only one deity should remind us that the Bible doesn't provide a tightly uniform testimony. Its witness, as I have shown elsewhere, is pluriform and polyphonic.[77] In the question of divine unity, therefore, we have another case in which systematic theologians must decide which biblical ideas to embrace and which to ignore or explain.[78]

A counter-intuitive view emerged early in Christianity as those early theologians sought to establish God's oneness. Most call it the doctrine of divine simplicity. The doctrine, still accepted by some

---

[75] For instance, see Robert Karl Gnuse, *No Other Gods: Emergent Monotheism in Israel* (Sheffield, England: Sheffield Academic, 1997); Mark S. Smith, *The Early History of God: Yahweh and the Other Deities in Ancient Israel*. 2nd ed. (Grand Rapids, MI: Eerdmans, 2002), *The Origins of Biblical Monotheism: Israel's Polytheistic Background and the Ugaritic Texts* (Oxford: Oxford University Press, 2001).

[76] Arguably, the Latter-Day Saint tradition is one exception to the solidifying of monotheism in Christianity.

[77] See Thomas Jay Oord, *Pluriform Love: An Open and Relational Account of Well-Being* (Grasmere, ID: SacraSage, 2023), chs. 2-3.

[78] Unity and Trinity. After the Bible was written, another obstacle to divine unity emerged. When trying to account for Jesus of Nazareth, many Christians embraced trinitarian theologies. Many trinitarian theologies seem, on their face, to undermine monotheism. Trinitarians typically say the one God is three persons, and the word "triune" is their way to affirm both divine oneness and threeness. Other Christians join Muslims, Jews, and Unitarians to criticize trinitarian thinking. They do so, in part, because saying God is three persons sounds like three agents rather than one. Some advocates of the social trinity even claim the three persons have unique wills, distinct actions, and each relates with the others. This sounds like polytheism. I will address these concerns later, but I raise them here to highlight controversies related to divine unity.

today, says God has no parts, properties, experiences, or attributes. The simple God is beyond any conceptual categories, and this deity doesn't respond to creatures, have experiences, or live timefully.

Augustine affirms this view. "God has no properties but is pure essence,"[79] he says. He also denies the philosophical category of "accidents," or things which are contingent, when affirming divine simplicity. Accidental properties "can be lost or diminished," says Augustine, and they exist "in relation to something." Examples include "friendships, relationships, services, likenesses, equalities, and anything else of the kind," he says. And accidental properties, for him, include "places and times, acts and passions."[80] According to Augustine, God neither has nor experiences any of these.

To the simple God, "*nothing* is said to be according to accident," says Augustine.[81] This means a simple deity can't act, relate, be a friend, experience time, have emotions, or be anything like creatures. All divine attributes collapse into one, with absolutely no distinctions. In God, according to this view, we find no plurality of any kind.

Conceptual problems arise for those who embrace divine simplicity. The act of loving, for instance, includes most, if not all, the accidents and activities Augustine denies of God. A simple deity can't act, relate, experience, feel emotion, or experience time. Consequently, a simple God can't love, at least not in any way we understand. It may ultimately be impossible to imagine a simple deity at all.

Take another problem: divine simplicity advocates say we should think of God's existing and creating as identical. We can't separate them. But think about it: if God necessarily exists, and God's existing and creating are identical, then God necessarily creates. Therefore, creation would exist necessarily.[82] Yet Augustine and others reject these

---

[79] Augustine, *On Trinity*, Book 6, 7.

[80] Ibid, Book 5, 17.

[81] Ibid.

[82] On this issue, see R. T. Mullins, "Classical Theism," in *T & T Clark Handbook of Analytic Theology*, James M. Arcadi and James T. Turner, Jr., eds. (London: Bloomsbury, 2021), 85-100;

implications lurking in their view of simplicity. This issue (and many others) points to inconsistencies in traditional theologies.[83]

Divine simplicity contradicts the logic of divine love.

## God's Essence is to Exist, Part Two

In an earlier chapter, we explored Thomas Aquinas's claim that God's essence is to exist (*ipsum esse subsistens*), which has various meanings. If it means the Spirit's nature isn't an object, entity, or thing, we should agree. An essence refers to an abstraction or definition, not an actual object. And if "God's essence is to exist" means deity exists necessarily, affirming that would be entirely appropriate. Saying God must exist can be a helpful way to understand divine aseity.[84]

But advocates of divine simplicity also use the phrase "God's essence is to exist" to say there can be no conceptual differences between the divine attributes. Because God has, or is, one essence, goes the argument, God has, or is, just one attribute or property. We might put this in a formula: the divine essence = divine existence = divine attribute/property. Combined with timelessness, advocates of divine simplicity end up saying God exists all at once and has no conceptual distinctions *at all*.

---

[83] James Dolezal is a contemporary advocate of divine simplicity. See his book, *God without Parts: Divine Simplicity and the Metaphysics of God's Absoluteness*, Eugene, OR: Pickwick Publications, 2011). For strong argument against classic divine simplicity, see William Hasker, "Is Divine Simplicity a Mistake?" *American Catholic Philosophical Quarterly*, 90:4 (2016): 699–725; R. T. Mullins, "Simply Impossible: A Case Against Divine Simplicity," *Journal of Reformed Theology*, 7 (2013): 181-203; Mullins, *The End of the Timeless God*, (Oxford: Oxford University Press, 2016); Timothy O'Connor, "Simplicity and Creation," *Faith and Philosophy*, 16 (1999): 405-412; Alvin Plantinga, *Does God Have a Nature?* (Milwaukee: Marquette University Press, 1980); Richard Swinburne, *The Christian God* (Oxford: Oxford University Press, 1994); Nicholas Wolterstorff, "Divine Simplicity," *Philosophical Perspectives 5*, J. Tomberlin, ed. (Atascadero: Ridgeview, 1991), 531–552.

[84] Divine Aseity. Divine aseity has come to mean many things, some of which I affirm, others I reject. If aseity means God necessarily exists, is everlasting, perfect, has an immutable and self-derived essence, is self-derived, and depends on nothing outside deity for God's existence (self-existent), I affirm it. If aseity means God is wholly independent, impassible, can exist alone, timeless, has no conceptual distinctions, and can create *ex nihilo*, I reject it. My reasons for affirming some meanings of aseity but rejecting others comes, ultimately, from my understanding of God's nature of love, which includes love for creatures.

This systematic theology of love rejects divine simplicity as traditionally understood.[85] Among many reasons for doing so, it's hard to imagine how a simple God could be a loving person. Or how God could live freely. Philosopher Alvin Plantinga puts it this way, "If God is a property, then he isn't a person but a mere abstract object; he has no knowledge, awareness, power, love, or life. So taken," says Plantinga, "the simplicity doctrine seems an utter mistake."[86] Theologian R. T. Mullins says this doctrine "should not be allowed to plague Christianity anymore."[87] I agree. I would add that divine simplicity shouldn't be embraced by *any* coherent theology of love, Christian or otherwise.

Systematic theologians can, and should, make distinctions about God's nature, actions, and experiences. They should also distinguish among a living Spirit's diverse experiences. A time-oriented deity undergoes a series of experiences that differ one from another. We can affirm this without saying God has parts, multiple personalities, or objective segments.[88] God can have multiple attributes and experiences but still be unified as a single person.

We best understand divine unity, therefore, as saying that God exists as just one deity, not many gods. This One has various traits and characteristics that persist in the divine nature as immutable attributes. This Spirit is one person who makes decisions from this unitive perspective as a Self and also receives from creation in this unity. The deity's multiple experiences, multiple actions, and multiple characteristics don't require the Spirit to be multiple in essences.

The one God loves in a myriad of ways.

---

[85] Katherine Sonderegger takes the unity of God as her orienting concern in systematic theology. Her work mirrors much of classical theology, including her affirmation of traditional notions of omnipotence and omniscience. Love isn't her orienting concern. See *Systematic Theology: The Doctrine of God* (Minneapolis: Fortress, 2015).

[86] Alvin Plantinga, *Does God Have a Nature?* (Milwaukee: Marquette University Press, 1980), 47.

[87] Mullins, *Eternal in Love*, 3. See also Timothy O'Connor, "The Unity of the Divine Nature: Four Theories," in *Classical Theism*, Jonathan Fuqua and Robert C. Koons, eds. (London: Routledge, 2023).

[88] On this issue, see Eberhard Jüngel, *God as the Mystery of the World*, Darrell L. Guder, trans. (Grand Rapids, MI: Eerdmans: Edinburgh: T&T Clark, 1983), 107.

## Conclusion

An adequate systematic theology of love will reject the views of Augustine and other theologians who claim God is timeless. A theology of love says the Spirit experiences the flow of time. Ongoing time must be real for God, because the loving Spirit temporally engages others. This means God doesn't see past, present, and future all at once, as if they were a timeless snapshot, as Augustine and Aquinas believed.[89] The loving Spirit is everlasting, living, and an unending series of divine experiences.

Divine omniscience includes knowing all that can be known—including everything actual and possible. A loving God can't know the actual future, because there is no actual future: it doesn't yet exist. But the Spirit directly feels creation moment by moment, in the present, with receptive empathy.

Biblical writers often depict God as making wise decisions. The authors of scripture portray the Spirit's wisdom not as timeless knowledge but as relational discernment within time. A timeless and foreknowing God can't undergo the process of being wise, because that deity would experience no processes. By contrast, the loving Spirit exercises wise discernment, while aiming at promoting overall well-being.

The Spirit knows not by detached seeing but through empathetic feeling. Scripture portrays God as one who risks in making covenants, granting freedom even when doing so might frustrate divine aims. The Spirit also entrusts creation with real responsibility and hopes for faithfulness in return. The wise One feels, risks, and trusts.

The Spirit's dynamic life is unified despite being an everlasting series of moments. This unity doesn't require classic simplicity, which erases all distinctions among attributes in the divine nature. Nor does it negate all moments in the divine experience. The universal Spirit enjoys a unity of life and nature, because God is love.

The Loving Spirit is everlasting, all knowing, and one.

---

[89] On these issues, see Vaughn Baker, "Timeless Eternity or Temporal Existence," in *Uncontrolling Love*, Chris Baker, et. al., eds. (Grasmere, ID: SacraSage, 2017).

CHAPTER TEN

# The Proper Role of Mystery

## THE BIG IDEAS

- I'm not certain God exists, but I think it's more plausible than not.
- Rather than rethink their views of God, some theologians play defense and appeal to mystery.
- Some theologians appeal to utter mystery by saying God is absolutely unknowable.
- Appropriate appeals to mystery say we can't be certain about God or know deity fully, but we aren't clueless.
- Saying God is transcendent and immanent means God is like creatures in some ways but different from them in others.
- Saying God is "infinite" leads to numerous problems, but the word can be salvaged.
- Good theologies are theopoetic, because they admit we construct our views of God in response to various influences.
- Good theologies portray God as neither too big nor too small, neither too different from us nor too similar, neither too vague nor too definite.

At the outset of this systematic theology of love, I explored both reasons to believe God exists and reasons to doubt. I mentioned my own journey from belief to unbelief and why I then returned to faith.

Today, I'm not certain of God's existence, but I think it's more plausible than not. I live in reasonable risk, affirming a universal, loving Spirit as real and active, and I try to pattern my life after that Lover. But I could be wrong.

I have argued that a systematic theology of love ought to be rationally consistent as it draws from the biblical witness, lived experience, and other sources. I've criticized traditional theologies for failing in these ways, including influential theologians like Augustine and Aquinas and contemporary theologians like Paul Tillich and Wayne Grudem. Many of my criticisms boil down to the problem that each of these theologians fails to account well for what we know firsthand about love.

I propose a multi-faceted doctrine of God that champions love. Some of my suggestions have been bold; some have been novel; others may seem less surprising. Much of the Bible aligns with my claims, but not all of it; scripture contains diverse and sometimes contradictory views. My proposals align with lived experience and strive to be, to my knowledge, rationally consistent. I advance a vision of an actual divine Spirit who is by nature loving and uncontrolling.

But how confident should any of us be when talking about *God*?[1]

## Defensive Mystery

When it comes to the divine, some theologians and people of faith readily appeal to mystery. Karl Rahner and Katherine Sonderegger embrace God as "Absolute Mystery," for instance.[2] Appeals to mystery can sometimes be helpful, but often they're not. To get clarity, we should distinguish the appropriate from the inappropriate appeals to mystery, identifying the legitimate appeals from cop-outs and smoke screens.

Some systematic theologians speak confidently—even certainly— about the truth of particular beliefs or doctrines. Those displaying the most confidence usually base their assurance on a sacred book they consider inerrant. They may argue for the perspicuity of scripture,

---

[1] This chapter is dedicated to Jay McDaniel. He more than any other has prompted me to think about the issues I discuss in this chapter. He has done so through his writings, personal conversations, and public discussions.

[2] See Karl Rahner, *Foundations of Christian Faith*, William V. Dych, trans. (New York: Seabury, 1982), ch. 2; Katherine Sonderegger, *Systematic Theology*, Vol. 1 (Minneapolis: Fortress, 2015), 24.

appeal to a "plain reading," or may say, "the Bible clearly says." They think a deity who doesn't err provides a document without error, and they typically assume their interpretation of it is correct. I reject these ways of thinking.

Others place their confidence in a religious tradition and cite its leader or prominent voices. Instead of "the Bible clearly says," they'll proclaim, "the church confesses" or something similar.[3] Some in Catholicism, for instance, believe God preserves the Church from error in its teaching "on matters of faith and morals." Some Catholic theologians act as if Thomas Aquinas found the whole truth; some Protestants act like John Calvin or Karl Barth captured it all.[4]

When these confident people encounter good alternative arguments, personal experiences, or scientific theories disputing their views, they can be tempted to appeal to mystery. Some cite God's inscrutability. Others admit their theologies have contradictions but cling to their allegedly inerrant authority and engage in what I call playing the mystery card to preserve their views. "God's ways are not our ways," they'll say. "I trust the wisdom of the tradition," or "the Bible is the infallible Word of God," or "we'll never know this side of heaven." I find these appeals frustrating.

I could cite numerous examples of this practice, but here's one pertaining to love: the problem of evil. Many theologians who are certain God must be omnipotent appeal to mystery when asked why an allegedly all-loving deity doesn't prevent unnecessary suffering. These same people may be quite sure about a theory of atonement, a particular miracle, the truth of a scripture passage, or the infallibility of a church teaching. But when it comes to the strongest objection to theism—the problem of pointless pain—they invoke the inscrutability of an infinite deity. Instead of rethinking their beliefs, they appeal to mystery.

---

[3] K. Steve McCormick helpfully describes how love can take priority in the church and doctrine in *Doctrine Made Flesh* (Digital Theological Library, 2025).

[4] For more nuanced views on the relationship between Catholic thinking and process thought, see Marc A. Pugliese and John Becker, eds., *Process Thought and Roman Catholicism: Challenges and Promises* (Lanham, MD: Lexington, 2022).

The first unhelpful appeal to mystery, therefore, occurs when people of faith refuse to reformulate strongly-held beliefs that oppose good evidence, experiences, moral sensibilities, or strong arguments. I'll call it "defensive mystery," because those who appeal to it defend beliefs they're unwilling to reconsider. Instead of adjusting their views, they play the mystery card.

Good appeals to mystery open doors to explore; bad appeals shut them.

## UTTER MYSTERY

The second unhelpful appeal to mystery occurs when theologians or other people of faith claim that *nothing* positive can be said about God. I call this absolute apophaticism. Apophaticism traditionally emphasizes the limits of human language and knowledge of God. In its extreme form, it denies that *anything* we say, think, or experience provides truth about the divine. Thomas Aquinas endorses apophatic thinking when he says, "We can't know what God is, but rather what he isn't. We have no means for considering how God is, but rather how He isn't."[5] In absolute apophatic theology, people assume God to be *entirely* incomprehensible.

Apophatic theology, when in its relative rather than absolute form, offers an important corrective to theologies of certainty.[6] Relative apophaticism rebukes theologians who talk or act as if they can understand God fully. It reminds us we have limited understanding, that we can't be certain, and that all sources of knowledge will be incomplete. So, we must be humble.

*Absolute* apophatic theology, however, goes beyond admitting we can't be certain or can't know God fully. It takes denials that we can't understand the Spirit to the extreme. It rejects *all* positive speculation about what God might be like. In fact, absolute apophaticism proves

---

[5] Thomas Aquinas, *Summa Theologica*, I, q. 3, introd. In his writings, Aquinas makes numerous additional claims that suggest he doesn't take his own apophatic reasoning seriously.

[6] See, for instance, Catherine Keller, *Cloud of the Impossible: Negative Theology and Planetary Entanglement* (New York: Columbia University Press, 2015).

self-refuting: If we can't say anything true about the divine essence, we shouldn't say, "we can't say anything true about the divine essence." No one can know. I doubt there's a difference between absolute apophatic theology and no theology at all.

Some who take the absolute apophatic approach say their mystical experiences of God give them certain, often non-rational knowledge of the divine. But they also claim these experiences as ineffable, that is, impossible to describe or share with others. This helps no one but the experiencer. While we won't be able to describe our experiences of the divine *fully*, we don't need to reject *all* descriptions of God.

Some theologians have embraced apophaticism to avoid reformulating their inconsistent theologies. Those who call themselves "Calminians," for instance, claim to unite Calvinist beliefs to contradictory Arminian beliefs. Affirming contradictions about God shouldn't strike us as an example of revelatory insight, however. Instead, call it what it is: nonsense.

Let's call this second unhelpful approach to theology the appeal to "utter mystery." I oppose this approach, because it denies all positive proposals about God. This way of talking leads to theological nihilism, because it rejects knowing God as a basis for meaning. It even rejects the statement "God is love" as being true, at least in any way we could understand.

Conservatives are more likely to engage in defensive mystery. Many think they have a sure and certain foundation, be it in scripture or tradition. Instead of tearing down or rethinking that foundation when issues like the problem of evil, evolution, or divine hiddenness arise, they play the mystery card.[7] They retrench rather than revise.

Liberals or progressives are more likely to appeal to utter mystery. Many grew up conservative, but now doubt that sure and certain foundations exist. They know from experience that smugness in theology leads to haughtiness and harm. But instead of making tentative

---

[7] I find especially unsatisfying the skeptical theist appeal to mystery in the face of the problem of evil. For a concise presentation of the view, see Stephen Wykstra, "A Skeptical Theist View," in *God and the Problem of Evil: Five Views*, Chad Meister and James K. Dew, Jr., eds. (Downers Grove, IL: InterVarsity, 2017). See my response to Wykstra in the same book.

proposals for what God *might* be like, some progressives go too far in the other direction and appeal to sheer mystery.

It's impossible, however, for progressives to believe in an *utterly* mysterious God. There's no content there to believe. We can't have a concept of a deity who remains beyond all concepts. So, we should beware the God of utter mystery; we'll never know who the devil he may be!

## Humble Mystery

Appealing to mystery can be appropriate in some cases. One helpful case recognizes that words can't account for God fully. Theological language can't comprehensively contain the Spirit or precisely portray the divine. In fact, words can't capture all truths of any object or experience. Philosopher Jacques Derrida makes this argument forcefully when he describes the dynamism of *differance*.[8] His work illustrates how language always slips away when we try to create and fix meaning about the world.

A second helpful appeal to mystery extends from the first: we can affirm not only that words fail to account fully for the Spirit, but that our minds, feelings, and experiences also fail to provide a complete account. We can't attain exhaustive truth, because we're limited. We face "limit" questions, or queries that point beyond the boundaries of what we know.[9] Therefore, God remains at least partially mysterious.[10]

Notice the word "fully" and its synonyms in the paragraphs above. To say our words, thoughts, feelings, or experiences can't capture God *fully* doesn't discount the possibility we might know *something*. The middle way between total knowledge and none is *some*. "We know in

---

[8] See, for instance, Jacques Derrida, *Writing and Difference*, Alan Bass, trans. (Chicago: University of Chicago Press, 2017).

[9] On the role of limit questions in theology, see Willem Drees, *Religion, Science, and Naturalism* (New York: Cambridge University Press, 1996); Douglas F. Ottati, *A Theology for the Twenty-First Century* (Grand Rapids, MI: Eerdmans, 2020), 32-33; David Tracy, *Blessed Rage of Order* (New York: Seabury, 1975), 91-118.

[10] Russell Pregeant gets at this when he distinguishes between appropriate mystery and "magic." See *Mystery without Magic*, 2nd ed. (Anoka, MN: Process Century, 2022).

part," to quote the Apostle Paul (1 Cor. 13:9). I'll address the basis for this partial knowledge in later chapters when I explore how the Spirit communicates.

A third helpful appeal to mystery acknowledges we can't be certain about God. Most modern people doubt often, because we can imagine good reasons to be skeptical. This lack of certainty might be less worrisome than we might think, however, because theists have long considered themselves people of *faith*, not defenders of certainty. We're believers, not "certainers." But believers wisely pursue plausibility and reject blind faith, because a measure of mystery always remains.[11]

The words "know" and "understand" often confuse people in discussions about God. When people of faith say they *know* God or *understand* the divine will, we can interpret them as meaning they *fully* comprehend God or are *certain* of what the Spirit desires. But "know" and "understand" can mean something humbler. And because our knowing will always be partial and understanding incomplete, even partial knowing and understanding are fallible.

On this issue we may find the words of love from the Apostle Paul helpful. He prays that readers would "grasp how wide and long and high and deep is the love of Christ, and to know this love that surpasses knowledge" (Eph. 3:18b-19a). This "grasping" and "knowing" that Paul identifies seem to involve experiential understanding. But the love of Christ can be known only in part, he implies, not fathomed in full, because it surpasses full knowledge.

I call the helpful appeals to mystery I've identified "humble mystery." Rather than getting defensive or appealing to utter inscrutability, the humble person of faith tentatively offers positive claims about the Spirit. These claims may be partially true, but they never rise to the

---

[11] Degrees of Certainty. Some believers appeal to "degrees of certainty" when it comes to belief in God. I find this appeal unhelpful, because I think certainty isn't a matter of degree. I recommend using the word "confidence" instead, because it better lends itself to the possibilities of greater or lesser confidence in particular beliefs. I affirm that we can be certain of self-referential statements like, "I'm thinking right now." And we can be certain about abstract forms, mathematics, and those things true by definition. But I doubt we can be certain about actualities external to us, such as God.

level of full truth. And they don't involve certainty.[12] Despite their inadequacies, we're justified in making them, and they can be productive.

But mystery remains.

## Transcendence and Immanence

Some theologians use the words "transcendent" and "immanent" to describe the Spirit. When used well, we shouldn't understand these words as descriptions of God's spatial distance from, or proximity to, creation.[13] Instead, the language of transcendent and immanent describes ways in which God differs from, or is similar to, creatures and creation. When we speak of a transcendent Spirit, we identify something unique about deity; when we speak of divine immanence, we identify similarities between God and creatures.[14]

Absolute apophatic theology assumes total divine transcendence. This creates insurmountable problems for any systematic theology, because the totally transcendent deity can't be known, experienced, imitated, or imagined. If God is in all ways transcendent, we'd have no idea what it means for the Spirit to love. I call theologies based on total divine transcendence "anthropophobic:" they fear saying God can be *anything* like us.

I conversely use the phrase "absolute anthropomorphism" to describe theologies that posit a totally immanent God. A deity *exactly* like us would be radically limited, morally compromised, and in many ways imperfect. This deity would love sporadically, not know some facts, have a beginning, be limited to some locations, and be as weak as we are. As I've indicated, this systematic theology of love doesn't describe God as entirely immanent.

Most systematic theologies fall somewhere on a continuum between absolute apophaticism and absolute anthropomorphism. In

---

[12] Eberhard Jüngel distinguishes between negative and positive mystery *God as the Mystery of the World*, Darrell L. Guder, trans. (Grand Rapids, MI: Eerdmans, 1983), ch. 4.

[13] Millard Erickson equates immanence and transcendence with God's nearness and distance. See *Christian Theology*, 2nd ed. (Grand Rapids, MI: Baker, 1998), ch. 15.

[14] Stanley J. Grenz and Roger E. Olson explore these issues in *20th Century Theology* (Downers Grove, IL: InterVarsity, 1992).

them, God differs from creatures in some respects, but is similar in others. Traditional or conservative theologies can overemphasize the differences; progressive or liberal theologies can overemphasize the similarities. A right-sized Spirit will be neither wholly like, nor wholly unlike, us.

Some theologians use "holiness" to describe differences between God and creation. Rudolf Otto famously appealed to holiness as God's radical otherness. He used the Latin phrase *mysterium tremendum et fascinans* to differentiate our experiences of God from other experiences. Thanks in part to Otto, some theologians say God is "wholly other."[15]

We can interpret the phrase "wholly other" in various ways. It might be helpful, in so far as it rejects pantheism and absolute anthropomorphism.[16] But historically, it's been a natural progression to move from saying God must be "wholly other" to proclaiming the death of God.[17] God, if utterly unknowable, becomes irrelevant.

When theologians link the idea of God as "wholly other" with claims about moral holiness, they often end up saying a wholly other God can't be in the presence of sin. This claim denies divine omnipresence, however, and it renders divine forgiveness either partial or nonexistent.

Calling the Spirit "wholly other" also undermines analogies between deity and creation. This includes denying that creatures are made in God's image (Gen. 1:26) or can partake in the divine nature (2 Pt. 1:4). God conceived as wholly other opposes the centrality of love—creaturely and divine—in systematic theology.

Holiness is better understood as intimately linked with divine love. "What is holiness?" asks John Wesley. He answers: "Is it not, essentially,

---

[15] See Rudolf Otto, *The Idea of the Holy*, 2nd ed., John W. Harvey, trans. (Oxford: Oxford University Press, 1950 [*Das Heilige*, 1917]).

[16] I appreciate Keith Ward's discussion of this issue in *Sharing in the Divine Nature* (Eugene, OR: Cascade, 2020), ch. 2.

[17] A significant body of literature explores "the death of God," a label made famous by Thomas J. J. Altizer and others. Some of those writings advocate reductive atheism, but other death of God writers simply oppose theologies that make no sense of reality or are internally inconsistent. For an edited collection of essays exploring this, see Daniel J. Peterson and Michael Zbaraschuk, eds. *Resurrecting the Death of God* (Albany, NY: SUNY, 2015).

love? The love of God and of all mankind? Love governing the heart and life, running through all our tempers, words, and actions."[18] Wesley also says, "God is love. Love is the very essence of His nature; yea, His whole nature is love. And love, if it be considered as it is in God, is holiness itself."[19] Wesley's way of holiness centers divine love that we can imitate, and this overcomes both absolute apophaticism and absolute anthropomorphism.

God is neither entirely unlike nor entirely like us.

## The Finite and Infinite

Many theologians identify differences and similarities between the Spirit and creatures using the language of "finite" and "infinite." "Infinite" proves a tricky word, as we saw in earlier chapters, and it carries both quantitative and qualitative meanings.[20] I agree with Keith Ward when he says it's "annoyingly vague."[21] For many theologians, "infinite" serves as the polar opposite of "finite." When they use the phrase "the infinite" to identify what lies beyond comprehension, the word supports absolute apophaticism. A God infinite in all respects would be unbelievable, as I've already said.

Theologians who use the language of "infinite" to portray God as utterly incomprehensible sometimes sound like children who end arguments with "times infinity!" Conversations cease. I find it difficult to know how anyone could adjudicate theological claims as accurate, or absurd, if God must be in all ways infinite. The infinite is indefinite.

A slightly better approach says the infinite encompasses the finite rather than opposing it. But this kind of thinking can reject qualitative

---

[18] See "The Scripture Way of Salvation," §II.4 (*Wesley Works*, ed. Outler, Vol. 2, p. 160).

[19] John Wesley, "The First Commandment," in *The Works of John Wesley, Volume 6: Doctrinal and Controversial Treatises II*, ed. Albert C. Outler (Nashville, TN: Abingdon, 1985), 193. See also Allan Bevere, *Holiness of Heart and Life* (Gonzalez, FL: Energion, 2023); Thomas Jay Oord and Michael Lodahl, *Relational Holiness* (Kansas City, MO: Beacon Hill, 2005); Mildred Bangs Wynkoop, *A Theology of Love* (Kansas City, MO: Beacon Hill, 1973).

[20] On the meanings of "infinite," see Benedikt Paul Gocke and Christian Tapp, eds., *Divine Infinity* (Notre Dame, IN: Notre Dame University Press, 2019).

[21] Keith Ward, *Sharing in the Divine Nature* (Eugene, OR: Cascade, 2020), 112.

differences between God and creation. When we consider all creation taken into, or part of, the Infinite, the result can sound like pantheism. Creation is divine.

The most helpful references to divine infinity refer to limitless superlatives: God has a limitless quantity, or quality, of some finite trait or activity.[22] God can be infinite as everlasting, for instance, if this means the Spirit experiences an unlimited succession of moments of time. God can be infinite as universal, if this means the Spirit is present to everything in every location. God can be infinitely loving, if we mean God always acts for the well-being of everyone and everything.[23] And so on.

Helpful uses of the concept of divine infinity require that God be subject to finite categories. The meaning of love, for instance, must apply to God and creatures, so it has a finite meaning. God's relation to time must be like creaturely relations to time. A unit of time is finite. If we want to talk meaningfully about God's relations, attributes, and actions, we must assume these traits and activities have finite meanings. To talk meaningfully about the Spirit of Love, we should say the Spirit must be finite in some respects but infinite in their extension.

The language of "finite" and "infinite" simply isn't required in theology. And many theologians avoid these terms because of the confusion the words create. Good theology can be done without using this language.

---

[22] Three Helpful Notions of Infinity. William Beardslee identifies three helpful views of infinity as 1) the infinity of possibility, 2) the total unification of reality, and 3) the infinity of the perfection of quality. Beardslee points out that even the infinity of possibility is differentiated, however. These possibilities represent the future rather than an undifferentiated present. And while they may reside in God's nature, they are not divine. Infinity as the total unification of reality, which is Beardslee's second meaning, is possible because of God's all-embracing experience. But this unification is temporary to each moment, because new unifications will come in future moments. So this is an ever-increasing infinite rather than fixed infinite. The second and third meanings of infinity that Beardslee identifies are what I call God's "limitless superlatives." See Beardslee, "The Infinite," in *Margins of Belonging* (Atlanta: Scholars, 1991), 101-116.

[23] This is the general approach taken by Lewis S. Ford as he lays out process notions of finitude and infinity. See "In What Sense Is God Infinite? A Process Perspective," *The Thomist* 42:1 (1978): 1-13.

## Theopoetics

If we can't be certain about God and no source provides indisputable data about the divine, then should we understand theology as sophisticated make-believe? Are theologian Ludwig Feuerbach and others correct that we just project our ideas onto a divine Someone who doesn't actually exist?[24] Are people of faith fantasy writers who build gods entirely from their imaginations, and might systematic theologies be sophisticated forms of fan fiction?

As I argued at the outset, I think we have plausible grounds to think an actual Spirit exists who loves. But we should admit systematic theologians and everyday believers *do* construct claims about God and reality, at least to some degree.[25] Put differently, the Spirit doesn't download crystal-clear truths directly into our minds. We, at least partially, create beliefs about a Spirit whom, I nevertheless believe, actually exists.

We shouldn't think of the creating when doing theology as something negative. We can use the term "theopoetics" to describe the constructive task of theology. *Poesis* translates as the Greek word for "making" or "creating," and *theo* refers to God. Theopoetics acknowledges that we create beliefs in response to the Spirit, culture, personal experiences, scripture, science, and so on. Theology is best done as an artistic endeavor; it's not a compilation of propositions burned into skulls by divine lightning.[26]

The work of theopoetics doesn't require us to think the Spirit is without ontological reality.[27] We "feel about" for an actual becoming

---

[24] See Ludwig Feuerbach, *The Essence of Christianity* (New York: Prometheus, 1989).

[25] Roland Faber calls this "God in the Making." See *Depths as Yet Unspoken* (Eugene, OR: Pickwick, 2020).

[26] For an introduction to theopoetics, see L. Callid Keefe-Perry, *Way to Water: A Theopoetics Primer* (Eugene, OR: Cascade, 2014). For essays in theopoetics, see Jeremy Fackenthal and Roland Faber, eds. *Theopoetic Folds* (New York: Fordham University Press, 2013). Bill Tammeus explores God as poet in "An Amipotent God is Both the Poet and the Poetry," in *Amipotence*, vol. 2, Brandon Brown, et. al., eds. (Grasmere, ID: SacraSage, 2025).

[27] Theopoetics comes in many forms. John Caputo's version can be interpreted as denying an ontology for God. Richard Kearney and Catherine Keller's versions of theopoetics don't require denying ontology of God. See John D. Caputo, *The Insistence of God* (Bloomington: Indiana University Press, 2013); Richard Kearney, *Anatheism* (New York: Columbia University Press, 2010); Keller, *Cloud of the Impossible*.

Spirit, as the Apostle Paul put it (Acts 17:27). Because God is "not far" from us, adds Paul, our feeling about, intuiting, and inferring may provide a measure of truth about deity. And that can include us believing God to be a loving Subject.

The "poetic" aspect of theopoetics refers to far more than written poetry. Postulating God takes many forms, written and unwritten, audio and visual, and even encompassing smelling and tasting. We often find the most aesthetically pleasing portrayals of the Spirit the most compelling. Theopoetics represents a process of art and creativity in service of theological work, and like all good art, theopoetics holds its construction tentatively.

Because theopoetics emphasizes human roles in formulating the ways of the Spirit, it doesn't assume God is a controlling potentate who reveals infallibly.[28] Just the opposite. Theologians aren't puppets dutifully writing words dictated by deity. They're free to speculate that the Spirit woos, nudges, calls, inspires, excites, and whispers. Alfred North Whitehead puts it well when he says, God "is the poet of the world, with tender patience leading it by his vision of truth, beauty, and goodness."[29] In doing theology creatively, the Spirit leads patiently, and we respond.

While we have grounds to believe an objective Lover exists, the language about that Lover will always be *our* language. We hope our rhetoric bears some resemblance to the Spirit, but we never know for sure. Theopoetics doesn't denounce reason, thinking, or knowing, but it rejects the idea that we have no role in imagining God.

Theology isn't divine dictation but our artfully imagining a Universal Lover.

## Your God is Too Vague

In his classic book *Your God is Too Small*, J. B. Phillips rightly points out that many people of faith imagine deity as inept, immoral, absent,

---

[28] Rubem Alves applies theopoetics to liberation. See *The Poet, The Warrior, The Prophet* (London: SCM, 1990). See also Oluwatomisin Olayinka Oredein and Lakisha R. Lockhart-Rusch, eds., *Theopoetics in Color* (Grand Rapids, MI: Eerdmans, 2024).

[29] Alfred North Whitehead, *Process and Reality: An Essay in Cosmology*, corrected ed., David Ray Griffin and Donald W. Sherburne, eds. (New York: Free Press, 1978), 346.

or imperfect in some way.[30] We shouldn't feel obligated to worship a God that's too small. In their book *Searching for an Adequate God*, John B. Cobb, Jr., Clark Pinnock, and others argue that we can also imagine God as too big.[31] An over-sized deity is all-determining, unaffected, impersonal, and utterly inconceivable. A God too big is also not worthy of worship.[32] We need a right-sized deity.

Some people of faith claim to know *too much* about God. This presumption of knowledge seems more common among conservatives. Their overconfidence may arise from literal readings of scriptures they believe to be inerrant. Or it comes from placing surety in a religious tradition, saint, or sage. Occasionally, a particularly self-assured person of faith says he's totally figured out God on his own. Beware of those who know too much.

I also worry about a much less-discussed problem found more often in liberal or progressive circles. Instead of having a deity that's too small, too big, or too definite, some appeal to a God that's too vague. In fact, people even praise vagueness in some circles, and the more opaque the deity, the better. On the positive side, those who prize vague theologies waste less time arguing on the internet. There's no reason to fight when we have few or no constructive theological beliefs.

Vagueness carries costs, however. And nebulousness has consequences. A verse in Proverbs identifies one problem: "Without a vision, the people perish" (29:18). Most people of faith need a vision of God to make sense of life and to motivate them to do hard things when times become difficult. Without some clarity about the divine, many will instead shape their lives around economic, cultural, or pleasure-based Ultimates. Theology matters.

We need a God neither too small nor too big, neither too definite nor too vague. We need an appropriately-envisioned deity. Helpful

---

[30] J. B. Phillips, *Your God Is Too Small* (New York: Macmillan, 1953).

[31] Clark Pinnock's legacy is far reaching. In addition to his own writings, see Barry L. Callen, *Clark H. Pinnock: Journey Toward Renewal* (Nappanee, IN: Evangel, 2000); Andrew Ray Williams, *Boundless Love: A Companion to Clark H. Pinnock's Theology* (Eugene, OR: Wipf and Stock, 2021).

[32] Keith Ward is among many who claim humans are, by nature, worshipers. See *Religion and Human Nature* (Oxford: Oxford University Press, 1998).

theologies, I believe, will be tentative, provisional, speculative, suggestive, multi-sourced, plausible, credible, open, and/or approximate. They'll be proposals in process.

I've repeatedly argued that love ought to be central to a winsome vision of the Spirit. The universal Lover of all isn't too small, nor too big. When carefully considered, we can see this Lover as neither too definite nor too vague. We can talk about a right-sized deity that makes sense of our experiences and gives us a plausible vision.

We'll never be certain about God, but we aren't clueless.

## RIGHT-SIZING

While exploring appeals to mystery, transcendence and immanence, the finite and infinite, God as wholly other, vagueness, and theopoetics, we've encountered a complex set of issues. Each deserves further reflection, and theologians have examined these issues. I've briefly explored them one by one to identify key issues for a systematic theology of love. Here are some of the implications.

I know of no good reason to write a systematic theology of love if words tell us *nothing* true about the divine. If God remains utter mystery, we have no grounds to believe our thoughts, words, and experiences tell us something true about the Lover of the Universe. If we think the Spirit wholly other in the sense of nothing like us, then describing a Spirit of love will be nonsense. No helpful analogies are possible for an entirely dissimilar deity.[33] And if God infinitely transcends the finite, constructive theology fails. To make sense of divine love, the Spirit must be similar to creatures and creation in some ways.

---

[33] Analogies Normally, we refer to analogies in the sense of bi-directional. One thing is similar to another, for instance, because that second thing is like the first. But many classical theists, such as Thomas Aquinas, think of Creator-creation analogies as uni-directional. Aquinas affirms such analogies when he says creature are "like" God, but God isn't "like" creatures (*Summa Contra Gentiles* [London-New York: 1928 & 1929], I: 29). Applied to love, this would mean the love creatures express is like God's love, but God's love isn't like creaturely love. My appeals to analogies of love reject uni-directional analogies and embrace bi-directional analogies.

God must differ from creatures in other ways, however.[34] We can only trust that the Spirit *always* loves, for instance, if love is an essential attribute of the divine nature. We can only believe God directly loves *all* creation if deity is universal. We can be confident that the God who knows all that's possible to know effectively loves us and creation while we move into an open future. And so on.

Words like "love," "relate," "act" and "well-being" need to apply to Creator and creatures to make sense of *how* God loves. Divine love must also be timely rather than timeless, for instance. The Spirit who loves can't be an exception to finite categories pertaining to love. If we're created in God's image (Gen. 1:27), if we can choose to imitate God when we love (Eph. 5:1), and if we can partake of the divine nature (2 Pt. 1:4), the Spirit must not be *wholly* different.[35]

Biblical writers often point to similarities between divine and creaturely love. They express the activity and character of God's love in analogies about masters and servants, grooms and brides, husbands and wives, fathers and sons, leaders and followers.[36] The writers say the Spirit is akin to a loving hen gathering chicks (Mt. 23:37) or an eagle protecting its offspring (Dt. 32:11). These analogies only make sense if the Spirit's love and our love are similar.[37]

Two preeminent theologians of love, Daniel Day Williams and George Newlands, described this issue well: "On the strictest biblical terms," says Williams, "there must be something in common between the words we use to speak about God's being and about our being."[38]

---

[34] Jordan Wessling argues for something similar in what he calls "the similarity thesis." See *Love Divine* (Oxford: Oxford University Press, 2020), 12.

[35] Eleanor O'Donnell explores this in "Like God," in *Amipotence, vol. 1*, Chris S. Baker, et. al., eds. (Grasmere, ID: SacraSage, 2025).

[36] For an extensive discussion of New Testament analogies, see Herbert M. Gale, *The Use of Analogy in the Letters of Paul* (Philadelphia: Westminster, 1965). For a philosophical explorations of the analogies of love, see Robert Merrihew Adams, *Finite and Infinite Goods* (Oxford: Oxford University Press, 1999) and Paul Ricoeur, "Naming God," in *Figuring the Sacred*, Mark Wallace, ed. (Minneapolis: Fortress, 1995).

[37] "To understand God using the analogy of love," says Gary Chartier, "is to allow our convictions to be shaped by a complex interplay of the church's narrative and affirmations about God on the one hand and our own experiences and reflection on the other" (*The Analogy of Love* [Charlottesville, VA: Imprint Academic, 2007], 13).

[38] Daniel Day Williams, *The Spirit and the Forms of Love* (New York: Harper and Row, 1968), 123.

And "if there is to be genuine communication," says Newlands, "there must be some sort of analogical relationship between God and our language about him."[39]

Insofar as Jesus provides a clear revelation of divine love and insofar as we can love like him, Jesus identifies similarities between divine and creaturely love. "We know love by this," says John, "that he laid down his life for us." So "we ought to lay down our lives for one another" (1 Jn. 3:16). The revelation of God in Jesus Christ implies that God is finite and immanent in at least those respects that make imitating deity possible.[40]

Without similarities between us and the Spirit, there is no revelation, no imitation, no relationship.

## Conclusion

A systematic theology of love should abandon traditional claims about God and love if they contradict our moral intuitions and widespread experiences. Good theology rethinks contradictory beliefs instead of defensively appealing to mystery. It opposes utter mystery too, because the absolutely mysterious One would be absolutely unbelievable.

If divine love is to be meaningful, we must speak of love with concepts that apply to both the Spirit and creatures. Otherwise, it will be neither intelligible nor imitable. And without bi-directional analogies, a theology of love becomes incoherent. A systematic theology of love, therefore, works to develop a conceptual framework to support rather than erase the language of loving relations between Creator and creatures.

A robust theology will also portray God as neither too big nor too small, neither too definite nor too vague. It aims for a rightly-envisioned theology of a loving Spirit, one that makes intellectual sense and fits life as we know it. Those who propose a right-sized vision should be humble. And the most adequate theologies employ the logic of love.

An adequate theology fits our experiences and intuitions of love.

---

[39] George M. Newlands, *Theology of the Love of God* (Atlanta: John Knox, 1980), 53.

[40] For more on this, see Thomas Jay Oord, "Analogies of Love between God and Creatures: A Response to Kevin Vanhoozer," In *Love, Human and Divine* (London: T & T Clark, 2020).

# Creation and Providence

CHAPTER ELEVEN

# *Creatio Ex Nihilo* and Other Creation Theories

## THE BIG IDEAS

- Most theists in the Western traditions believe God initially created the universe from absolutely nothing (*creatio ex nihilo*).
- The creation from nothing theory isn't supported by the Bible.
- Biblical authors repeatedly say or imply that God creates out of or alongside creation.
- The claim that God speaks something into existence and biblical claims about a beginning don't require God creating something from nothing.
- Gnostics originally conceived of *creatio ex nihilo,* because they thought a holy God would not associate with an unholy world.
- There are eleven reasons to reject *creatio ex nihilo*, perhaps the most powerful being the theory's implications for God and evil.
- Various theories other than creation from nothing have advantages and disadvantages but are not adequate in themselves.
- The current scientific consensus is that our universe began billions of years ago with a Big Bang.
- The fine-tuning of the universe suggests the activity of a Tuner.
- Multiverse theories weaken the fine-tuning argument, but some versions make little sense.
- In light of both theology and science, a new doctrine of creation is needed.

Just about every theist—Christian or otherwise—says God creates. Most hold theories about how God originally created our universe and whether this creating continues. But the details of creation theories differ, sometimes drastically.[1]

Some theories or theologies take Christian scripture as a historical-literal account of the origin of the universe. This approach leads many to think the earth must be relatively young, evolution is false, and contemporary science suspect.[2] This view not only contradicts contemporary science but is also not consistently supported by the biblical authors.

Biblical writers describe a three-tiered cosmology that differs greatly from how contemporary scientists think about the universe. They depict heavens and a "firmament" above a flat earth, and they describe the sky in way that sounds like it's an inverted bowl or tent. These writers say that under the earth lies a place for the dead (*sheol*), a watery chaos, and large pillars supporting the earth.[3] The details of these descriptions simply aren't reconcilable with the universe we observe.[4]

Other theories or theologies of creation embrace key ideas in contemporary science. They claim God created the universe at the Big Bang, for instance, and God used evolution thereafter when creating diverse life forms. These views are sometimes called "theistic evolution" or "evolutionary creationism." They are more promising.

Many theologians link with science their claims that God created the universe from nothing. They say deity can and does intervene in creation. In some mysterious way, goes one often argued position, God

---

[1] This chapter is dedicated to Philip Clayton. Philip's work in science and religion is groundbreaking and a model that I aim to imitate. I also appreciate his friendship and encouragement.

[2] Wayne Grudem is a systematic theologian who regards Genesis as providing a historical account of God's creating. Among other things, this means he rejects the idea that God creates through evolution. See *Systematic Theology* (Grand Rapids, MI: Zondervan, 1994), ch. 15.

[3] Mark Harris explores biblical claims about creation in *The Nature of Creation: Examining the Bible and Science* (Durham: Acumen, 2013).

[4] Fortunately, a growing number of Christians, including Evangelicals, embrace evolution and interpret biblical passages in light of it. For short testimonials on this, see Kathryn Applegate and J. B. Stump, eds., *How I Changed My Mind about Evolution* (Downers Grove, IL: InterVarsity, 2016). See also J. B. Stump, *Science and Christianity* (Oxford: Wiley Blackwell, 2017).

is the primary cause that determines all secondary causes. Most who take this approach think scientific explanations differ entirely from theological ones, because divine causation and creaturely causation are different in kind. On their view, God isn't a cause among others in the universe.

This systematic theology of love draws from scripture and science but proposes new ways to think about God as Creator. It affirms major scientific theories like the Big Bang and evolution, and it aligns with the general features of contemporary cosmology. This theology rejects the idea that the Bible gives an accurate historical-literal description of the universe. It draws from theological claims in the Bible, while criticizing long-held theories about how God created the world. And it aims to portray God's actions as similar in kind to other actions we know. My overall aim will be to offer an internally consistent theory that aligns with science, our experience, reason, and key creation themes in the Bible.

Before laying out the creation theory of this systematic theology of love, we need to look at ways theologians have explained God and the origin of the universe.

## THE THEORY OF *CREATIO EX NIHILO*

Since roughly the third century, major Christian theologians have speculated that God initially created our universe from absolutely nothing.[5] Many Jews, Muslims, and other theists have adopted this theory too.[6] Scholars today often use the Latin phrase *creatio ex nihilo* to refer to this idea.

---

[5] For essays focusing on particular advocates of creatio ex nihilo in history, see chapters in David B. Burrell, Carlo Cogliati, Janet M. Soskice, and William R. Stoeger, eds., *Creation and the God of Abraham* (Cambridge: Cambridge University Press, 2010) and "Creation 'Ex Nihilo' and Modern Theology," Modern Theology (special issue, ed. Janet Martin Soskice) 29, no. 2 (2013).

[6] Islamic scholar Saida Mirsadri says, "the doctrine of *creatio ex nihilo*—advocated later by Muslim theologians, and closely tied with the concept of divine omnipotence—isn't rooted in the Qur'an." See her essay, "S/He Who Cares about Every Tear," *Amipotence*, vol. 1, Chris. S. Baker, et. al., eds. (Grasmere, ID: SacraSage, 2025), 144.

Advocates of the creation from nothing view say God initially existed alone, without creation. Maimonides puts it simply: "In the beginning, God alone existed, and nothing else."[7] Then, at some point and for some reason, the solitary One created the universe out of absolutely nothing. God made all things, says Augustine, "not from [God's] own substance . . . but out of nothing."[8]

Theologians of this ilk offer various reasons for why God decided to create. Wayne Grudem follows the logic of Calvinist theologians by saying God wanted to display glory.[9] Clark Pinnock says the members of the Trinity wanted to share their love with something not divine.[10] But according to each, God could have remained alone, without ever creating.

If we look closely, we'll see *creatio ex nihilo* isn't actually in the opening verses of Genesis. They say, "In the beginning, when God created the heavens and the earth, the earth was a formless void and darkness covered the face of the deep, while a wind from God swept over the face of the waters" (1:1, 2). "When" begins a temporal clause, important because it doesn't point to an absolute beginning of time.[11] And we find no definite article such as "the" in the Hebrew text, so it could just as well be translated, "In *a* beginning," rather than "In *the* beginning." Perhaps it's best translated "When God began to create the heavens and the earth . . ."[12]

According to these verses, the divine Spirit (*ruach elohim*) creates while hovering or vibrating over a "formless void," "face of the deep," and "face of the waters." These phrases suggest something was present

---

[7] Moses Maimonides, *The Guide for the Perplexed*, M. Friedlander, trans. (New York: Dover, 1956).

[8] Augustine, *Confessions*, Henry Chadwick, trans. (Oxford: Oxford University Press, 1991), book 12:27.37, p. 269.

[9] Grudem, *Systematic Theology*, ch. 15.

[10] Clark Pinnock, *Most Moved Mover* (Grand Rapids, MI: Baker, 2001), ch. 3.

[11] Jon D. Levenson explains this point in *Creation and the Persistence of Evil* (Princeton, NJ: Princeton University Press, 1994), 121.

[12] Dan McLellan explains these issues succinctly in *The Bible Says So* (New York: St. Martins, 2025), ch. 3.

when God began to create the universe.[13] Liane Feldman interprets this as "mire and muck."[14] Whatever the language, the Spirit engaged materials and forces, and God established a life-sustaining order by creating from what was present.

The phrase "formless void" in verse two of Genesis is *tohu wabohu*. Some translators render it "primordial chaos;" others call it an "amorphous state" or "undifferentiated mass."[15] God transforms this chaos. These verses also speak of darkness covering the "face of the deep." This *tehom* refers to something nondivine. "The *tehom* signifies the primeval waters," says Brevard Childs, which also point to something present in the beginning.[16]

A number of influential biblical scholars say Genesis doesn't endorse creation from nothing:

- "Creation out of nothing is foreign to both the language and the thought of the unknown author of Genesis," says Claus Westermann.[17]
- "God's creating in Genesis one," says Terrence Fretheim, "includes ordering that which already exists ... God works creatively with already existing reality to bring about newness."[18]
- "'Nothingness' isn't the picture of the situation at the beginning," says Mark S. Smith. "Unformed as the world is, *tohu va bohu* is far from being nothingness or connoting nothingness."[19]

---

[13] Early translations of Genesis tended to separate verses one and two of chapter one. This gave the impression that the second verse was an explanation of the first. But most contemporary biblical scholars see the second verse as an explanation of how God began creating in relation to chaos. On the possible ways to interpret these verses, see Terence Fretheim, *God and the World in the Old Testament* (Nashville, TN: Abingdon, 2005), 35.

[14] Liane Feldman, *The Consuming Fire* (Oakland, CA: University of California Press, 2023), 53.

[15] Levenson prefers "primordial chaos" (*Creation and the Persistence of Evil*, xx). David Toshio Tsumura and William P. Brown say God created from something like an amorphous state or undifferentiated mass. See Tsumura, *The Earth and the Waters in Genesis 1 and 2* (Sheffield: JSOT, 1989); Brown, *The Ethos of the Cosmos* (Grand Rapids, MI: Eerdmans, 1999). For a theological exploration, see Eric M. Vail, *Creation and Chaos Talk* (Eugene, OR: Pickwick, 2012).

[16] Brevard S. Childs, *Myth and Reality in the Old Testament* (London: SCM, 1960), 33.

[17] Claus Westermann, *Genesis 1–11*, John J. Scullion, trans. (London: SPCK, 1994), 110.

[18] Terence E. Fretheim, *God and the World in the Old Testament*, 5.

[19] Mark S. Smith, *The Priestly Vision of Genesis 1* (Philadelphia, PA: Fortress, 2010), 50.

- "It can be said that Yahweh is the creator of the world," says Rolf P. Knierim, "because he is its liberator from chaos."[20]
- "Properly understood," says Jon Levenson, "Genesis 1:1–2:3 can't be invoked to support the developed Jewish, Christian, and Muslim doctrine of creation *ex nihilo*."[21]
- "The storytellers were not thinking of what later philosophical and theological traditions, speaking Latin as they often did, called *creatio ex nihilo*," writes Edwin Good. "In this story, something was there—the empty, shapeless 'earth,' darkness, the 'abyss,' the wind across the waters."[22]
- "At the outset of God's creation," says David Carr, "there were three main precursors, with the description of each element building on the others: the uninhabitable formless mass of earth (1:2a), the dark primeval ocean in which that earth was submerged (1:2a), and God's breath/primeval wind moving over the face of the waters (1:2b)."[23]

The list of scholars saying Genesis doesn't support creation from nothing is long, and it includes both liberals and conservatives.[24] But

---

[20] Rolf P. Knierim, *Task of Old Testament Theology* (Grand Rapids, MI: Eerdmans, 1995), 210.

[21] Jon D. Levenson, *Creation and the Persistence of Evil*, 121.

[22] Edwin Good, *Genesis 1–11, Tales of the Earliest World* (Stanford, CA: Stanford University Press, 2007), 11.

[23] David M. Carr, *Genesis 1–11, IECOT* (Stuttgart: W. Kohlhammer, 2021, Kindle), Introduction.

[24] In addition to those cited, see Joseph Blenkinsopp, *Creation, Un-Creation, Re-Creation* (London: T & T Clark, 2011); William P. Brown, *The Ethos of the Cosmos* (Grand Rapids, MI: Eerdmans, 1999); Keith Norman, "Ex Nihilo: The Development of the Doctrines of God and Creation in Early Christianity," *BYU Studies* 17/3 (1977): 291–318; Shalom M. Paul, "Creation and Cosmogony: In the Bible," *Encyclopedia Judaica* (Jerusalem: Keter, 1972), 5:1059–63; David Toshio Tsumura, *The Earth and the Waters in Genesis 1 and 2* (Sheffield, UK: JSOT, 1989); Bruce K. Waltke, *Creation and Chaos* (Portland, OR: Western Conservative Baptist Seminary, 1974); John H. Walton, *The Lost World of Genesis One* (Downers Grove, IL: IVP, 2009); David Winston, "The Book of Wisdom's Theory of Cosmogony," *History of Religions* 11/2 (1971): 187–91; Frances Young, "Creatio Ex Nihilo: A Context for the Emergence of Christian Doctrine of Creation," *Scottish Journal of Theology* 44 (1991): 139–51. One exception to this list would be a book from Paul Copan and William Lane Craig. Careful readers will note that in this book, the authors reference few, if any, contemporary biblical scholars, and they use shoddy biblical arguments. In addition, they overstate the philosophical and scientific arguments. See *Creation out of Nothing* (Grand Rapids, MI: Baker, 2004).

given the prominence of *creatio ex nihilo*, it's hard to overemphasize its absence in scripture. So, I'll say it again:

Genesis doesn't support the idea that God creates from nothing.

**Other Biblical Passages**

Other biblical passages also say God creates from something. The writers of the Hebrew Bible use a dozen or so Hebrew words that scholars translate "create." The writers of Genesis typically use the verbs *bara* and *asah*. These words refer to both divine and creaturely creating, and we find no Hebrew word that means God created something out of nothing.[25]

The writers of the Psalms praise God as creator. Their praise portrays the Spirit's creating in ways that complement or contrast with Genesis. But no passage in the Psalms says God creates something from nothing.[26]

Sometimes advocates of the creation from nothing view appeal to a passage in 2 Maccabees. (This book isn't recognized as canonical by Protestants, but Roman Catholic and Orthodox theologians cite it.) In the passage, a mother speaks to her son:

> She leaned over close to him and, in derision of the cruel tyrant, said in their native language: "Son, have pity on me, who carried you in my womb for nine months, nursed you for three years, brought you up, educated and supported you to your present age. I beg you, child, to look at the heavens and the earth and see all that is in them; then you will know that God did not make them out of existing things. In the same way, humankind came into existence (7:27–28).

Some have taken the phrase "God did not make them out of existing things" to refer to creation from nothing. But the context of the

---

[25] See Fretheim, *God and the World in the Old Testament*, 10-13.

[26] Job 26:7 says, "He stretches out Zaphon over the void and hangs the earth upon nothing." A few have argued this refers to creation out of nothing, but hanging the earth on nothing doesn't mean creation from nothing.

passage suggests otherwise: the mother witnesses to carrying, nursing, and educating her son. "In the same way," says 2 Maccabees, "humankind came into existence." That's not an example of *creatio ex nihilo*.

The mother plays the key role in creating children, but her egg requires a male's sperm. The growth of the fetus also requires a womb and nutrients, and environmental factors affect its growth. In short, natal and developmental analogies for creation require multiple causes and prior entities, so they don't align with God creating from nothing.[27]

If we consider Catholic and Orthodox creation passages not in the Protestant canon, we should note one other passage. "For your all-powerful hand, which created the world out of formless matter," says the Wisdom of Solomon, "did not lack the means to send upon them a multitude of bears or bold lions" (11:17). This passage reflects the ancient Greek view that God creates by bringing form to matter. But matter is something, not nothing.

Furthermore, we find no explicit references to *creatio ex nihilo* in the New Testament. The book of 2 Peter offers the most direct statement about God's creating, but it points to God creating in relation to something. It says that "by the word of God, heavens existed long ago and an earth was formed out of water and by means of water" (2 Pet. 3:5).

The reference to heavens and earth in this passage parallels the reference to heavens and earth in the first verses of Genesis. The comments about creating "out of" and "by means of" water aligns with how ancient people associated chaos with water. The verb in the Peter passage usually translated "formed out of" means to organize and combine, not create from nothing.[28]

Other New Testament passages speak of God creating out of "unseen things" (Heb. 11:3), creatures (2 Cor. 5:17), and creation generally.

---

[27] On the possible meanings of this passage, see Jonathan A. Goldstein, *II Maccabees*, The Anchor Bible Series (New York: Doubleday, 1983), 307-315. I'm grateful to Steven Joseph Bruening for alerting me to this resources and others.

[28] On these issues, see Richard J. Bauckham, *Jude, 2 Peter* (Waco: Word, 1983), 297–302; Blake T. Ostler, "Out of Nothing: A History of Creation ex Nihilo in Early Christian Thought," *Review of Books on the Book of Mormon 1989–2011*, 17:2 (2005): Art. 9. Available at: https://scholarsarchive.byu.edu/msr/vol17/iss2/9

But unseen things are still things. And the oft-cited Colossians passage about divine creating doesn't identify "invisible things" with absolute nothingness. It says, "for in him were created all things in heaven and on earth: everything visible and everything invisible, thrones, ruling forces, sovereignties, powers—all things were created through him and for him. He exists before all things" (1:16–17).

Ancient people do sometimes refer to children being created by their parents "from what doesn't exist."[29] Obviously, sperm, egg, and womb come into play in this creating, however, and we know that various factors contribute to a fetus's development. Examples of parents creating children, therefore, point to making from something, not nothing.[30]

## Speaking into Existence

Some advocates of the creation from nothing theory cite biblical passages that say God creates by speaking or calling things into existence (e.g., Ps. 33:6-9). An oft-cited passage is Romans 4:16-18:

> For this reason the promise depends on faith, in order that it may rest on grace, so that it may be guaranteed to all his descendants, not only to the adherents of the law but also to those who share the faith of Abraham (who is the father of all of us, as it is written, "I have made you the father of many nations"), in the presence of the God in whom he believed, who gives life to the dead and calls into existence the things that don't exist. Hoping against hope, he believed that he would become "the father of many nations," according to what was said, "So shall your descendants be."

---

[29] Gerhard May cites ancient writers such as Plato, Xenophon, and Philo as using this creation analogy. See *Creatio Ex Nihilo: The Doctrine of "Creation out of Nothing" in Early Thought*, trans. A. S. Worrall (Edinburgh: T&T Clark, 1994), 8.

[30] See Jonathan A. Goldstein, *II Maccabees*, 309-313.

The key line here is "calls into existence the things that don't exist." Looking at the context, however, reveals Paul isn't referring here to creation from nothing. He's talking about people coming together as a nation under Abraham and his descendants. This assembling doesn't mean people emerged from nothing; instead, an already-existing people and their offspring respond to God's call to form a group. And their descendants come thereafter. That's creation out of something (or someones), not nothing.

The 2 Peter passage mentioned previously also says God creates "by the word" (3:5). It specifically identifies creating the earth from water by the word. So the Peter passage proves a clear example that speaking something into existence doesn't require bringing something into being from nothing.

The wedding ceremony provides a good illustration of how spoken words create something new by drawing upon something already present. An officiant speaks a marriage into existence when saying, "I now pronounce you husband and wife." Or consider schoolteachers. They sometimes call lines of children into existence when they say, "Line up, class." In these examples and others, creators call upon others to respond, and others' cooperation enacts a new state of being. "God commands in the way that an ancient monarch might have commanded," says Douglas Ottati, but ancient monarchs were able to create only if others followed their commands.[31]

The claim that God speaks or calls when creating, if taken literally, faces another challenge. It suggests the Spirit has vocal cords or a mouth. But an incorporeal God doesn't have the physical features required for speaking. One could respond by saying the divine speaking should be taken as metaphorical, of course, but if true, this metaphor shouldn't be asked to carry the metaphysical weight of claims about God bringing something from nothing. While I think we would be wise to believe the incorporeal Spirit literally communicates, I don't

---

[31] Douglas Ottati, *A Theology for the Twenty-First Century* (Grand Rapids, MI: Eerdmans, 2020), 172. Unfortunately, Ottati doesn't take his own claim here seriously enough. He elsewhere suggests (wrongly, I believe) that God's calling or speaking supports *creatio ex nihilo*.

think this communicating requires a literal mouth, vocal cords, or other bodily parts.

In sum, no biblical passage explicitly says divine speaking creates something out of nothing.

## "From the Beginning" Not the Same as "Out of Nothing"

Some advocates of *creatio ex nihilo* read that view into scripture when the text just doesn't support it. As an example, I note Millard Erickson's appeal to creation from nothing in his systematic theology.

In a section Erickson titles "Elements of the Biblical Teaching on Creation," he admits that the Hebrew Bible doesn't clearly advocate for creation from nothing. "The idea of *ex nihilo* creation can, however, be found in a number of New Testament passages," he claims. "In particular," Erickson says, "there are numerous references to the beginning of the world or the beginning of creation."[32] He then lists the following biblical citations:

- "from [since, before] the foundation of the world" (Matt. 13:35; 25:34; Luke 11:50; John 17:24; Eph. 1:4; Heb. 4:3; 9:26; 1 Peter 1:20; Rev. 13:8; 17:8)
- "from the beginning" (Matt. 19:4, 8; John 8:44; 2 Thess. 2:13; 1 John 1:1; 2:13-14; 3:8)
- "from the beginning of the world" (Matt. 24:21)
- "from the beginning of the creation" (Mark 10:6; 2 Peter 3:4)
- "from the beginning of creation which God created" (Mark 13:19)
- "since the creation of the world" (Rom. 1:20)
- "Thou, Lord, didst found the earth in the beginning" (Heb. 1:10)
- "the beginning of God's creation" (Rev. 3:14)

None of these passages explicitly affirm *creatio ex nihilo*. In citing these examples, Erickson projects his metaphysical position upon the biblical text. He assumes references to a beginning imply creation from nothing. But we could find many ways to interpret God's creating

---

[32] Millard Erickson, *Christian Theology*, 2nd ed. (Grand Rapids, MI: Baker, 1998), 395.

at "the beginning," and they don't require creating something from nothing.

While I value metaphysics, there's no indication that New Testament writers equated "beginning" with "from nothing." And this equation doesn't fit how other biblical passages refer to beginnings or with how you and I speak of them. Each of us had a beginning, after all, but none of us were created *ex nihilo*. Our parents engaged in sexual intercourse; that's *something*. And everything we know began by emerging from something prior.

Saying our world had a beginning can't be the same as saying nothing existed prior to its start.

## THE GNOSTIC ORIGIN OF *CREATIO EX NIHILO*

Early Christian and Jewish theologians believed God created the world out of something. Philo, for instance, postulated pre-existent matter alongside God. Justin, Hermogenes, Athenagoras, and Clement of Alexandria wrote that God created the world out of something. "These theologians," says historian Gerhard May, "could hold an acceptance of an unformed matter was entirely reconcilable with biblical monotheism and the power of God."[33] Origen of Alexandria and John Scotus Eirugena argued God has always been creating,[34] which implies that God never existed entirely alone.

*Creatio ex nihilo* has suspect beginnings. In his authoritative work subtitled *The Doctrine of 'Creation out of Nothing' in Early Christian Thought*, Gerhard May points to the Gnostic theologian Basilides as the originator of *creatio ex nihilo*. Gnostics were known for their view that matter must be inherently evil, says May, and they took a "very negative estimate of the world."[35]

---

[33] May, *Creatio Ex Nihilo*, 74.

[34] In addition to May's historical work, see James N. Hubler, "Creatio ex Nihilo: Matter, Creation, and the Body in Classical and Christian Philosophy through Aquinas" (Ph.D. diss., University of Pennsylvania, 1995); Blake T. Ostler, "Out of Nothing: A History of Creation ex Nihilo in Early Christian Thought," *FARMS Review*, 17, no. 2 (2005): 253–320.

[35] May, *Creatio Ex Nihilo*, 39.

Gnostics saw the world so negatively that they couldn't attribute its origin to a creative act of a good God. Marcion, for instance, thought any "God who uses this [evil] material can't be the true God."[36] Consequently, Basilides the Gnostic speculated that God first created a seed from nothing, out of which the universe grew without any divine help.[37] He also denied any analogy between divine creating and a human artist creating from material at hand.[38]

After other Gnostics joined Basilides in proposing creation from nothing, more "orthodox" Christians took up the theory. By the start of the third century, the doctrine began to settle in as the central creation theory of the church. May points to the church father Irenaeus as the decisive voice in this development.

We find in Irenaeus's doctrine of God an early articulation of the classical theism I've been showing is at odds with love. The deity he affirms not only creates *ex nihilo* but is impassible, simple, immutable, self-sufficient, eternal, and needs nothing.[39] And God's creating and sustaining, according to Irenaeus "isn't a necessary consequence of the goodness of God."[40]

The idea of omnipotence was central to why Irenaeus affirmed the doctrine of creation from nothing that he found in Basilides and other Gnostics. As Irenaeus puts it, "Neither the nature of any created thing, nor the weakness of the flesh, can prevail against the will of God. For God isn't subject to created things, but created things to God; and all things yield obedience to his will."[41] "The almightiness and freedom of God," says May, "dominates [Irenaeus's] whole theological position."[42] It was important to this early theologian that God be omnipotent.

---

[36] Ibid., 57.

[37] Some early Gnostics speculated that angels or the demiurge created matter. Like most early Christians, most Gnostics assumed God formed the universe from eternal matter. See May, *Creatio Ex Nihilo*, ch. 2, 3.

[38] Ibid., 73.

[39] Ibid., 164-178.

[40] Ibid., 176.

[41] Irenaeus of Lyons, *Against Heresies*, in *The Ante-Nicene Fathers*, edited by Alexander Roberts and James Donaldson (Grand Rapids, MI: Eerdmans, 1985), 5.5.2.

[42] Ibid.

Eventually, most major systematic theologians rejected the Gnostic notion that matter must be intrinsically evil. Some even cite creation from nothing to argue that we should see all creation as valuable exactly *because* God created it.[43] And unlike Irenaeus, some said love motivates God to create and thereafter relate with impure creatures.[44] But few contemporary advocates of *creatio ex nihilo* seem to know about the theory's Gnostic origin, or that biblical writers and many early Christians didn't affirm it.

Contemporary proponents of the creation from nothing theory point to several advantages they believe it has: it draws a clear distinction between God and creation, for instance, thereby avoiding pantheism. It implies that creatures depend upon God for their existence, whereas God, to exist, doesn't depend upon them. In the doctrine we clearly find God as creation's originator. And proponents emphasize the theory's implications for divine power: a God who can create from nothing seems more powerful than a God who creates in relation to creatures.[45]

The God who creates *ex nihilo* also seems freer and more independent, say advocates of this view. The deity who essentially exists alone doesn't need creatures. "The driving motive which underlies the Christian doctrine of *creatio ex nihilo*," concludes May, "is the attempt to do justice to the absolute sovereignty and unlimited freedom of the biblical God."[46] Jon Levenson agrees: "When it comes to creation, there remains a strange but potent tendency to resort to static affirmations of God's total power."[47]

*Creatio ex nihilo* supports the theology of an omnipotent, radically free, and essentially independent deity. We've already looked at the many problems for love these ideas entail.

---

[43] This is a major reason Ian A. McFarland says he embraces *creatio ex nihilo*. See *From Nothing* (Louisville, KY: Westminster John Knox, 2014).

[44] Michael Lodahl writes eloquently about the God who "bends down" to engage creatures. See *When Love Bends Down* (Kansas City, MO: Beacon Hill Press of Kansas City, 2006).

[45] Brian Robinette makes these kinds of arguments and others. See *The Difference Nothing Makes* (Notre Dame, IN: University of Notre Dame Press, 2024).

[46] May, *Creatio Ex Nihilo*, viii.

[47] Levenson, *Creation and the Persistence of Evil*, xxi.

## Problems with *Creatio Ex Nihilo*

The creation from nothing theory leads to a host of problems, and I've hinted at some above. Perhaps the most pressing: the problem of evil. An omnipotent deity who can create from nothing would be culpable for failing to prevent genuine evil. The God who creates *ex nihilo* singlehandedly can determine all creaturely abilities, systems, and trajectories. This all-powerful deity could instantly create obstacles to prevent evil doers from committing their heinous crimes. The creation from nothing view, therefore, intensifies the problem of evil.[48]

Some who say God once created from nothing will also claim God never creates that way today.[49] We find this aligning with the "voluntary divine self-limitation" view noted earlier: an omnipotent God initially created from nothing but freely chooses not to do so now.

But the problem of evil remains for those who embrace this view. After all, this all-powerful deity voluntarily chooses not to control, or create from nothing, to stop evil. This deity could, in theory, become un-self-limited to rescue the harmed and abused. On a whim, this God could create barriers to evil from nothing.

Let me illustrate: suppose a disturbed individual enters a restaurant with a machine gun and begins firing. The God who can create something out of nothing could instantly fashion miniature walls to deflect each bullet. In doing this, deity wouldn't violate the assailant's free will. If creating such obstacles would violate the laws of nature—laws the *ex nihilo* God alone decided—this violation would be justified because it

---

[48] Clarence Graham White responds to this criticism in *A Brief Process Reappraisal of Creatio Ex Nihilo* (Clarence Graham White, 2025). See also Rem Edwards, *What Caused the Big Bang?* (Amsterdam and New York: Rodopi/Brill, 2001).

[49] Not Even Once? Philip Clayton and Steven Knapp propose the strongest version of this argument. They call it the "not even once" view and say a loving God will not control creatures after creating *ex nihilo*. In response, I argue that if God once existed alone and voluntarily created from nothing, it stands to reason that acting as sufficient cause is something essential to deity. So, God can control creatures, if God wants to do so. Divine decisions not to control, in other words, would be contingent for this "not even once" God. But if God *can* control, the evils we experience, one would think, are awful enough to prompt a loving deity to prevent them. See Philip Clayton and Steven Knapp, *The Predicament of Belief* (Oxford: Oxford University Press, 2011), 66.

saved lives. A deity who can create something from nothing should, in the name of love, use this ability to stop genuine evil.

Some answer this objection by saying God's periodic interruption of the natural laws would lead to an unstable world. But they also typically say simultaneously that God alone decided the fundamental structures, laws, and systems of existence. And they're often the same people who claim God already *does* interrupt the laws of nature when doing miracles.

The unexamined implication of this thinking? Every murder, rape, torture, or genocide must, sadly, not have been important enough for God to prevent. Once we begin to imagine the ways a God capable of instantly creating something from nothing *could* prevent genuine evil, the problem of evil mushrooms. This deity seems either asleep, or doesn't care enough.

It's impossible for me—and I think for most people—to believe a God capable of creating obstacles out of nothing would allow every evil we've witnessed because they somehow make the world better. To believe this, we are forced to affirm that God permits every rape, holocaust, genocide, murder, or torture because, overall, we're better off. The way we live, however, suggests we don't actually believe the world becomes better when evils occur. Our intuitions rightly tell us that a *loving* God wouldn't permit the harm that an omnipotent deity could stop.[50]

*Creatio ex nihilo* has other problems too. I list eleven below, although I include some I've already mentioned. Some of these problems are more acute than others. But even the less consequential would be legitimate reasons to question the creation from nothing view.

---

[50] Is Uncontrolling Love Essential to God's Creating? Those who affirm creation from nothing might claim God has an attribute that prevents deity from controlling creatures, once they are created. But for a "God-can't-control-creatures" attribute to be essential to the divine nature, it must be expressed necessarily and, presumably, everlastingly. And it could only be an everlasting expression of God if there are always creatures alongside God. If God always creates alongside creatures, however, this would undermine any reason for affirming creation from nothing. On the other hand, if "God-can't-control-creatures" is a contingent divine attribute, God could decide to control from time to time. And the problem of evil emerges. Austin Pounds wrestles with these options in "Must Omnipotence Die so that Amipotence May Live?" in *Amipotence*, vol. 1 (Grasmere, ID: SacraSage, 2025); and "Love as the Foundation of Creation," Substack, https://evolvingtheologian.substack.com/p/love-as-the-foundation-of-creation

1. The Theoretical Problem – Absolute nothingness can't be conceived. It's intellectually impossible to fathom.[51]
2. The Historical Problem – Creation out of nothing was first proposed by Gnostics who assumed creation must be inherently evil.
3. The Empirical Problem – We have no empirical evidence that our universe originally came into being from nothing. Science doesn't tell us what occurred before the Big Bang.
4. The Creation at an Instant Problem – We have no evidence that creatures or creaturely entities today can emerge instantaneously from absolute nothingness.
5. The Solitary Power Problem – Creation out of nothing assumes God once acted alone. But power only makes sense when understood in relation to others.
6. The Timeless Creator Problem – Theologians who claim God is timeless before creating the universe *ex nihilo* can't account for how a timeless God timefully acts when creating.[52]
7. The Errant Revelation Problem – A God who can create something from nothing could guarantee an inerrant revelation. But we have good evidence no inerrant revelation exists.
8. The Evil Problem – God can omnipotently create from absolutely nothing, this deity is culpable for failing to use that ability to prevent genuine evil.
9. The Empire Problem/Status Quo Problem – The power needed to create something from nothing supports the idea that God establishes or permits oppressive empires or the evil status quo.[53]
10. The Biblical Problem – The Bible itself doesn't endorse creation from nothing. Writers say God creates out of something: water, deep, chaos, invisible things, mire and muck, and so on.

---

[51] Sjoerd L. Bonting argues this point well in *Creation and Double Chaos* (Minneapolis: Fortress, 2005), 70.

[52] Ryan Mullins addresses this problem in several books, often citing William Lane Craig's view as problematic. See R. T. Mullins, *From Divine Timemaker to Divine Watchmaker* (New York: Routledge, 2024).

[53] Whitney A. Bauman argues that *creatio ex nihilo* justifies colonialism. See "Creatio ex Nihilo, Terra Nullius, and the Erasure of Presence," in *Ecospirit*, Laurel Kearns and Catherine Keller, eds. (New York: Fordham University Press, 2007), 354.

11. The Ecological Problem – A God who can create something from nothing could prevent ecological disasters or make another world to replace this one. *Creatio ex nihilo*, therefore, demotivates us in our love of and sacrifice for the world.[54]

The idea of omnipotence lurks at the heart of most of these problems. A God who can bring about something from nothing has the all-powerful ability to bring about results singlehandedly. But omnipotence not only conflicts with what many people say about God's love and creaturely freedom, the above list suggests it's not empirically justifiable. And it undermines ethical motivations.

To overcome these problems, we need a creation theory that says God *never* has and *can't* create something from nothing.[55] A strong alternative would follow the logic of love when considering the Spirit's creating. This theory would say the Creator can't control anyone or anything at any time, even at the beginning of our universe. It would describe the Spirit as essentially relational, pantemporal (existing in all times), and whose freedom is shaped by love. To be strong, this alternative view would be consonant with general biblical claims about the Spirit's creating from something and mesh with general claims of contemporary science. And it would support, rather than undermine, our motivations to love God, one another, other creatures, and the planet.

---

[54] Michael Zbaraschuk argues this point in "*Creatio ex Deo*: Incarnation, Spirituality, Creation," in *Theologies of Creation*, Thomas Jay Oord, ed. (New York: Routledge, 2014). Michael Lodahl puts it well: "The biggest danger I see on *nihilo's* horizon, then, is that this concept tends to give us a rather cheap universe, a kind of throwaway world." Lodahl, *Theologies of Creation*, "*Creatio Ex Amore?*" 102.

[55] I address many of these problems as they relate to climate change in "God's Initial and Ongoing Creation, "in *Christian theology and Climate Change*, Hilda P. Koster and Ernst M Conradie, eds. (London: T&T Clark, 2019). See also John Culp, *Rebuilding After Collapse* (Anoka, MN: Process Century, 2018).

## Alternatives to *Creatio Ex Nihilo*

The creation from nothing theory has dominated Christianity and other religions for roughly 1,700 years. But other creation views preceded it, and theologians have proposed alternatives since that view's origin.

### Creation through Violence

Some alternatives to *creatio ex nihilo* prove less than savory. The *Enuma Elish* is a Babylonian creation story that predates the Genesis scriptures. At the heart of the narrative we find a battle in which a male god named Marduk defeats a female sea monster named Tiamat. After the battle, Marduk splits Tiamat's body to create the sky and earth. According to this theory, this battle and its aftermath comprise the origin of the universe.

The *Enuma Elish* story has several similarities with Genesis, which leads many scholars to think biblical writers were familiar with it. Both stories refer to a watery chaos or sea existing before creation, and the Hebrew word for this chaos, *tehom*, is similar to Tiamat. Both narratives speak of separating heaven and earth, which are in turn created from chaos. The order of creation is similar in each story too, with a period of rest after creating.

But it's not difficult to see patriarchal implications to the story of a male Marduk defeating and instrumentalizing the body of the feminine Tiamat. The battle narrative establishes the authority of a male God over the female other. "This narrative of omnipotent origin," says Catherine Keller, "vaporizes any residual, female-tinged chaos."[56] The story implies male dominance must be built into existence.

Important differences exist between the *Enuma Elish* and Genesis, however. The Babylonian cosmogony (i.e., story about ultimate origins) relies upon a violent battle and killing to initiate the creating process. The Genesis account doesn't. The Bible speaks of one God creating,

---

[56] Keller makes this argument and many others when advocating for a creation out of *chaosmos* or *profundis*. See *Face of the Deep* (New York: Routledge, 2003), 44.

although the word for deity is plural. By contrast, the *Enuma Elish* assumes polytheism. Some biblical passages assume the chaotic sea monster continues to exist, and some writers portray Israel's God opposing this chaos.[57] Other passages, however, assume God created it.[58]

The similarities between the *Enuma Elish* and Genesis sufficiently undermine the historical-literal view that the Bible gives a scientific account of the universe's origin. Put another way, studies in archeology and ancient mythology undermine the Young-Earth perspective. The first chapter of scripture likely represents a creation poem or liturgical hymn instead of a literal account.[59] We don't have to believe Genesis gives an eye-witness description of the Spirit's creating.

*Other Ancient Creation Myths*

Other ancient creation stories vary widely. A Chinese folk-tale speaks of a huge egg, from which came chaos, yin-yang, and a creator named Pan Ku. Greek creation myths typically involve stories of divine sex and family violence. The primary Norse creation story starts with a frost giant named Ymir who forms creation from primordial vapors. One Egyptian story starts with the god Atum who contained within himself the potential for everything. Another speaks of a bird from whose throat creation comes.

Hindu creation myths come in many forms. One of the most familiar says the primordial female creator Aditi gives birth to another creator, who in turn creates Aditi, and this is an ongoing cycle of creating. Another Hindu myth speaks of Vishnu sleeping in a cosmic ocean out of which the universe comes.

Australian aboriginal creation stories appeal to "The Dreamtime," and creating is a form of dreaming. A Rainbow Serpent awakens from sleep, emerges from the earth, and calls other creatures forth. From this, the world is created.

---

[57] See Job 26:12-13; Ps. 74:12-14; 89:10-11; Isa. 51:9.

[58] See Ps. 148:4-6.

[59] See Conrad Hyers, *The Meaning of Creation* (Atlanta: John Knox Press, 1984); John H. Walton, *The Lost World of Genesis One*.

Creation stories from the Americas typically involve multiple worlds in which our world is one among an everlasting succession. Some myths speak of creator gods, others of animal spirits working together to create. In Mayan creation stories, the silent sky and sea are interrupted when Plumed Serpent arises as creator. The Aztecs appealed to the Plumed Serpent as well, but they added that our world is one in a cycle of creation and destruction.

The Hopi of North America tell a creation myth in which the Sun God above and Spider Woman on earth split themselves to create. The Chumash tell of a female goddess forming and nurturing when creating. The Intuit speak of the Raven who instigates creating by bringing together the animals as co-creators. The Crow people tell of Coyote blowing on mud.[60]

### Creation Using Pre-Existing Materials

Until roughly the third century CE, most Jews and Christians thought God used pre-existing matter to create the universe. Following the Latin wording, this alternative has been called *creatio ex materia*. Plato influenced early people of faith who affirmed it, and he argued we should imagine God (*demiurge*) as a craftsman who created everything from pre-existing materials or prime matter.[61] More specifically, Plato says divinity has imposed order, reason, and soul upon material chaos and pressed the forms onto a void called the Receptacle.[62]

Advocates of *creatio ex materia* made an empirical argument against *creatio ex nihilo*. "Out of nothing, comes nothing," they said: *ex nihilo, nihil fit*. The first-century poet Lucretius is most associated with the idea that, as he put it, "nothing can be created out of nothing." We don't witness something coming from nothing in our daily

---

[60] For details on these stories, see Bryan E. Penprase, *The Power of Stars*, 2nd ed. (Cham, Switzerland: Springer, 2017), ch. 3.

[61] Often noted in these discussion are the Greek phrases *ouk on*, which means absolute nothingness or utter absence, and *me on*, which means a state of indeterminate possibilities. Most creation from nothing advocates appeal to *ouk on*.

[62] Plato's book *Timaeus* and its ruminations about the universe have influenced questions of origins since its writing (Desmond Lee, trans. [New York: Penguin, 1977]).

lives, he argued, and if it were to occur, it would undermine creation's regularities.[63]

Today, the Latter-Day Saint tradition is perhaps the largest religious group to say God originally created from pre-existing matter. According to *Doctrine and Covenants*, "the elements are eternal. They had no beginning, and they can have no end."[64] Latter-Day Saint scriptures point to multiple creators too. "And there stood one among them that was like unto God, and he said ... we will go down ... and we will make an earth whereon these may dwell."[65] This making "doesn't mean to create out of nothing," argued Mormonism founder Joseph Smith, it "means to organize."[66]

According to most *ex materia* theories, the pre-existing materials out of which God created our universe existed independently of deity's creative power and will. If true, the common biblical claim that God creates all things would be false: the writer of the book of Revelation, for instance, says that God "created all things, and by your will they existed and were created" (4:11). We find similar statements elsewhere in scripture.[67] If *creatio ex materia* were correct, at least some matter would be eternal and was once independent of God.

### Creation through Emanation

Another creation theory says God emanates the universe into existence from divine being. Philosophers such as Plotinus championed this view, although it comes in various forms and has diverse advocates. One of the most developed forms says creation flows from the divine being without God intending it, analogous to how rays shine forth from the sun or sparks come from flames. In this view, God doesn't actively choose what to create, just as the sun or fire makes no choice

---

[63] See Stephen Mumford's discussion of this in *Absence and Nothing* (Oxford: Oxford University Press, 2021).

[64] *Doctrine and Covenants* 93:33.

[65] Abraham, 3:24

[66] Joseph Smith, *King Follett Discourse* (April 7, 1844). For an explanation of Mormon philosophy, see Brittney Lowe Hartley, *Mormon Philosophy Simplified* (2019).

[67] See, for instance, Jn 1:3; Acts 17:24; 1 Cor. 8:6; Col. 1:16; Heb. 11:3.

in what they produce.⁶⁸ Plotinus also believed God's emanating to be timeless, and that creatures are, therefore, non-temporal gradations of divinity.⁶⁹

Other creation theories are straightforwardly pantheistic. One simply says God created the universe out of Godself: *creatio ex dei*. If God creates the world and its creatures from the divine being, of course, all beings would presumably be divine. This creation theory undermines distinctions between God and the universe, because created objects must also be divine objects.⁷⁰

*Creatio ex dei* isn't attractive to most who take evil and sin seriously and also believe in a perfectly loving God. According to *creatio ex dei*, after all, whatever occurs—including horrific evils—would be an expression of the divine. If true, all crooked politicians would be deities—literally. Every instance of sexual abuse and every natural disaster would be the outcome of the divine. Pantheistic creation theories, therefore, exacerbate the problem of evil, or deny its reality.

### *Creatio Ex Christi*

Several New Testament texts suggest a *creatio ex Christi* doctrine. This view says God creates in, through, by, or out of Christ.⁷¹ When Christ is seen as agent, instrument, or source of creating, this view can function alongside *creatio ex nihilo, creatio ex materia,* and other theories. If we think Christ to be the material used in the creating, this view veers toward *creatio ex dei* and pantheism.⁷²

Theologian Jürgen Moltmann advances a *creatio ex Christi* theory. "If we proceed from the inner-trinitarian relationships of the Persons

---

⁶⁸ Muslim theologians Ibn Sīnā and al-Fārābī offered similar emanation theories. See H. Pehlivan, "İbn Sînâ'ya göre duaya icabet ve duanın tesiri," *İslâmî Araştırmalar Dergisi*, 31:2 (2020), 383–405. I'm grateful to Dini Cevaplar for alerting me to this.

⁶⁹ Plotinus, *The Enneads*, A. H. Armstrong, trans. 7 vols. (Cambridge, MA: Harvard University Press, 1984).

⁷⁰ Mary-Jane Rubenstein, *Pantheologies* (New York: Columbia University Press, 2018).

⁷¹ See, for example, 1 Cor. 8:6, Col. 1:15-20, John 1:1-3, Heb. 1:2.

⁷² For a fine discussion of this, see Stephen H. Webb, "Creatio A Materia Ex Christi," in *Theologies of Creation,* Thomas Jay Oord, ed. (New York: Routledge, 2012).

in the Trinity," he says, "then it becomes clear that the Father creates the one who is his Other by virtue of his love for the Son."[73] This means that "from eternity God has desired not only himself but the world too, for he did not merely want to communicate himself to himself; he wanted to communicate himself to the one who is other than himself as well." Therefore, it was "through the eternal Son/Logos [that] the Father creates the world."[74]

We might interpret Moltmann's proposal in at least two ways. One says God everlastingly makes the world through the Son, because the world was created out of divine substance. This would imply, however, that the world essentially *is* God.[75] Although Moltmann speaks of "the creation of the world out of God" and claims, "God acts on himself when he acts creatively," he also rejects pantheism.[76]

The second interpretation of Moltmann's proposal engages his claim that "the idea of the world is inherent in the nature of God himself from eternity."[77] This means, Moltmann says, that "the idea of the world is already inherent in the Father's love of the Son."[78] In fact, the Son "is the divinely immanent archetype of the idea of the world."[79]

This interpretation of *creatio ex Christi* faces the limits inherent in abstract ideas.[80] Ideas have no materiality, so they can't be the "stuff" required for the construction of the universe. Ideas can't create, and they don't function as efficient causes. Although likely necessary for creative activity, ideas neither act nor can be acted upon. At best, therefore, the *ex Christi* theory says God engages *potentialities*.[81] But

---

[73] Jürgen Moltmann, *The Trinity and the Kingdom* (San Francisco: Harper and Row, 1981), 122.

[74] Ibid., 108.

[75] Joy Ann McDougall explores the trinitarian implications of Moltmann's thought in *Pilgrimage of Love* (Oxford: Oxford University Press, 2005).

[76] Ibid., 110-113.

[77] Ibid., 106.

[78] Ibid., 108.

[79] Ibid., 112.

[80] Samuel Youngs offers a coherent view of Moltmann's Christology in *The Way of the Kenotic Christ* (Eugene, OR: Cascade, 2019).

[81] Eberhard Jüngel makes similar arguments for the Father creating through the Son, and he's influenced by Karl Barth in this speculating. But Jüngel doesn't lay out a clear creation theory. See Eberhard Jüngel, *God as the Mystery of the World* (Grand Rapids, MI: Eerdmans,

Moltmann would have needed to develop his view for it to make good sense.

## Vague Theories

Some theologians who endorse *creatio ex nihilo* actually think God created out of or in relation to a "nothing-something."[82] Karl Barth, for instance, affirms *creatio ex nihilo*. But by the time he describes the influence and characteristics of "nothingness," it sounds like something. Similarly, Jürgen Moltmann affirms both "creation out of chaos and *creatio ex nihilo*."[83] He claims that "creation [is] God's act in Nothingness and . . . God's order in chaos."[84] Combining something and nothing in these ways confuses rather than illuminates; it breaks the law of noncontradiction.

Theologians John B. Cobb, Jr. and David Ray Griffin distinguish between creation from *relative* and *absolute* nothingness. This affirmation of the relative would allow for the existence of disorder, forms, and simple entities but no enduring entities. Something exists, but not anything complex.

This language can confuse, however, because it seems there's no metaphysical difference between what Cobb and Griffin call "relative

---

1983). Marit A. Trelstad makes a stronger argument for creation from possibilities in "The Fecundity of Nothing: A Proposal of *Creatio ex Potentia* in Conversation with Quantum Cosmologies," in *Theologies of Creation*, Thomas Jay Oord, ed. (New York: Routledge, 2014).

[82] Augustine uses the unfortunate phrase "nothing-something" in his affirmation of creation from nothing. See *The Confessions of St. Augustine*, John K. Ryan, trans. (Garden City, NY: Image/Doubleday), XII, 6. Catherine Keller addresses Augustine and the idea in "'Nothingsomething' On My Mind: *Creatio Ex Nihilo* or *ex Profundis*?" in *Theologies of Creation*, Thomas Jay Oord, ed. (New York: Routledge, 2014).

[83] Moltmann, *The Trinity and the Kingdom*, 109, 110; see also 113.

[84] Ibid., 109. Drawing from Jewish sources, Moltmann also appeals to *zimzum* as a creating tactic. "The God who within himself," says Moltmann, "indwells so widely and in so reciprocal a way, corresponds to himself when he cedes his creation space besides himself, before he creates it. God gives space, God makes room, God withdraws in order to let a non-divine reality exist with himself and in himself. This divine conferral of space provides the free and open scope for the existence, life and enduring being of those whom God creates. See "The Origin and Completion of Time in the Primordial and in the Eschatological Moment," *Science and Wisdom*, Trans. M. Kohl (Minneapolis: Fortress, 2003), 119.

nothingness" and chaos. If God did not create and can't control relative nothingness, a primary reason to affirm *creation ex nihilo* disappears.[85]

Still others say the Spirit's decision to create comes neither from external forces nor God's own nature. They appeal to mystery. Millard Erickson, for instance, says God "freely chose to create, for reasons not known to us."[86] Erickson and others like him want to avoid speculating about the Spirit's reasons so as to allow maximal freedom to God. They choose refuge in vagueness. This appeal seems to be another example of prioritizing divine freedom at the expense of relational love.

## *Creatio ex Amore*

A more promising creation theory says God creates out of love. Michael Lodahl argues for *creatio ex amore*, in part, because doing so begins "to lure our attention toward the *moral character* of the Holy Mystery we call 'God.'" This, says Lodahl, offers us "a measure of enlightenment regarding the question of *why* God has created, and continues to create, a world such as the one in which we live."[87] In short, love motivates divine creating.

Lodahl's version of *creatio ex amore* also positively depicts creation as a divine gift rather than necessary emanation. He doesn't portray divine giving as a one-off in the distant past, but as an expression of God's continual loving. The Spirit creates so that creatures can fulfill their purpose by loving in response. God creates, Lodahl says, so that love might flourish.[88]

Lodahl's vision holds promise as an alternative theory of creation, but its details aren't developed. He helpfully says love serves as God's motive for creating. But *creatio ex amore* could also easily mean that love is the "stuff" from which God creates. And, unfortunately, Lodahl

---

[85] David Ray Griffin and John B. Cobb, Jr. address the relative vs. absolute nothingness distinction. See *Process Theology* (Louisville, KY: Westminster John Knox, 1976), 65.

[86] Erickson, *Christian Theology*, 378.

[87] Michael Lodahl, "*Creatio Ex Amore!*" in *Theologies of Creation*, Thomas Jay Oord, ed. (New York: Routledge, 2014), 99. Italics are Lodahl's.

[88] Ibid., 103-105.

also says *creatio ex amore* "doesn't necessarily contradict *creatio ex nihilo*."[89]

As I see it, *creatio ex amore* as Lodahl describes it, needs significantly more development.[90] And I believe a view of God's creating that prioritizes love should reject *creatio ex nihilo* and, thereby, avoid problems the traditional doctrine generates.[91] Those problems not only include the problem of evil, but also claims about God's essential non-relations with creation and sovereign freedom. While Lodahl rightly prioritizes love, we should reject creation theories that support divine isolation and control.[92]

## Scientific Considerations

Until the 1960s, most major scientists believed the universe was eternal. Today, the view is less common and, in some circles, off the table as a possibility. Now, the dominant view is popularly known as the "Big Bang theory" but in the sciences, it is known as "the standard model of cosmology." It says the universe began as an extremely hot, dense point billions of years ago. From this initial singularity, the universe has been expanding.

Physicists speculate that within the first second after the Big Bang's explosion, basic physical forces and fundamental particles of matter emerged. Over time, these fundamental elements of existence were

---

[89] Ibid., 99.

[90] Of those who develop *creatio ex amore* more than Lodahl, I find James H. Olthuis's work most helpful. But he's reluctant to make bold metaphysical claims, often appealing to apophatic mystery. See "Creatio Ex Amore," in *Transforming Philosophy and Religion*, Norman Wirzba and Bruce Ellis Benson, eds. (Bloomington, IN: University of Indiana Press, 2008).

[91] Norman Wirzba offers an even less compelling version of *creatio ex amore*. He not only embraces creation from nothing, but he also says God is beyond being, is timeless, and adopts other tropes from classical theism. See his explanation in *The Sacred Life* (Cambridge: Cambridge University Press, 2021).

[92] For Lodahl's most developed and most helpful writings on creation, see Michael E. Lodahl, *God of Nature and of Grace* (Nashville, TN: Kingswood, 2003). Others scholars exploring the notion of creation out of love include Paul Fiddes, "Creation Out of Love," in *The Work of Love*, John Polkinghorne, ed. (Grand Rapids, MI: Eerdmans, 2001); J. Richard Middleton, *The Liberating Image* (Grand Rapids, MI: Brazos, 2005); Jürgen Moltmann, "God's Kenosis in the Creation and Consummation of the World," in *The Work of Love*, and Jordan Wessling, *Love Divine* (Oxford: Oxford University Press, 2020).

drawn together by gravity and other forces. From this emerged the basic and the massive structures of existence, including nuclei, atoms, molecules, dust, rocks, planets, stars, galaxies, galaxy clusters, and superclusters. The emergence of life and the formation of more complex entities gives reason to speak of the universe's development in evolutionary terms.

Big Bang theory can't be based on eye-witness accounts of the beginning, obviously. But it does build from other observations. First, the discovery of a cosmic microwave background radiation supports it. Scientists detect a faint glow apparently left over from the hot start of the universe. Observation of a redshift in galaxies also support the Big Bang theory, and this shift seems to indicate that the distant galaxies keep moving away from us. This expansion seems to be accelerating, likely driven by an unknown force called "dark energy."

No one knows the conditions of the universe's beginning at time zero ($t = 0$). The purview of science limits scientific speculation about what, if anything, existed prior to the Big Bang. Much of the standard model of cosmology relies upon mathematical extrapolations from what's known in the present. Scientists often focus on what might have occurred in the initial milliseconds. It's all *highly* speculative.

Physicists offer a number of proposals to account for the mathematical oddities and dark energy associated with the Big Bang. Some propose an exponential inflation of the universe in the beginning, others talk about a subsequent "big bounce;" some appeal to string theory; others speak of "branes" in multi-dimensional space; some propose cyclical models that say our universe is part of an everlasting chain; others point to vacuum fluctuations; some say our universe bounced out of a black hole; and so on.[93] Each proposal has variations and details.

---

[93] For accessible explanations of these options, see Andrei Linde, "The Self-Reproducing Inflationary Universe," *Scientific American*, November 1994; Paul J. Steinhardt and Neil Turok, "The Myth of the Beginning of Time," *Scientific American*, May 2004; David Deutsch and Michael Lockwood, "The Quantum Physics of Time Travel," *Scientific American*, March 1994; Max Tegmark and Dennis Sciama, "Parallel Universes," *Scientific American*, May 2003. George Ellis evaluates these proposals in "Does the Multiverse Really Exist?" *Scientific American*, August, 2011. See also Enrique Gaztanaga, "Gravitational bounce from the quantum exclusion principle," in *Physics Review*, (May, 2025) DOI: https://doi.org/10.1103/PhysRevD.111.103537

Results from the James Webb Space Telescope research expose gaps in the best theories about what might have come before and after the Big Bang. Many unanswered questions remain, especially about the origin of space, time, and energy.

Perhaps the most scientifically remarkable discovery about the universe consists in what has come to be called its "fine-tuning."[94] The constants of nature, which include the mass of the electron, the strength of gravity, the capacities of nuclear forces, and more, have the remarkably precise values needed for life to emerge.[95] If these constants had been ever so slightly different, we couldn't exist.[96] We live in a Goldilocks universe where the conditions are "just right." "Most scientists concede," says physicist Paul Davies, "that there are features of the observed Universe that appear ... ingeniously and felicitously arranged in their relationship to the existence of biological organisms in general and intelligent observers in particular."[97]

The precision of this fine-tuning suggests a Tuner. In fact, some prominent atheists have become theists, in part, because of the fine-tuning discovery.[98] However, what the fine-tuning argument for God gives as an advantage—the idea that deity precisely[99] formulated

---

[94] Key texts explaining the anthropic principle, fine-tuning, and their various features include John Barrow and Frank Tipler, *The Anthropic Cosmological Principle* (Oxford: Clarendon, 1986) and Paul Davies, *The Accidental Universe* (Cambridge: Cambridge University Press, 1982). Among the better books on the subject, see Karl Giberson, *The Wonder of the Universe* (Downers Grove, IL: InterVarsity, 2012).

[95] George Ellis and Nancey Murphy explore these issue in *On the Moral Nature of the Universe* (Minneapolis: Fortress, 1996). I find their work helpful, except insofar as they accept *creatio ex nihilo* and insofar as they say, "God voluntarily withholds divine power" (246). See my response to them in "An Open Theology Doctrine of Creation," in *Creation Made Free* (Eugene, OR: Wipf and Stock, 2009).

[96] Robin Collins addresses this issue well in "The Teleological Argument: An Exploration of the Fine-tuning of the Cosmos." In *The Blackwell Companion to Natural Theology*, edited by W. L. Craig and J.P. Moreland (Oxford: Blackwell, 2009), 202-81.

[97] Paul C. W. Davies, "Universes Galore: Where Will It All End?" in *Universe or Multiverse?* Carr, ed. (Cambridge: Cambridge University Press, 2007), 487.

[98] Antony Flew explains his shift from atheism to belief in God in *There Is a God* (New York: HarperOne, 2007). Philip Goff explains his shift from fictionalism to theism in *Why? The Purpose of the Universe* (New York/Oxford: Oxford University Press, 2023). Sy Garte explains his journey in *The Works of His Hands* (Grand Rapids, MI: Kregel, 2019).

[99] Keith Ward offers an accessible explanation and assessment of five versions of the multiverse. See *Why There Almost Certainly Is a God* (Oxford: Lion, 2008).

the fundamental laws of the universe—gets erased by the problem of evil. Why doesn't the God who initially created in such a precise way do a *better* job of reducing suffering? If God could manipulate creation in the past, why not prevent pointless pain in the present?[100]

The more finely tuned the universe, the more we might doubt a divine Tuner loves perfectly.

An influential approach to explaining (or explaining away) fine-tuning has gained prominence in recent decades: the multiverse. It imagines our universe as one among a massive number of differently-conditioned universes. According to this view, this multiverse contains an immensely large, perhaps infinite, number of universes. Consequently, it's not remarkable that we should find one universe, by pure chance, to be finely tuned. "If there are an infinite number of worlds that take on all possible parameters through infinite time," explains Mary-Jane Rubenstein, "then strange as our particular parameters may seem, they were bound to emerge at some time."[101] To put it simply, we got lucky.

Multiverse theories come in various forms: some imagine a massive number of universes spatially separated by mind-boggling expanses across space-time. Others imagine an endless number of successive universes, in the temporal sense of one emerging after another. Others see universes emerging from the moment-by-moment "branching" of decisions made at all levels of existence, even at the quantum level.

Perhaps the most controversial posits that an infinite number of worlds *necessarily* exist, but they're inaccessible to one another, because each resides in its own space and time. (This, of course, is unverifiable.) Though the multiverse hypothesis can sound fantastical, each of these proposals has varying degrees of plausibility and has gained supporters.

Some adopt the multiverse perspective to avoid saying God created our universe. As the physicist Bernard Carr puts it, "if you don't want

---

[100] Lawrence Cahoone addresses these questions well in "Cosmology and the Problem of Evil: God and the Second Law," *Zygon: Journal of Religion and Science* 60:3 (2025), 779–801.

[101] Mary-Jane Rubenstein, *Without End: The Many Lives of the Multiverse* (New York: Columbia University Press, 2014), 17.

God, you'd better have a multiverse."[102] But it isn't that simple. After all, an entirely inaccessible and incomprehensible multiverse proposal provides no explanatory grounds for conducting scientific work. What's to observe?

An infinite number of universes seems conceptually fruitless too. Without limits, comparisons seem impossible. And an infinite number of simultaneous universes wouldn't be falsifiable, because, as Paul Steinhardt notes, "it allows every conceivable possibility."[103] The multiverse, therefore, isn't scientifically proven, nor is it provable.

Lest theists scoff at the infinite multiverse hypothesis, however, they should remember how many traditional theologians similarly describe God. Some theists claim an infinite, incomprehensible, and inaccessible deity serves as the ultimate explanation for all that exists.[104] Those who appeal to an infinite and inaccessible deity would be hypocritical to scoff at alternative appeals to an infinite and inaccessible multiverse. In fact, neither is proven nor provable.

In most versions of the multiverse, speculation amounts not to doing science but is really speculative metaphysics. There's nothing wrong with metaphysics, of course, or speculation. In fact, an adequate doctrine of creation for a systematic theology of love *requires* metaphysical speculation. Although metaphysics can neither be proven nor provable in the scientific sense, the best metaphysical proposals account for reality better than alternatives.

Science can't, on its own, answer the question of why there is something rather than nothing. But theology also can't answer this question alone.[105] The most plausible doctrines of creation, therefore, integrate insights from science, theology, and metaphysics. Or as Alfred North Whitehead put it, "You can't shelter theology from science, or science

---

[102] Tim Folger, "Sciences Alternative to an Intelligent Creator: The Multiverse Theory." [Interview with Andrei Linde.] *Discover*, November 10, 2008.

[103] Maggie McKee, "Ingenious: Paul Steinhard," *Nautilus* 25 (Sept. 2014).

[104] Mary-Jane Rubenstein explores these issues and many others in her wonderful book, *Worlds Without End*.

[105] On theology and fine-tuning, see George Ellis, "The Theology of the Anthropic Principle," in *Quantum Cosmology and the Laws of Nature*, Robert John Russell, et. al., eds. (Vatican Observatory/CTNS, 1993).

from theology; nor can you shelter either of them from metaphysics, or metaphysics from either of them. There is no short cut to truth."[106]

## Conclusion

The theory that God created the universe out of absolutely nothing—*creatio ex nihilo*—has dominated theological discourse for centuries. But it faces devastating and, I think, insurmountable problems. I believe it should be rejected.

The idea that an omnipotent God can create something from nothing intensifies the problem of evil, because this deity would be culpable for failing to use this omnipotent ability to prevent unnecessary suffering. In addition, the Bible doesn't endorse *creatio ex nihilo*, because biblical writers variously depict God creating from pre-existing chaos, water, unformed matter, or something else. Problematically, Gnostics invented this theory to separate a pure deity from an evil world. And *creatio ex nihilo* depicts God as essentially independent from creation rather than essentially loving it.

Each alternative to *creatio ex nihilo* has advantages and deficiencies. Some deficiencies derive from vagueness; for instance, saying God both creates from nothing and yet also from chaos. We saw how other cultures offer accounts that rely on violence, portray God as unloving, or imply that deity isn't omnipresent. Some make God's creating so inconceivable that we can't draw analogies to creaturely creating and, consequently, "God creates" becomes incomprehensible. Other alternatives lead to pantheism, which undermines helpful distinctions between a loving Spirit and creatures who sometimes harm. Some theories assume God didn't create all things, and others remove all freedom from God's creating. Some creation theories remain underdeveloped. And so on.

Contemporary science offers insights and theories about the origin of the universe. Although grounded in some empirical data, the Big Bang model leaves key questions unanswered—particularly about

---

[106] Alfred North Whitehead, *Religion in the Making* (New York: Fordham University Press, 1996), 76-77.

the state of reality at, or before, the initial singularity. Attempts to answer those questions include inflation theory, cyclical cosmologies, or string-based multiverses, but these all remain highly speculative, relying on mathematical extrapolations. These cosmological models, while valuable, show the limits of scientific inquiry when pondering ultimate origins.

The universe's apparent fine-tuning proves to be one of the most provocative findings of contemporary science. The precise balance of constants necessary for life remains either an extraordinarily improbable accident or suggests the work of a divine Tuner. Some cosmologists offer multiverse theories as an alternative to God as an explanation for fine-tuning, but these theories stay in the realm of metaphysical speculation without empirical grounding. Ironically, defenders of an infinite and inaccessible multiverse face similar credibility challenges to those who invoke an infinite and inaccessible deity.

In light of both theology and science, a new doctrine of creation is warranted. An adequate creation theory would align with general aspects of contemporary cosmology, honor theological insights from the biblical witness, and center love in God's creating. The new doctrine would reject both *creatio ex nihilo* and the doctrine of omnipotence that supports it. And it would present a vision of a creating Spirit who never acts in isolation, never controls, and isn't culpable for evil.

I offer this alternative theory in the next chapter.

CHAPTER TWELVE

# Ever Creator

## THE BIG IDEAS

- God is the ever creator.
- The Spirit always creates out of or alongside creation in love (*creatio ex creatione sempiternalis en amore*).
- The new theory overcomes various problems associated with *creatio ex nihilo*, and it centers love in God's creating.
- The motive, method, modes, measure, materials, and meaning of the Spirit's creating revolve around issues of love.
- *Creatio ex creatione sempiternalis en amore* fits the biblical witness to God's creating better than *creatio ex nihilo*.
- The scriptural emphasis upon God's everlasting love (*hesed, olam*) aligns with the new creation theory.
- *Creatio ex nihilo* isn't fully aligned with science; *creatio ex creatione sempiternalis en amore* aligns with a cyclical model of the universe.
- The new theory says our universe isn't co-eternal with God nor part of an infinite regress.
- The new theory says God freely creates in one sense but must create in other, and God depends on creation in one sense but not in another.
- The new theory says God is uncreated, and God always creates out of entities God previously created.
- The new theory says the always and necessarily creating Spirit is the transcendent One worthy of worship.

*I*n the beginning... was love.

*Before* the beginning of our particular universe, the Spirit was loving and creating. God loved creatures before the Big Bang and has loved moment by moment throughout evolutionary history. The Spirit creates and loves every entity, organism, creature, ecosystem, and civilization on every planet, universe, and multiverse that might exist. God will everlastingly create and love in the future too.[1]

As the last chapter indicated, most theologies say God creates all things. But many ignore love or marginalize it when considering this creating. Even theologians who start with love usually fail to develop its full implications. Or they offer confusing proposals.

This chapter offers a new doctrine of creation in which the Spirit's creative love plays the central role.[2] This theory fits the general drift of scripture, which consistently portrays God as both loving and creating in relation to something. It aligns with leading theories in science, accounting for the Big Bang, evolution, and multiverse possibilities.[3] And the new theory builds from the logic of uncontrolling and pluriform love I've offered.[4]

The loving Spirit, I will argue, is the Ever Creator.

## GOD EVERLASTINGLY CREATES OUT OF CREATION IN LOVE

I offer what I call *creatio ex creatione sempiternalis en amore* as a more adequate theory of creation. This is a mouthful, but the Latin phrase means "God everlastingly creates out of creation in love." Here's a summary of the components of what I'll advocate in this new theory:

---

[1] This chapter is dedicated to Tripp Fuller. Tripp's friendship has motivated me to think deeply and creatively, exploring new ways to talk about theology in our present age.

[2] Although I came to my creation views independently, I've discovered they share some similarities with those of Ibn Taymiyya. For an explanation of Taymiyya, see Jon Hoover, *Ibn Taymiyya* (London: Oneworld Academic, 2019). I'm grateful to Ryan Mullins for alerting me to this. See Mullins, *From Divine Timemaker to Divine Watchmaker* (New York: Routledge, 2025).

[3] For the scientific implications of and associates with various creation theories, see Mary-Jane Rubenstein, *Worlds without End* (New York: Columbia University Press, 2015).

[4] See Thomas Jay Oord, *The Uncontrolling Love of God* (Downers Grove, IL: IVP Academic, 2015) and *Pluriform Love* (Grasmere, ID: SacraSage, 2022).

- The Spirit was creating other universes before ours and will create others after it (which amounts to successive universes). God may create universes alongside ours (which amounts to simultaneous universes), but the idea of an absolutely infinite number of universes is incoherent.[5]
- The Spirit always creates out of, or in relation to, what God previously created. Even at the Big Bang, the Spirit created in relation to what this loving deity created earlier. God always creates out of something.
- The Spirit never creates singlehandedly, as a sufficient cause. There have always been creatures and creation out of or in relation to which God creates. The always loving deity never began to create, as if not doing so previously. God is the Ever Creator.
- Love motivates the Spirit's creating, and God always wants the best, given the circumstances. In the creative process, there's something rather than nothing because God everlastingly loves and creates.
- Creation isn't self-sufficient, because it relies upon God moment-by-moment. Creatures are also not self-explanatory, because they depend upon God and other creatures for their existence. Every universe that exists—however many there are—has the Spirit as its Source.
- The Creator is uncreated, in the sense that God everlastingly and necessarily exists. But the Spirit's moment-by-moment experiences are partially created by creaturely co-creators.
- "Love for creation" is a necessary divine attribute. The Spirit necessarily creates and loves others. How and what God creates will be contingent upon what's possible in each situation and upon the contributions of creatures.

---

[5] The claim that God necessarily creates an infinite number of universes simultaneously has numerous metaphysical problems. But those problems don't apply to my claim that God everlastingly creates a succession of universes. The theory I propose says God can't create in unloving ways. Consequently, the universes that could *actually* exist will be characterized by the action of a loving Creator. This view isn't the same as positing an infinite number of possible universes. In addition, every universe that exists will share particular metaphysical laws. This is another reason why "infinite" is problematic.

The theory that God creates out of creation everlastingly in love overcomes the problems of *creatio ex nihilo*. It doesn't ask us to conceive the inconceivable: absolute nothingness. We avoid the Gnostic view that creation must be inherently evil. This theory better fits the empiricism of science, which says something always emerges in relation to something else. It overcomes creation-from-nothing-at-an-instant obstacles, which also makes solving the problem of evil impossible. Saying God creates out of creation everlastingly assumes God's power as social, not overpowering or conjuring by fiat. It affirms the notion of successive universes, aligns with the possibility of simultaneous universes, but doesn't affirm (because this would be incoherent) an absolute infinite number of universes. And this theory matches the general witness of scripture, which always portrays God creating in relation to something.

The God who everlastingly and in love creates something out of, or in relation to, what deity previously created isn't omnipotent, at least not in the usual meanings of the word. The Spirit has never controlled creation nor ever created singlehandedly and never could. The Spirit's creative love is essentially uncontrolling—now, at the beginning of our universe, and everlastingly. The Ever Creator is amipotent.

The Spirit didn't singlehandedly set up the conditions that make genuine evil possible. The systems and law-like regularities of the universe have never been the result of the Spirit's unilateral decisions, because God can't singlehandedly determine outcomes. Even at the Big Bang, deity worked with other actors, factors, and forces, because God collaborates with creaturely co-creators, conditions, law-like regularities, and/or chaos.[6]

God everlastingly creates something *new* in each moment alongside creaturely input, and the possibilities for good and evil inherently emerge from God's creative love and creation's response.[7] Sometimes

---

[6] Matthew David Segall argues similarly in "Amplifying Amipotence Through a Theopoetic Re-Reading of Creation," in *Amipotence, vol. 2*, Brandon Brown, et. al., eds. (Grasmere, ID: SacraSage, 2025).

[7] On the importance of possibilities for creating, see Marit A. Trelstad, "The Fecundity of Nothing: A Proposal of *Creatio ex Potentia* in Conversation with Quantum Cosmologies," in *Theologies of Creation: Creatio Ex Nihilo and its New Rivals*, Thomas Jay Oord, ed. (New York: Routledge, 2014). The role of possibilities is also crucial for Ruth Page in *God and the Web of Creation* (London: SCM, 1996).

creatures collaborate poorly, or the conditions aren't conducive for flourishing. When that happens, evil occurs. But the universal Spirit of love doesn't create, will, cause, or permit evil. Creatures and creation are to blame.

## Six M Words to Describe the Ever Creator's Work

Here's a summary of my new view of God's creating. For convenience, we can identify the six main ideas with words that begin with the letter "M."

### Motive

The Spirit doesn't primarily create to seek glory; love motivates God's creating.[8] The Spirit always wants to promote the well-being of creaturely others. The answer to the question, "Why is there something rather than nothing?" would be, in part, that love everlastingly motivates God to create what is nondivine. Love is the Ever Creator's motive for creating.

### Materials

The Spirit always creates from or in relation to material creation. But all the material entities and organisms from which deity creates in each moment were previously created by God. The "stuff" from which the Spirit creates, therefore, are the creaturely entities, organisms, and actors God created previously.

The Spirit doesn't create from the divine being nor from ideas about the Son. The Spirit didn't "stumble upon" materials that predate or pre-exist deity. Creation isn't the result of a violent battle nor involuntary divine emanation. God doesn't create from ideas or possibilities alone, although they play a role in the Spirit's creating. The Ever

---

[8] For an accessible discussion of divine motives for creating, see Jordan Wessling and Ross Park, *Divine Motivation and Humanity* (Cambridge: Cambridge University Press, 2025). See also Jordan Wessling, *Love Divine* (Oxford: Oxford University Press, 2020).

Creator uses materials when creating, materials that deity created previously. And there is no absolute beginning to the Spirit's creating these materials.

## Method

The Spirit's method of creating is collaborative, cooperative, and invitational. God's creating is direct, calling creatures and creation to co-create.[9] In this process, the Spirit woos as an efficient cause each entity, organism, and actor, but God never acts as a sufficient cause. Life as we know it emerges as jointly created by Creator and creation.

It's not just that the Spirit's method for creating involves collaboration.[10] An adequate doctrine of creation acknowledges that the creaturely spontaneity, agency, and activity proves essential to the creative process. Using abilities God necessarily gives them, creatures can cooperate well or poorly with the Spirit's creating. And a loving God can't control them. The Ever Creator's creative methods are collaborative not solitary.

## Modes

The Spirit creates necessarily in one sense and contingently in another. Unlike the God of traditional theologies, the Spirit *necessarily* creates, because it's God's nature to do so. But what and how the Spirit creates are contingent, being influenced by various actors and factors, forces, and possibilities that emerge in the creative process.

*Whether* the Spirit creates is decided by the divine nature; God must create. *How* and *what* the Spirit creates freely emerges in ongoing, open-ended collaboration with creatures. This is contingent, because creatures and creation could have been different than they are. The Ever Creator faces an open future and creates in the modes of both necessity and contingency.

---

[9] Philip Hefner has done extensive work arguing for the cogency of the label "created co-creators." See *The Human Factor* (Philadelphia: Augsburg Fortress, 2000).

[10] Mark Umstot puts this succinctly, "If love is the center, control can't be the method."

## Measure

The measure of the Spirit's creating is everlasting. There are no sets or calculations that can measure its duration, so in this sense, it's measureless. Although each individual universe has a beginning and end, the temporal series of successive multiverses would have no absolute beginning and no absolute end. *Creatio ex creatione sempiternalis en amore* aligns with this repeated phrase in scripture: "the steadfast love of the Lord endures forever!"

If there are universes simultaneous with ours, the Spirit created them too. But no universe could exist without the loving creating and presence of the Spirit, so an absolute infinite number of universes is impossible. But the Ever Creator's creating is everlastingly measureless.

## Meaning

The meaning of the Spirit's creating is thus: A divine Lover creates beloved creatures and inspires them to love others, God, themselves, and creation in diverse ways. The primary meaning of life, then, is love. Put another way, the universal Spirit of love creates a universe of potential lovers and calls them to express pluriform love so that all will flourish. The Ever Creator's love gives life meaning.

## BIBLICAL SUPPORT

The writings of scripture provide resources, inspiration, and ideas a systematic theologian can marshal to support a creation theory. Because we find so much diversity in scripture, various biblically-supported creation theories are possible. But the diversity isn't so extreme that *any* creation theory is consonant with scripture's major ideas and general drift.

My proposed theory, *creatio ex creatione sempiternalis en amore*, fits scripture better than *creatio ex nihilo*. Biblical writers *repeatedly* say God creates out of, or in relation, to creation. They *never* say God creates out of nothing, in the sense of bringing something out of absolute nothingness. On this crucial issue, therefore, God's creating from creation fits the Bible better than creation from nothing.

The Bible neither explicitly affirms nor explicitly denies my claim that God's creating is *everlasting*. This is metaphysical issue. One can make a case from scripture to support this idea, and my proposal follows logically from the assumption that the Spirit everlastingly loves. When love of creatures (not just love of self) is the primary attribute of an everlasting deity, believing God everlastingly creates comes naturally.

While I may be the first to call God "the Ever Creator," I'm not the first to speculate that deity always creates.[11] The church father Origen, for instance, believed God creates successive worlds, and he pointed to biblical passages to support that view. He cites Isaiah, for instance, which portrays God saying, "there will be new heavens and a new earth, which I will make to abide in my sight" (65:17). Origen also cites passages about the end of our particular universe, such as "the heavens will perish" (Ps. 102:26) and "heaven and earth shall pass away" (Mt. 24:35).[12] Instead of thinking these new creations are spiritual metaphors, we can believe they point to an everlasting succession. Even Thomas Aquinas speculated God might create an infinite number of universes.[13]

The widespread scriptural emphasis upon God as *always* loving forms the most important biblical support for the new theory. Love's prominence and persistence prompt me to speculate that it is the Spirit's primary attribute. And it leads me to interpret the other divine attributes in light of it. Consequently, I believe that the attribute "Creator" and divine creating will always be shaped by love. When biblical authors write passages such as "the spirit of God has made me, and the

---

[11] Jon Paul Sydnor also endorses the notion that God everlastingly creates. See *The Great Open Dance* (Eugene, OR: Pickwick, 2024).

[12] See Origen, *De principiis*, in *The Ante-Nicene Fathers*, Alexander Roberts and James Donaldson, eds. (Buffalo, NY: Christian Literature, 1885), 4:239-382. For a concise explanation of Origen's views, see Mary-Jane Rubenstein, *Worlds Without End*, 62-64. Rubenstein cites other theologians who believed God everlastingly creates.

[13] See *Summa Theologica*, I. 47.3. Aquinas mistakenly believed Genesis required the creation out of nothing view.

breath of *Shaddai* gives me life" (Job 33:4), I consider this creating an expression of love.

This new theory of creation has strong biblical support, insofar as it stresses that God works with creation rather than overpowering it. This seems rather obvious when considering free creatures such as humans. But the Spirit also worked with non-human forces, such as the face of the deep, *tehom*, when initially creating. The Spirit doesn't overpower even these chaotic materials or conjure them from nothing.

As the Genesis 1 creation story unfolds, the Spirit continually shares power in the creative process. And God shares with increasingly complex creatures. On day two, for instance, the Spirit grants the firmament the function of separating waters above from waters below. On days three, five, and six, God invites earth and waters to bring forth living creatures. Over and over, the Spirit blesses creatures with the capacity for co-creative fertility and invites them to multiply and fill the earth.[14] And God repeatedly calls "good" or "very good" what emerges from this co-creating process.

The oft-repeated "let there be" lines attributed to God in Genesis 1 are not imperative coercions. They take the form of Hebrew jussives, a form of speech not perfectly duplicated in English but serve as invitations requiring creaturely responses. This means that "the process of creation [is] God's sharing power with creation," says Richard Middleton, "inviting creatures to participate (as they are able) in the creative process itself."[15] William Brown agrees, saying Genesis describes the Spirit's "invitations to enter into the grand creative sweep of God's designs."[16]

In the second creation story in Genesis, God grants Adam a task reserved only for deity in other religions: naming the animals. But

---

[14] For a persuasive *tehomic* theology, see Catherine Keller, *The Face of the Deep* (New York: Routledge, 2003); See also Andre Rabe, *Creative Chaos* (Eugene, OR: Andre Rabe Publishing, 2019).

[15] Richard Middleton, *The Liberating Image* (Grand Rapids, MI: Brazos, 2005), 287. Terence Fretheim argues similarly in *God and the World in the Old Testament* (Nashville, TN: Abingdon, 2005), 38.

[16] William P. Brown, "Divine Act and the Art of Persuasion in Genesis One," in *History and Interpretation*, M. P. Graham, William Brown, and Jeffrey Kuan (Sheffield: JSOT, 1993), 32.

*Yahweh-Elohim* determines that animals can't satisfy Adam's need for relationship. So God creates another—Eve—out of the first human rather than conjuring her from nothing. In other words, God works with, and relies upon, creatures when creating something new and when seeking to establish well-being. The Spirit relies upon these others to maintain overall well-being, including asking humans to avoid doing what will harm (e.g., eat from the tree in the Garden).

Although we shouldn't interpret the claims of Genesis as historical-literal, we can affirm the repeated emphasis upon the Spirit creating alongside creatures as important theologically. The Genesis creation stories point "to a God who is generous with power," says Richard Middleton. Terence Fretheim says, "God works creatively with already existing realities to bring about newness." And "while God is certainly the initiator and primary actor in creation," says Fretheim, "God involves both the human and the nonhuman in the continuing process of creation."[17] Middleton concludes that Genesis "depicts God's founding exercise of creative power in such a way that we might appropriately describe it as an act of love."[18] In fact, "Genesis 1:1-2:3 converges with John 3:16," he says, because "in both creation and redemption, 'God so loved the world. . . .'"[19]

According to scripture, the loving Spirit creates alongside, rather than overpowers, creation.

## ESSENTIAL *HESED* AND EVERLASTING CREATING

Perhaps the strongest biblical support for my new creation theory is the oft-repeated biblical phrase, "the steadfast love of the Lord endures forever."[20] "Steadfast love" is an English translation of the Hebrew

---

[17] See Fretheim, *God and the World in the Old Testament*, 5, 48.

[18] Richard J. Middleton, "Creation Founded in Love: Breaking Rhetorical Expectations in Genesis 1:1-2:3," in *Sacred Text, Secular Times: The Hebrew Bible in the Modern World*, Leonard Jay Greenspoon and Bryan F. LeBeau, eds., (Omaha, NE: Creighton University Press, 2000), 57.

[19] Middleton, "Creation Founded in Love," 67.

[20] "The steadfast love of the Lord endures forever" occurs in all twenty-six verses of Psalm 136 and repeatedly in Psalms 89 and 118. Exodus says the "merciful and gracious" God "abounds in steadfast love and faithfulness" (Ex. 34:6). Nehemiah describes God as "gracious and

word *hesed* (or *chesed*).[21] Divine *hesed* brings blessing, health, flourishing, and goodness. Steadfast love "is used in the Old Testament only of God, never of human beings," says Katherine Doob Sakenfeld, and in it we find an "attitude and action of God."[22] To use my language, *hesed* acts intentionally, in relational response, to promote overall well-being.

*Hesed* links intimately with God's covenants with creatures and creation.[23] In these covenantal contexts, it portrays the beneficial love a person with greater resources expresses toward those with fewer. While the parties aren't equal, they engage in real reciprocity, with each contributing to what emerges.[24] The Spirit's *hesed* is, therefore, not controlling: God commits to creatures, and expects them to commit in response.

The covenantal love of *hesed* is unconditional in one sense and conditional in another. "It is unconditional," says Jon Levenson, "in that the love comes into, and remains, in force even when nothing has been done to deserve it." But the covenant is conditional "in that it involves expectations and stipulations, and it suffers and turns sour if they are not met."[25] These two senses of conditionality fit nicely with my saying that God, in one sense, necessarily loves and creates but, in another sense, contingently loves and creates.

---

merciful" and "abounding in steadfast love" (Neh. 9:17). According to Lamentations, the Lord's "mercies never come to an end" (Lam. 3:22). God repeatedly tells Israel his love is steadfast, and God loves Israel with an "everlasting love" (Is. 54:8). See also 1 Chron. 16:34, 41; 2 Chron. 5:13; 7:3, 6; 20:21; Exod. 3:11; Ps. 105.

[21] Among the renderings are "continual doing good," "covenantal love," "devotion," "faithfulness," "goodwill," "grace," "love," "loyal helpfulness," "loyal kindness," "mutual reciprocity," "reliable solidarity," "steadfast love," and "sure-love." Most scholars credit Nelson Glueck for launching the contemporary discussion of *hesed* (*Das Wort hesed im alttestshatuamentlichen Sprachgebrauche als meschiliche und gottliche gemeinschaftgemasse Verhaltungswise*, translated by Alfred Gottschalk as *Hesed in the Bible* (Cincinnati, OH: Hebrew Union College, 1967 [1927]). See a reprint with Gerald A. Larue's introductory essay on 20th century explorations of *hesed* (Eugene, OR: Wipf and Stock, 2011). Most of the translations listed here are in Larue's summary essay. See also Harold M. Kamsler, "*Hesed* — Mercy or Loyalty?" *Jewish Biblical Quarterly* 27, no. 3 (1999): 183-85.

[22] Katherine Doob Sakenfeld, *Faithfulness in Action* (Philadelphia: Fortress, 1985), 49, 56.

[23] On this, see Jon D. Levenson, *The Love of God* (Princeton: Princeton University Press, 2016); Norman H. Snaith, *The Distinctive Ideas of the Old Testament* (London: Epworth, 1944), 95.

[24] Levenson, *The Love of God*, 6.

[25] Ibid., 61-62, 121.

Although biblical writers speak often of God's *hesed* for Israel,[26] they also say the Spirit expresses *hesed* for all nations and all creation.[27] "The earth is full of the steadfast love of the Lord," says the Psalmist (33:5), and "the earth, O Lord, is full of your steadfast love" (119:64). Biblical writers portray God's *hesed* as revealed throughout the cosmos.[28] Incidentally, the term *hesed* isn't ever used scripturally to describe God's love for Godself, so it doesn't support the claim that God loves in Trinity.

The word *olam* translates to the English word "forever" in the phrase "the steadfast love of the Lord endures forever." It refers to unending duration.[29] "Give thanks to the Lord, for he is good," says the Psalmist, "his steadfast love (*hesed*) endures forever (*olam*)" (106:1). And "great is his steadfast love (*hesed*) toward us, and the faithfulness of the Lord endures forever (*olam*)" (117:2).[30] We best understand unending duration as a series of everlasting moments in which God loves creatures; *olam* doesn't refer to divine timelessness.[31]

Given the frequency with which "steadfast love" combines with "forever" in biblical references to the Spirit's love for creatures, it seems

---

[26] E.g., Ps. 147:8-10.

[27] See Ps. 117:1-2; Jonah 4:2; Ruth 1:8; 2 Sam. 15:20. Shai Held argues that traditional Jewish thinkers say the mandate to *hesed* extends beyond human beings to all living creatures. See *Judaism is About Love* (New York: Farrar, Straus, Giroux, 2024). John C Merkle addresses these issues in "Jewish Insights on God's Power and Love," in *Amipotence, vol. 2*, Brandon Brown, et. al., eds. (Grasmere, ID: SacraSage, 2025).

[28] See Psalm 33, 36, 103, 117, 147. See also Walter Brueggemann, "Psalm 109: Three Times 'Steadfast Love,'" *Word and World* 5, no. 2:144-54; John Goldingay, *Psalms: Vol. 3, Psalms 90-150* (Grand Rapids, MI: Baker Academic, 2008).

[29] See, for instance, Ben-Yehuda, Eliezer, *A Complete Dictionary of Ancient and Modern Hebrew*, Vol. 10 (Jerusalem-Berlin: Ben-Yehuda Hozaa La'Or, 1940), 4998; James Strong, *The New Strong's Exhaustive Concordance of the Bible* (Nashville, TN: Thomas Nelson Publishers, 1990), 5769, 5956.

[30] See Rolf A. Jacobson, "'The Faithfulness of the Lord Endures Forever': The Theological Witness of the Psalter," in *Soundings in the Theology of Psalms*, Rolf A. Jacobson, ed. (Minneapolis: Fortress, 2011).

[31] I'm not claiming every passage in the Hebrew Bible confirms God's love as everlastingly *hesed*. Scripture is inconsistent. In advocating essential *hesed*, I'm making a theological decision to privilege "the steadfast love of the Lord endures forever" as telling the truth about who God essentially is and how God always acts. Privileging *hesed* and considering it essential to God is in many ways fruitful. Saying God *necessarily* and *everlastingly* expresses *hesed* for creatures and creation assures creatures of their Creator's steadfast love.

appropriate to say God *always* loves others. Everlastingly. And God can love creatures everlastingly only if there are always creatures for God to love. Therefore, people of faith would be wise to embrace a theory that says God always creates creatures to love.

I have previously coined a phrase to identify *hesed* as a necessary divine attribute. I call this "essential *hesed*." It says we should understand *hesed* as a necessary and eternal aspect of the Spirit's essence, so God *must* love creatures everlastingly.[32] "The steadfast love of the Lord endures forever," therefore, tells us the truth about who God essentially is and how God always acts. Essential *hesed* for creation characterizes the One who *everlastingly* creates.

The phrase "the steadfast love of the Lord endures forever" makes no sense if *creatio ex nihilo* were true. Everlasting love for creatures isn't possible if God once existed alone and then created something from nothing.[33] *Hesed* for creatures isn't essential to an independent One who once existed without creatures.[34] By contrast, the creation theory that says God, in love, everlastingly creates out of, or in relation to, creation well fits this oft-repeated phrase, "the steadfast love of the Lord endures forever."

God's everlasting creating expresses essential *hesed*.

---

[32] Karl Barth comes close to affirming essential hesed when he calls *hesed* "an inner mode of being in God Himself." Karl Barth, *Church Dogmatics*, II/1, G. W. Bromiley and T. F. Torrance, eds. (Edinburgh: T & T Clark, 1957), 353.

[33] Some Christians appeal to the idea of the social Trinity as a metaphysical foundation for saying God always and essentially loves. Essential hesed doesn't require this claim, because it says God always and essentially loves creatures and creation. But neither does essential *hesed* deny the trinity. Christians who embrace the social Trinity should also embrace essential *hesed*. Doing so allows one to say God everlastingly expresses love among members of the Godhead *and* everlastingly loves creation. For an argument on the compatibility of the Trinity and the theology I propose, see Thomas Jay Oord, "Analogies of Love Between God and Creatures: A Response to Kevin Vanhoozer," in *Love, Divine and Human* (New York: T & T Clark, 2020).

[34] While the majority of biblical passages portray God as always, and essentially, loving creatures, there's a minority report that doesn't portray God this way. In some passages, God threatens to withdraw *hesed*. In others, God can't withdraw *hesed* and must keep covenant (e.g., Exod. 34:6-7; Jer. 16:7). Biblical writers are inconsistent on many issues, including this one. But the majority report in the Bible describes a God whose steadfast love for creation is everlasting and, I think, essential to deity.

## *Eros, Philia,* and *Agape* Creating

In this new view of God as Ever Creator, divine love creates the universe and all of its inhabitants. The desire for diverse beauty drives God's creating in love and creatures contribute in response. "Creative love" shouldn't be thought of as a thing, however, and it's not an independent energy. It's the activity of actors, both creaturely and divine. Something new arises each moment from the creative synergy of Creator and creatures.

As I explained in earlier chapters, the Spirit's love takes various forms depending on the circumstances and possibilities. Specific entities, organisms, occasions, species, eco-systems, and civilizations will express specific types of love. Love is a pluriform and many-splendored activity.

In earlier chapters, we saw that wisdom is an important attributes of an everlasting and universal Spirit of love. Wisdom's love created the world, according to the writers of Proverbs, Job, Psalms, and Ecclesiasticus. God's creating wasn't haphazard or ill-advised, but included intelligence, dreams, and desire. Jürgen Moltmann rightly says that "what [we] say about Wisdom can be said about God's Spirit too."[35] The wise Spirit creates using various loves.

*Eros* will always be a motive in Wisdom's creating. Divine *eros* imbues creatures with value, and it creates to enhance or expand value. The Spirit enjoys creatures and creation as One who truly appreciates their beauty, integrity, and worth. The Spirit also desires greater expressions of complexity, relationality, and goodness. So, in *eros,* deity creates to manifest these expressions.

The Spirit of Wisdom desires both the good of creation and Her own good, as One both perfectly altruistic and egoistic. When an omnipresent God acts to enhance the well-being of all creation, the cooperative responses of creatures enhance God's own well-being. The Spirit seeks both the glory of others and its own glory. Only a universal Lover can perfectly love Self and others in harmony. God isn't fighting the world.

---

[35] Jürgen Moltmann, *The Spirit of Life* (Minneapolis: Fortress, 1992), 46.

*Eros* is a driving force in God's everlasting creating.

*Philia* also plays a role in the Spirit's creating. *Philia* is love that seeks collaboration, friendship, and solidarity with others in the effort to promote overall well-being. The God who always creates out of or in relation to creaturely others is One for whom *philia* is essential. The Creator calls upon created co-creators when creating in love.

Divine *philia* is essential to *creatio ex creatione sempiternalis en amore*. To say it another way, the Spirit's method of creating will always be collaborative. Rather than being essentially independent, the One who expresses *philia* toward creation always creates through the methods of relational love. Rather than being a backup plan or afterthought, *philia* is the Spirit's creative *modus operandi*.

*Philia* is a relational force in God's everlasting creating.

Creatures sometimes thwart the Spirit's creative plans. Sometimes, chance events, law-like regularities, or inanimate conditions just aren't conducive for the flourishing God desires. Sin and evil frustrate the Creator's work too. Both experience and scripture tell us all's not well in the created order.

Consequently, the Spirit sometimes expresses *agape* when creating. This form of love works for well-being *despite* negative actions of creatures or inhospitable conditions in creation. In the creative process, *agape* repays evil with good. Despite ill-being, God creates with well-being in mind. Because deity always creates with an aim for what's good, and because creatures don't always cooperate with this aim, the Spirit sometimes expresses *agape* when creating.[36]

*Agape* is sometimes a factor in God's creating.

The film director Orson Welles purportedly said, "The enemy of art is the absence of limitations."[37] He's pointing to the fact that creative constraints prove necessary for creative art, because limitations force

---

[36] Jordan Wessling and Ross Parker argue for an agapist framework to explain God's motive for creating. They seem to use *agape* in a general sense and not the precise sense of acting for good in spite of creaturely actions that harm. For Wessling and Parker's arguments, see *Divine Motivation and Humanity*.

[37] Henry Jaglom, "The Independent Filmmaker," in *The Movie Business Book*, Jason E. Squire, 2nd ed. (New York: Simon & Schuster, 1992), 78.

artists to find innovative solutions, and they give direction to their work.

The same can be said of the Spirit's creative love. The Creator's love takes many forms when creating alongside creatures and their limits. These forms will often be mixed and intermingled as they arise in relation to creation, both its possibilities and limitations. The beauty of the Spirit's diverse loves generates diverse beauty amid constraints.

Diverse forms of love provide ultimate answers to existence.

## Scientific Evidence?

In a number of books and articles, William Lane Craig argues that the Big Bang supports *creatio ex nihilo*.[38] In his work with Paul Copan, Craig presses the argument in various ways. After looking at evidence for the expansion of the universe and thermodynamics, Craig concludes, "At a minimum we can say confidently that those who believe in the doctrine of *creatio ex nihilo* will not find themselves contradicted by the empirical evidence of contemporary cosmology but on the contrary will be fully in line with it."[39]

Craig's claims prompt frustration in the physicist Victor Stenger. The evidence shows "that *our* universe had a beginning," says Stenger, "but it need not have been the beginning of *everything*." Something could have existed prior to the first moment of our universe, he says. Stenger lists other leading physicists who agree.[40] They contend that "even if we identify a point in the past as the beginning of the Big Bang, that need not have been the beginning of everything."[41] Physicist John Barrow puts it more precisely: "It is possible for any particular domain to have a history that has a definite beginning in an inflationary

---

[38] William Lane Craig, *The Kalam Cosmological Argument* (London: Macmillan, 1979).

[39] Paul Copan and William Lane Craig, *Creation out of Nothing* (Grand Rapids, MI: Baker, 2004), 248.

[40] Victor J. Stenger, *God and the Multiverse* (Amherst, NY: Prometheus, 2014), 318.

[41] Ibid., 320. While I find Stenger's criticisms of Craig appropriate, Stenger doesn't consider the model of God offered in this systematic theology. Consequently, he seems unable to imagine God as creator in the sense I have suggested.

quantum event but the process as a whole could just go on in a steady fashion for all eternity, past and present."[42]

Craig's claim that empirical evidence doesn't *contradict* the creation from nothing theory is modest and likely correct. How could *creatio ex nihilo* contradict science, given that science engages *something*, not nothingness? But science also doesn't contradict my theory that the Spirit everlastingly creates out of that which God created previously. My theory fits the Big Bang too.

Craig is wrong, however, to say *creatio ex nihilo* is "fully in line" with contemporary cosmology. It isn't. Contemporary cosmology doesn't and can't make empirical claims about God creating something from nothing. It can't make this claim on methodological nor empirical grounds. So, creation out of nothing isn't fully in line with the Big Bang, as understood by science.

Some physicists, like Barrow, argue for an everlasting series of universes. Take, for example, the cyclical model advocated by Paul J. Steinhardt and Neil Turok. In *Endless Universe: Beyond the Big Bang*, the Princeton and Cambridge physicists say the "big bang might not be the 'beginning' of the universe after all, but instead a physically explicable event with a 'before' and an 'after.'"[43] Theories that propose an absolute beginning to the universe from nothing are problematic, say these physicists, because "there are no rigorous physical principles that dictate how to go from 'nothing' to 'something.'"[44]

Steinhardt and Turok propose a particular cyclical model of creation. In it, "galaxies, stars, and life have been formed over and over again long before the most recent Big Bang, and will be remade cycle after cycle far into the future."[45] They speculate that "the big bang was triggered by the decay of dark energy that existed before."[46] Some

---

[42] John D. Barrow, "The Far, Far Future," in *The Far-Future Universe*, George F. R. Ellis, ed. (Philadelphia: Templeton, 2002), 30.

[43] Paul J. Steinhardt and Neil Turok, *Endless Universe* (New York: Doubleday, 2007), 15.

[44] Ibid., 226. Roger Penrose argues for a beginningless series of universes in *Cycles of Time* (New York: Knopf, 2011).

[45] Steinhardt and Turok, *Endless Universe*, 61.

[46] Ibid., 60.

features of the universe were present in and influenced by previous universes. Before and after each big bang, say Steinhardt and Turok, "the fabric of space remains intact, the energy is always finite, and time proceeds smoothly."[47]

This cyclic universe model isn't a Nietzschean eternal recurrence of the exact same. Cyclical models don't require time to be a closed circle occupied by creatures doomed to repeat the same events endlessly. In the Steinhardt and Turok model, only the most basic metaphysical features are passed from one universe to the next. In each new universe, genuine novelty emerges, while some metaphysical continuity is maintained universe to universe.[48]

The *creatio ex creatione sempiternalis en amore* view fits cyclic models that involve genuine novelty and metaphysical continuity. But my theory isn't inescapably linked to Steinhardt and Turok's model; it could link with other models that reject creation from nothing. *Creatio ex creatione sempiternalis en amore* adds a measure of directionality and value-rich novelty, which are made possible by a loving Spirit who always creates out of, or in relation to, creation.

Science contributes to questions of ultimate origins but can't settle them alone. We must bring other sources to bear. I bring the metaphysical, biblical, ethical, and theological reasons I identified in the previous chapter and this one when comparing creation models. For a host of reasons, I (and others) conclude that *creatio ex creatione sempiternalis en amore,* or something like it, is preferable to *creatio ex nihilo.* It matches scripture better, and it doesn't imply God is culpable for evil. It overcomes problems associated with creation out of nothing. And in this new creation theory, love is the motive, method, measure, modes, and meaning of the Spirit's creating.

---

[47] Ibid., 61-62.

[48] Paul Davies, "Eternity: Who Needs It?" in *The Far-Future Universe,* George F. R. Ellis, ed. (Philadelphia: Templeton, 2002), 45.

## WHAT THE NEW THEORY DOES *NOT* MEAN

New theories should naturally and properly be scrutinized. The theory that God everlastingly, in love, creates out of or in relation to what God previously created has already received scrutiny. Not surprisingly, some people misunderstand these claims. It seems appropriate here to address the most common misunderstandings.

### *No Universe is Co-Eternal with God.*

While it's true that the new theory says God always relates to and creates from creaturely others, it doesn't imply that *our* or *any* particular universe is eternal. Rather, it suggests an everlasting chain of creaturely entities the Spirit creates who co-create. No single entity, organism, society, world, or universe is eternal or necessary. But at least one universe exists at a time, and it was preceded by others.

Our universe apparently had a Big Bang billions of years ago. But there is no empirical evidence to tell us out of what that bang occurred.[49] My theory of *creatio ex creatione sempiternalis en amore* speculates that the chaos and dark matter of a previous universe existed prior to the Big Bang. And a great deal of dark matter remains.

The entities the preceded the Big Bang would have been simple and diffuse, although not entirely formless, as the previous universe "died" due to increasing entropy. In its last moments, it may have been entirely composed only of quarks and subatomic particles in radical disorder. But even these basic entities would possess basic metaphysical features characteristic of all existing things—including features of self-causation, agency, value, and structural integrity. Consequently, we might say that God sometimes creates from "scratch," but never out of nothing at all.

No entity, organism, or universe is itself eternal.

---

[49] One of the strongest arguments in favor of creatio ex nihilo comes from Rem B. Edwards. For reasons I outline in previous chapters, I'm not convinced by Edwards. But see his arguments in *What Caused the Big Bang?* (New York Rodopi, 2001).

## The Spirit Never Creates Out of Uncreated Entities.

God exerts creative influence upon every actual things that exists.[50] No actual entities can be entirely self-existent, because God and other entities creatively influenced their coming to be. No materials are uncreated, predate God, or are independent of divine influence. Put positively, the new theory agrees with biblical writers who say God created all actual things.[51]

The theory that God creates everlastingly, in love, out of, or in relation to, creation says the Spirit creates in each moment. No universe, world, creature, or "thing" existed before God created it. The Spirit doesn't create out of eternal "stuff" or entirely independent, formless matter. Everything that influences God was first created and influenced by God. And the materials and creatures of the universe are not divine, nor did they emanate unintentionally from deity.

God never "stumbles upon" uncreated materials.

## The Universe Isn't an Infinite Regress.

Some scholars object to the notion of an everlasting series of universes. There aren't any infinite sets of actual entities, they argue. I have also criticized the notion of infinite sets. Sets assume boundaries; but infinity has no boundaries. While it may make sense to talk about abstract infinite sets in mathematics, an "infinite set" makes no sense if we're talking about actualities. For this reason, I avoid using the word "infinite" to characterize my theory.

We should also avoid the word "regress" when talking about the Spirit's everlasting creating. Our experience tells us that time and causation always move forward, never backward. Therefore, we should reject both the notion of retrocausation and the idea of timeless efficient causality. I use "everlasting" rather than "eternal" when talking

---

[50] Like most philosophical theologians, I don't think God creates numbers, possibilities, and other abstract objects. I think these realities reside everlastingly in the divine mind. For God to deny or contradict them, therefore, God would have to deny Godself . . . which God can't do.

[51] See, for instance, Isa. 45:18; John 1:3; Acts 4:24; Col. 1:16; Rev. 4:11.

about the always creating Spirit and an open future. And I appeal to the experiential truth of the presentist theory of time, which says only the present moment is actual.

In this new theory, God and creation are numerically distinct. They are not identical, although Creator and creatures share similarities. My theory isn't pantheism.[52] Each creaturely entity, organism, person, or universe depends upon the Spirit's creating for its existence. No creature or universe is entirely self-explanatory.

The new theory doesn't appeal to, nor embrace, an infinite regress.

## *God Depends on Creation in One Sense but Not in Another.*

In earlier chapters, I argued that a Spirit of love depends upon creatures in some ways but not others. Love is relational, so dependent relations are essential to an essentially loving Spirit. But God doesn't depend upon creation for God's existence. Creation didn't bring God into being. The Spirit exists necessarily, and no creature or creation could end deity. The Spirit is *a se,* to use the ancient words, which means self-existent.[53]

There is no logical contradiction in saying that to exist, God doesn't need creation, *and yet* the Spirit needs creation in each moment of divine loving and creating. Because God always creates others, God can necessarily exist and necessarily create through dependent loving relations. Creatures don't decide *whether* God exists, therefore, but they influence *how* the Spirit loves and creates. The Spirit's love depends upon the existence of recipients of that love, because love requires genuine others.[54]

Because it's God's nature to create everlastingly, the fact that creaturely entities exist presents us with a *conditional* necessity. God

---

[52] Lina Langby compares models of God and creation in *God and the World* (Uppsala: Acta Universitatis Upsaliensis, 2023).

[53] I agree with Richard Rice who argues that God doesn't rely upon creation for God to exist. See "*Creatio Ex Nihilo:* It's Not about Nothing," in *Theologies of Creation*, Thomas Jay Oord, ed. (New York: Routledge, 2014).

[54] Keith Ward argues similarly when criticizing David Bentley Hart. See *Sharing in the Divine Nature* (Eugene, OR: Cascade, 2020), 74.

necessarily creates so, necessarily, there will be creaturely others. But no single entity, creature, world, or universe will be *unconditionally* necessary. Each might not have existed, and each depend upon God's creating activity.

It's necessary that a chain of universes exists, but no single universe is necessary.

### An Everlasting Chain of Universes is Logical.

Some may object to *creatio ex creatione sempiternalis en amore* by saying they can't imagine an everlasting chain of creaturely entities. It's mind-bogglingly inconceivable, they'll say. The logic of an everlasting chain, however, amounts to the same logic used to say God exists everlastingly. The concept of "everlasting" is unimaginable in both cases, but not illogical. Few people of faith would object to saying God exists everlastingly just because they can't imagine it. It's the same with my theory.

Others insist that there must be a first moment of creating. But asking for a first moment in an everlasting chain of creative moments is like asking for the first in an everlasting chain of moments in the divine life. There is no "first" in everlasting. It's equally logical to say God's everlasting series of moments in the divine life had no first moment than to say an everlasting chain of universes had no first universe.

The biggest difference between saying the Spirit exists everlastingly and saying a chain of creaturely entities exists everlastingly is that the Spirit is an *individual*. The one God is an everlasting series of divine occasions of experience. By contrast, the everlasting chain of creation describes a plurality of actual creatures. To put it another way, the Spirit is the only everlasting individual, but because God creates moment by moment, a chain of multitudinous creations everlastingly develops.

As the Ever Creator, the Spirit everlastingly creates universes.

### A Wild Mare Analogy Can Help.

To help conceptualize how God creates a chain of creations, I offer a horse analogy. Suppose a mare in an Idaho wild horse herd lived a million years. Suppose the rest of the herd, including her offspring, each lived 15-20 years. This mare would give birth to foal after foal, some of them colts who become mature stallions. The mare would then mate with her offspring to produce more foals. And so on.

In this analogy, the one mare stays the same, but stallions come and go in succession. Stallions are born and die, but the mare lives on. The mare and each stallion contribute in each generation to what the mare will birth in a seamless sequence. But only the mare remains constant.

Analogously, one Spirit creates new universes, creatures, and entities, one after another. Each creature and creation has a beginning and end, and God creates them in relation to previous creatures and creations. Creatures co-create with the Creator. Because God always creates in relation to what God previously created, however, there will always be creaturely others with whom God creates.

This analogy isn't perfect, of course. No mare lives everlastingly; all are born and die. Furthermore, the mare is localized, and she doesn't give birth moment by moment. By contrast, God is everlasting, universal, and always creates. Despite these differences, the wild mare who co-creates in relation to those she co-created illustrates the Spirit's co-creating in relation to those created.


### *God Freely Creates in One Sense But Must Create in Another.*

The Spirit necessarily creates in one sense and creates contingently in another. God acts freely when choosing *how* to create, given the creaturely conditions, possibilities, and collaboration. Even God can't create the impossible, of course, given the circumstances generated by creaturely causes, factors, and actors. Logical and ontological limitations apply. But God freely and lovingly chooses while creating in relation to the past and a yet-to-be-determined future.[55]

God isn't free *not* to create, however. To say it positively, creating constitutes a necessary activity for the Spirit in whom creative love comes logically first. To grasp this, think of it this way: God isn't free

---

[55] Open and relational theology's view that the future is open overcomes William L. Rowe's worry that a perfectly loving God can't be free when creating. The God who can't foreknow with certainty freely chooses among possible choices when creating. See Rowe's argument in *Can God Be Free?* (Oxford: Oxford University Press, 2004).

to be something other than God. The Spirit is, by nature, a creator. So, God *must* create.

In an important sense, the deity I'm describing is Creator with a capital C. The capitalized word is appropriate when it's God's nature to create. The deity of most theologies may or may not create, because it's not in that God's nature to do so.[56] The traditional God could have remained alone, without ever creating. The traditional deity is an occasional creator (lower case) rather than an everlasting Creator.

The God who everlastingly creates is Creator with a capital C.

### *The Transcendent Spirit Who Always Creates is Worthy of Praise.*

Advocates of *creatio ex nihilo* sometimes imply that a God who brings something from nothing is more worthy of praise. The ability to create *ex nihilo* means God transcends us, and transcendence should elicit our worship. These advocates see as an advantage the fact that there is no scientific evidence of something coming from absolute nothingness. To them, lack of evidence proves God's creating is unique.

The Spirit who everlastingly and by nature creates is transcendent in a way the traditional God isn't. The Spirit of *creatio ex creatione sempiternalis en amore* necessarily and everlastingly creates. By contrast, the God of *creatio ex nihilo* may or may not create, which means creating is not essential to deity. Consequently, the new theory portrays the Spirit as transcendent in a way the traditional God isn't. If transcendence is a factor in worship-worthiness, the new theory also offers a transcendent Creator worthy of praise.

*Creatio ex creatione sempiternalis en amore* affirms other transcendent divine attributes. It says, for instance, that God is the only uncreated existent. The Spirit is the only existent who necessarily and everlastingly exists. God is the only existent who knows all creative possibilities. And so on. The new creation theory doesn't reduce the transcendent Spirit to a creature.

---

[56] On this and related issues, see *Creation Made Free: Open Theology Engaging Science*, Thomas Jay Oord, ed. (Eugene, OR: Pickwick, 2009).

Advocates of the creation from nothing theory sometimes express amazement at the deity they claim brings something from nothing. "Isn't it mind-bogglingly glorious what God can do?" they say. "No mortal can comprehend God's infinite ways!" The fact that no one fathoms what it means to bring something from absolutely nothing is, from this perspective, cause for awe.

The new theory claims the Spirit *everlastingly* creates out of creation, which means the chain of creaturely others is everlasting. But some say they can't imagine God creating a chain of universes with no absolute beginning. "Doesn't there have to be an absolute first moment?" they ask. "Didn't God have to start the creating process?"

As I said earlier, we find no logical reason there must be a first moment in an *everlasting* chain of creaturely moments, just as there is no logical reason there must be a first moment in the *everlasting* divine life. Everlasting is everlasting. If being "mind-bogglingly glorious" prompts worship, *creatio ex creatione sempiternalis en amore* is mind boggling too. And it privileges love.

When it comes to praising the Creator, I suspect the major difference between the new creation theory and creation from nothing is familiarity. I suspect that with increased familiarity, the new creation view will breed increased creativity for imagining reasons to praise God. God as Ever Creator is a belief with untapped wellsprings for worship and precious gems yet to be mined.

Great is the loving Ever Creator and greatly to be praised!

### *God is Uncreated.*

In an oft-cited passage, Alfred North Whitehead says that "It is as true to say that God creates the World as that the World creates God."[57] This passage comes in a series of contrasting statements, and it might seem to undermine the traditional notion that God is uncreated. But Whitehead prefaces the series of statements with these words: "In each antithesis there is a shift of meaning which converts the opposition

---

[57] Alfred North Whitehead, *Process and Reality*, 348.

into a contrast." In the case of this quote, the meaning of the word "create" shifts.

My new creation theory affirms God as uncreated. By this, I mean the Spirit necessarily and everlasting exists, and nothing brought deity into existence. All creatures have beginnings, but the Creator is beginningless. We best understand Whitehead's line about the world creating God to mean that creatures affect the Spirit's moment by moment experience. As I see it, no creatures predate God, and none created deity.

The everlasting Creator is uncreated.

## Other Issues

The doctrine of *creatio ex creatione sempiternalis en amore* can embrace the positive aspects of *creatio ex nihilo* while rejecting the negative ones. For instance, the new theory similarly denies an eternal dualism of good and evil beings, as well as denying an eternal dualism of good and evil matter. Like *creatio ex nihilo*, it affirms that God creates creatures and creation as intrinsically good, although they sometimes do evil. My theory agrees with *creatio ex nihilo* by saying all creation depends upon God, and nothing in creation serves as its own explanation.

The new theory denies that God simply rearranges what already exists. It says, instead, that God creates something new each moment. It provides a conceptual basis for literally affirming the biblical claim that God "makes all things new" (2 Cor. 5:17; Rev. 21:5) Although various metaphysical principles will remain true in all universes, the actualities created in each moment will always be novel. All actual entities are *de novo*, to use the Latin, because the Spirit always does and creates new things.

Making new things is a necessary attribute of the loving Ever Creator.

## Conclusion

Most creation theories fail to put love at the center. They emphasize divine omnipotence or trumpet God's sovereign freedom in ways that directly, or indirectly, undermine a coherent theology of creative love.

The few theories that do emphasize love often fail to develop its implications. Some have attempted to combine love with divine control, or say God can be both relational yet also essentially isolated prior to creating. I find these incoherent.

I've offered a new creation theory that says God everlastingly creates out of creation in love. Rendered in Latin, this is *creatio ex creatione sempiternalis en amore*. This theory says the spirit always creates; God should be called the *Ever Creator*.

Love motivates divine creating, and rather than creating from nothing, the Spirit creates from or in relation to what God previously created. Everlastingly. Creation is therefore an unending, relational, and cooperative process, as the Spirit works with creaturely co-creators and factors. God never creates in solitude.

This view proposes a temporal succession of universes, each being unique, with a beginning and end. But each universe adds to an everlasting sequence. The Spirit creates through persuasive, collaborative means that involve creaturely agency, contributions, and spontaneity.

Divine creating involves *eros* (valuing), *philia* (collaboration), and *agape* (repaying evil with good). Because this theory conceives of creative love as essential to God's nature, there will always be creaturely others, although no particular creature or universe is necessary.

This new theory draws upon scripture, which always describes God creating in relation to creation. Passages from Genesis, the Psalms, prophetic literature, and the New Testament portray the Spirit sharing power, inviting co-creating, and responding to the conditions and contributions of creatures.

The Hebrew concept of *hesed*—steadfast love—plays a central role in this theory, framing God's everlasting creating as a covenantal commitment to the flourishing of creation. I regard the biblical phrase, "the steadfast love of the Lord endures forever" as a metaphysical claim about God's everlasting creating and loving. This is what I call "essential *hesed*."

By denying creatio ex nihilo, this new theory avoids a host of theological and metaphysical problems. The new theory avoids having to posit the incoherence of absolute nothingness, and it avoids the problem of evil. It avoids the problems associated with saying God creates before time. It says the Spirit loves creatures in concert with an evolving and responsive cosmos, and divine love is pluriform.

I could be wrong about all of this, of course. Just as I'm not certain God exists, I'm not certain how, when, or why the Spirit creates. But I believe the theory I've proposed—that God, in love, everlastingly creates out of or in relation to what God previously created—makes better sense of the Spirit and existence than *creatio ex nihilo* or any other theory I know.

And it prioritizes love, which is essential.

CHAPTER THIRTEEN

# Amipotent Providence

## THE BIG IDEAS

- Traditional accounts of providence assume an omnipotent God rules over creation.
- Adequate accounts of providence say humans and (probably) other complex creatures have genuine but limited free will.
- Creatures co-create with the Creator, and the Spirit necessarily collaborates with all creatures, great and small.
- A necessarily loving and creative Spirit would not and could not annihilate creation.
- God provides agency to all creatures, and God can't withdraw, override, or fail to provide it.
- Free will emerged smoothly in evolutionary history from simpler creatures with simpler agency.
- The Spirit loves the smallest entities, in the sense of enjoying their value and acting for their well-being.
- A material-mental monist ontology accounts for God and creatures better than idealism, materialism, or dualism.
- Random events and law-like regularities occur because of God's steadfast love for all, and God can't suspend regularities nor control randomness.
- The best theory of panentheism says all creatures affect God and, therefore, are in the Spirit's experience.
- The best theory of theoenpanism says God affects all creatures and, therefore, is in all creaturely experiences.

Most systematic theologians have said an all-powerful God created the universe from nothing in the distant past. Consequently, they assume deity has the ability to control creation in the present. God so understood could fix any problem or attain any goal by determining any creature or outcome singlehandedly.

Some quote the Bible to support this assumption: "With God, all things are possible" (Mt. 19:26). Given this, most theologians consider the idea of providence as referring either to God's persistent, or occasional, control of creation. On most accounts, providence explains how God rules.[1]

It's natural for theists to say God providentially engages creatures in history. We typically understand this engagement as purposive, with both creatures and Creator having aims, goals, and aspirations. Theologies that consider God timeless, however, can't account well for historically-dependent purposes.[2] Amipotence-based theologies can. If we take God's action in history seriously, theologies that consider deity timeless fail.

To the extent that theologians consider the Spirit's love in accounts of providence, most limit it to an idea of benevolence. *Providentia* is then reduced to divine provision, according to this thinking, and God gives good gifts.[3] Benevolence-only theologies assume a non-relational deity never receives from or responds to creation, however.[4] When providence is considered the work of an impassible and omnipotent God, creatures don't *really* matter.

Amipotence-based providence says a loving Spirit gives *and* receives, always collaborates, and never controls. God expresses uncontrolling love moment-by-moment, because it's the divine nature to do so. Amipotent providence involves God receiving causal, informational,

---

[1] This chapter is dedicated to Karl Giberson. Karl's friendship over the years, both personally and in matters of science and faith, has opened doors and pushed me to think in new ways.

[2] I address this issue in "Providence and Process," in *T&T Clark Handbook of the Doctrine of Creation*, Jason Goroncy, ed., (London: T& T Clark, 2024).

[3] David Fergusson provides an overview of major options of providence in *The Providence of God: A Polyphonic Approach* (Cambridge: Cambridge University Press, 2018).

[4] Robert Adams offers a strong criticism of benevolence-only theologies and affirms the idea that God desires loving relationships with creatures for the sake of those relations. See Robert Merrihew Adams, *Finite and Infinite Goods* (New York: Oxford University Press, 1999), ch. 5.

and emotional input. As a result, the Spirit alone neither decides the grand scope of history, nor its details. Creation matters.

Some traditional theologians flatly deny free will; others affirm it but also say God controls all. Amipotence providence, in contrast, celebrates the fact that complex creatures act freely. It embraces libertarian free will, which says that complex creatures express genuine but limited freedom. Rather than rule over and overrule, the amipotent Spirit empowers, inspires, and provides freedom.

Traditional accounts of providence underappreciate or deny contributions from simpler creatures, smaller organisms, and actors in the micro realm. Instead of thinking smaller entities alive, most assume entities at the micro level function like mindless cogs in a machine.[5] The fallacy of *Deus ex machina* ("God from the machine") applies literally when we think God controls matter unable to resist nor cooperate with deity. It's hard to conceive of how the traditional God loves dead and inert cogs, however, in the sense of promoting their well-being. Most theories of providence fail to consider what *all* creatures—great and small—provide *God*.

Historically, most systematic theologians have assumed that chance, luck, and randomness should be seen as expressions of the divine will. As such, they only *appear* to be random; they're actually God's activities. Theologies that reject randomness compound the problem of evil, however, because they imply (though they may not admit) that deity ordains bad luck, unfortunate accidents, and harm-producing chance events. Rejecting the random also ends up undermining explanations in cosmology, biology, economics, political science, and jurisprudence. Most accounts of providence are literally out of luck.

Many theologians say that God, by fiat, installed and sustains the law-like regularities of nature. They are, therefore, susceptible to divine interruption. This view also intensifies the problem of evil, however,

---

[5] For a summary of the scientific, philosophical and theological considerations of mechanism, see John Hedley Brooke, *Science and Religion* (Cambridge: Cambridge University Press, 1991), chs. 2–4. In various books, John Polkinghorne explains why the mechanistic view of existence is unhelpful. See, for instance, *The Polkinghorne Reader*, Thomas Jay Oord, ed. (West Conshohocken, PA: Templeton, 2010), 21-24. Alister McGrath argues against nature as mechanistic in *The Reenchantment of Nature* (New York: Doubleday, 2002).

because a deity who omnipotently installs and upholds the natural laws should occasionally suspend them to rescue victims. An all-powerful deity who can interrupt or suspend law-like regularities would seem to care more about maintaining them than liberating people!

This chapter lays out an account of providence that prioritizes an amipotent Spirit. The universal Lover it describes provides freedom to complex creatures and agency to all. The Spirit never controls the large or tiny, but acts for the flourishing of everyone and everything. Creation is *in* this universal Spirit's experience, and the Spirit is *in* creation. Amipotent providence affirms evolution and says creatures co-create with the Creator. This account of providence, therefore, will speculate not only about the becoming Spirit of love but also about the free becoming of complex creatures and the dynamic agency of all creatures.

Amipotent providence prioritizes God's moment-by-moment love for all.

## Genuine but Limited Freedom

When pondering providence, Christians often debate the reality of creaturely freedom. Arguments between followers of John Calvin and Jacob Arminius deserve special focus.[6] Arminians rightly appeal to the authenticity of freedom and reject the idea that God always controls.[7] But most say or imply that an omnipotent God could, and sometimes does, guarantee outcomes by unilaterally determining circumstances or individuals. A primary difference between Arminians

---

[6] Don Thorsen explores this in terms of the theologies of John Calvin and John Wesley. See *Calvin Vs. Wesley* (Nashville, TN: Abingdon, 2013).

[7] For an explanation of Arminian free will, see Paul W. Chilcote, "Wesley's Theology of Grace and Holiness," *Wesleyan Theological Journal* 28 (1993): 5–26; Geordan Hammond, "Reflections on Responsible Grace after Twenty-Five Years," *Wesleyan Theological Journal* 56, no. 1 (2020): 127–150; Mary Elizabeth Mullino Moore, "Wesley on Prevenient Grace and the Church's Mission," *Wesleyan Theological Journal* 55, no. 1 (2021): 45–68; Roger E. Olson, *Arminian Theology* (Downers Grove, IL: InterVarsity, 2006); Keith D. Stanglin and Thomas H. McCall, *Jacob Arminus* (Oxford: Oxford University Press, 2012); Jason Vickers, *The Grace of God, the Will of Man* (Nashville, TN: B&H Academic, 2016).

and Calvinists, therefore, would be how the two imagine the frequency of divine control.

This systematic theology of love recognizes and builds from the truth that we make free choices. I take at face-value freedom as a lived reality, and there are few things we know better than our experience of choosing.[8] In the way we act, we presuppose our choosing is at least partly free. This represents another experiential nonnegotiable. Our emotions confirm this reality, because we sometimes feel blameworthy, guilty, praiseworthy, or proud. We have similar feelings in response to what others do, believing they act freely, at least sometimes. And we presuppose the reality of free will when we hold ourselves and others accountable.

A theological argument for freedom appeals to the reality of sin. To be morally responsible, a person must be freely response-able. If God were to determine entirely how creatures act, they would not be free to act any way other than how this controlling deity decides. A God who controls all, therefore, is culpable for whatever occurs, including sin. But if sin is real, this leads to a major problem: God can't love perfectly *and* be morally culpable.

Debates about God and freedom generally lead to three positions. Theological determinists deny that we choose freely. They reject our first-person experiences of freedom and, when consistent, are forced to say God actually wills creaturely sin. As John Calvin put it, "nothing happens contrary to [God's] will, even that which is contrary to his will."[9] This view embraces the definition of divine omnipotence I identified as "God exerts all power." Many determinists also say sin ruined us from the beginning, so we can't trust our experience of free choosing.

The second group—theological compatibilists—try to account for free choosing. But they also say that, in some mysterious way, a sovereign God still controls everything we do. Hermann Bavinck puts it this

---

[8] Thomas Reid made this point centuries ago and called it "common sense" (See Norman Daniels, *Thomas Reid's 'Inquiry'* (Stanford, CA: Stanford University Press, 1989). David Ray Griffin makes a similar point but calls this a "hard-core commonsense notion." See *Reenchantment without Supernaturalism* (Ithaca, NY: Cornell University Press, 2001).

[9] John Calvin, *The Secret Providence of God*, Paul Helm, ed. (Wheaton, IL: Crossway, 2010), 81.

way: "There is no division of labor between God and his creature, but the same effect is totally the effect of the primary cause [God] as well as totally the effect of the proximate cause [creatures]."[10] I criticized this view earlier.

It makes no sense to say creatures are free and yet God controls them.[11] If "control" means God acts as the sole cause of creaturely action and "free" means creatures exert self-causation, "control" and "free" are *incompatible*.[12] The same effect can't be totally caused by God but also partly caused by creatures. "When God is seen as totally in control," says Anna Case-Winters, "any credible concept of freedom and autonomy for human beings is relinquished, and human actions lose their significance."[13]

People of faith who affirm *genuine* creaturely freedom are often called "libertarian free will theists." They say freedom is irreconcilable with being fully determined to act in a particular way; free creatures have the ability to do other than what they did. A free chooser can't be controlled by anything or anyone, including God. The particular libertarian free will view I affirm says creaturely freedom is "genuine but limited."

The genuine but limited freedom view has three dimensions.[14] The first pertains to the power of the chooser. Timothy O'Connor uses "agent causation" to describe it, and by this he means the chooser's

---

[10] Herman Bavinck, *Reformed Dogmatics*, John Bols, John Vriend, trans., Vol. 2 (Grand Rapids, MI: Eerdmans, 1989), 605. Some versions of Thomas Aquinas's primary-secondary causal scheme assume compatibilism. For an example of a Thomist who embraces compatibilism using the primary-secondary scheme, see Michael Dodds, *Unlocking Divine Action* (Washington, DC: The Catholic University of America Press, 2017).

[11] See Simon Kittle's work on this, including "The Incompatibility of Universal, Determinate Divine Causation with Human Free Will," In Vicens, L. and Furlong, P. *Theological Determinism* (Cambridge University Press, 2022), 100-118.

[12] A number of philosophers make this argument, but see Peter van Inwagen, "The Incompatibility of Free Will and Determinism," in *Agency and Responsibility*, Laura Wadell Ekstrom, ed., (Boulder, CO: Westview, 2001).

[13] Anna Case-Winters, *God's Power* (Louisville, KY: Westminster/John Knox, 1990), 9.

[14] I explain "genuine but limited freedom" in "Genuine (but Limited) Freedom for Creatures and for a God of Love" in *Neuroscience and Free Will*, James Walters and Philip Clayton, eds. (Eugene, OR: Pickwick, 2020). For an accessible argument for why neuroscience studies have not disproven free will, see Alfred Mele, *Free: Why Science Hasn't Disproved Free Will* (Oxford: Oxford University Press, 2014).

decision is necessary for freely acting one way instead of another.[15] Kevin Timpe calls this "sourcehood," and he says the agent is the source of its actions.[16] I agree with both: a free agent plays a primary causal role in free choosing.[17]

The second dimension of the genuine but limited freedom view says various options or possibilities are available when an agent chooses. Without multiple possibilities, a chooser can't do other than what circumstances dictate.[18] Put another way, free choice requires live options. Choosers select among viable possibilities in the moment of their deciding.

The third dimension of the genuine but limited freedom view addresses what "limited" means. Deniers of freedom sometimes identify activities an agent can't do. From these, deniers go on to claim free will is an illusion. But few if any freewill theists say creatures have *unlimited* freedom. Every chooser is constrained by forces, history, logic, culture, body, gravity, etc. So we select from *limited* options in each moment, and our choices are, consciously or not, influenced by a host of factors.

A systematic theology of love will value free choosing, because freedom is an aspect of loving. Forced love is a contradiction. Free will also proves important to make sense of how we develop loving characters and become loving people. Consistent lovers adopt habits of care,

---

[15] See Timothy O'Connor, "Agent-Causal Theories of Freedom," in *The Oxford Handbook of Free Will*, ed. Robert Kane, 2nd ed. (Oxford: Oxford University Press, 2011), 309-28. See also Randolph Clarke, "Alternatives for Libertarians," in *The Oxford Handbook of Free Will*, ed. Robert Kane, 2nd ed. (Oxford: Oxford University Press, 2011), 329-48; Robert Kane, *The Significance of Free Will* (Oxford: Oxford University Press, 1998); and Timothy O'Connor, "The Agent as Cause," in *Free Will*, ed. Robert Kane (Oxford: Wiley-Blackwell, 2001), 196-205.

[16] Kevin Timpe, *Free Will: Sourcehood and Its Alternatives*, 2nd ed. (New York: Bloomsbury, 2013), 11.

[17] Among others who argue well for libertarian freewill, see Julian Baggini, *Freedom Regained* (Chicago: University of Chicago Press, 2015); Christian J. Barrigar, *Freedom All the Way Up* (Victoria, BC: Friesen, 2017); Jeffery F. Keuss, *Freedom of the Self* (Eugene, OR: Pickwick, 2010).

[18] See William Hasker, "Divine Knowledge and Human Freedom," *The Oxford Handbook of Free Will*, ed. Robert Kane, 2nd ed. (Oxford: Oxford University Press, 2011), 40-56; Laura W. Ekstrom, "Free Will Isn't a Mystery," in *The Oxford Handbook of Free Will*, ed. Robert Kane, 2nd ed. (Oxford: Oxford University Press, 2011), 366-80.

compassion, and generosity. Free choosing is an ongoing exercise necessary for consistent loving.

Love makes little sense if freedom is a fraud.

## GOD CO-CREATES AND CAN'T ANNIHILATE

I champion the view that free creatures function as creative agents. They contribute to the making of themselves and the making of creation. Although only God is universally creative, creatures co-create in each location. Therefore, it's not merely that the Spirit everlastingly and by nature creates, the creatures that God makes co-create.[19]

Creaturely co-creating obviously includes the procreative activities of sexual intercourse. But it also includes every moment-by-moment action we and other creatures take, because those actions affect minds, bodies, the world, and God. All we witness in the universe involves creaturely actors, factors, and forces. Creatures are created to create.

God and creatures engage in *creatio continua:* continual creating.[20] From the smallest to the largest, the Spirit creatively empowers all, and, together, God and creation bring about something new, moment by moment. This *concursus*—acting together—involves multiple causal actors, factors, and forces but always the creaturely and divine together. This is libertarian co-operative, rather than compatibilist, concurrence. And God preserves existence moment by moment as One who necessarily creates, relates, and loves.

To put it another way, the Spirit's creating wasn't a one-time event in the distant past. Of course, what's creatively possible now differs drastically from what was possible then when the Spirit hovered over the chaotic deep. But just as Genesis portrays God calling upon creatures to "bring forth" others, creatures bring forth today as co-creators.

---

[19] Philip Hefner has done extensive work arguing for the cogency of the label "created co-creators." See *The Human Factor* (Philadelphia: Augsburg Fortress, 2000).

[20] Tyron Inbody does a fine job of arguing for continuing creation in his book *The Faith of the Christian Church* (Grand Rapids, MI: Eerdmans, 2005). Jeffrey Pugh argues similarly in *Entertaining the Triune Mystery* (Harrisburg, PA: Trinity, 2003).

Affirming co-creating should alter the way we talk. Saying, "God created that," for instance, would never be strictly true, if by this we mean deity *alone* did it. All that exists has divine and creaturely input; none comes through the Spirit's effort alone.

Although the loving Creator always acts for good, creatures don't always do the same. Affirming this truth helps us account for evil, injustice, and ugliness, because they occur when creatures don't respond well to the Universal Lover's prompting. The Spirit should not be blamed, therefore, when creatures fail to promote flourishing. The negative aspects of creation aren't God's will.

Many traditional theologies say God could decide at any point to stop creating and preserving creation. These activities, they believe, are voluntary choices for an omnipotent and essentially independent deity who created the universe from nothing. As T. J. Mawson puts it, God "could annihilate [the universe] at any moment."[21] Deity so conceived could either actively destroy everything, or passively let it slip (back) into nothingness.

By contrast, an amipotent God can't annihilate. Doing so doesn't align with the nature of the Spirit who necessarily creates in love. A thief might steal, kill, and destroy, but the amipotent One that Jesus reveals gives life, and that more abundantly (Jn. 10:10).[22] Therefore, the universal Spirit can't eliminate worlds, people, or entities, even if they go awry. As the necessary source of life, the Lover of the Universe *must* sustain creation.

All of this matters for providence. If creatures are truly free, a wise God takes into account their actions when seeking the well-being of all. The deity who desires loving relationships can't override the freedom creatures need to express love. The wise Spirit responds to creaturely co-creating when seeking flourishing, and this Lover wouldn't, and couldn't, annihilate.

---

[21] T. J. Mawson, *The Divine Attributes* (Cambridge: Cambridge University Press, 2018), 19.

[22] Steve Watson explores this issue well in his concise essay, "Faith in a God that Does Not Kill," in *Amipotence, vol. 1*, Chris S. Baker, et. al., eds. (Grasmere, ID: SacraSage, 2025).

## The Origins of Creaturely Freedom

How is it that humans and (likely) other complex creatures find themselves able to choose freely?

This question proves crucial for accounts of providence, because it addresses the nature and extent of the Spirit's love. The best answer will propose a theory for how robust freedom emerged in evolutionary history in conjunction with divine influence and creaturely factors. This answer says God provides freedom to complex creatures and agency to organisms, cells, and even the simplest entities.

The well-established theory of evolution assumes complex creatures emerged slowly and smoothly from less complex ones.[23] New species emerge due to a host of causal factors, including creaturely actions, random genetic mutations, and environmental pressures.[24] Evolution occurs, therefore, through gradual increases in creaturely complexity and capacities, not through radical "jumps." That is, there are no insertions of factors of differing metaphysical kinds.[25]

---

[23] Among the better books arguing for the compatibility of theism and evolution, see Ilia Delio, *Christ in Evolution* (Maryknoll, NY: Orbis, 2008); Karl Giberson, *Saving Darwin* (New York: Harperone, 2008); Karl Giberson and Francis Collins, *The Language of Science and Faith* (Downers Grove, IL: InterVarsity, 2011); John Haught, *God after Darwin* (Boulder, CO: Westview, 2000); Bradford McCall, *Evolution: Secular or Sacred?* (Eugene, OR: Wipf and Stock, 2020); Ted Peters, *Can You Believe in God and Evolution?* (Nashville, TN: Abingdon, 2006); Janet Kellogg Ray, *Baby Dinosaurs on the Ark?* (Grand Rapids, MI: Eerdmans, 2021); Paul Wallace, *Stars Beneath Us* (Minneapolis: Fortress, 2015).

[24] While Neo-Darwinian claims about the importance of genes for evolutionary change have not been dismissed entirely, contemporary biologists readily acknowledge many other factors, actors, and mechanisms at play in evolutionary history. On this, see Sy Garte, *Beyond Evolution: How New Discoveries in the Science of Life Point to God* (Carol Stream, IL: Tyndale, 2025).

[25] Punctuated Equilibria. This view of how evolution proceeds challenged the gradualist view that held sway for decades. Stephen Jay Gould, Niles Eldridge, and others used paleontological evidence to propose that not all evolutionary change is gradual. Periods of rapid evolution could punctuate periods of more gradual (equilibrium) change. Recent work suggests the truth is likely somewhere in between the strong argument made by Eldridge and Gould and the strong gradualism insisted upon in earlier decades. My view of providence allows for punctuated equilibria. But my view rejects the idea of supernatural insertions or emergences of different metaphysical kinds. See Niles Eldredge and Stephen Jay Gould, "Punctuated Equilibria: An Alternative to Phyletic Gradualism," in *Models in Paleobiology*, ed. Thomas J. M. Schopf (San Francisco: Freeman, Cooper, 1972), 82–115; Stephen Jay Gould, *Punctuated Equilibrium* (Cambridge, MA: Harvard University Press, 2007). I'm grateful to Bev Mitchell for engaging me on this and other issues.

The most plausible account for how freedom emerges in creatures rejects the idea that God supernaturally provides free agency, in the sense of singlehandedly inserting it from outside the evolutionary process.[26] Supernatural insertions would entail radical jumps that introduce new metaphysical factors. So, while believers can and should say God creates through the evolutionary process, they are wise to oppose the idea the Spirit interrupts the natural causal processes to insert freedom by fiat.

Not only does the notion of supernatural insertions not align with evolution, but it also heightens the problem of evil. It stands to reason, after all, that a deity who supernaturally could provide freedom could, at any time, also withdraw, override, or fail to provide it. It's entirely up to God. Using this reasoning, presumably a loving and omnipotent God would also, on occasion, interrupt or intervene to prevent horrific evils. And yet horrific evils occur. Theologies of providence that say God supernaturally provides freedom, therefore, can't answer well why deity doesn't fiddle with or foil freedom to prevent pointless pain.

### The Spirit Necessarily Provides Freedom to Complex Creatures and Agency to All

Rather than saying God supernaturally inserts freedom in an evolving universe, we should follow the logic of the Spirit's uncontrolling, collaborative, and persistent love. This means that while the Spirit's love *does* provide freedom to complex creatures, God doesn't act supernaturally to do so, in the sense of overriding creation's causal processes.[27]

---

[26] For strong arguments against supernaturalism understood as divine unilateral determination, see Chad Bahl, *The Death of Supernaturalism* (Grasmere, ID: SacraSage, 2025); David Ray Griffin, *Reenchantment without Supernaturalism* (Ithaca, NY: Cornell University Press, 2001).

[27] Although John Wesley's view of providence included a vital place for human freedom, he also said that God sometimes omnipotently secures outcomes or suspends the laws of nature. These arguments lead to inconsistencies and make his theology susceptible to charges that Wesley's God is culpable for failing to prevent evil. For a helpful summary of Wesley's view of providence, see Douglas M. Strong, "Strangely Warmed, Strangely Free: Wesley's Depiction of God's Particular Providence," in *Wesleyan Theological Journal*, 60:2 (Fall 2025): 39-56.

To make sense of this, we need to add several additional ideas to the claim that God's love is the source of creaturely freedom.

The first addition says the Spirit *necessarily* provides freedom to humans and (likely) other complex creatures. This giving is a necessary expression of the divine nature, so deity can't withdraw, override, or fail to provide freedom. God must give. Rather than supernaturally deciding to give freedom—as if God could choose not to—it's the Spirit's nature to give freedom to complex creatures.

God's giving isn't confined to humans and other complex creatures, however. The second additional idea says deity provides agency to all in creation, even the smallest entities. These gifts—even if in some cases nearly trivial—are necessary expressions of the Spirit's love. Whether quarks, quinoa, quail, queers, or quasars, the Spirit loves all and provides agency to each, depending on their constitution and complexity. God-given agency is essential to the moment-by-moment becoming of everything that exists, because everything is, as Alfred North Whitehead puts it, "a process: it is a becomingness."[28] In God, all creation lives and moves and has its being (Acts 17:28).

This thinking differs from how theologians such as Thomas Aquinas think about divine giving to creation. God "has granted being to other things, not by a necessity of His nature," says Aquinas, "but according to the choice of His will."[29] But when granting good gifts is God's arbitrary choice, deity can freely choose *not* to give. By "arbitrary choice," I mean that the God whom Aquinas envisions is constrained neither by the divine nature nor by creation. In radical freedom, the traditional God decides to grant agency or not. By contrast, the amipotent One necessarily, by nature, provides agency to all.

Giving good gifts is what love does.

---

[28] Alfred North Whitehead, *Science and the Modern World* (New York: Free Press, 1967), 175.

[29] Thomas Aquinas, *Summa Contra Gentiles*, bk. 3, ch. 1, sec. 1, trans. Vernon J. Bourke (Notre Dame, IN: University of Notre Dame Press, 1975), 31.

## Smooth Emergence

The third additional idea we need for an adequate explanation says the Spirit's love plays an essential role in the smooth emergence—through evolutionary history—of robust freedom in complex creatures.[30] This gradual and smooth emergence arises naturally from the agency God provides less complex creatures. To quarks, deity supplies the agency underlying the indeterminacy we witness at the quantum level. To cells and related entities, the Spirit supplies the agency of spontaneity and multiplication. To simpler creatures, deity provides the agency necessary for self-organization and homeostasis.[31] And to the most complex creatures, the Spirit enables full-fledged free will, because they have evolved levels of complexity that make free will possible.

Greater degrees and types of agency emerge smoothly, therefore, as species complexify over time.[32] Both Creator and creatures contribute to this. Because the Spirit necessarily provides agency throughout evolutionary history, deity doesn't need to insert freedom supernaturally into humans when they appear. There were no jumps. The robust freedom we experience as humans emerged slowly and uniformly in continuity with expressions of simpler agency preceding it.[33]

The complexity of the organism determines the degree of agency or freedom the Spirit provides. God can't arbitrarily choose to give

---

[30] Smooth Emergence. I first heard the phrase "smooth emergence" from Joanna Leidenhag at a meeting of the European Society for the Study of Science and Theology. She used it in contrast to "brute" emergence. I'm using it as an alternative to strong emergence theories that say mind can emerge from matter that has no mental dimensions. My students also suggest "rolling emergence," "expansiveness," "growth," and "dynamic complexification." For Leidenhag's helpful book on these issues, see *Minding Creation: Theological Panpsychism and the Doctrine of Creation* (London: T & T Clark / Bloomsbury, 2021).

[31] On this, see David Nikkel, "Self-Organizing Systems and Divine Action," *Zygon: Journal of Religion and Science* 60:3 (2025), 736–54.

[32] Harold Morowitz identifies twenty-eight steps of emergence in life. See *The Emergence of Everything* (Oxford: Oxford University Press, 2002).

[33] Uniformitarianism. While evolution accounts for the slow emergence of new species over time, it allows for occasional rapid change so long as this involves natural causes. The biologist Charles Lyell famously argued for uniformitarianism, by which he said the evolution of life can be explained by the same basic set of causal factors. David Ray Griffin explains the importance of this doctrine for theology and science in *Religion and Scientific Naturalism* (Albany, NY: State University of New York Press, 2000).

less or more agency or freedom. Love seeks the greatest expressions of well-being in each creature and, therefore, God gives the utmost possible to each creature, given its capacity.

Notice that my proposal doesn't require that all creatures—even quarks and cells—have robust free will. As I see it, "free will" connotes conscious choosing among a wide range of possible choices. Simple entities don't seem to do this. But my proposal regards all creatures as expressing a measure of agency, no matter their size or complexity.[34] The agency of self-causation is ubiquitous, in other words, and this was necessary for the eventual emergence of full-fledged free will among complex creatures.

Because the Spirit supplies agency to all and can't control any, the positive and negative activities of even the smallest creatures matter. This means, in part, that what we often call "natural evils" are rightly blamed on agents in creation and creaturely conditions rather than God.[35] Pandemics, violent weather, random genetic mutations, tsunamis, and other natural disasters aren't caused nor permitted by the amipotent Spirit who can't control even the simplest elements and conditions of creation.[36] But positive actions at the microlevel can also contribute to creation's beauty and harmony as the tiniest creatures co-create with the Creator.

The Spirit provides agency to all creatures, depending on their complexities and capacities.

## GOD LOVES THE LEAST OF THESE

Adequate accounts of providence say the Spirit provides agency to all creatures and robust freedom to humans. But it's not just that adequate

---

[34] Philip Clayton explores these issues in a number of books, including *Mind and Emergence: From Quantum to Consciousness* (Oxford: Oxford University Press, 2004).

[35] Bethany Sollereder addresses animal suffering and God's love in *God, Evolution, and Animal Suffering* (New York: Routledge, 2020), as does Christopher Southgate, *The Groaning of Creation* (London: Westminster John Knox, 2008). Ilia Delio addresses love and evolution in *The Unbearable Wholeness of Being* (Maryknoll, NY: Orbis, 2013).

[36] John Culp shows how amipotence overcomes the problem of natural evils in "Amipotence Overcomes Two Problems with Omnipotence," in *Amipotence, vol. 2,* Brandon Brown, et. al., eds. (Grasmere, ID: SacraSage, 2025).

theories of providence will account for the contributions of smaller actors, simple entities, and indeterminate elements. And it's not just that the Spirit isn't culpable for the natural evils caused by simpler creatures, tiny organisms, and weather patterns. An adequate theory of providence will also account for how God actually *loves* the smallest entities in the universe.

The writers of John's gospel probably had only humans in mind when they quote Jesus saying, "For God so loved the world (*cosmos*) . . ." (3:16). But we can rightly wonder what it means for God to love creatures beyond humans, especially the simplest in existence. How can God *literally* love the world, we might ask, in the sense of acting for the well-being of everyone and everything, including the tiniest?

To answer these questions, we should recall that love acts intentionally, in relational response to God and others, to promote overall well-being. It's not hard to imagine a universal Spirit acting intentionally or relating with all creation, assuming we follow the biblical witness of God as a relational agent. And it's not hard to imagine how complex creatures like us can have our well-being enhanced. But it's still not clear how God can promote the well-being of the simplest entities.[37]

For the Spirit to love the least of these in existence, the simplest entities must be capable of experiencing a measure of well-being. Rather than mindless and inert, therefore, simpler entities must be capable of at least a rudimentary level of experience. These capacities are likely minuscule compared with what complex creatures possess, of course. But to enjoy the flourishing God promotes, even the simplest need to enjoy an iota of well-being.[38] An adequate account of providence, therefore, would assume the Spirit's love can enhance the experience of even the last, the least, and simplest. Little ones are loved.

---

[37] In earlier chapters, I said God also responds in light of God's past moments. I said lovers relate to their past selves, so "others" includes our past moments of existence. And this also applies to God.

[38] I explain this accessibly in "Can Creatures Experience Our Love? Beholding, Befriending, Bewelling," in *The Love of Nature and the Nature of Love*, Thomas Jay Oord, ed. (Grasmere, ID: SacraSage, 2026).

To put it another way, all creatures—minuscule and macro, small and large, basic and developed—enjoy values.[39] The most complex are likely capable of a wider range and depth of enjoyment, and the simpler have smaller abilities and ranges. But even the smallest have the capacity to experience a degree of flourishing.[40] The Spirit loves both the simple and the complex, because all creatures are both valuable and enjoy values.

We find here important ecological reflections in an age of climate change. If even the smallest can enjoy a measure of well-being, this means that loving creation involves not merely wanting it to function well so that humans might flourish.[41] It also means acting for the well-being of the tiniest in their own experiencing.[42] All creatures matter for what they contribute to human well-being, and yet they also matter for their own flourishing.

## Ontologies?

Claiming that all creatures have agency and can enjoy the Spirit's love implies a theory about the fundamental characteristics of what it means to exist. It implies an ontology or theory of being/becoming. Many theologies of providence sidestep ontological speculation. Creaturely ontology doesn't really matter if we conceive of God as omnipotent in the classical sense, because an all-powerful deity could accomplish ultimate goals without creaturely input.

To simplify a complex discussion, I briefly identify four ontologies. And I'll advocate for the final of these four.

---

[39] Andrew M. Davis offers a sophisticated exploration of God and values in *Mind, Value, and Cosmos* (New York: Lexington/Bloomsbury, 2020). See also Keith Ward, *Morality, Autonomy, and God* (London: One World, 2013).

[40] Frederick Ferre describes this as the "kalogenic universe." See *Being and Value* (Albany, NY: SUNY, 1996).

[41] Among the growing number of good books on caring for the earth, see Philip Clayton and Wm. Andrew Schwartz, *What is Ecological Civilization?* (Anoka, MN: Process Century, 2019); Mary Elizabeth Moore, *Ministering with the Earth* (St. Louis, MO: Chalice, 1998).

[42] See, for instance, Gary Chartier, *Loving Creation* (Minneapolis: Fortress, 2022).

Idealist ontologies claim minds and ideas are ultimate.[43] These ontologies excel in describing human experiencing, decision-making, freedom, values, possibilities, and such, and some versions of idealism extend these abilities to other creatures. This ontology privileges consciousness, which is why many Eastern religions assume idealism. Theistic versions typically center around the actions of an immaterial deity or Ultimate Consciousness.[44]

Idealist ontologies usually do poorly, however, when accounting for the material realities we experience, and which science presupposes. According to idealism, mind voluntarily manifests materiality, and so it's not ultimately consequential. But we don't create the physical world by thinking about it, and neither does God. While theistic versions of idealism describe well interactions between the divine Mind and human minds, they fail to account well for how an entirely immaterial Mind interacts with mindless materiality.[45]

Materialist ontologies, by contrast, excel in describing the physical aspects of existence. For them, the materiality we sense, and its causal effects, are what's ultimately significant. Materialism accounts for the "stuff" of which we are composed and what we perceive with our five senses. For this reason, philosophers of science have often been attracted to materialism, at least initially.

Materialism fails to account well, however, for our subjective experience, decision-making, freedom, values, and possibilities.[46] And it can't make good sense of consciousness. In fact, reductive versions

---

[43] For arguments in favor of a divine mind as essential for reality, see Lothar Schafer, *In Search of Divine Reality* (Fayetteville, AR: University of Arkansas Press, 1997).

[44] For a theological defense of idealism, see *Idealism and Christianity*, Joshua Farris, et. al., eds. (New York: Bloomsbury, 2017). See also Keith Ward, *Sharing in the Divine Nature* (Eugene, OR: Cascade, 2020). I encourage Ward to adopt material-mental monism in "Keith Ward and a Metaphysics of Love" in *God and Faith,* Ian S. Markham and J.D. Bauman, eds. (Eugene, OR: Pickwick, 2025).

[45] Charles Taliaferro raises this important question in *A Contemporary Philosophy of Religion* (Oxford: Blackwell, 1998), 78.

[46] In various books, Keith Ward has carefully described the many drawbacks to materialism. For one particularly accessible account of materialism's weaknesses, see *God and the Philosophers* (Minneapolis, MN: Fortress, 2009), ch. 11.

of materialism discount these realities altogether.[47] Theistic versions typically assume God must be immaterial, which puts the divine in a unique metaphysical category. This means that they, like idealist ontologies, can't account well for how an immaterial deity interacts with material creation.

Third are dualist ontologies. To their credit, these ontologies acknowledge the reality of both materiality and mentality. This option understands creaturely minds as entirely mental but just about everything else as entirely material. Mind-matter dualism says, then, that existence divides neatly into what's material and what's mental. Two kinds of entities exist.

Dualist ontologies notoriously fail to account for how purely mental entities and purely material entities interact, especially the human mind and body. Dualism also has difficulty accounting for the evolutionary emergence of an immaterial mentality from material entities. There's no continuity. Dualist ontologies face the theological problem found in both idealist and materialist ontologies: accounting for how an immaterial deity interacts with the material entities in creation. And they incline many who adopt them to value immaterial souls, and disvalue, or undervalue, material bodies and the world.[48]

## MATERIAL-MENTAL MONISM

My claims about the Spirit's love for all creation fit best in a fourth ontology. I call it "material-mental monism."[49] It says all existing entities—

---

[47] John Haught argues powerfully against the reductive materialism in *Is Nature Enough? Meaning and Truth in the Age of Science* (Cambridge: Cambridge University Press, 2006).

[48] Although somewhat technical, David Ray Griffin's book *Unsnarling the World-Knot* offers an excellent overall criticism of standard ontologies and defense of what I call material-mental monism and what he calls panexperientialism. See *Unsnarling the World-Knot: Consciousness, Freedom, and the Mind-Body Problem* (Berkeley, CA: University of California Press, 1998).

[49] I'm indebted to Alfred North Whitehead for the basis of this ontology. When I say that all existing actualities have mental and material dimensions, Whitehead talked about physical and mental poles. For instance, Whitehead says these "aspects will be called the physical and the mental poles of an actual entity. No actual entity is devoid of either pole; though their relative importance differs in different actual entities" (*Process and Reality*, Corrected edition by David Ray Griffin and Donald W. Sherburne (New York: Free, 1978 [1929]), 239. One of the

no matter their size or complexity—are events with both material and mental dimensions. The word "monism" indicates one general type. This single type includes the smallest, the simplest, and micro entities, along with the largest, most complex, and macro creatures.

Material-mental monism is a form of panpsychist ontology. John Polkinghorne and others call it "dual-aspect monism," and David Ray Griffin calls it "panexperientialism."[50] I prefer "material-mental monism," because the phrase clearly identifies both subjective and physical aspects as part of the ontology that applies to all existing entities. "Panpsychism" is easily confused as a form of idealism, some forms of which fail to consider materiality a necessary aspect of reality. "Panexperientialism" rightly points to the primary status of experience, but it fails to identify mentality and materiality as its essential aspects. "Dual-aspect monism" doesn't explicitly identify the materiality and mentality of existing entities.

Material-mental monism says human minds and body parts have mental and material dimensions. It rejects the idea that the mental and material are two different kinds of substances or entities. Instead, every entity that exists has mental and material aspects.

Material-mental monism also overcomes the problem of conceptualizing how purely mental agents interact with purely material objects, because it says there are no purely mental agents and no purely material objects.[51] It provides a conceptual framework for understanding how mind and body interact: both have material and mental aspects.[52] And it says the divine Spirit has both dimensions, which provides a framework for making sense of interactions between God and creation.[53]

---

better introductions to panpsychism is from Philip Goff, *Galileo's Error* (New York: Vintage, 2020). On the fruitfulness of panpsychism for theology, see Godehard Brüntrup, et. al., eds., *Panentheism and Panpsychism* (Mentis Verlag/Brill, 2020) and Joanna Leidenhag, *Minding Creation* (London: T & T Clark, 2021).

[50] For Polkinghorne's views, see *The Polkinghorne Reader*, Thomas Jay Oord, ed. (London: SPCK, 2010; Philadelphia: Templeton, 2010).

[51] Pierre Teilhard de Chardin offers a version of this theory in *The Heart of Matter*, René Hague, trans. (New York: Harcourt Brace Jovanovich, 1979).

[52] Matthew Benton explores this in *The Case for a Living Universe* (London: Postbridge, 2024).

[53] Sarah Lane Ritchie explores this issue in *Divine Action and the Human Mind* (Cambridge: Cambridge University Press, 2019).

The mental dimension of each creature and of the Spirit goes by many names, but it affirms a measure of experiential subjectivity.[54] This subjectivity comes in various types and degrees, which means it accounts for various interactions, interiorities, and, in complex creatures, consciousness.[55] Whether we give this "the name of feeling, receptiveness, response to stimuli, volition, or something else," says Hans Jonas, "it harbors, in some degree of 'awareness,' the absolute interest of the organism in its own being, agency, and continuation."[56] The word "mental," therefore, accounts for a wide swath of subjectivity-based activities.

The material dimension also comes in types and degrees. It sometimes goes by terms like "physical," "objective," "concrete," or "substantial." Matter is dynamic, according to physicists, in the sense of exhibiting energy, and it's what philosophers associate with efficient causation.[57] Alfred North Whitehead points to the material dimension of reality when he says, "the physical pole [of an entity] is the inheritance of the efficient cause."[58] It's stubborn fact. We witness this dimension when a boxer's fist impacts an opponent or a lover's embrace warms a partner. Materiality is fundamental to existence and is present even when we can't perceive it with our five senses. Dark matter in the universe illustrates this causal influence even when invisible.

I submit that material-mental monism fits human experience better than the other ontologies I've described. It begins with what we know best: ourselves. Material-mental monism aligns with the mental awareness we experience when thinking, choosing, dreaming, solving problems, consciousness, and so on. Rene Descartes's famous line, "I

---

[54] The implications of material-mental monism for spirituality are immense. For one example, see Sarah Lane Ritchie, "Panpsychism and Spiritual Flourishing," *Journal of Consciousness Studies*, 28:9–10 (2021): 268–88.

[55] Timothy Eastman offers a sophisticated philosophy of science that incorporates key principles in material-mental monism. See Timothy E. Eastman, *Untying the Gordian Knot* (Eugene, OR: Wipf and Stock, 2020).

[56] Hans Jonas, *Mortality and Morality* (Evanston, Ill: Northwestern University Press, 1996), 63.

[57] Alfred North Whitehead called this energy "creativity." See his *magnum opus*, *Process and Reality*.

[58] Whitehead, *Process and Reality*, 237.

think, therefore, I am," identifies mentality as an experiential nonnegotiable for humans: we are thinking creatures.

Material-mental monism also aligns with the material realism of science. It fits with what science says about the physical universe and that our bodies consist of mutually influencing cells, organs, muscles, and other parts.[59] Material-mental monism fits our experience of being impacted physically and impacting others. Self-described solipsists stuck in their own minds can't consistently live as if nothing material exists beyond their own thinking, because they so obviously materially influence creation, and it materially influences them.

Building from first-person experience, material-mental monism speculates that other creatures have less developed mental and material dimensions. Rather than following a dualist ontology that divides existence into mental subjects and material objects, material-mental monism says both are aspects of everything that exists.[60] All ontologies speculate, of course, but material-mental monism better aligns with our experience.[61]

Material-mental monism supports smooth emergence in evolutionary history. Complex creatures with highly sophisticated abilities, freedom, and consciousness evolved from simpler entities with lesser agency, lesser mentality, and limited abilities. "Thought and behavior in people are rendered far less mysterious," says biologist Lynn Margulis, "when we realize that choice and sensitivity are already

---

[59] John Pohl explores these issues well in *A Theology of the Microbiome: An Intersection of Divinity and the Microbial Life Within Us* (Grasmere, ID: SacraSage, 2024). See also his essay, "Do Our Bacteria Love Us?" in *Amipotence, vol. 1*, Chris S. Baker, et. al., eds. (Grasmere, ID: SacraSage, 2025).

[60] A number of theologians have explored this general approach to ontology. In addition to those cited in other footnotes, see Nancy R. Howell, *A Feminist Cosmology* (Humanities Press, 2000).

[61] Combination Problem. Material-mental monism provides a framework for overcoming the combination problem, which asks how consciousness can arise from simpler nonconscious creatures. It makes sense to believe consciousness arises because mentality goes all the way down to the simplest. Through evolutionary forces that affect both the mental and material dimensions of nature, consciousness emerged as mentality developed in complexity in relation to aspects of embodiment and material environment. On the combination problem, see Jaegwon Kim, *Physicalism or Something near Enough* (Princeton: Princeton University Press, 2005). On overcoming it, see essays in Godehard Brüntrup, et. al., eds., *Panentheism and Panpsychism* (Mentis Verlag/Brill, 2020).

exquisitely developed in microbial cells that became our ancestors."[62] Consequently, we don't need to posit supernatural insertions of agency, freedom, or mentality in evolutionary history.

Material-mental monism also applies to the Spirit. Rather than being entirely immaterial, God has material and mental aspects. I will argue in Volume 2 of this systematic theology that we perceive the Spirit through non-sensory perception. Here I simply say that material-mental monism offers a coherent conception of how a God with both material and mental dimensions interacts with and loves creatures and creation, all of which also have material and mental aspects.

I might summarize this way: The universe isn't made up of mindless matter nor matter-less minds. It's made up of relational, temporal agents of various sizes and diversities with both material and mental aspects. So, we should be mindful that everything matters.

## What about Rocks?

We often find the strongest objection to material-mental monism expressed by a question like this: "Are rocks agents who think and make choices?" This good question has a good answer.[63]

Material-mental monism *doesn't* say rocks must be thinking agents who make choices. It distinguishes between two general ways in which creation organizes. Animate organisms are comprised of simpler agents organized around a dominant agent or idea. In human individuals, this dominant agent is the mind. In human communities, it may be a leader. Simpler organisms typically orient around a function or form, so they have an inclusive experience. They act more or less as a whole. Cells are a good example.

Whether simple or complex, animate organisms act as unified agents composed of simpler agents as they respond to their environments, possibilities, and other factors. Bacteria, cells, algae, fungi,

---

[62] Lynn Margulis, "Gaia is a Tough Bitch," in *The Third Culture*, John Brockman, ed., (New York: Simon & Schuster, 1995), ch. 7.

[63] Wm. Andrew Schwartz and I explain this in "Panentheism and Panexperientialism for Open and Relational Theology," in *Panentheism and Panpsychism,* Godehard Brüntrup, et al., eds.

worms, insects, vertebrates of various types, and large communities are animated organisms.

By contrast, rocks are inanimate aggregates composed of unorganized entities. Rocks aren't oriented around a mind or dominant entity, so they don't think, make choices, or possess consciousness. Examples of other aggregates include dust particles, minerals, desks, and computers. Although inanimate aggregates are composed of agents with a measure of mentality, they are not organized so that these agencies coalesce.[64] To say all creatures and creation has materiality and mentality, therefore, requires that we distinguish between animated organisms and inanimate aggregates.[65]

Material-mental monism provides a conceptual framework for affirming an enchanted existence, both in our lives and existence generally. By "enchanted," I don't mean life is a supernatural myth or magical fairytale. I mean that rather than being a mindless machine composed of puppets and pinions, the world and her creatures are, like us, alive and experiential. Vital becoming is widespread; responsive resonance abounds. The enchantment of the universe is real because other-than-human creatures like animals, plants, organisms of various sizes, and even the simplest entities also have mental and material dimensions.

Material-mental monism fits the worldview that biblical writers assume. In scripture, we encounter dancing trees, talking donkeys, rocks crying out, and more. While we don't need to think of these claims as literally true, they express the truth of material-mental monism that creation is alive rather than mechanical. It's enchanted. Love-based accounts of providence, therefore, would be wise to adopt the material-mental monist ontology when considering the nature of providence.

The material-mental monist idea that existence is enchanted aligns also with wisdom in indigenous cultures. Many First Nations people live close to nature, and they collaborate with creation. It's "our

---

[64] I explore what it means for God to love inanimate computers in "Love, Society, and Machines," in *Love, Technology, and Theology*, Scott A. Midson, ed. (London: T&T Clark, 2020.)

[65] David Ray Griffin calls the organismic and aggregate dimensions of material-mental monism "panexperientialism with organizational duality." See *The Christian Gospel for Americans*, 84-86.

responsibility as Indigenous people to be keepers of the land," says Native American and open and relational theologian Randy Woodley. He points to the similarities among creatures expressed by material-mental monism when he calls other creatures his "relatives." "Our role is to maintain harmony and balance," says Woodley.[66] He criticizes the "Western Worldview" and calls us to *shalom* with creation.[67]

We are enchanted creatures in an enchanted universe communing with an enchanted Spirit.

## Chance and Randomness

Contemporary accounts of the world affirm what may seem a contradiction. On the one hand, we find existence characterized by law-like regularities, which are crucial for the order life requires. On the other hand, chance, accidental, and random events also occur. An adequate account of providence will address both chance and regularities. It sees both made possible by the Spirit's steadfast but uncontrolling love for creatures and creation.

The Heidelberg Catechism, a Christian Protestant document dating from the 16th century, explicitly denies chance and randomness. Its writers define providence as "the almighty and ever-present power of God whereby he still upholds, as it were by his own hand, heaven and earth together with all creatures, and rules in such a way that . . . everything comes to us not by chance but by his fatherly hand."[68] The catechism aligns with those who believe, as Thomas Aquinas puts it, "there is no such thing as fortune or chance."[69]

---

[66] Randy S. Woodley, *Indigenous Theology and the Western Worldview* (Grand Rapids, MI: Baker, 2022), 58. See also Ryan Remington, *Peelakiiya Ankwi: Processing Liberation Through an Indigenous American Lens* (Chico, CA: Quoir, 2025).

[67] See Randy S. Woodley, *Shalom and the Community of Creation* (Grand Rapids, MI: Eerdmans, 2012).

[68] *The Heidelberg Catechism*, Allen O. Miller and M. Eugene Osterhaven, trans. (Philadelphia: United Church Press, 1962).

[69] Thomas Aquinas, *The Sermon-Conferences of St. Thomas Aquinas on the Apostle's Creed,* 29-33. For other examples, see Augustine, *Enarrationes in Psalmos I* 18, v. 12 (Vienna: Austrian Academy of Sciences, 2011); John Calvin, *Institutes of the Christian Religion* I.16.2 (Louisville, KY: Westminster, 1960), 198; R. C. Sproul, *Not a Chance* (Grand Rapids, MI: Baker, 1994), 3.

Quantum physics and contemporary biology play key roles in why genuine chance and randomness play crucial roles in contemporary explanations of life.[70] The Copenhagen interpretation of the collapse of the wave function, for instance, says that indeterminacy occurs at the quantum level of existence.[71] The implication is that past occurrences don't entirely determine what happens among even the tiniest entities.[72] We also can't perfectly predict the behavior of more complex entities and organisms, because some behavior is, apparently, random. Because of chance and randomness, we can't be certain how life will play out.[73]

The story biologists tell includes random genetic mutations in the reproductive processes of life.[74] Sometimes, genetic mutations affect only one individual; other times, they pass to subsequent generations. Random changes in the DNA and RNA sequences have led to changes within species and between them. Sometimes genetic mutations prove advantageous, sometimes disadvantageous, and sometimes inconsequential. Randomness played a key role in the slow emergence of complex life.

It's not hard to see chance and randomness also play essential roles in our daily lives. Accidents happen, for instance, and we take this into account when holding ourselves and others accountable. We morally evaluate our children, siblings, or strangers based, in part, upon whether we think what they did was intentional or accidental.

---

[70] For a summary of the scientific, philosophical, and theological considerations of mechanism, see John Hedley Brooke, *Science and Religion* (Cambridge: Cambridge University Press, 1991), ch. 2-4.

[71] Two interpretations of the wave function collapse dominate. In the Copenhagen interpretation, the collapse is what it appears to be: nondeterministic. This interpretation is most common among physicists. In the Bohmian interpretation, however, physicists view the collapse as deterministic.

[72] See John Polkinghorne, *Quantum Theory* (New York: Oxford University Press, 2002).

[73] See David J. Bartholomew's *God, Chance and Purpose* (Cambridge: Cambridge University Press, 2008). James Bradley offers a concise article laying out various aspects of the God and randomness issues ("Randomness and God's Nature," in *Perspectives on Science and Christian Faith*, 64:2 (June 2012): 75-89.

[74] See Heather Hassan, *Mendel and the Laws of Genetics* (New York: Rosen, 2005); Anthony J.F. Griffiths, *Introduction to Genetic Analysis*, vol. 10 (New York: Macmillan, 2008).

Sometimes we're the victims of bad luck; other times we benefit from good luck. Our games, scientific studies, polls, mathematics, businesses, and arts involve chance. The way we react to unintended events, coincidental circumstances, deliberate randomizations, or chance-based outcomes suggests we don't *actually* think God providentially controls all.[75]

Genuine randomness seems at play—to some degree—top to bottom.[76]

## Law-Like Regularities

Randomness and chance are only part of the story. To make sense of existence, we must account for regularities, too. If not for regularity, in fact, we wouldn't call some events random at all.

Traditional systematic theologians have championed life's regularities. Many claim an omnipotent deity installed them as laws of nature.[77] When creating the world from nothing, goes the argument, God inserted natural laws to maintain the order and consistency necessary for life. But this omnipotent "God isn't limited by the laws of nature," says Richard Swinburne, because "he makes them, and he can change or suspend them—if he chooses."[78] A deity who freely installs natural laws can freely suspend or supersede them.

A God who could supersede or suspend the laws of nature would, presumably, exercise this ability to prevent genuine evil. At least a loving deity would. And yet genuine evils occur, many of which could have been prevented by a temporary interruption of the natural laws. This therefore makes the deity conceived by traditional accounts culpable for failing to prevent unnecessary suffering and evil.

---

[75] I explore in more detail the specifics of chance and randomness in *The Uncontrolling Love of God* (Downers Grove, IL: IVP Academic, 2015), ch. 2.

[76] See John Polkinghorne's discussion of the relationship between scientific unpredictability and philosophical adjudication on the epistemic and ontological levels in *One World* (West Conshohocken, PA: Templeton, 2007), 47-49.

[77] Jeffrey Koperski explores God's relation to the laws of nature in *Divine Action, Determinism, and the Laws of Nature* (New York: Routledge, 2020).

[78] Richard Swinburne, *Is There a God?* (New York: Oxford University Press, 2010), 7.

To explain the reality of law-like regularities, we should begin with the steadfast love of the Spirit for each entity in particular and the universe as a whole. From the smallest to the largest, God's love is relentless. It empowers creatures and creation to exist and inspires all toward life, beauty, love, justice, and all that's good. The Spirit's steadfast love, therefore, is a factor in the persistence of existence and the regularities that emerge.

A love-based theory of providence doesn't say God unilaterally installed the law-like regularities of existence. Instead, these regularities emerge from the steadfast love of the Spirit and the intrinsic characteristics of creatures and creation.[79] Consequently, the uncontrolling Lover can't by divine decree interrupt or suspend the law-like regularities of creation.

Law-like regularities are more evident among the simpler entities than among complex creatures. This isn't surprising, because the agency of the simplest is far less than the agency of the complex. Consequently, the options for change and variety are far fewer among the smallest, because the range of possibilities is narrower. Tiny entities engage in repeated actions over vast periods of time, and this is partly what generates law-like regularities.

Regularities are also more evident among inanimate aggregates. Rocks, chairs, and computers, for example, change less often than cells, worms, and people. We all know this. The entities that compose inanimate aggregates are not organized, the individual agencies of those entities will be statistically diminished almost to zero. For the most part, they cancel one another out. Aggregates often function with narrow ranges of variability in the same way as the simplest entities, therefore, and this contributes to the regularities of existence.

The predictable patterns among groups of aggregates and organisms generates the law of large numbers. Statistics can be used to predict what entities will do. The patterns among a massive sample can be

---

[79] A number of physicists reject the idea that the law-like regularities of the universe are eternally immutable. For a discussion of this, see Roberto Mangabeira Unger and Lee Smolin, *The Singular Universe and the Reality of Time* (Cambridge: Cambridge University Press, 2015).

so statistically consistent that we (would wrongly) think the creatures in that sample entirely determined. Despite free will among the humans, we can predict with high probability what percentage in a given culture will marry. And despite occasional randomness at the quantum level of my computer, for instance, it maintains stability. So my computer functions consistently . . . most of the time.

Law-like regularities also emerge from the habits of both simple and complex creatures. We know the power of habits—good and bad—from our first-person experiences. We make free choices over and over, and this repetition leads to regularities, which creates metaphorical grooves in our lives that can be hard to get out of. This experience of habituated patterns provides grounds to speculate that even more ingrained habits can be present in smaller agents with fewer options.

Finally, the law-like regularities we witness also partly stem from the relations among creatures and Creator. These relations have histories and structures, and they rely upon what's possible in each moment.[80] Their ubiquity prompts Alfred North Whitehead to call the law-like regularities "widespread habits," rather than natural laws.[81] They arise organically from interactions between God and creatures and between creatures and creatures.[82] The aren't imposed from the outside.

An adequate account of providence, therefore, affirms the law-like regularities of existence, without saying God supernaturally inserted or omnipotently sustains them.[83] The regularities arise naturally because of the Spirit's persistent love and the characteristics and relations among creatures. Both law-like regularities and chance events make sense, therefore, when God is thought to be others-empowering and

---

[80] Eternal Objects. What's "possible" in each moment affects not only what each entity will become but also the regularities that might emerge. Alfred North Whitehead called these possibilities "eternal objects," although he included other realities as well. Their influence is present at all moments of existence in ways similar to what Aristotle called formal and final causation.

[81] Alfred North Whitehead, *Modes of Thought* (New York: The Free Press, 1968 [1938]), 154.

[82] Alfred North Whitehead, *Adventures of Ideas* (New York: The Macmillan Company, 1933), 112.

[83] I explore in more detail the law-like regularities of life in *The Uncontrolling Love of God* (Downers Grove, IL: IVP Academic, 2015), ch. 2.

uncontrolling.[84] The Spirit who necessarily loves creation can't control chance events nor suspend law-like regularities.

The Spirit's love makes both randomness and regularity possible.

## Panentheism

The intimate connection between the universal Spirit and all creation is sometimes called "panentheism." Although coined in the 19th century, this label has gained attention in the 20th thanks to the process philosopher Charles Hartshorne.[85] It depicts a model of the God-universe relationship that differs both from pantheism and the divine impassibility most systematic theologians assume. In panentheism, "pan" means "all," "en" means "in," and "theism" means "God." Panentheism says all creation is *in* God.[86]

We find at least a dozen versions of panentheism on offer today, and each builds from ontological and theological claims.[87] At stake in this diversity? The meaning of "in" and various views of God. I don't find helpful those versions of panentheism that understand "in" spatially. They imply that all creatures exist "inside" a divine container. Other unhelpful versions of panentheism understand the finite nested within the infinite. These versions confuse, because "infinite" is

---

[84] Arthur Peacocke makes this point in several of his books. See, for instance, *Theology for a Scientific Age* (Minneapolis: Fortress, 1993), 119.

[85] The word was apparently coined by Karl Christian Friedrich Krause. On this and Krause's particular version of panentheism, see Benedikt Paul Göcke, *The Panentheism of Karl Christian Friedrich Krause (1781–1832)* (Berlin: Peter Lang, 2018). On Hartshorne's use of the term, see Charles Hartshorne and William L. Reese, *Philosophers Speak of God* (Chicago: University of Chicago Press, 1953).

[86] For an articulate explanation of panentheism, see the work of Michael W. Brierley, including "Naming a Quiet Revolution: The Panentheistic Turn in Modern Theology," in *In Whom We Live and Move and Have our Being*, Philip Clayton and Arthur Peacocke, eds., (Grand Rapids, MI: Eerdmans, 2004), 1–15.

[87] For an example of the variety, see Clayton and Peacocke, eds., *In Whom We Live and Move and Have Our Being*. See also Philip Clayton, "How Radically Can God Be Reconceived before Ceasing to Be God? The Four Faces of Panentheism," *Zygon: Journal of Religion and Science* 52, no. 4 (December 2017): 1044–1059. For more on the history of panentheism and its various meanings, see John Culp, "Panentheism," *The Stanford Encyclopedia of Philosophy* (Fall 2023 Edition), Edward N. Zalta & Uri Nodelman (eds.) https://plato.stanford.edu/archives/fall2023/entries/panentheism/, (accessed 6/19/2005).

ambiguous at best and a negation of the finite at worst. In other forms of panentheism, advocates say the world "participates" in God.[88] But little explanation is given of what "participate" actually means.[89]

When it comes to the meaning of panentheism, confusion reigns.

### *In the Divine Experience*

When I affirm panentheism, I'm embracing at least three ideas. First, panentheism as I understand it says all creatures and all creation are in God's *experience*. The universal, becoming Lover experiences creaturely others moment by moment, and all creation affects God. Everything influences the Living One.

Let me illustrate what it means to be in someone's experience. As you read or hear the words of this book, they enter your experience. They affect you. Although you're distinct from them, they influence your thinking and, therefore, your living. When you feel a change in temperature, your experience also changes, because the temperature affects you. And so on. Analogously, panentheism says every creature—great and small—affects the universal Spirit's experience. Moment by moment, we all enter God's life.

I often use the word "influence" when describing panentheism. The word has Latin roots and means "to flow into." In terms of God's experience, influence describes the causal and emotional sway of creatures upon the experience of the Loving One. All creatures flow into the divine life.

---

[88] John Cooper's criticism of panentheism draws from or is predicated upon various theories I also find problematic. Cooper's helpful criticisms don't apply to the version of panentheism I offer. See John Cooper, *Panentheism—The Other God of the Philosophers* (Grand Rapids, MI: Baker Academic, 2006). See also Gregory Peterson, "Whither Panentheism?" *Zygon*, 36 (2001): 395-405; R. T. Mullins, "The Difficulty with Demarcating Panentheism," *Sophia*, 55 (2016): 325-346.

[89] Andrew Davison does a better job than most theologians in explaining what he means by "participation in God." See *Participation in God* (Cambridge: Cambridge University Press, 2019).

## Directly with and Entangled

The second idea central to panentheism denies the Spirit is located somewhere outside creation. It rejects the popular idea that God sits on a throne in the clouds or resides at the edges of the universe.[90] Panentheism says the universal Spirit entangles with creation, in the sense that creatures directly relate to, and affect, deity.[91] God is never "over there" but always "right here." I call this theo-cosmo-entanglement.

I add to this second point the claim that God has *never* existed without creaturely others.[92] The loving Spirit everlastingly and necessarily relates, creates, empowers, inspires, and loves creation. It's God's nature to relate with whatever God creates. Therefore, a necessary relationship exists between the universal Spirit and creation, although individual creatures and universes come and go.

Some people criticize pantheism by associating it with women and non-white traditions. These critics worry that the God of pantheism would be intimately related to creatures and lack independence. Consequently, these critics endorse radical differences between God and creation. This points to some of the ethical implications of the traditional view for women and non-white people; radical separations of God and creation are not neutral.[93]

Panentheism, as I conceive it, proudly embraces the idea of divine intimacy with creation, and it embraces creaturely plurality. It affirms that God isn't identical with creation but emphasizes a God-universe entanglement.[94] And it has better ethical implications for those who haven't traditionally been in charge.

---

[90] See Amos Yong, *The Spirit of Creation* (Grand Rapids, MI: Eerdmans, 2011).

[91] Kirk Wegter-McNelly offers something similar in *The Entangled God* (New York, NY: Routledge, 2011).

[92] Many versions of panentheism *don't* say God necessarily and everlastingly relates to creatures. See some of this variety in *In Whom We Live and Move and Have our Being*, Clayton and Peacocke, eds.

[93] See Mary-Jane Rubenstein, *Pantheologies: Gods, Worlds, Monsters* (New York: Columbia University Press, 2018).

[94] Michael M. Rose expresses well the primacy of love and God-creation entanglement in *Made by Love, for Love* (Grasmere, ID: SacraSage, 2026).

My claim that God *necessarily* relates with creation is uncommon among systematic theologies.[95] The Christian scriptures don't deny this view, but they also don't explicitly endorse it either. It's a metaphysical claim. But I agree with Terence Fretheim when he says, "God and creation must be considered together, because again and again the [biblical] texts keep them together."[96] Fretheim puts it simply: "Where there is world, there is God; where there is God, there is world."[97]

Other voices affirm this necessary relationship between Creator and creation. "God is always a God for a world," says Raimon Panikkar.[98] Teilhard de Chardin puts it this way, "the universe contributes something that is vitally necessary to God."[99] Henri Bergson says, "the mystics unanimously bear witness that God needs us, just as we need God." And he asks rhetorically, "Why should [God] need us unless it is to love us?"[100] I put it this way: The Spirit is both the Ever Creator *and* Ever Relator, because creating and relating are necessary aspects of the One whose nature requires loving entanglement with creation.

### God and Creation Are Not Identical

The third key idea to my version of panentheism says God is more than, and not identical to, creation. Although the Spirit and creation always entangle in intimate mutual influence, deity isn't another creature nor the whole of creation. It would make no sense to say, as I do, that the Spirit and creation "entangle" if the two were identical.

---

[95] My claim is rare among the contributors of an accessible book on panentheism edited by Andrew Davis and Philip Clayton. See *How I Found God in Everyone and Everywhere* (New York: Monkfish, 2018).

[96] See *God and the World in the Old Testament* (Nashville, TN: Abingdon, 2005), xvi. For more on the meaning of theocosmocentrism, see Thomas Jay Oord and Wm. Andrew Schwartz, "Panentheism and Panexperientialism for Open and Relational Theology," in *Panentheism and Panpsychism*, Godehard Brüntrup, et. al., eds., (Mentis Verlag/Brill, 2020).

[97] Terence E. Fretheim, *The Suffering of God* (Philadelphia: Fortress, 1984), 37-38.

[98] Raimon Panikkar, *The Rhythm of Being* (New York: Orbis, 2013), 207.

[99] Pierre Teilhard de Chardin. *Christianity and Evolution,* René Hague, trans. (New York: Harcourt, Brace & Jovanovich, 1974) 177.

[100] Henri Bergson, *The Two Sources of Morality and Religion* (London: Macmillan & Co., 1935), 255.

Entangling requires difference. God transcends the universe by differing from it, but deity isn't so radically different as to have no similarities with creatures.[101] God is numerically distinct from but relationally entwined with the universe.

The analogy of the mind's relation to the body—if carefully explained—helps make sense of God as entangled with, but not identical to, creation.[102] For the analogy to work well, we must think of the mind as a series of experiential entities with material and mental dimensions. And we must think the mind directly influences the body (especially the brain), and the body directly influences the mind. We can't see this mutual influence by opening our craniums, of course, but we infer it through our experience.[103]

Analogously, the divine Spirit is a series of divine moments with material and mental dimensions. The Spirit has direct influence upon every creature, each of which also has material and mental dimensions. All that exists, therefore, directly influences God, and God directly influences all. But God and creation aren't identical. And just as we can't open our craniums to see our minds at work, we also can't see the invisible Spirit working in the world. But we infer the Spirit's work by what we observe and directly experience.

God isn't apart *from* the whole, nor an exception *to* the whole, but a part *of* the whole, without being identical *with* the whole.

## Theoenpanism

It's not simply that all creation is in God's experience. An account of providence that takes love seriously also says God is in every creature's experience. The Universal Lover affects all others, from micro to

---

[101] Michael Brierley argues similarly in "The Potential of Panentheism for Dialogue between Science and Religion," in *The Oxford Handbook of Religion and Science,* Phillip Clayton and Zachary Simpson, eds., (Oxford: Oxford University Press, 2006), 635–651.

[102] Hartshorne preferred this analogy. See his discussion in "Pantheism and Panentheism," *The Encyclopedia of Religion*, vol. 11, Mircea Eliade, general editor (NY: Macmillan, 1987), pp. 165-171.

[103] On the fruitfulness of combining panentheism and material-mental monism, see *Panentheism and Panpsychism*, Godehard Brüntrup, et. al., eds.

macro. This is theo-en-panism: God is *in* all.[104] The view also supports the long-standing claim that the universal Spirit sustains us and all creation. God is in us too.

Typical accounts of providence portray God's sustaining activity through external causation. Many theologians imagine a transcendent and unaffected deity exerting causal force upon what amounts to the "machine" of creation and its creaturely "cogs." Divine power so described isn't inherently empowering or invitational; it overpowers and imposes.

This way of thinking construes God like a football player tackling another or, as the Heidelberg Confession puts it, "a fatherly hand." But unlike football players and hands, the traditional deity is thought to be immaterial and invisible. This way of talking erases any analogy between a primary divine cause and secondary creaturely causes, rendering God's action inconceivable.

Theoenpanism thinks about God's presence differently. Without reducing deity to merely a "spark" or "energy," it says the Spirit indwells all creation. *All* creatures are *always* affected by a loving deity, because the Spirit is truly *within* the experiences of all. Material-mental monism is at play here as well.

Although John Wesley didn't explicitly say the Spirit and creatures are experiencing agents, his words illustrate theoenpanism. "God is in all things," he says, and "we are to see the Creator in the glass of every creature." That means "nothing [is] separate from God" and "his intimate presence holds them all in being." The Spirit "pervades and actuates the whole created frame," and God is "the soul of universe."[105]

---

[104] A few others use "theoenpanism" and related words, but they mean something different than what I mean. See Joas Adiprasetya, "Dua Tangan Allah Merangkul Semesta: Panentheisme dan Theenpanisme," *Indonesian Journal of Theology*, 5:1 (2017): 24-41; Alan J. Torrance, "Creatio Ex Nihilo and the Spatio-Temporal Dimensions, with Special Reference to Jürgen Moltmann and DC Williams," in *The Doctrine of Creation*, Colin E. Gunton, ed. (London: T & T Clark, 2004), 91; N. T. Wright, *Paul and the Faithfulness of God* (Minneapolis: Fortress, 2013), 1093.

[105] John Wesley, "*Upon Our Lord's Sermon on the Mount, Discourse the Third (Matt. 5:8-12),*" in *The Works of John Wesley*, ed. Albert C. Outler et al., vol. 1 of the Oxford Edition (Nashville, TN: Abingdon, 1984). Joanna Leidenhag explores this issue in light of amipotence. See "Is the Amipotent God the World-Soul?" in *Amipotence, vol. 1*, Chris S. Baker, et. al., eds. (Grasmere, ID: SacraSage, 2025).

Theoenpanism also affirms creaturely union with God, without characterizing that union as complete identification or a loss of creaturely identity.[106] Rather, we can see the Spirit as united with creation by being *within* every creaturely experience, while yet not *being* a creature.[107] This is part of what it means to be internally related to God and one another.

The strong version of theoenpanism says the loving Spirit is *necessarily* in each creature's moment-by-moment experiencing. No entity, organism, creature, world, or universe can exist without divine influence. As John's gospel puts it, without God's empowering, we can do nothing (Jn. 15:5). But the requirement of divine influence extends to all creatures. The Spirit will never withdraw nor abandon creation, because the Universal Lover necessarily indwells the experiences of creaturely others. God *can't* leave us.

Both panentheism and theoenpanism reject divine intervention. An uncontrolling Spirit who is always in creaturely experiences never interrupts, interposes, interferes, or intrudes. Those words imply that creation has causal closure that doesn't include divine influence. And if "supernatural" means the Spirit overrides creaturely causation, panentheism and theoenpanism reject supernaturalism too.[108] Instead, an uncontrolling God always entangles with creation as One who is in creation's experiences, and they are in divine experiences.

In loving providence, panentheism complements theoenpanism, and vice versa.

## Conclusion

Most accounts of providence don't begin with the universal Spirit of uncontrolling love. They assume, instead, that deity must be impassible and all-powerful, and providence is how God rules. Amipotent

---

[106] Jeff Wells explores divine love in humans in his essay, "God's Powerful Love in Us, Too," in *Amipotence, vol. 1*, Chris S. Baker, et. al., eds. (Grasmere, ID: SacraSage, 2025).

[107] Brian Claude Macallan explores how God influences creation in "How Are We Influenced by God's Love?" in *Amipotence, vol. 2*, Brandon Brown, et. al., eds. (Grasmere, ID: SacraSage, 2025). See also his book *Forgiving God* (Anoka, MN: Process Century, 2023).

[108] See Bahl, *The Death of Supernaturalism* and Griffin, *Reenchantment without Supernaturalism*.

providence, by contrast, says the universal Spirit always loves and never controls. It says the divine Lover necessarily collaborates with creaturely co-creators, great and small. God also receives causal, informational, and emotional input, and the Spirit endeavors to establish flourishing.

Complex creatures express freedom the Spirit of love necessarily supplies. This freedom is genuine, in the sense that creaturely free agents aren't controlled by others. But it's limited, in the sense of being constrained by factors, actors, and forces within and beyond the agents. The universal Spirit provides agency even to the simplest entities of existence, and deity can't withdraw, override, or fail to provide these gifts, even when creatures use them wrongly. Divine giving also accounts, in part, for the chance and randomness in creation. It scales as complexity increases, which means simpler entities possess minimal yet real agency, while complex creatures have full-fledged free will.

A particular ontology supports amipotence-based accounts of providence. I call it material-mental monism, and it says that every existent—from gluons to gophers to God—has both material and mental aspects. Inanimate aggregates (such as rocks) lack unified mentality, however, so they aren't intentional actors. Material-mental monism supports the smooth emergence of complex creatures from those with low-grade agency. This emergence requires the Spirit's uncontrolling love in each moment, but it allows for no supernatural insertions in the evolutionary process. And this framework affirms that even the least can, in measure, be loved by God and humans.

The God of traditional theologies imposes natural laws but could suspend them on occasion. This deity can also annihilate creation. Amipotent providence, by contrast, says law-like regularities can't be suspended. They emerge from the relentless but uncontrolling love of the Spirit interacting with creaturely agents, their relations, and their habits. And God can't annihilate.

Finally, amipotence accounts of providence cast the God-world relation in panentheistic and theoenpanist terms. This means that every creature is in God's experience and God indwells every creature's experience. Although intimately entangled, Creator and creation aren't identical. This systematic theology of love understands providence, then, as the universal Lover's ceaseless, uncontrolling, and life-giving work alongside co-creating creatures and creation.

It matters when a theory of providence puts uncontrolling love first.

CHAPTER FOURTEEN

# Solving the Problem of Evil

## THE BIG IDEAS

- The problem of evil asks, "Why doesn't an all-powerful and all-loving God *prevent* genuine evil?"
- The more horrific, inexplicable, or expansive the evil, the stronger the evidence against believing in an all-powerful and all-loving deity.
- Evil isn't best defined as the privation of good. Evils are events that, all things considered, make the world worse than it might have been.
- The Bible doesn't provide a solution to the problem of evil.
- A helpful solution to the problem of evil makes six claims:
  - *God can't prevent evil singlehandedly.*
  - *God empathizes with creaturely suffering.*
  - *God works to heal, but can't singlehandedly.*
  - *God works to squeeze good from bad.*
  - *God needs creaturely cooperation.*
  - *God doesn't create evil, but its possibility is present in creation.*
- This systematic theology of love is agnostic on whether a literal devil or demons exist.
- Biblical references to lament often describe the frustration and pain of sufferers, but some wrongly say God causes evil, withdraws, or waits to rescue.

Atheists and agnostics give many good reasons for why they don't believe in God. Most revolve around the problem of evil and divine silence. The omnipotent deity of traditional theology could prevent evil singlehandedly and provide crystal-clear communication.[1] But evil occurs, and God often seems hidden. These problems lead sincere people to doubt God exists, as I have argued elsewhere.[2]

In previous chapters, I offered an alternative view of divine power. It rejects omnipotence and embraces amipotence, which I define as the power of uncontrolling love. This alternative solves the theoretical aspect of the problem of evil, because a Lover who can't control anyone or anything can't prevent evil singlehandedly. God's not culpable.

I'll explain in Volume 2 how amipotence solves the divine silence and hiddenness problems. I'll argue that the Spirit communicates but can't control interpreters. God's consistent but relationally-conditioned communication always intertwines with creaturely input and requires creaturely discernment.

This chapter continues exploring providence from the perspective of amipotence. In it, I address the problem of evil directly, while defining evil and considering its origin. Along the way, I bring scripture to bear, as I explore the work of Bart Ehrman and N. T. Wright. I also consider the possible existence and role of a devil and demons.

The bold claim of this chapter? I believe the problem of evil can be solved. Yes, solved. In showing how, I identify six dimensions of the solution. While this multi-faceted proposal isn't explicitly found in scripture, it builds from biblical themes, it's reasonable, and it accounts for broad experience. Accounting for evil seems crucial if a systematic theology strives to portray God as perfectly loving.

## INADEQUATE ANSWERS TO THE PROBLEM OF EVIL

We often find the problem of evil stated in question form: "Why doesn't an all-powerful and all-loving deity *prevent* genuine evil?" I highlight

---

[1] This chapter is dedicated to David Ray Griffin. His thinking on the problem of evil influenced me long before he became my doctoral advisor, and his theological and philosophical reflections have shaped me profoundly.

[2] See Thomas Jay Oord, *The Uncontrolling Love of God* (Downers Grove, IL: IVP Academic, 2015); *God Can't* (Grasmere, ID: SacraSage, 2019); *The Death of Omnipotence and Birth of Amipotence* (Grasmere, ID: SacraSage, 2022).

the word "prevent," because some theologians say God *allows* evil.[3] Saying this, however, doesn't solve the problem, because a God who permits evil that could have been prevented isn't consistently loving. Love prevents preventable evil. Those who allow hurt, horrors, and holocausts that they could have stopped aren't exemplars of love.

Some theologians respond to the problem of evil by saying an omnipotent God allows evil to build our characters or teach us lessons.[4] This pedagogical view doesn't provide a solution either. Saying God allows evil to strengthen us doesn't account well for those victims who don't survive. They're not strengthened. And instead of getting better, some survivors grow bitter. One wonders why an omnipotent creator didn't make strong-character people in the first place. Or why an omnipotent God (one with allegedly no limits) created a world in which lessons needed to be learned.[5]

Other theologians say the omnipotent One causes or allows evil as punishment. In this view, we and others deserve the pain we endure.[6] This response is also unsatisfying. Not only do undeserving victims and innocent children suffer needlessly, but the agony of the guilty often far exceeds the harm of their disobedience. The punishment doesn't fit the crime. More importantly, this punishment proves irreconcilable with divine mercy.[7] A loving God *forgives*.

Analytic theologians like to claim Alvin Plantinga has proved there's no logical contradiction between belief in God and the occurrence of evil.[8] But surely this is a minor win; few ordinary people

---

[3] For one example, see theologian Jack Cottrell, "The Nature of Divine Sovereignty," in *The Grace of God, the Will of Man*, ed. Clark H. Pinnock (Grand Rapids, MI: Zondervan, 1989).

[4] John Hick offers the most influential contemporary form of this argument in *Evil and the God of Love*, 2nd ed. (London: Macmillan, 1977). One of the best criticisms of this view comes from C. Robert Mesle, *John Hick's Theodicy: A Process Humanist Critique* (London: MacMillan, 1991).

[5] For a discussion of major options in theodicy, see Chad Meister and James K. Dew, Jr., eds., *God and the Problem of Evil: Five Views* (Downers Grove, IL: IVP Academic, 2017).

[6] As an example, see Jonathan Edwards, "Sinners in the Hands of an Angry God," in *The Works of Jonathan Edwards, Vol. 22: Sermons and Discourses, 1739–1742*, Harry S. Stout, Nathan O. Hatch, and Kyle P. Farley, eds. (New Haven, CT: Yale University Press, 2003).

[7] Pete Shaw addresses this from a pastoral perspective in "Smite Our Enemies, Loving God?" in *Amipotence, vol. 1*, Chris S. Baker, et. al., eds. (Grasmere, ID: SacraSage, 2025).

[8] See Alvin Plantinga, *God, Freedom, and Evil* (Grand Rapids, MI: Eerdmans, 1977).

lose sleep over the logic of the problem. Most of us want emotionally and ethically *plausible* solutions to the problem of evil, not just logical ones. Besides, it doesn't help an abuse survivor to tell her it's logically possible a loving God allowed her harm. The same goes for victims of genocide, pandemics, torture, cancer, and more. We want believable answers, not just logically possible ones.

Skeptical theists appeal to mystery in response to the problem of evil. God "will indeed have a good reason for permitting evil," says Plantinga. "But why suppose the theist must be in a position to figure out what it is?"[9] This response provides no solution and isn't even a defense.[10] I find it particularly annoying when analytic theists seem confident they've solved far less important problems but appeal to mystery in response to the problem that leads countless people to unbelief. Why worry about solving trinitarian conundrums, for instance, if the problem of evil provides good grounds to doubt the trinity even exists?

More promising are the "greater good," "creation project," and "only way" theodicies. They implicitly, if not explicitly, admit God can't do everything we might want. According to these approaches, God can't always get good results . . . given creaturely freedom, natural processes, divine goals for creaturely moral growth, the limits of logic, the reality of time, incompatible goods, law-like regularities, chance, and so on.

Most who advance these types of theodicies also say God is omnipotent, however. What they mean by "omnipotent"—given the many qualifications such as those I just listed—differs radically from both traditional and popular meanings of literally being all-powerful. Worse, saying an omnipotent God allows evil for some greater good, as a general policy, or not to interfere in a creation project won't convince

---

[9] Alvin Plantinga, "Reply to the Basingers on Divine Omnipotence," *Process Studies* 11/1 (Spring, 1981), 28.

[10] Antitheodicy. Some unsatisfied with answers to evil that appeal to soul-building, greater good, free will, etc. dispense with seeking any solution. They rightly reject bad arguments, but they don't radically formulate divine power in attempts to find satisfying solutions. For an explanation of how amipotence theodicy overcomes worries of antitheodicy and typical theodicies, see Mark Waters, "A Middle Way Between Theodicy and Antitheodicy," in *Amipotence, vol. 2*, Brandon Brown, et. al., eds. (Grasmere, ID: SacraSage, 2025).

survivors that the Spirit cares about them.[11] A deity who allows evil that could be prevented must have had more important issues on His plate than the horrors survivors endure and that kill some victims.

What analytic theologians call "the evidential" dimension of the problem of evil has long formed the center of concern. We want to know why a loving and powerful God didn't prevent *this* particular evil, such as a rape or murder. Why doesn't deity prevent large-scale evils too, such as plagues, pandemics, and genocides?[12] Why do infants and animals suffer unnecessarily? Why doesn't God stop accidental deaths and random mutations that lead to intense pain? And so on.

The more horrific, inexplicable, or expansive the evil, the stronger evidence we have against believing in an all-powerful and all-loving deity.

## Defining Evil

One way to slip off the problem-of-evil hook? Deny that evil is actually real. This typically takes one of two forms, each based on different definitions of evil. One denial considers evil the privation or imperfection of things. The other understands evil as the harmful consequences of an event or action.

### *Privation*

Augustine defines evil as the privation or defectiveness of a good thing. According to this perspective, evil shouldn't be understood as an object. It's the lack of perfection in things that God created, things that remain fundamentally good. "Evil has no positive nature," says Augustine, "but the loss of good has received the name 'evil.'"[13]

---

[11] Chad Bahl makes this point beautifully in his response to William Hasker's "General Policy" creation project theodicy. See "Bad Theodicy: An Open Theism Approach" (https://chadbahl.substack.com/p/bad-theodicy-an-open-theism-approach -accessed 11/18/2025).

[12] Clifford Cain addresses natural evil from a perspective very similar to my own. See Clifford Chalmers Cain *God, Pandemics, and the Holocaust* (Eugene, OR: Wipf and Stock, 2025).

[13] Augustine, *City of God* (Edinburgh: Murray and Gibb, 2014), 447.

Asking "Why did God make evil?" would be the wrong question, according to Augustine.[14] Evil isn't created; it's the defect of an intrinsically good thing. He believes, therefore, in what some interpreters call "evil goods."[15]

Defining evil as the privation of good is unsatisfying, however, even to Augustine. When we think God to be the sole creator and absolute ruler of all, saying evil is a privation makes no sense. Evil is explained away, and Augustine admits this in a prayer:

> To Thee there is no such thing as evil, and even in Thy whole creation taken as a whole, there isn't; because there is nothing from beyond it that can burst in and destroy the order which Thou hast appointed for it. But in the parts of creation, some things, because they don't harmonize with others, are considered evil. Yet, those same things harmonize with others and are good, and in themselves are good.[16]

What we consider evil, says Augustine, must actually be good from a God's-eye point of view. In some mysterious way, what *seems* imperfect and defective contributes to the beauty of the whole. For "the Omnipotent God . . . and Supreme Power of all would not allow any evil in his works unless . . . he is able to bring forth good out of evil."[17] He's saying privations don't actually make the world worse, overall.

Augustine's view of evil as privation also doesn't fit the broad biblical witness or the way we live our lives. It assumes a substance-based ontology, rather than tying evil to actual actions and events. Applied to humans, it means we are defective substances rather than dynamic experiencers; we're imperfect things rather than becoming agents. For

---

[14] On Augustine's view of evil, see G. R. Evans, *Augustine on Evil* (Cambridge: Cambridge University Press, 1982).

[15] Samantha Thompson, "What Goodness Is: Order as Imagination of Writing in Augustine," *The Review of Metaphysics* 65:3 (March 2012), 525.

[16] Augustine, *Confessions*, Henry Chadwick, trans. (Oxford: Oxford University Press, 1998), 7:13.

[17] Augustine, *The Enchiridion on Faith, Hope, and Love*, in *Augustine*, John Burnaby, ed. (Philadelphia: Westminster, 1955), ch. 3.

these reasons, we should reject the idea that evil is the privation of a good thing.

We would be wise to retain Augustine's claim that nothing is wholly evil, however. Acknowledging the intrinsic goodness of everyone and everything helps us honor the inherent value of all people, even those who do evil habitually. And it helps us to respect and protect creation in general and particular creatures we might be tempted to destroy (e.g., spiders and snakes!). Although we and other creatures sometimes do evil, nothing and no one should be considered intrinsically evil.

*Events*

A better definition understands evil in terms of events or occurrences. This view says genuine evils are events that, all things considered, make the world worse than it otherwise might have been.[18] Evils are harmful happenings when better ones could have occurred.

Consider the evil involved in molesting a child. This heinous action involves harmful events instead of helpful ones, such as hugging or encouraging them. Molesting children makes life worse, all things considered, than what it could have been. Or consider murder. It's an unnecessary occurrence that ends the life of an intrinsically valuable person. Or take embezzlement. It's a series of events that involves stealing money, and life would have been better had the embezzling not happened. Or bullying. A strong individual threatens and often inflicts harm on a weaker one when avoiding this bullying action was possible.

Genuine evils are events that didn't *have* to happen, and they make the world, all things considered, worse than it otherwise might have been.

The event-oriented definition of evil faces an objection. We might wonder how anyone could ever judge whether a particular event makes the world worse, all things considered. None of us has a God's-eye perspective; our vision remains limited. Because of our limits, some

---

[18] David Ray Griffin defines evil similarly. See *God, Power, and Evil* (Louisville, KY: Westminster John Knox, 2004). I compare genuine evil to the concepts of necessary and gratuitous evil in *The Uncontrolling Love of God*, ch. 3.

people deny the reality of evil by saying we can't know the good *at all*. Or they say all events *must* contribute to a greater good, because they were caused or allowed by an omnipotent deity.

Most greater good and creation project theodicies are sophisticated denials of genuine evil.[19] Those who embrace them admit that horrific pain, bad accidents, or intentional harm do occur. But they say even the most horrific suffering must be necessary for God to secure some benefit, or else to maintain some pledge of non-interference in creation. Or they say the overall creation project would run aground if God made an exception and rescued those in harm's way. Hence, any particular evil—e.g., the torture of a child—doesn't make the world worse than it might be if God were to have stopped that event.

Denying any occurrence is genuinely evil or saying we can't know evil from good, has dire consequences. If true, every murder, rape, pandemic, or deception that's ever occurred must, in some way, make the world better. Or God's stopping it would have led to worse consequences. Those who affirm an omnipotent deity but appeal to greater good, creation project, or only-way theodicies are implicitly denying that even the greatest horrors must be *genuinely* evil. Or they retreat to the claim we have no clue which events are evil, and which are loving. That's extreme moral relativism.

### *Experiential Nonnegotiable*

No one lives as if they think every event was good and none evil. Some people might say, "everything's good" and by this mean evil never occurs, but they nevertheless *act* as if some events make their lives or the lives of others worse than they *could* have been. Few people can look a survivor of repeated sexual abuse in the eye and say, "What happened to you isn't genuinely evil."[20] Few could respond to the Rwandan genocide survivors and say the same. Few people think that their child getting tortured isn't bad. We all *live* as if evil is genuine.

---

[19] I explain this in reference to the work of John Sanders. See *The Uncontrolling Love of God*, ch. 6.

[20] Tambry Harris addresses sexual trauma in *Awakening the Light* (Spark, 2020).

The fact that genuine evils occur is another experiential nonnegotiable. We all act as if, deep down, we think some events make life worse than it might have been. We can't actually live as if evil is an illusion, at least not consistently. We're wise to assume, therefore, that our valuation of events as good and evil—flawed as they might sometimes be—tell us something true about the values and disvalues of reality.

We also implicitly acknowledge the reality of genuine evil when we try to improve nature, which includes trying to improve ourselves. If we thought we and the world were just as good as they could be, no one would ever seek improvement. By our actions we show we think that our lives and other aspects of our world are worse than they otherwise might have been.[21] Things could have been better.

In addition to evil being something we experience, Christians have a conviction that requires they affirm the category of evil: all have sinned (Rm. 3:23).[22] If God wants the salvation of us and all creation, and if sin undermines this salvation, then sin must make creation, all things considered, worse than what God wanted it to be. Sin does evil. That seems to be the assumption of biblical writers and a reality Augustine misses when he defines evil simply as the privation of a good thing.

To be clear, then, when I talk about "genuine evil," I'm referring to happenings, occurrences, or events that make existence, all things considered, worse than it might have been. I think some events are genuinely evil, and I think God regards some events as genuinely evil. I'll explain the relation between sin and evil in Volume 2 of this systematic theology of love.

## Evil and Scripture - Bart Ehrman

Many Christians have searched scripture for a solution to the problem of evil. In *God's Problem: How the Bible Fails to Answer our Most Important Question—Why We Suffer*, biblical scholar Bart Ehrman

---

[21] John Hedley Brooke and Philip Hefner make a similar argument. See John Hedley Brooke, "Improvable Nature," in *Is Nature Ever Evil?* Willem B. Drees, ed. (New York: Routledge, 2003); Philip Hefner, "Nature good and evil: a theological palette," in *Is Nature Ever Evil?* Willem B. Drees, ed. (New York: Routledge, 2003).

[22] Many Christians exempt Jesus of Nazareth from this "all humans have sinned" statement.

explores what biblical writers say about God and suffering.[23] The Bible offers a range of answers.[24]

Many biblical authors believe pain and suffering to be divine punishment. The book of Amos, for instance, describes God punishing humans for their transgressions. This includes deity inflicting burning, nakedness, famine, isolation, drought, pestilence, death, and other disasters (1:3-4, 6-8). It's brutal! But divine punishment isn't just found in Amos. It's "the point of view of the majority of authors who produced the biblical texts," concludes Ehrman.[25]

If an omnipotent deity punishes the wicked, it would seem that people who suffer more than others would be more wicked. But this doesn't fit life as we know it nor the witness of other biblical texts, such as the story of Job. Innocent babies sometimes suffer, and the wicked sometimes prosper. More importantly, the idea that evil is God's punishment stands at odds with the fundamental concept of divine forgiveness. If true, God doesn't always "turn the other cheek," even though Jesus tells his disciples they must do so (Mt. 5:39). Therefore, the punishment view of evil portrays God as not always forgiving.

A second biblical view says suffering is the natural consequence that comes from sin—ours, or the sins of others. The book of Judges, for instance, offers examples of victims who suffer because of the violence others do. The apostle Paul recounts suffering caused by humans and other creaturely factors, not God (2 Cor. 11:23-26). And New Testament writers say a sinless Jesus suffered and died at the hands of religious and political authorities.

The idea that sin brings natural negative consequences is the closest biblical writers come to free-will theodicy.[26] But people of faith who embrace this explanation, says Ehrman, usually believe in an "all-powerful Sovereign of this world who foreknows all things." If an omnipotent and foreknowing deity causes or allows evil, says Ehrman,

---

[23] Bart Ehrman, *God's Problem* (New York: HarperOne, 2008), 16.

[24] See also James L. Crenshaw, *Defending God* (Oxford: Oxford University Press, 2005); J. Richard Middleton, *Abraham's Silence* (Grand Rapids, MI: Baker, 2021).

[25] Ehrman, *God's Problem*, 61.

[26] Theodicy. A theodicy can be defined as a theory that justifies believing in God despite the occurrence of evil and other arguments against belief.

"there is very little we could do about it."²⁷ In other words, it must be God's will.

A third biblical response says evil must be redemptive: God wants it for some good. Some think the story of Joseph illustrates this (Gen. chs. 37-50), says Ehrman. Joseph was sold into slavery, but this evil made it possible for him, to later, save his brothers. The story of Moses leading people out of Egypt could be interpreted as God allowing evil (slavery) for some greater good (the promised land). Many say God wanted the death of Jesus, because "by his wounds we are healed" (Isa. 53:5). The idea that suffering is redemptive, says Ehrman, "is found throughout the Bible."²⁸

This answer fails to account for the fact that *genuine* evils lead to less good than what was otherwise possible. Take genocide as an example, or rape. Whatever goods come from them surely would be less beneficial than if these horrors had never occurred. If they aren't, we should rejoice when mass killings and sexual abuse occur. But we don't. In fact, "*most* suffering isn't positive," claims Ehrman. It "doesn't have a silver lining, isn't good for the body or soul, and leads to wretched and miserable, not positive, outcomes."²⁹

Ehrman labels the final biblical answer to evil "apocalypticism."³⁰ This stance says evil forces work against God and harm creatures. Those who embrace the apocalyptic view, says Ehrman, believe "God handed over control of the world to these forces of evil." Those forces will eventually be overcome, however, when the kingdom of God has come in power (Mk 9:1). According to this view, says Ehrman, "God will reassert himself and wrest control of this world from the forces that now dominate it."³¹

The apocalyptic answer is rife with problems, because most who hold this view think God is omnipotent. To overcome evil, therefore, an all-powerful deity wouldn't need to wait on anyone or anything; He

---

[27] Ehrman, *God's Problem*, 120, 122.

[28] Ibid., 153.

[29] Ibid, 155-56.

[30] Ehrman also offers a chapter on biblical appeals to mystery as no answer (see chapter 6).

[31] Ibid., 227.

can do it now. Besides, a perfectly loving deity would never give control to evil forces and figures. That's like hiring a babysitter whom we know tortures children. And thinking God will eventually overcome evil singlehandedly should, logically, lead us into complacency about solving life's problems. Why make sacrifices now if, no matter what we do, God will later fix things singlehandedly?

After considering the Bible's answers to the problem of evil, Ehrman found none satisfying. Like atheists and agnostics, therefore, Ehrman stopped believing God exists. He "felt compelled to leave Christianity," he says, although he left "kicking and screaming, wanting desperately to hold to the faith."[32] He "could no longer explain how there can be a good and all-powerful God actively involved with this world, given . . . a cesspool of misery and suffering."[33]

The Bible doesn't solve the problem that leads hundreds of millions to unbelief and billions to confusion.

## Evil and Scripture - N. T. Wright

In his book *Evil and the Justice of God*, N. T. Wright also explores what scripture says about God and evil. Wright doesn't address as many biblical passages as Ehrman does, but his exploration leads him to agree with Ehrman on some points and disagree on others.

Wright explicitly tells readers he doesn't have an answer to why God fails to prevent evil. And like Ehrman, he believes biblical writers don't solve the problem, let alone reveal evil's true origin. "We are not told—or not in any way that satisfies our puzzled questioning," says Wright, "how and why there is radical evil within God's wonderful, beautiful, and essentially good creation."[34]

Several of Wright's comments do address well-known responses to the problem of evil. He's skeptical of the view that God permits evil so

---

[32] At the conclusion of his book, Ehrman considers Harold Kushner's view that God can't prevent evil.

[33] Ibid., 3.

[34] N. T. Wright, *Evil and the Justice of God* (Downers Grove, IL: InterVarsity, 2006), 164. See also page 40.

that virtue can flourish, for instance.[35] Wright never says God allows evil to bring a greater good.[36] He sometimes talks about God's "project" for creation and, in several comments, takes the view that sin is self-defeating.[37]

Wright never directly says, as I do, that God *can't* prevent evil singlehandedly. But he makes statements that say, or imply, that divine power has limits. He says, for instance, that "God can't undo the good creation, even though it has gone wrong."[38] That's a "God can't" statement. Wright says God's work to overcome evil isn't easy. "God has had to work to bring the world out of the mess," he says. Deity "has to get his boots muddy" and "his hands bloody."[39] That suggests limits on divine power.

Importantly, Wright rejects the idea that "God is the omnicompetent managing director of a very large machine."[40] This assertion seems to admit God can't do some things. But Wright says that for a reason he can't understand, "the Creator God will not simply abolish evil from this world."[41] His words "will not" suggest that God could abolish evil but chooses not to do so.

Wright's main proposal for understanding God and evil involves a central role for the crucifixion of Jesus. The cross represents "an event in which the living God deals with [evil]."[42] Evil is "confronted," "defeated," and "exhausted," says Wright.[43] The cross becomes "the sign that pagan empire, symbolized in the might and power of sheer brutal force, has been decisively challenged by a different power, the power of

---

[35] Ibid., 28. One exception is when Wright says, "The story of God's action to deal with evil at every level by letting it do its worst to his own incarnate self" (102). Saying God "lets" evil do its worst sounds like permission. But here he's restricting this to God allowing evil to harm Godself, not creation.

[36] Ibid., 40.

[37] Ibid., 109. Unfortunately, Wright sometimes talks about *the* Christian view of evil rather than acknowledging many Christian views (e.g., 40).

[38] Ibid., 73-74.

[39] Ibid., 58-59.

[40] Ibid., 73.

[41] Ibid., 55.

[42] Ibid., 93.

[43] Ibid., 142.

love, the power that shall win the day."⁴⁴ In other quotes similar to the last one, Wright prioritizes love over power.

God doesn't defeat evil by the cross alone, however, according to Wright. We also have a role to play. We "act as God's wise agents . . . to bring his wise and healing order to the world, putting the world to rights under his just and gentle rule."⁴⁵ He says we must "implement the victory of God in the world *through suffering love*."⁴⁶

How will God do this? Wright doesn't provide specific details. But he does point to forgiveness. Overcoming evil and bringing new creation involves God's forgiving love. We must also forgive so that we "will no longer be affected or infected by [evil]."⁴⁷ The following sentence summarizes Wright's view: "When we understand forgiveness, flowing from the work of Jesus and the Spirit, as the strange, powerful thing it really is, we begin to realize that God's forgiveness of us, and our forgiveness of others, is the knife that cuts the rope by which sin, anger, fear, recrimination and death are still attached to us."⁴⁸

*So, how should we evaluate Wright's proposals?*

We could rightly say that because Wright doesn't solve the problem of evil, the book is, on that issue, a failure. He leaves readers with their main question unanswered: Why doesn't God *prevent* genuine evil? And because that question remains, others arise. If God has the ability to abolish evil eventually, as Wright contends, wouldn't a loving deity do so *now*? Why wait? If God could resurrect Jesus without "undoing" creation, how can God resurrect the rest of us without undoing it? What's the relation between sovereignty and suffering love?

The fact that the Bible fails to solve the problem of evil—something both Wright and Ehrman admit—*doesn't* mean the issue is inconsequential. The absence of an explicit biblical answer doesn't provide an excuse for us to pretend the problem doesn't need solving. It does.

---

⁴⁴ Ibid., 100.

⁴⁵ Ibid., 139.

⁴⁶ Ibid., 98.

⁴⁷ Ibid., 142.

⁴⁸ Ibid., 164-65.

Wright's focus on forgiveness can be partly helpful. The Spirit's forgiveness delivers us from worries about divine punishment: that's important. Our forgiving delivers us from resentment, bitterness, and self-loathing. That's important too. But God's forgiving and ours don't deliver us from the actual *harm* we experience when we and others do evil. Worse, a deity who allows evil just to forgive it doesn't really love victims. Solving the problem of evil requires more than affirming the power of forgiveness.

Although a failure in one sense, Wright's book can be helpful in others. He shuns inadequate answers to evil, for instance, and admits that divine power has limits. Wright doesn't dismiss evil as privation or say God allows suffering for some greater good. He never says God *alone* overcomes evil and often points to the role creatures play. Most promisingly, Wright rejects divine omnicompetence and brutal force.[49]

According to Wright, God's power is suffering and gentle love.

## SOLVING THE PROBLEM OF EVIL

The view of a loving Spirit I've laid out in previous chapters, alongside Ehrman's and Wright's exploration of scripture, provide a basis to solve the problem of evil. I offer a six-fold solution, because the problem of evil has various dimensions. While this solution isn't explicitly found in scripture, it aligns with key biblical ideas.

*1) The Uncontrolling Dimension: God can't prevent evil singlehandedly.*

The most important claim for solving the problem of evil denies that God is omnipotent. The loving Spirit can't control anyone or anything, because an amipotent God loves everyone and everything, and

---

[49] Chris Baker argues that N. T. Wright ought to embrace an open and relational theological vision to make a better case for many of Wright's convictions. See *The Invitation: How Open and Relational Theology Enhances N. T. Wright's Use of Vocation in Atonement* (Grasmere, ID: SacraSage, 2025).

amipotence never controls.[50] To the question, "Why doesn't God prevent evil," therefore, we should say God isn't all-powerful. God doesn't exert all power, can't do everything we might imagine, and can't control creatures or circumstances. Consequently, the Spirit whose nature is uncontrolling love *can't* prevent evil singlehandedly, because "God can't deny himself" (2 Tim. 2:13).

This emphasis upon an uncontrolling God within a six-fold solution to the problem of evil affirms what's best in the free-will defense.[51] But my view essentializes and expands it. It essentializes by saying the Spirit *necessarily* gives free will to complex creatures and *can't* withdraw, override, or fail to provide it. We're essentially free.[52] Rather than "permit" or "allow" the evil that free-will creatures cause, the God of uncontrolling love can't prevent it singlehandedly. By nature, the amipotent Spirit loves all by self-giving and others-empowering.

The full solution to the problem of evil also expands the free-will theodicy. My view says the Spirit supplies agency to all creatures and creation. Consequently, God can't control smaller creatures, simpler organisms, and inanimate entities. The Spirit can't control the tiniest nor the largest, those with minimal agency and those with maximal. For reasons I laid out in previous chapters, God also necessarily sustains and can't suspend the law-like regularities of the universe. Therefore, the Spirit can't interrupt the laws of nature to stop evil.

Saying God can't control also explains why the Spirit can't prevent evil associated with random and chance events. Deity gives agency to all, and can't control any. So freak accidents aren't part of some divine plan, and God doesn't permit them for some greater purpose. They're

---

[50] I've explained these dimensions to my solution to evil in previous books, including *The Uncontrolling Love of God* (Downers Grove, IL: IVP Academic), *God Can't* (Grasmere, ID: SacraSage, 2019), and *The Death of Omnipotence and Birth of Amipotence* (Grasmere, ID: SacraSage, 2023)

[51] Garry DeWeese offers a good overview of the free-process defense in "Natural Evil: A 'Free Process' Defense," in *God and Evil*, ed. Chad Meister and James K. Dew Jr. (Downers Grove, IL: InterVarsity Press, 2013), 53-64. John Polkinghorne defends a version of the free-process defense. See *Science and Providence* (West Conshohocken, PA: Templeton, 2005).

[52] Earlier in my career as a theologian, I called the view I'm proposing "essential freewill theism." See "A Process Wesleyan Theodicy" in *Thy Name and Thy Nature is Love*, Bryan P. Stone and Thomas Jay Oord, eds. (Nashville, TN: Kingswood, 2001).

just unlucky events generated by creaturely agents of all sizes, and the Spirit can't control them.⁵³ Consequently, God can't stop natural evils caused by random and chance events.⁵⁴ It's the way the universe works.

God is amipotent rather than omnipotent.

## 2) *The Empathetic Dimension: God empathizes with our suffering.*

In previous chapters, I argued that God is relational and empathetic. This means creatures influence the Spirit, and deity feels emotion. Saying God is relational and empathetic proves crucial to affirming a second dimension to solving the problem of evil, which says God feels our suffering as One who co-suffers.⁵⁵ The "God of all consolation," says the Apostle Paul, "consoles us in all our affliction" (2 Cor. 1:3b,4a).

Unlike us, the Spirit will never be overwhelmed nor incapacitated by negative emotions. And the suffering God won't ever be tempted to be wicked. The Spirit whose unchanging nature is love will *never* do evil. In this sense, God can't. But the God whose experience changes moment by moment suffers with sufferers. In this sense, God can. These two truths comprise what I've called the Spirit's essence-experience binate, which I explained in earlier chapters.

Too often, those who address evil seek primarily to honor the freedom of evil's perpetrators. This sidelines victims. Most free-will defense theodicies, in fact, make freedom their primary concern. When asking questions of God and evil, however, we should privilege the experience of victims and survivors. Good solutions to the problem of evil account for both the experiences of the sinned-against and the freedom of the sinners.⁵⁶

---

⁵³ I explain the meaning and role of randomness and chance in *The Uncontrolling Love of God* (Downers Grove, IL: InterVarsity, Academic, 2015), ch. 2.

⁵⁴ John E. Culp addresses this in "Amipotence Overcomes Two Problems with Omnipotence," in *Amipotence, vol. 2*, vol. 2, Brandon Brown, et. al., eds., (Grasmere, ID: SacraSage, 2025).

⁵⁵ Many theologians argue that the oppressed can find comfort in a passible God. See James Cone, *God of the Oppressed* (London: SPCK, 1977); Adam Hamilton, *Why?* (Nashville, TN: Abingdon, 2011); Roberto Sirvent, *Embracing Vulnerability* (Eugene, OR: Pickwick, 2014).

⁵⁶ On this, see Andrew Sung Park and Susan L. Nelson, eds., *The Other Side of Sin* (Albany, NY: SUNY, 2001). Park has addressed this topic in other books using the Korean concept of *han*. For instance, see *From Hurt to Healing* (Nashville, TN: Abingdon, 2004).

Believing God empathizes with the harmed doesn't, in itself, solve the problem of evil. An omnipotent God who would allow pointless pain just to empathize with victims wouldn't be loving. That's like permitting a vicious attack just to sympathize with the sufferer. Saying God empathizes with creaturely suffering must be supplemented with saying God isn't omnipotent.

An empathetic and amipotent Spirit feels our pain.

### 3) The Therapeutic Dimension: God works to heal.

The third dimension of my six-fold solution to the problem of evil addresses healing.[57] Most people who are hurt want to recover, be restored, or get better. An omnipotent God could heal everyone in an instant, but instantaneous healing rarely occurs. So, the sick and abused are left to wonder if God has abandoned them. Or they might think deity punishes.

Instead, the amipotent Spirit works to heal *all* who hurt from accidents, disease, self-harm, abuse, or injustice. But healing *always* requires creaturely cooperation or the alignment of inanimate conditions. It *never* comes through control. Therapeutic healing requires the uncontrolling love of the Great Physician and creaturely cooperation—often including human physicians and therapists—or needs conducive conditions in creation.[58] The amipotent One works to "heal the brokenhearted and bind up their wounds" (Ps. 147:3).

Sometimes, our bodies don't cooperate with God, even when we want them to. Sometimes, the general conditions of creation aren't aligned with the wholeness the Spirit wants, even if we are. Sometimes, we collaborate with God's healing efforts, but our communities or societies don't. Despite our collaboration with the Comforter, other forces,

---

[57] I address questions of healing in *God Can't*, ch. 3 and *Questions and Answers for God Can't*, ch. 2-3. See also Bruce Epperly, *Praying with Process Theology* (Anoka, MN: River Lane, 2017); Mark Karris, *Divine Echoes* (Glen Oak, CA: Quoir, 2018); Ryan Lambros, *Eumorphosis: A Process-Relational Framework for Healing* (Doctoral Dissertation at Northwind Theological Seminary, 2023).

[58] Shannon Davy Mimbs addresses this beautifully and succinctly in "No Quick Fix," in *Amipotence, vol. 2*, Brandon Brown, et. al., eds. (Grasmere, ID: SacraSage, 2025).

factors, and actors can thwart the healing God always desires. But God never gives up.

This dimension of my solution has proven attractive to some postcolonial and liberation theologians.[59] Monica Coleman says making sense of suffering—especially the abuse of Black women and LGBTQ people—requires a suffering God. And Coleman rejects omnipotence. "God can't make us do one thing or another," she writes. "Rather, God influences, persuades, lures, or 'calls' us to embrace the principles of God's vision in every context."[60] This means "the quest for health and healing in the midst of violence, oppression, and evil is a lifelong cooperative process between God and us."[61]

Both recovery and its absence make sense if God works to heal, but isn't omnipotent.

### 4) *The Pedagogical Dimension: God works to squeeze good from bad.*

The fourth dimension to my solution to the problem of evil says the amipotent Spirit doesn't want, cause, or allow any unnecessary suffering. But when it occurs, God doesn't give up on or abandon the harmed. The Lover of us all squeezes whatever good can be squeezed from the bad that the Lover didn't want in the first place. The Spirit "works for good, in all things, with those who love" (Rom. 8:28).

The insights found in soul-building, creation project, and greater good theodicies can be salvaged if we detach them from omnipotence. Doing so means we don't have to believe "everything happens for a reason."[62] Genuine evil isn't part of some foreknown plan designed to build our characters or make the world better. And God isn't maintaining

---

[59] For example, see Ekaputra Tupamahu, "A Decolonial View of God," in *Uncontrolling Love*, Lisa Michaels, et. al., eds (Grasmere, ID: SacraSage, 2017) and Randy S. Woodley, *Indigenous Theology and the Western Worldview* (Grand Rapids, MI: Baker, 2022).

[60] Monica A. Coleman, *Making a Way Out of No Way: A Womanist Theology* (Minneapolis, MN: Fortress, 2008), 59.

[61] Ibid., 169. See also Coleman's handbook for congregational response to sexual violence, *The Dinah Project* (Eugene, OR: Wipf and Stock, 2004).

[62] For a popular criticism of the idea that everything happens for a reason, see Kate Bowler, *Everything Happens for a Reason . . . and Other Lies I've Loved* (New York: Random House, 2018).

some voluntary pledge of non-interference or permitting some pain for a greater good.

To put it another way, the Spirit works alongside creation to bring something beautiful from what is ugly, something healthy from what is ill, and something good from evil. God redeems. Some good results aren't possible, of course, and growth isn't inevitable, but something beneficial may emerge.

The amipotent God works for good in the aftermath of evil.

### 5) The Synergistic Dimension: God needs creaturely cooperation.

The fifth dimension to a solution to the problem of evil says the Spirit *needs* creaturely cooperation for love to win. God needs us. Put another way, Creator-creature love synergy is indispensable for goodness to prevail.[63] It's not all up to us; but it's not all up to God, either: it takes both. So the Spirit invites us to be "fellow workers" (1 Cor. 3:9).

We earlier saw that N. T. Wright's reading of scripture leads him to believe God will eventually overcome evil. He says the Spirit overcomes evil through forgiveness, the cruciform love of Jesus, and creaturely cooperation. Although Wright sometimes dismisses the idea that God controls, he should explicitly reject it. In earlier chapters, I've shown that omnipotence isn't biblical. Wright should be more explicit about the Spirit's reliance upon creatures and creation for overcoming evil. God needs creatures.

This cooperation dimension returns us to the importance of affirming divine incorporeality. The universal Spirit doesn't have a localized body with which to exert impact. Most creatures do. So, God calls upon creatures to use their bodies to prevent evil. When they respond positively, they don't control others, in the sense of being the *only* (sufficient) causes. But embodied creatures can do bodily activities a bodiless God can't. To rescue, for instance, a loving God requires the help of creaturely bodies cooperating with divine desires. Liberation and protection requires embodied beings cooperating with the Spirit.

---

[63] I explain indispensable love synergy in *God Can't*, ch. 5.

For love to bloom, a bodiless God needs embodied creaturely cooperation.

## 6) *The Origin Dimension: God doesn't create evil.*

The final dimension to a six-fold solution to the problem of evil addresses why evil events are even possible. It answers the oft-asked but misguided question, "Why did God create evil?"

With Augustine, we should understand that genuine evils aren't objects existing in the world. But instead of understanding evil as privation, we should define it as events, occurrences, or happenings that, all things considered, make the world worse than it otherwise might have been.

With Augustine, we can affirm creation as intrinsically good. The Spirit co-creates intrinsically good creatures who, in their moment-by-moment becoming, can use their God-provided agency for good or ill. Even chance and random events can help or harm. But against Augustine, we should deny that everything that happens is good in God's sight. Genuinely evil events occur.

On the question of the possibility of evil, it's helpful to return to our discussion of how God creates. And we'll find that my proposed *creatio ex creatione sempiternalis en amore* offers a distinct advantage over *creation ex nihilo*. The new creation theory denies that God alone decides the existence of anyone or anything. Creator and co-creating creatures collaborate in relation to what was previously created. This means that the possibilities for evil will always be present.

The deity who allegedly created the world *ex nihilo* is, by contrast, solely responsible for the possibility of evil. Nothing else could be. In fact, some theologians even say the God who creates from absolute nothingness could have made a universe of robot creatures and automata.[64] This implies that deity could have made a universe in which evil was never a possibility.

---

[64] Alan Rhoda also says God "could have created exactly the sort of world that theistic determinists believe God has created." And "God sovereignly chose not to be an all-determining micro-manager." Alan Rhoda, *Open Theism* (Cambridge: Cambridge University Press,

*Creatio ex creatione sempiternalis en amore* says God necessarily creates alongside creation, and the Spirit necessarily gives agency to all. Possibilities for good and evil will, therefore, be present when creatures—both complex and simple—have agency. God's creating something new from something old always includes the possibilities for good and evil. The amipotent Spirit who co-creates alongside creatures and creation can't remove those possibilities. They're "baked into" creaturely existence.

Affirming the smooth evolution of complex creatures from simple ones can help us make sense of the complex possibilities of good and evil we encounter. As evolving creatures increased in complexity, they experienced an increase in both the ability to enjoy positive values and to suffer from negative ones. They also experienced an increase in the ability to cause positive and negative outcomes. Because agency increases through evolution, the most complex creatures have greater possibilities to cause good or evil.

It was *impossible* for the uncontrolling Spirit who joins co-creating creatures to make humans who could enjoy immense pleasure but not be capable of suffering immense pain. These possibilities rise together. And the Spirit could not make humans capable of expressing profound love but unable to do profound evil.[65] These possibilities correlate. This insight shows what's right about "only way" theodicies.

The claim that we find possibilities for good and evil co-extensive with creation *doesn't* mean the actual occurrence of evil is necessary. Nor does it mean evil can never be overcome. Belief in an always active and persuasive Spirit of love provides us grounds to hope that all creation will respond favorably to the Spirit's calls to love. And this responding will, over time, develop habits of existence that make the reoccurrence of evil unlikely. I'll explain this view further in the third volume of this systematic theology of love.

Possibilities for good and evil are inherent in the creatures God necessarily creates and the agency God necessarily provides.

---

2024), 45. John Sanders affirms this possibility in *The God Who Risks* (Downers Grove, IL: InterVarsity, 1998). See pages 52, 116, 174, 185, and 198.

[65] I am indebted to David Ray Griffin for these insights. See *The Christian Gospel for Americans* (Anoka, MN: Process Century, 2019), 69-70.

## Does this Solve the Problem of Evil?

After hearing this six-fold solution, most see its logic and find it satisfying. But others claim the problem of evil has not been solved, because evil events still occur. Solving the problem of evil, they assume, means ending evil entirely. This six-fold solution doesn't do that.

My solution doesn't forevermore thwart evil. But as typically stated, the problem of evil doesn't wonder why evil remains. Instead, it wonders why a loving and powerful God doesn't prevent evil. *That's* the issue that leads many to atheism and many more to confusion.

I've solved that problem by denying that God is all-powerful. The Spirit *can't* prevent evil singlehandedly. I've also solved other problems related to God and evil in other dimensions of my six-fold solution.

Evil ends when creatures and creation respond well to the Spirit. This statement is perfectly reconcilable with the existence of an all-loving, impassible, healing, instructive, cooperative, and uncontrolling Creator. The deity I describe empowers all creation toward love, but creatures and creation must cooperate. Neither God alone nor creatures alone can end evil; the triumph of good over evil requires the relational love of both.

My solution to the problem of evil also doesn't guarantee that creatures will collaborate with God. But it explains how the Spirit loves in relation to creatures whom deity can't control and who must respond appropriately to divine calls to promote well-being.
God is not to blame.

## THE DEVIL AND DEMONS?

Exploring evil leads naturally to considering the possible existence of a devil and demons. For many people of faith, these evil characters seem ontologically real and at least partly why evil occurs. Belief in evil spiritual beings predates scripture, can be found in the Bible, and continues today.

Like N. T. Wright, I reject the idea of an eternal dualism of good and evil. I think an essentially good God exists and creates everlastingly. I also reject the eternal dualism of good and evil found in some forms of Zoroastrianism and Manichaeism. Elements of these ancient belief systems permeate some theologies and persist to this day.

If the devil exists, I don't believe it has the unique divine abilities I mentioned in earlier chapters. For instance, the devil isn't all-knowing. He isn't universal, isn't maximally powerful, isn't all-wise, isn't everlasting, and so on. If the devil and demons exist, they have limits typical of creatures. The devil and demons would be unable to control others, for instance, in the sense of being sufficient causes. Claims about demon "possession" would be inaccurate, if by this some mean demonic forces control us or others.

Many people think the devil and demons are spiritual agents, primarily due to their being invisible. Although localized, they apparently have a composition like the invisible, divine Spirit. Material-mental monism stipulates that the devil and demons, if they exist, have mental and material dimensions that can't be seen.

People also believe demonic beings influence creatures negatively. As spiritual beings, however, they don't have the physical capacity to pick up objects like we and other creatures have. They wouldn't be able to control the weather through bodily impact, for instance. Their influence would primarily be mental or psychological, by luring or threatening. They might induce those with bodies to do evil.

Beyond scripture, the evidence for a devil and demons typically comes from experiencing profoundly negative events or strangely harmful behavior in creatures. Some people attribute hallucinations, temporary changes of voice, flying objects, predictions, extraordinary strength, and other strange activities to demonic influence. Some people who believe in a devil or demons attribute *all* evil to them. But others agree with St. James that "each person is tempted when they are dragged away by their *own* evil desires" (1:16).

All this remains highly speculative, of course. And the biblical witness doesn't settle these questions. Biblical writers can be wrong about various aspects of nature and cosmology, so they could be wrong about the existence of a devil or demons. Scriptural references to them could be metaphors. But in assessing their possible existence, we should ponder fairly the possibility that a devil and demons exist as ontological beings. And we should consider the possibility that their existence partly accounts for profoundly negative and odd occurrences. It's an open question.

### How should we respond to the question of the devil and demons?

I've offered a description of what these negatively-inclined beings could be like, and we can see how they're generally described in the Bible. This systematic theology is agnostic on whether they actually exist. When it comes to a devil, demons, or even angels, I find the words of the cosmologist Laplace appropriate: "I have no need for that hypothesis." This systematic theology of love doesn't outright reject the possibility of a literal devil, demons, or angels, but it doesn't require them to make sense of reality.

If a devil or demons do exist, these spiritual beings would be negative influences in creation. Their negativity and tempting are freely chosen and likely have become habitual. But like all creatures, demonic beings could repent and, thereby, join in God's salvation. They are not inherently evil; even the devil is redeemable.

If the devil and demons *don't* exist, we can account for unusual and strangely negative behaviors in other ways. The material-mental monism model I've proposed provides a conceptual framework for this accounting. In an enchanted and unpredictable world of dynamic creatures, strange things can happen. Events some think the result of demonic spirits might instead be the influence of dynamic entities and creatures with unusual mental and material dimensions. The more we explore the implications of material-mental monism, in fact, the greater its ability to account for the diverse and unusual expressions of existence. The world can be a strange place.

A growing awareness of how systems lead to evil has prompted many theologians to appeal to the demonic not as ontological beings, but as a way of describing negative systems, habits, and propensities. I'll address this issue in later chapters when I explore sin. I simply note here that invisible systemic forces do incline us toward injustice. But those forces may not be actual demons or a devil.

## Lament and Deliverance

I close this chapter by examining an oft-misunderstood biblical response to evil. Scholars typically call that response "lament." Numerous scripture passages offer the laments of those who suffer, and some passages even speak of God lamenting.[66] Most lament scriptures describe the frustrations of people who wait for deliverance, often perplexed that Yahweh has not saved them.

To illustrate lament, I look at segments of Psalm 44. But the themes in this passage can be found in other biblical examples.

> We have heard with our ears, O God;
>   our ancestors have told us
> what deeds you performed in their days,
>   in the days of old:
> you with your own hand drove out the nations,
>   but them you planted;
> you afflicted the peoples,
>   but them you set free . . .
> In God we have boasted continually,
>   and we will give thanks to your name forever . . .
> Yet you have rejected us and shamed us
>   and have not gone out with our armies.
> You have made us like sheep for slaughter
>   and have scattered us among the nations.
> You have sold your people for a trifle,
>   demanding no high price for them.
> Our heart has not turned back,
>   nor have our steps departed from your way,
> yet you have broken us in the haunt of jackals
>   and covered us with deep darkness.
> Because of you we are being killed all day long
>   and accounted as sheep for the slaughter.

---

[66] For biblical references on divine lament, see Jer. 4:14; 13:27; and Hos. 8:5.

> Rouse yourself! Why do you sleep, O Lord?
>> Awake, don't cast us off forever!
> Why do you hide your face?
>> Why do you forget our affliction and oppression?
> For we sink down to the dust;
>> our bodies cling to the ground.
> Rise up, come to our help.
>> Redeem us for the sake of your steadfast love.[67]

If we are to take these words at face value, we find a number of claims present. First, in the passage the speaker says the Lord isn't rescuing, even though God has rescued previously. Second, the author believes God shames, rejects, sells, breaks, allows killing, and covers the people with darkness. It appears the Lord causes or allows immense evil. But third, the author says this evil can't be the result of the Lord punishing the people for their wickedness, because they have not departed from righteousness. Their hearts have not turned from God. So, fourth, we have a statement that the Lord needs to be awakened and reminded of the covenant. God must be prompted to help, to come out of hiding, to remember their suffering. After all, fifth, helping and redeeming are the activities the author expects from a covenantal God of steadfast love.

In another well-known Psalm of lament, we find the author adding a surprising, disturbing statement. The psalmist speaks of the happiness of those who smash infants on rocks. Some scholars even translate the passage as God killing these children.

> By the rivers of Babylon—
>> there we sat down, and there we wept
>> when we remembered Zion . . .
> O daughter Babylon, you devastator!
>> Happy shall they be who pay you back
>> what you have done to us!
> Happy shall they be who take your little ones
>> and dash them against the rock! (Ps. 137:1, 8, 9)

---

[67] Psalm 44:1-2, 8-12, 18-19, 22-26.

### *What are we to make of lament passages such as these?*

If we ask theologians of love, many will say God never rejects, shames, kills, sells, or wants children dashed against rocks. God loves. Lament passages express the deep pain of those who suffer and their longing for deliverance. They truthfully describe the raw feelings of those in deepest pain. Given other descriptions of divine love and forgiveness in scripture, therefore, we are wise to believe lament passages often give *inaccurate* portrayals of God. The Spirit of love isn't in the harming business.

Lament scriptures express human pain but inaccurate views of God.

Many progressive theologians who dismiss what lament passages imply about God's love would say those passages indicate that an omnipotent God *could* deliver and will someday do so singlehandedly. These theologians reject what the Bible says about divine neglect or punishment, but they assume biblical authors believe God can control. I pointed out earlier, however, that biblical writers never say God singlehandedly brings about outcomes. And I know of no lament passages that explicitly say God rescues unilaterally or rights wrongs by fiat.

Put another way, we're not required to interpret lament passages as saying the Spirit will someday wake up, show up, and rescue omnipotently. Whether the authors thought that would happen isn't explicitly in the text. But we can believe a steadfastly loving God *always* works to deliver but needs cooperation from creatures. Rather than asleep, the universal Spirit of love is always acting for good. This cooperation God desires may come when oppressors are convinced to stop their evil ways and the oppressed resist their bondage.

God delivers when creatures—both oppressors and the oppressed—collaborate with the Spirit's aims for liberation.

In addition to expressing the pain and anger of the persecuted, lament passages in scripture point to another important truth: evil is real. To use the language I've developed, *genuinely* evil events occur that make the world worse than it otherwise might have been. Unnecessary suffering doesn't make the world better. It's gratuitous. Both God and creatures yearn for a time in which evil will be overcome. Passages that portray God lamenting also support the notion that time is real for the Spirit, and God doesn't know the future.[68]

Both God and creatures cry out, "How long . . . ?"

## Conclusion

Atheists and agnostics often reject belief in God because of the evil they experience or witness. They rightly conclude that an all-loving and all-powerful God must not exist.

Theists have offered a range of responses to the problem of evil, but few have succeeded in solving it. Appeals to divine permission, character-building, punishment, free will, mystery, only way, or greater-good justifications fall short. They offer no persuasive explanation for why a supposedly good and all-powerful deity doesn't prevent evil.

By "evil," I mean occurrences that, all things considered, make the world worse than it might otherwise have been. Genuine evil is an experiential nonnegotiable, and an adequate systematic theology of love must explain why God doesn't prevent it.

The Bible offers no explicit solution to the problem of evil, nor a plausible explanation of evil's origin. But scripture does help us as a resource for a six-fold solution. This solution begins by denying omnipotence and affirming amipotence: the power of God's uncontrolling love. An amipotent deity isn't culpable for failing to prevent evil, because the Spirit can't do so singlehandedly. This solution also says the Spirit empathizes with those who suffer, works to heal alongside creation, endeavors to bring something good from the bad, and calls creatures to join in overcoming evil with good.

Evil isn't something created by God. The Spirit necessarily creates creatures with real agency, and thus potential for both good and harm. These possibilities are inherent in creaturely existence and can't be removed. Evil isn't created by the devil or demons, if they exist: I remain

---

[68] Terence Fretheim remarks, "The [Bible] witnesses to a God who shares in our history . . . in such a way that . . . even [God] can cry out: 'How long?'" Terence E. Fretheim, *The Suffering of God* (Philadelphia: Fortress, 1984), 44.

agnostic on their existence. Finally, biblical examples of lament don't accurately portray God as causing or allowing evil. But they express the heart-felt cries of those in pain and indicate that evil is genuine.

An amipotent Spirit neither causes nor allows evil, but calls creatures to join the work in overcoming evil with good.

CHAPTER FIFTEEN

# The Problem of Good, Miracles, and God's Will

## THE BIG IDEAS

- The problem of good wonders why good occurs and why we intuit ultimate goodness if a good God doesn't exist.
- Just as belief in evil is an experiential non-negotiable, belief in goodness is too.
- It makes the best sense to believe a universal Spirit serves as the transcendent Standard of goodness and prompts creatures to do good.
- Amipotence solves both the problem of good and the problem of evil.
- Most theologians have defined miracles as events God does alone by supernaturally overriding nature.
- The traditional view of miracles creates a host of difficulties, including the problem of selective miracles and scientific conflicts.
- We shouldn't call every event a miracle nor deny miracles altogether.
- We better define miracles as extraordinary, good events that involve divine and creaturely causation.
- Believing deity predestines and foreknows all undermines a plausible view of following God's will.
- The Spirit has a general will, specific wills, and vocations to which creatures are called.

While the problem of evil stymies most theists, the problem of good stymies most atheists. At least it should. We ought to wonder why there's so much love, beauty, friendship, positivity, cooperation, order, humor, and excellence in the world . . . if there is no God.[1]

---
[1] This chapter is dedicated to Jon Paul Sydnor. His creative thinking in systematic theology has influenced me, and I appreciate his friendship.

People intuit a standard of goodness that transcends their personal and social preferences, even though they differ in their values, and culture influences them. It's natural to seek an *ultimate* explanation for our deepest intuitions about goodness. Amipotence provides one.

Traditionally, systematic theologians point to miracles as evidence of divine providence. But as typically defined, miracles raise severe problems. The problem of selective miracles, for instance, says we should expect far more miracles if God were omnipotent and loving. But where are they?

We rightly wonder why a deity with almighty power to do miracles doesn't use that ability to stop pointless pain. And then there's the problem that a traditional view of miracles presents to scientific explanations. As typically understood, miracles confuse and confound, and they inadvertently portray God as stingy when it comes to love.

Given these issues, some theologians reject miracles as objectively real. Others claim *everything* should be considered miraculous. I'm unsatisfied with both responses. A better view accounts for the broad biblical witness to miracles and contemporary examples, while overcoming the real problems associated with the traditional view. It considers miracles good and extraordinary events that involve creaturely actions and/or the conditions of creation, alongside the activity of an amipotent God.

Questions about miracles, goodness, and evil lead to pondering God's will. Traditional theologies portray God as timeless, predestining, and/or controlling, ideas that cause a host of problems for discerning what it means to following divine desires. Traditional theologies also say God foreknows all, which makes no sense if creatures can *freely* choose to follow God's call or do otherwise. To conclude my exploration of providence, I propose a love-based explanation of God's will, featuring what I will call a general divine will, specific wills, and vocations.

Goodness, miracles, and God's will can make sense if the Spirit's love is uncontrolling.

## THE PROBLEM OF GOOD

The authors of scripture assume that creatures do good and evil. We assume this too, and we show this assumption by the way we live every day. Our lives constantly revolve around values, and we cannot escape this fact. Biblical writers also say God evaluates what's good and evil, and our ability to evaluate is analogous to God's, despite our limits. "If you who do evil know how to give good gifts to your children," asks Jesus, "how much more will your Father in heaven give good things to those who ask him?" (Mt. 7:11).

In the previous chapter, we looked at the problem of evil. It's the primary reason many people don't believe in God and a source of confusion for those who do. Most systematic theologians can't solve it because they cling to notions of divine omnipotence, impassibility, divine punishment, and other love-undermining ideas. I laid out a six-fold solution, the heart of which replaces omnipotence with amipotence.

Atheists and agnostics face a different problem: it's the problem of good. In a nutshell, it doubts that anyone can give a satisfying explanation for truly good events and ultimate goodness while denying the existence of a good God. If deity doesn't exist, this problem asks why is there so much positivity, cooperation, generosity, altruism, self-sacrifice, desire for justice, heroism, and love? And without an Ultimate Standard, on what basis can we possibly judge some actions or events as better than others?

Systematic theologians have an answer to the problem: God.[2] Grounding goodness in deity, says Keith Ward, "gives to moral experience an objectivity, authority, and effectiveness that would immensely strengthen the motivating force of morality and its consilience with a more general worldview."[3] I agree. Especially when we consider love

---

[2] Many religious traditions see God as the source and inspiration of what is good, loving or merciful. On this, see selections from Thomas Jay Oord, ed., *The Altruism Reader* (West Conshohocken, PA: Templeton, 2008).

[3] Keith Ward, *Morality, Autonomy, and God* (London: Oneworld, 2013), 214.

logically first in the divine nature and an essential divine attribute, belief in a good God overcomes the problem of good.

Not all views of God prove equal, however. The best will solve the problem of good *and* the problem of evil. Amipotence says a universal Spirit—one in whose nature love comes first—prompts us to act in good ways and live good lives. This means that God's nature is the ultimate measure of goodness and the wellspring for the possibility of well-being. Believing these claims can motivate us to do good deeds and become good people, as we cooperate with the Spirit's calls to goodness.[4] "Love is from God, and everyone who loves knows God," says the Apostle John. "The person who doesn't love doesn't know God, for God is love" (1 John 4:7, 8).

Those who say they don't believe in God can't appeal to deity as the Ultimate source, inspiration, or standard of the goodness they witness or want in the world. And without an Ultimate source, goodness becomes a preference rather than a universal norm. "Good" becomes whatever I decide, whatever my tribe requires, or whatever the most powerful person decrees. Extreme relativism ensues.

Some people admit to having no transcendent standard for goodness, but they say science dismisses the need for one. Researchers in sociobiology and evolutionary psychology acknowledge that they witness altruistic behavior and cooperation within and even across species.[5] But they say creatures are *ultimately* selfish, because every creature acts only for its own reproductive success. Above all, goes the argument, we all selfishly want to further our genetic lineage.

---

[4] This is a main theme in Thomas Jay Oord and Michael Lodahl, *Relational Holiness* (Kansas City, MO: Beacon Hill, 2005).

[5] Some of the more influential arguments are found in Robert Axelrod, *The Evolution of Cooperation* (New York: Basic, 1984); Samuel Bowles and Herbert Gintis, *A Cooperative Species* (Princeton, NJ: Princeton University Press, 2011); Lee Alan Dugatkin, *Cheating Monkeys and Citizen Bees* (Cambridge, MA: Harvard University Press, 1999); W. D. Hamilton, "The Evolution of Altruistic Behavior," *American Naturalist* 97, no. 896 (1963): 354-56; Elliot Sober and David Sloan Wilson, *Unto Others* (Cambridge, MA: Harvard University Press, 1998); Robert L. Trivers, "The Evolution of Reciprocal Altruism," *Quarterly Review of Biology* 46, no. 1 (1971): 35-37; Edward O. Wilson, *On Human Nature* (Cambridge, MA: Harvard University Press, 2004 [1978]). I discuss these and other types of altruism as they relate to love in my book *Defining Love*, 97-136.

If this were true, "good" becomes simply a name for acting to benefit our offspring or furthering our genetic line.[6] And we only cooperate to help ourselves and our family and friends. "What passes for cooperation turns out to be a mixture of opportunism and exploitation," says Michael Ghiselin. "Scratch an 'altruist' and watch a 'hypocrite' bleed."[7]

Others have rejected the category of goodness on nihilistic grounds. In *Beyond Good and Evil*, philosopher Friedrich Nietzsche says, "There are no moral phenomena at all, but only a moral interpretation of phenomena."[8] Therefore, this implies, goodness is *entirely* what the individual decides. "The noble type of [person] experiences itself as determining values," says Nietzsche, "[they do] not need to be approved; [they] judge, 'what is harmful to me is harmful in itself.'"[9] Scientist Richard Dawkins gives contemporary expression to this notion when he says, "The universe that we observe has precisely the properties we should expect if there is, at bottom, no design, no purpose, no evil, no good, nothing but blind, pitiless indifference."[10]

Whether on scientific grounds, to embrace nihilism, or for another reason, some people say there is no transcendent goodness. But such claims don't fit our experience.[11] Denying transcendent goodness contradicts the way we all live our lives practically. We act as if some events make the world better, all things considered, than it otherwise might have been. This action implies our more basic, implicit belief in an Ultimate Standard for goodness.

Just as belief in evil is an experiential non-negotiable, belief in goodness is too.

---

[6] Richard D. Alexander advocates this view. See his book *The Biology of Moral Systems* (New York: De Gruyter, 1987), 93-94.

[7] Michael T. Ghiselin, *The Economy of Nature and the Evolution of Sex* (Berkeley, CA: University of California Press, 1974), 247.

[8] Friedrich Nietzsche, *Beyond Good and Evil*, trans. Walter Kaufmann (New York: Vintage Books, 1966), 82.

[9] Ibid., 202.

[10] Richard Dawkins, *River Out of Eden: A Darwinian View of Life* (London: Weidenfeld & Nicolson, 1995), 133.

[11] Brittney L. Hartley addresses nihilism and her experience of values in *No Nonsense Spirituality: All the Tools No Belief Required* (Grasmere, ID: SacraSage, 2024).

We sometimes choose to help others at our own expense. We try to save the planet, improve our lives, protect the vulnerable, or do good to strangers. Sometimes, we love our enemies and repay evil with good. We sometimes act against our genetic self-interest, such as when people adopt children or care for kids with whom they share no genetic lineage.[12] Whether consciously or not, we assume Goodness sometimes calls us to act in ways that transcend personal pleasure and what furthers our genes.

This prompts me to respond to Richard Dawkins and say we all live as if goodness is real, and, at bottom, there's *more* than blind, pitiless indifference. And I respond to Michael Ghiselin that if we scratch what he calls a hypocritical altruist, we'll often find someone who acts for a good greater than their own. In fact, those who deny transcendent goodness are the hypocrites: they deny with their mouths a reality they live in their practice. That's hypocrisy.

Deniers of transcendent goodness have a response. They say evolution has tricked us into *thinking* we do good and *believing* in transcendent goodness. We've evolved, goes the argument, so that our incessant selfishness remains hidden, even to us. We've been duped. When we think we're responding to a higher calling, our better angels, or God, we're actually just doing what our genes have programmed us to do. So, they say, we can't trust our beliefs about transcendent goodness.

This argument backfires. If evolution undermines our capacity to have true beliefs, those who deny transcendent goodness have no grounds to think *their* beliefs are true either. No one could know. If, as they say, there are no standards, then we can't ever know which beliefs are accurate, and that includes arguments against transcendent goodness. And if we see all our practices as inherently untrustworthy, even the practice of criticizing goodness can't be trusted. Their argument ends up being self-refuting.

---

[12] Important books exploring this theme include Philip Clayton and Jeffrey Schloss, eds., *Evolution and Ethics* (Grand Rapids, MI: Eerdmans, 2004); Frans DeWaal, *Good Natured* (Cambridge: Cambridge University Press, 1996); Andrew Michael Flescher and Daniel L. Worthen, *The Altruistic Species* (West Conshohocken, PA: Templeton, 2007); Robert Wright, *The Moral Animal* (New York: Vintage, 1994).

Without some transcendent Measure, we have no objective basis for truth or falsity, good or evil, better or worse. And yet, we all assume, explicitly or implicitly, a transcendent standard and that our judgments should be assessed by it. This Standard exceeds personal or cultural preferences, although those preferences also influence us.[13]

In fact, science itself *requires* standards of truth and value, because scientists assume grounds to claim some theories are truer or better than others. And scientists need to justify to themselves and the public why some research programs would be worth pursuing, on purely practical grounds.

Affirming transcendent goodness aligns with our lived experience.

## God as Source of and Prompt for Goodness

The best way to account for an ultimate source of goodness appeals to a metaphysics that includes a transcendent Source. This doesn't have to be a theistic metaphysics; some people have an ultimate belief system that doesn't include a deity. But I think theism has more advantages overall. The best versions of theism propose God as the transcendent Source and Standard for values. This helps them to account for *ultimate* goodness better than atheism, reductive "altruism," or nihilism.

This systematic theology of love embraces a theistic metaphysics that says a universal Spirit of love acts as the ultimate Source of goodness. The ultimate measures of the Spirit transcend personal or cultural preferences. This universal Lover plays a central role in explaining why creatures sometimes do good, because it says God calls and empowers creatures toward goodness. Theologies that portray God as *actively* providing creatures possibilities for truth, beauty, goodness, and love offer a satisfying framework not available in, for instance, a god-less Platonic metaphysics.[14]

---

[13] Keith Ward argues this point in several books, including *God, Chance, and Necessity* (Oxford: Oneworld, 1996).

[14] As an example of someone who attempts to have a god-less Platonic metaphysics, see Iris Murdoch, *Metaphysics as a Guide to Morals* (London: Chatto & Windus, 1992).

The best metaphysician in the contemporary era arrived at this conclusion. Alfred North Whitehead was an avid reader of theology and the son of a Christian minister. Whitehead first made his scholarly name in Cambridge and London as a world-class mathematician, co-writing the most ambitious mathematics and logic book to date.[15] Like many math-minded scholars, Whitehead appreciated Plato's formal categories. He believed that we encounter transcendent truths already in reality, waiting to be discovered. Plato called these truths "The Forms;" Whitehead called them "eternal objects" or "pure possibilities."[16]

As a middle-aged man, Whitehead rejected belief in God. Like other atheists and agnostics, the problem of evil led him to unbelief, and the death of his son Eric provided a pivotal moment in this journey. Whitehead sold his theology books and turned his genius to the subjects of philosophy, science, and intellectual history. In his early sixties, he accepted an invitation to teach metaphysics at Harvard University, which provided him a formal opportunity to explore life's biggest questions.[17]

The problem of good eventually led Whitehead back to belief in God.[18] To account for existence well, he realized he needed a metaphysics that includes something like a universal, good Mind. He concluded that a theistic hypothesis offered the best framework to make sense of his intuitions—especially creation's advance toward increased goodness. "The essence of life is to be found in the creative advance into novelty," said Whitehead, "conditioned so as to secure attained goodness . . ."[19]

---

[15] See Alfred North Whitehead and Bertrand Russell, *Principia Mathematica*, 3 vols. (Cambridge: Cambridge University Press, 1910–13).

[16] "Eternal objects are the pure potentials of the universe; and the actuality of the universe is the process by which these potentials are selected for realization." Alfred North Whitehead, *Process and Reality: An Essay in Cosmology*, Corrected Edition, ed. David Ray Griffin and Donald W. Sherburne (New York: Free Press, 1978), 22.

[17] Andrew M. Davis writes beautifully about both Whitehead's life and his ideas in *Whitehead's Universe: A Prismatic Introduction* (Maryknoll, NY: Orbis, 2026).

[18] To my knowledge, Whitehead never used the phrase "the problem of good." But it describes the issue at the heart of his return to theism.

[19] Alfred North Whitehead, *Adventures of Ideas* (New York: Macmillan, 1933), 284.

Whitehead needed an explanation for why the past doesn't always repeat itself. Not only do new things occur, but a wide view of reality points to evidence of increasing order, beauty, moral sensibility, and complexity in cosmological history. And we each sense a nudge toward what's better.

The explanation for these ideas can't come from the cosmos itself, because the cosmos in general and individuals in particular can't evaluate moment by moment an almost infinite number of possibilities. We need a ground for limitation, said Whitehead.[20] The best explanation for increasing values and the nudge we each feel involves a universal Mind. Whitehead came to believe a deity must exist whose nature divides good from evil and urges creation toward beauty, order, love, and more.[21]

I agree with Whitehead on this. The best account of existence involves a transcendent Standard and universal Agent who prompts and nudges creation toward increased value. Without belief in God, we can't explain well our intuitions about—and the actualization of—the good, true, beautiful, just, and loving. We need a metaphysical vision uniting Plato's concept of the Good with the Living God we find in scripture.[22]

Whitehead's view of divinity differs from traditional theologies, however, and two differences are especially important. First, Whitehead conceived of God not simply as a transcendent, abstract depository of values, as important as that may be. He also conceived of God as timefully immanent and ever-active, *personally* providing value-laden options to creatures and receiving input from them. For Whitehead, the Spirit lures all creatures to the best possibilities and apprehends their decisions in ongoing interaction.

I draw upon this transcendent Source and active Provider that Whitehead describes when proposing my idea of a universal Spirit of

---

[20] See Alfred North Whitehead, *Science and the Modern World* (New York: Free Press, 1967), 178.

[21] Ibid., 179. Andrew Davis explains Whitehead's views on God and goodness in "The Goodness of Whitehead's God," in *Process Studies*, 53:2 (Fall-Winter 2024): 192-212.

[22] For an explanation of this uniting God and Good, see Diana Lobel, *The Quest for God and the Good* (New York: Columbia University Press, 2015).

Love with an essence-experience binate.[23] As I see it, God's essence is the standard for goodness, truth, beauty, love, and other values. It's immutable and transcends creation.

God's experience interacts directly with all creatures and creation, calling and empowering each to goodness, and responding to the cosmos. This Living Lover is the Ultimate source of goodness and the One who invites all to promote well-being. This view solves the problem of good.

The second significant way Whitehead's theology differs from traditional theologies pertains to his view of divine power. Whitehead rejected the concept of omnipotence, in the sense of God having the ability to determine outcomes by unilateral coercion. Instead, he believed God acts through persuasion, in the sense of inviting and inclining creatures toward increasing goodness and other values. My theory of amipotence has been influenced by this Whiteheadian vision, because it says the amipotent Spirit influences all but can't control any. This view solves the problem of evil.

None of this *proves* God exists, of course. Atheists and agnostics have rational grounds for their skepticism. After all, it's logically possible there's no transcendent Source of goodness, despite the fact we act like there is, and despite the fact that we see increased order, beauty, and complexity in the natural world. We might call unbelievers not bothered by the problem of good, "skeptical atheists." Like the skeptical theists I discussed earlier, their views are logically possible, despite good evidence and strong arguments to the contrary.

I regard both skeptical atheism and skeptical theism as profound mistakes. Neither view accounts well for reality as we know it, especially those dimensions—like the reality of transcendent goodness and genuine evil—central to life. Unfortunately, neither skeptical theists nor skeptical atheists seem willing to rethink their concepts of deity, including their assumption that God must be omnipotent.

By contrast, amipotence rethinks divine power and love. It says a loving, universal Spirit is the source and inspiration for all that's good

---

[23] In earlier chapters, I explain what I mean by God's essence-experience binate. It bears similarities to what Whitehead calls God's "primordial" and "consequent" natures.

and for other values central to existence.[24] Amipotence also says the Spirit can't prevent evil singlehandedly, because this Lover can't control anyone or anything.[25] Amipotence overcomes skeptical atheism and skeptical theism by accounting for good and evil.

"The moral arc of the universe is long," said Martin Luther King, Jr., "but it bends toward justice."[26] I believe the arc bends toward justice because an amipotent Spirit calls creatures to promote overall well-being. When creatures respond well to God's call, they do good and act justly in ways appropriate to their contexts.

The moral arc "bends" because the Spirit doesn't coerce; God can't control the universe. When creatures respond poorly to divine calls for love and justice, we witness evil, ugliness, and apathy. The degree and length of the arc's bend depend on creaturely responses to the Spirit.

A good God acts as the goad toward goodness.

## Miracles

Systematic theologies typically address miracles in their accounts of providence. In fact, people of faith often consider such events decisive evidence of divine action. Not only does the Bible include miracle stories, but they're also mentioned in various religious texts, and many people say miracles still occur today.

A number of problems arise when assessing the nature and occurrence of miracles, however. Some concern problems related to divine action. There's also the fact that people's belief in miracles can be

---

[24] Two of the better scholarly examinations of nature and ethics are Craig A. Boyd, *A Shared Morality* (Grand Rapids, MI: Brazos, 2007); and Celia E. Deane-Drummond, *The Ethics of Nature* (Malden, MA: Blackwell, 2004).

[25] I explore this in "A Relational God and Unlimited Love," in *Visions of Agape*, Craig A. Boyd, ed. (Farnham, UK: Ashgate, 2008), 135-48.

[26] This line originated from Theodore Park. King uses it in his sermons, including Martin Luther King Jr., "Remaining Awake Through a Great Revolution," sermon delivered at the National Cathedral, Washington, DC, March 31, 1968, in *A Testament of Hope* (San Francisco: HarperCollins, 1986), 269. King was also influenced by Whitehead. On this see, Brian Henning, "A. N. Whitehead's Influence on Martin Luther King Jr." whiteheadresearch.org. https://whiteheadresearch.org/2022/01/17/a-n-whiteheads-influence-on-martin-luther-king-jr/. accessed January 17, 2022).

explained psychologically, belief in miracles seems influenced by culture, and some may simply reflect the trickery of religious hucksters. Other problems emerge when science offers convincing explanations that oppose miracles. These problems have led a fair number of theologians and everyday people of faith to reject the category of miracles altogether.

People in some cultures—often non-Western—seem more apt to witness miracles. Advocates for believing in literal miracles and their allies sometimes complain that those who don't witness miracles must be blinded by modern culture, science, and Western enlightenment.

To people skeptical of miracles, however, the fact that those in less scientifically developed cultures witness more miracles indicates that some people are less advanced. If they just understood the world better, goes the thinking, they'd witness fewer events they'd call miraculous. Ironically, both advocates for miracles and deniers point to the influence of science and culture when assessing whether miracles actually happen.

Personality and personal preference also influence belief. Theists attracted to the dramatic and sensational seem more likely to believe in miracles. By contrast, reserved and restrained theists in general prove less likely to believe.

As like-minded people congregate, confirmation bias grows. Those who believe in miracles form groups of individuals who—not surprisingly—witness numerous miracles. Those who don't believe form groups who tend to conclude that miracles never or rarely occur. Many Pentecostal congregations would be examples of the first; many Presbyterian congregations give examples of the second. The Catholic church contains significant numbers of people huddled within their own groups.

Some people try to prove miracles exist. But some miracles turn out to be hoaxes, hysteria, or misunderstandings. Dishonest faith healers and shifty evangelists can trick the faithful, and this adds support to the view of some skeptics that *all* miracles must be fake. Suggestibility can incline some people to believe they, or others, have been healed when they haven't been—especially when respected religious authorities do the suggesting.[27] In addition, many healing miracles just can't be objectively verified by qualified experts such as medical doctors.[28]

The above issues point to the role human interpretation plays in miracles. How we each understand reality depends on a host of factors, both within us and in our environments. Two people believing in God could stand side by side and witness an event, and one calls it miraculous, while the other doesn't. One appeals to special divine action, the other points to natural causes. Diverse interpretative frameworks largely explain these differing explanations.

Perspective matters. People's view of miracles can also be altered over time. Sometimes, an extraordinary event convinces one not inclined to believe in miracles to begin believing. Other times, someone who once embraced the miraculous decides science, medicine, or other factors offer better explanations. None of us remain locked into our current perspective of God and life. People change.

## Defining Miracles

Given the factors I've noted, defining miracles can prove difficult. Writers of scripture tell stories of signs, wonders, and extraordinary events, but they don't clearly define the miraculous, or explain how it works. Consequently, definitions among theologians vary.

Most theologians assume God must be the sole cause at play in the miraculous. Thomas Aquinas says, "God alone" does miracles, for instance, and they are "beyond the order of created nature."[29] Martin Luther says miracles are "wrought by God alone."[30] Charles Hodge de-

---

[27] Tom Rundel addresses the problems omnipotence creates for abuse of leadership. See "Omnipotence Justifies Leadership Abuse," in *Amipotence, vol. 2,* Brandon Brown, et. al., eds. (Grasmere, ID: SacraSage, 2025).

[28] Candy Gunther Brown explores this issue documenting healing in *Testing Prayer* (Cambridge: Harvard University Press, 2012), ch. 3. See also Joshua W. Brown, *Proving a Miracle* (San Francisco: Harper, 2026).

[29] Thomas Aquinas, *Summa Theologiae*, vol. 1, *Prima Pars*, Q.105, Art.7, trans. Fathers of the English Dominican Province (New York: Benziger Brothers, 1947).

[30] Martin Luther, *Lectures on Genesis: Chapters 1–5*, vol. 1 of *Luther's Works*, ed. Jaroslav Pelikan (St. Louis, MO: Concordia, 1958), 60.

fines a miracle as "an event in the external world brought about by the immediate efficiency or simple volition of God, without the mediation of natural secondary causes."[31]

This emphasis on solitary divine causation becomes even more accentuated by the explicit denial of creaturely causation. "A miracle is a suspension or control of the established laws of nature," says Adam Clarke.[32] The New Catholic Encyclopedia says a miracle is "an event which lies outside the normal pattern of physical causes and is attributed to the immediate action of God, who thereby manifests the supernatural." "Miracles represent God's invasive grace," says Cheryl Bridges John, "moments in which the Spirit disrupts ordinary experience to reveal divine compassion and restore creation."[33] Others speak of God's "intervention"[34] in, or "interruption"[35] of, creation's causation. I've discussed the problems with appeals to external intervention in earlier chapters.

It's one thing to claim an event can't be explained by natural causes *alone*. Every theologian who says God must be a necessary cause for each event should affirm that claim. But most definitions of miracles say that God *alone* brought about some result, irrespective of nature. Words like "intervene," "interrupt," and "invade" imply that an omnipotent God occasionally shows up where previously absent to secure an outcome singlehandedly.[36]

---

[31] Charles Hodge, *Systematic Theology*, vol. 1 (New York: Charles Scribner's Sons, 1872), 619.

[32] Adam Clarke, *The Holy Bible Containing the Old and New Testaments, with a Commentary and Critical Notes*, vol. 5 (New York: Abingdon-Cokesbury, n.d.), 366.

[33] Cheryl Bridges Johns, *Pentecostal Formation: A Pedagogy Among the Oppressed* (Sheffield, UK: Sheffield Academic, 1993), 87.

[34] Karl Rahner and Herbert Vorgrimler, *Theological Dictionary*, trans. Richard Strachan (New York: Herder and Herder, 1965), s.v. "Miracle."

[35] Gordon D. Fee, *God's Empowering Presence* (Peabody, MA: Hendrickson, 1994), 709.

[36] Although I'm often critical of Wayne Grudem, his view of miracles is better than most theologians. He says, "a miracle is a less common kind of God's activity in which he arouses people's awe and wonder and bears witness to himself." I'd want to add an explicit claim about creaturely contributions to miracles, but at least Grudem doesn't speak of interruptions, interventions, or the supernatural. See Wayne Grudem, *Systematic Theology* (Grand Rapids, MI: Zondervan, 1994), 355.

## Problems with Miracles as Traditionally Understood

### The Problem of Selective Miracles

The way most theologians define miracles leads to numerous problems. One of the most egregious I call "the Problem of Selective Miracles." It arises because people who pray for miracles usually don't get them. The vast majority of requests to God seem to go unanswered, in the sense that those praying don't get miraculous results for others or themselves.[37] Even saints in scripture weren't healed, although they requested it.[38] "The complete absence of miracles in my life when they should have been abundant," says Stephen Bradford Long, "led me to question the veracity of all miracle claims.[39]"

The problem of selective miracles stems from believing God must be omnipotent. If deity were all-powerful and all-loving, we'd expect *many* more miracles than we witness. Christine Overall states the issue well: "In choosing to favor just a few individuals, God shows himself to be arbitrary in his beneficence to some and cruel and unfair in his neglect of others."[40] Apparently, the omnipotent God doesn't care enough to help consistently.

Those who say God alone does miracles often use the word "supernatural" to describe divine action. The word has several meanings, but saying a miracle occurs supernaturally sounds like an omnipotent God occasionally controls creatures or creation in some unnatural way. *Super*natural suggests God overrides or disrupts the natural course of events.[41]

---

[37] David and Randall Basinger explore this in *Philosophy and Miracle* (Lewiston, NY, and Queenston, Ontario: Edwin Mellen, 1986).

[38] See examples of this in Gal. 4:13-14; Phil. 2:27; 1 Tim. 5:23; 2 Tim. 4:20.

[39] Stephen Bradford Long, "Why I am Not A Christian: The Problem of Miracles," (https://stephenbradfordlong.com/2023/08/23/why-i-am-not-a-christian-the-problem-of-miracles/ accessed 12/5/2025)

[40] Christine Overall, "Miracles and Larmer," *Dialogue* 42 (2003): 131.

[41] One of the better arguments against the notion that miracles require divine coercion is found in David Ray Griffin, *Religion and Scientific Naturalism: Overcoming the Conflicts* (Albany, NY: State University of New York Press, 2000). See also Chad Bahl, *The Death of Supernaturalism* (Grasmere, ID: SacraSage, 2025).

## The Problem of Evil

The second problem with miracles as traditionally understood is similar to the first. Instead of asking why an omnipotent deity doesn't do *more* miracles, however, it wonders why God doesn't use those miracle-working abilities to *prevent* evil in the first place. The kind of power God uses to do miracles, "acting alone," could stop unnecessary suffering and pointless pain. What kind of God refrains from helping the oppressed and hurting?

"It would seem strange that no miraculous intervention prevented Auschwitz or Hiroshima," says Maurice Wiles on this point, "while the purposes apparently forwarded by some of the miracles acclaimed in traditional Christian faith seem trivial by comparison."[42] If God miraculously shortens the line at Starbucks or finds a parking place for someone, we might ask, why doesn't deity stop genocides? If God can cure grandma's arthritis, why doesn't deity use that ability to prevent your sister's rape, control the spread of global viruses, oust oppressive political tyrants, or stop the ravages of climate change?

The problems associated with miracles heighten when connected to "faith healers." When a charismatic pastor claims to have the gift of healing but fails to use every waking moment walking up and down hospital halls healing everyone, we wonder whether the person loves consistently. After all, they could be doing much more than they currently are. A deity who could control *all* entities or interrupt natural processes, but didn't do it to help the hurting, would love even less consistently.

Most theologians say God never grows tired. But when evil events occur, we understandably assume an omnipotent deity must be asleep on the job. Or just doesn't love lots of hurting people. This view of God creates massive problems for people who earnestly seek divine help but fail to receive it.

---

[42] Maurice Wiles, *God's Action in the World* (London: SCM, 1986), 29. Andrew Hronich addresses the question by responding to my proposals and others in "The Problem of Selective Miracles," *Eleutheria: John W. Rawlings School of Divinity Academic Journal* 9:1 (2025): 57–74.

## Problem of Scientific Explanation

There's also an intellectual problem with which many struggle. Most definitions of miracles say God ignores, interrupts, or overrides natural causes. Miracles involve "a suspension or control of the established laws of nature," says Adam Clarke.[43] Contemporary scholars often cite the 18th century philosopher David Hume as tying miracles to the suspension of natural laws,[44] but Aquinas also said miracles go "beyond the order of created nature."[45]

A tension arises between claims about miracles and scientific explanations. If God occasionally determines outcomes singlehandedly, scientists who point to natural causes for those outcomes will be wrong, by definition.[46] They won't be able to give *any* natural account of a miracle if God is the sole and supernatural cause.[47] This proves empirically problematic, and it undermines the process of science.

In addition, we have the issue that most who claim to observe miracles, if asked, could also identify creaturely causes at play. When defined as events beyond or overriding nature, therefore, miracles aren't just problematic for scientific explanation; they stand at odds with the typical explanations of everyday people.

A theological problem also arises when we call miracles "interventions." This way of talking implies that God normally resides outside nature and then "enters into" a closed system of natural causes. To say God "invades" also undermines claims about the Spirit's continual and

---

[43] Adam Clarke, *The Holy Bible Containing the Old and New Testaments, with a Commentary and Critical Notes*, vol. 5 (New York: Abingdon-Cokesbury, n.d.), 366.

[44] See David Hume, "An Enquiry Concerning Human Understanding," in *On Human Nature and the Understanding*, Antony Flew, ed. (New York: Collier, 1962 [1748]).

[45] Thomas Aquinas, *Summa Theologiae*, vol. 1, *Prima Pars*, Q.105, Art.7, trans. Fathers of the English Dominican Province (New York: Benziger Brothers, 1947).

[46] Amos Yong identifies the problems that come from thinking miracles amount to violations of the laws of nature in *The Spirit of Creation: Modern Science and Divine Action in the Pentecostal-Charismatic Imagination* (Grand Rapids, MI: Eerdmans, 2011), ch. 4.

[47] Howard Van Till addresses this issue by affirming what he calls the "functional integrity" of creation. See "Basil, Augustine, and the Doctrine of Creation's Functional Integrity," *Science and Christian Belief*, 8:1 (1996): 21-38.

necessary causation alongside and in creation. It implicitly says God isn't universally present.

## Problems with *Non-Traditional* Definitions of Miracles

Given the problems that arise with the traditional definitions of miracles, it's not surprising some have offered alternative definitions. In fact, I'll be providing my own. Before doing so, though, I want to look at other alternatives to the traditional view of miracles. I'll identify problems with each of these too.

### *Is Everything Miraculous?*

One response to traditional definitions of miracles says all events are miracles, and all of life is miraculous. Albert Einstein explains this approach. "There are only two ways to live your life," says Einstein. "One is as though nothing is a miracle. The other is as though everything is a miracle."[48] He recommends the second way. Paul Tillich argues for the idea that all of life is miraculous when he says, "Being itself is the true miracle, the ongoing act in which God sustains the world."[49]

But saying everything is miraculous faces major problems. First, it doesn't fit either biblical or common views that assume some events are extraordinary and others aren't. To most people, miracles are isolated incidents, not ubiquitous.

There's an even more important problem, and it's moral. Saying all events are miraculous means horrifically evil ones must be miracles too. On this definition, the Nazi Holocaust and the Russian Gulags were miracles, as was every genocide in history. All instances of sexual abuse, deceit, murder, humiliation, and destruction would be miracles if all that happens is miraculous. Saying everything is a miracle risks trivializing evil.

We shouldn't say everything is a miracle.

---

[48] Albert Einstein, quoted in Alice Calaprice, ed., *The Ultimate Quotable Einstein* (Princeton, NJ: Princeton University Press, 2010), 474.

[49] Paul Tillich, *Systematic Theology*, vol. 1 (Chicago: University of Chicago Press, 1951), 282.

## Nothing is Miraculous?

Einstein's other option says, "nothing is a miracle." Given the problems I've outlined of selective miracles, the problem of evil, and scientific obstacles associated with traditional views, it's not surprising that some people of faith deny miracles altogether. Biblical scholar Rudolf Bultmann takes this position when he says, "[The] modern man ... does not acknowledge miracles because they do not fit into his lawful order. When a strange or marvelous accident occurs, he does not rest until he has found a rational cause."[50]

When we can give plausible natural explanations for sensational events traditionally thought to be miraculous, we're tempted to believe miracles never occur. A crying statue of a saint might be thought miraculous, for instance, until a scientist explains condensation. The miraculous exorcism of a person thought demon-possessed can apparently be duplicated with a few pills from the psychiatrist's prescription. And so on. When naturalistic explanations sound more plausible than supernatural ones, it's easy to assume science explains away *all* miracles.

Saying nothing is miraculous faces problems too, however. First, it dismisses the experience many people have that some events in life are extraordinarily and surprisingly good. Saying "nothing is miraculous" flattens life, ignoring the wild and often wonderful diversity of existence.

Second, denying miracles can lead to thinking God isn't active in the world. Despite their many problems, at least traditional claims about miracles support belief in the activity of deity. Extraordinarily good events can remind us of an extraordinarily good Lover.

We don't need deny *all* miracles, but we do need a *plausible* account of them.

## Are Miracles Just in Our Heads?

Another modern option for understanding miracles capitalizes on the fact that we all interpret the world through our own experience. No

---
[50] Rudolf Bultmann, *Jesus Christ and Mythology* (New York: Charles Scribner's Sons, 1958), 37-38.

one knows the full truth of an event or can be certain of the truthfulness of their interpretation. Given this, some say miracles are *entirely* a believer's subjective assessment, irrespective of what actually occurred or what God does. Miracles are just in our heads.

Friedrich Schleiermacher is often cited as advocating this view. He says a miracle "is simply the religious name of an event" that "refers purely to the mental condition of the observer."[51] Edward Schillebeeckx seems to agree: "A miracle is . . . a human experience interpreted as God's salvation."[52] Those who understand omnipotence as meaning God controls all things say "miracle" is simply a label we give some events. But all events are entirely caused by deity.[53]

Admittedly, this view of miracles has advantages. It acknowledges the role interpretation plays for making sense of life. It rejects certainty and avoids claiming that God breaks natural laws. This way of understanding the miraculous also seems to account for why people in some cultures or with certain kinds of personalities seem more inclined to witness miracles.

Saying miracles must be *entirely* a matter of our subjective interpretation presents problems, however. It undermines the realism we need for science, morality, and everyday life. If we claim miracles are just in our heads, perhaps everything else is just in our heads. If reality is whatever we decide it will be, extreme relativism and skepticism arise.

Saying *all* miracles can be *entirely* explained by our subjectivity also dismisses extraordinary events that make an objective difference in the world. Sometimes the sick experience healing unexpectedly, for instance. Sometimes the visually impaired begin to see. Sometimes those pronounced dead on an operating table revive, to everyone's

---

[51] Friedrich Schleiermacher, *On Religion: Speeches to its Cultured Despisers* (New York: Harper and Brothers, 1958), 88.

[52] Edward Schillebeeckx, *Christ: The Christian Experience in the Modern World* (New York: Crossroad, 1980), 220.

[53] Some use the word "occasionalism" for this view, which denies the category of the natural altogether. It says what we consider natural causation is really God producing outcomes without any creaturely contributions. For an advocate of this position, see G. C. Berkouwer, *The Providence of God* (Grand Rapids, MI: Eerdmans, 1952).

surprise. Sometimes cancer disappears without medical explanation. Some events are extraordinarily good, and they rightly prompt us to wonder about the activity of an extraordinarily good God.

We have reason to think we sometimes witness extraordinary and objectively good events.

## A Better Definition of Miracles

To deny miracles altogether means denying an important feature of existence.[54] We can't easily dismiss the vast numbers of people throughout history who say they've witnessed a miracle. Some miracle stories in scripture or told today are likely not historically true, of course, but others likely are. An adequate systematic theology of love should, therefore, account for authentic miracles.

To overcome the problems we encounter with traditional and alternative views of miracles, we need a new and viable definition of miracles. Below I give my simple proposal. Following it, I explain what the definition entails:

> *A miracle is an extraordinary, good event that involves divine and creaturely causation.*

### Miracles are Extraordinary

Instead of saying everything is a miracle, we should reserve the word only for exceptional, unusual, or atypical events. Saying *every* event is a miracle collapses the exceptional into the commonplace. Worse, it risks identifying horrors and holocausts as miracles. Neither mundane moments nor evil events should be seen as miraculous; miracles are extraordinary occurrences.

---

[54] This is a main argument in Craig S. Keener's two volume work, *Miracles: The Credibility of The New Testament Accounts*, vols. 1 & 2 (Grand Rapids, MI: Baker, 2011). See also Paul Alexander, *Signs and Wonders* (San Francisco: Jossey-Bass, 2009); Candy Gunther Brown, *Global Pentecostal and Charismatic Healing* (Oxford: Oxford University Press, 2011); Harold Koenig, *The Healing Power of Faith* (New York: Touchstone, 1999).

We can (and should) believe the Spirit gracefully influences every creature, in every moment, and all creation, all the time. And we can (and should) say the Spirit invites creatures to do what's beautiful, loving, just, and so forth. God's invitations take different forms for different creatures, and they will vary depending on the circumstances. But saying the Spirit is necessarily present to and influencing all creation *doesn't* require us to say that everything occurring is miraculous.

Much of the time, God's influence goes unnoticed or is ignored. This isn't surprising, given that the invisible, universal, and incorporeal Spirit isn't perceptible to our five senses. But sometimes extraordinary events draw our attention to the divine. Some people of faith call them "God moments." But it's not divine influence *alone* that makes an event miraculous, as I'll explain shortly. The work of the Spirit is *part* of the reason some moments are extraordinary.

### *Miracles are Good*

Miracles aren't just extraordinary—they're also good. We sometimes witness unusual events that are awful, horrific, or destructive. I've said evil events, no matter how extraordinary, shouldn't be considered miracles. The slaughter of a village or people group may be extraordinary, but it's not miraculous. Genocides are—thankfully—unusual, but we shouldn't call them "miracles."

A few theologians define miracles with language that suggest they're good and extraordinary.[55] Theologian of the Spirit Amos Yong, for instance, defines miracles as "extraordinary manifestations of the Spirit, events in which God's presence becomes available, tangible, and transformative beyond conventional explanation."[56] Mildred Bangs Wynkoop says "miracles are personal acts of God's self-revealing love,

---

[55] For one of the better concise attempts to define miracles, see David Basinger, "What is a Miracle?" in *The Cambridge Companion to Miracles*, Graham H. Twelftree, ed. (Cambridge: Cambridge University Press, 2011).

[56] Amos Yong, *Renewing Christian Theology* (Waco, TX: Baylor University Press, 2014), 228.

events in which God's presence breaks through human experience in ways that cannot be accounted for by ordinary explanation."[57]

Neither Yong nor Wynkoop go far enough, however. Neither really clarifies the roles God and creation play in the miraculous. Consequently, their definitions are susceptible to the criticisms I've mentioned, namely that the deity they describe does miracles selectively, could prevent evil, suspends natural causes, or can determine outcomes singlehandedly. An adequate definition of miracles should include language that portrays the universal Spirit working *with* creatures and creation in uncontrolling ways.

### Miracles Involve Divine and Creaturely Causation

The final phrase of my definition of a miracle says *both* the Spirit and creatures/creation play a causal role in the miraculous. Miracles are *never* the work of God alone; deity *never* intervenes or invades; the Spirit *never* controls creatures or creation. God can't control, because the universal Spirit's love—even when enacting miracles—is always uncontrolling.

Creatures and creation co-operate with God in diverse ways. But, as I explained earlier, we can divide existence roughly into animate and inanimate.[58] Animate creatures—from cells to squid to sailors—use their agency variously when cooperating with deity in miraculous moments. Inanimate objects in creation don't have agency in the same way. But miracles can happen when large or small aggregate in creation are aligned with, or become conducive to, the miraculous events the Spirit desires.

Generally speaking, what I'll call "agent miracles" involve animate creatures cooperating with the Spirit—from the smallest to the largest,

---

[57] Mildred Bangs Wynkoop, *A Theology of Love* (Kansas City, MO: Beacon Hill Press, 1972), 216.

[58] Some entities have both animate and inanimate dimensions. For instance, many plants have aspects with agency (leaves) but other aspects that are aggregates (inner trunk). Human cyborgs (like me) can have organismic entities and aggregates. For instance, I have inanimate medical devices in my chest and plates in my legs, but most of my body is comprised of animated organisms. I explain these issues in "Love, Society, and Machines," in *Love, Technology, and Theology*, Scott A. Midson, ed. (London: T & T Clark, 2020).

from the tiniest to the grandest. Agent miracles include healings, personal transformations, and the like.

The second type are typical of what many call "nature miracles." They occur when inanimate creation becomes conducive to God's working to enact extraordinary and good events. Examples include parting the Red Sea.

The designations "agent miracles" and "nature miracles" are not hard and fast, of course, since all creatures and all created entities are part of nature. We're all natural. And even inanimate objects are composed of disorganized micro-agents, as I explained in earlier chapters.

My definition easily explains the most common miracles. In those, we see the changed lives of people who shift from living a way of life oriented toward destruction and ill-being to one being oriented toward flourishing and well-being. That's the miracle of salvation, as typically understood. These miracles include synergistic creaturely cooperation with the Spirit.

My definition aligns well with healings too, probably the second most common type of miracles. These extraordinary and good events involve cells, muscles, organs, smaller organisms, and so forth, entities that have a measure of agency to respond. These entities and organisms are influenced by the Spirit and other agents in their environments. The material-mental monism framework I introduced in earlier chapters helps explain how this influence works, because it posits that even the smallest entities have agency and are related to others and God.

Nature miracles are the rarest, but we can explain them too. They occur when the inanimate conditions and/or aggregates of creation are conducive to the Spirit's working for what is extraordinary and good. Nature miracles are rare because the smallest entities and inanimate objects have the least flexibility and, therefore, are the most inclined toward law-like regularity.[59] The greater the complexity and agency in creatures, the greater the possibility of miracles.

Miracles *always* involve both divine and creaturely causes.

---

[59] I have addressed the implications of this definition of the miraculous in other books. See, for instance, Thomas Jay Oord, *The Uncontrolling Love of God: An Open and Relational Account of Providence* (Downers Grove, IL: IVP Academic, 2015), ch. 8; Thomas Jay Oord, *Questions and Answers for God Can't* (Grasmere, ID: SacraSage, 2021), ch. 2.

## What About . . . ?

### *What about Miracles in the Bible?*

My definition of miracles fits the biblical witness well. Most scriptural reports of miracles explicitly mention creaturely factors, actors, and forces. No biblical passages say creatures or forces in creation made absolutely *no* contribution to miraculous outcomes. No scripture verse says God brought about a miraculous outcome by solitary fiat.[60]

Despite our radically different systematic theologies, Reformed theologian Wayne Grudem agrees with my claim that scripture points to creaturely factors and actors in miracles. If miracles are "God working *without means*," says Grudem, this "leaves us with very few if any miracles in the Bible, for it is hard to think of a miracle that came about with no means at all." He specifically identifies healing as involving both God and creation. "Some of the physical properties of the sick person's body were doubtless involved as part of the healing," he says. He sees even nature miracles as involving creaturely causation. "When Jesus multiplied the loaves and fish," says Grudem, "he at least used the original five loaves and two fishes that were there. When he changed water to wine, he used water and made it become wine."[61]

My theology differs from Grudem's in many other ways, however, including when he says God does "100% of the work" in miracles, but creatures also "do 100%." As I said in earlier discussions, I find this view nonsensical, besides being bad math. (See my discussion of divine power in earlier chapters.)

We can make better sense of miracles if we understand them to involve *both* creaturely and divine action, but with *neither* doing 100%

---

[60] In *The God of Miracles*, John Collins admits that biblical writers regard creation as endowed with natural properties and causal powers. He argues that special divine action "goes beyond the natural causal powers of the parties involved" (87). But all of the biblical passages he cites don't require us to think that this power "beyond" natural causes is God determining outcomes unilaterally. See C. John Collins, *The God of Miracles* (Wheaton, IL: Crossway, 2000).

[61] Grudem, *Systematic Theology*, 355-56.

of the work.[62] Saying both the Spirit and creatures contribute to miraculous events, as I do, overcomes the problems I identified with traditional and non-traditional views.

My view doesn't require one to think *every* miracle story true. I doubt every miracle mentioned in the Bible or allegedly occurring today actually happened. Some authors likely told a story to make a theological point or inspire hearers. Some biblical miracles are teaching moments, not historical happenings. And some alleged miracles in the past and today arise from misunderstandings, myths, or fabrications.

We can admit all of this without dismissing miracles outright. But insofar as *some* events are authentic, extraordinary, and good, we rightly call them miracles, because the Spirit and creation collaborated.

## *What About Special Divine Causation?*

In earlier discussions of divine causation, I rejected the claim that God ever controls anyone or anything. I also rejected the idea that the Spirit sometimes works a little harder than at other times. I said instead God always does all God can do in every situation, influencing at full capacity. The universal Spirit in whose nature love comes first will *always* love and *never* control.

Those beliefs about uncontrolling love apply to God's work in miracles, but I also believe the Spirit's action varies moment to moment.[63] Although God constantly loves, the *ways* that deity loves vary depending on the situations and the possibilities. The *fact* that God loves never varies, but *how* deity loves varies occasion to occasion. That's variable divine action.

Extraordinary and good events occur because God worked with what was possible in each situation, empowering and inspiring creatures to do what promotes overall well-being. Although God never sometimes "tries harder," the possibilities for each situation vary, which

---

[62] On this issue in Mark's gospel, see Russ Dean, "Amipotence in the Gospel of Mark," in *Amipotence, vol. 1,* Chris S. Baker, et. al. eds. (Grasmere, ID: SacraSage, 2025).

[63] Andre Rabe questions the meaning of "special" divine action in miracles. See "The Miraculous Nature of Our World," in *Amipotence, vol. 2,* Brandon Brown, et. al., eds. (Grasmere, ID: SacraSage, 2025).

means the Spirit's calls for the best vary. The responses of creatures and the conditions of creation also vary. Something unexpected, atypical, or unusual can occur because the Spirit called creatures to embrace new opportunities for something beautiful, excellent, or valuable.

Because the Spirit knows the past fully and knows all possibilities in the present, God knows which options are most likely to promote overall well-being. Creatures have limited knowledge. This view fits well the words of the writer of the book of Ephesians: "To him who by the power at work within us is able to accomplish abundantly far more than all we can ask or imagine..." (3:20). The "him" to which the author refers is God, but note the passage doesn't say deity does everything. God does more than we imagine, but we can still assume creatures cooperate. This "far more" includes miracles, as I have defined them.

In one sense, divine action varies, because creatures, situations, and possibilities vary. But God always exerts the most loving influence possible.

## What About Blaming the Victim?

Scripture often explicitly mentions creaturely contributions to miracles. After miracles occurred, Jesus sometimes makes statements like, "Your faith has saved and healed you" (Mk. 10:52), "You are now well because of your faith" (Mk. 5:34), or "your faith has made you well" (Lk. 17:19). The cooperative aspect necessary for miracles also comes to the fore when Jesus *can't* do miracles, such as happens in his hometown failures, "because of their lack of faith" (Mt. 13:58).

Although these passages and others clearly support the necessary role of creatures in miracles, they've unfortunately been used to clobber those who've not experienced healing. Saying "you didn't have enough faith" heaps condemnation on the heads of many who suffer. Instead of offering hope, this phrase and others like it blame victims. Many assume that those who suffer lack faith.[64]

---

[64] Joshua Reichard appeals to the logic of amipotence to avoid blaming victims. See "A Call for an Amipotent Pentecostal-Charismatic Renewal," in *Amipotence, vol. 2*, Brandon Brown, et. al., eds. (Grasmere, ID: SacraSage, 2025).

Those who blame victims make a mistake relational metaphysics can fix. Accusers forget that we're relational people in a relational universe, and we don't control our bodies or others. And we're always affected by other actors and factors. We can't control other creatures, our environments, or our bodies, when "control" means determining them as a sufficient cause.

People wanting miraculous healing may in fact cooperate with the Spirit as best they know how. They may trust God's love with full faith. And yet other factors, actors, and forces may oppose the healing both they and the Spirit want. Cells and organisms in our bodies—and agents and forces outside them—may not cooperate with God's healing initiatives. And because the uncontrolling Spirit of love can't control any, healing doesn't occur in these cases. We can't know all the factors at play, so we shouldn't be quick to judge.

Rather than blaming victims, therefore, my definition of miracles points consistently to an amipotent Spirit who wants everyone healed. But miracles require creaturely cooperation or conducive conditions in creation. We should blame neither the cooperating victim nor God when miraculous healing doesn't occur, or when things don't align sufficiently.

For these reasons, we wisely acknowledge the possibility of the miraculous, *while also* using traditional medical options and promising nontraditional ones. We can wisely treat our bodies and environments in ways that increase the overall chances of health and wholeness. In a relational world of multiple actors and forces, shaming and blaming victims have no place when love is the aim.[65]

## Conceptual Confidence

I began this discussion on miracles by noting that some people seem more disposed to witness miracles than others. And I noted that interpretations vary. Skeptics often dismiss claims about miracles, especially

---

[65] I address blaming the victim, miracles, and healing in greater depth in *God Can't: How to Believe in God and Love After Tragedy, Abuse, and Other Evils* (Grasmere, ID: SacraSage, 2019), ch. 3.

when those claims lack verification by recognized authorities. And yet numerous people seem to witness miracles, even some who previously doubted.

My definition of miracles provides conceptual confidence for acknowledging the reality of the miraculous. If miracles occur but we don't have to interpret them as God intervening, suspending the laws of nature, or controlling, the best arguments against miracles lose their force. And this means that even those most skeptical of miracles might decide they can accept some as authentic because those are good and extraordinary events that involve both divine and creaturely causation.

A good definition gives confidence to be believing in miracles.

## God's Will

To conclude my exploration of providence, I look at what people of faith often call "God's will." I argued earlier that the universal Spirit of love empowers and invites creatures to do good in each moment. This empowering and inviting takes various forms, but with the ways of love as primary. My view of providence assumes God has aims for creatures and creation, and those aims involve promoting well-being, justice, beauty, truth, and other values.

Many systematic theologians understand God's "will" in ways that undermine the primacy of the Spirit's uncontrolling love and free creaturely responses. Some say God predestined all events from all eternity, and life plays out in lock-step, from a detailed, preordained blueprint. Because they believe God is the sole cause of whatever happens, they argue all that occurs reflects God's will. To quote John Calvin again, "Nothing happens contrary to [God's] will, even that which is contrary to his will."[66] Of course, what "happens" in life includes sin and evil. For good reason, critics of all-determining predestination doubt that the deity it describes loves perfectly.

Fortunately, a growing number of people of faith now reject predestination, at least as understood by Calvin and his followers. These

---

[66] John Calvin, *The Secret Providence of God*, Paul Helm, ed. (Wheaton, IL: Crossway, 2010), 81.

people typically still think deity is omnipotent, but they think God also gives creatures agency, and they can freely veer away from divine plans.[67] God so conceived could control and suspend the law-like regularities of existence, but they'd say divinity does so only on occasion.[68] But as I've repeatedly indicated, this view implies that every genuinely evil event wasn't important enough for an omnipotent deity to prevent.[69]

Both those who say God determines all things and those who say God only determines some often respond to tragedy by saying, "It must have been God's will." This implies that an omnipotent God either caused or allowed the tragedy. The phrase "It must have been God's will" also implies that physicians who worked tirelessly but unsuccessfully to save a patient must have somehow been acting contrary to the divine will. And the social worker helping people with suicidal ideation would be, when the work proves unsuccessful, opposing God's will.[70]

Many who say God causes, or allows, death also believe God foreknows everything that will occur. But here's the problem: the deity who foreknows but doesn't prevent a physician's or caregiver's futile efforts seems like an evil mastermind who prompts people to make great sacrifices, while yet knowing their efforts will be unsuccessful. If a mistake-free God knows with certainty all that will occur, after all, everything that will occur must already be settled. It can't be otherwise. But as I've said in previous chapters, a settled future is incompatible with creatures freely choosing among live options now.

---

[67] For instance, see Richard A. Muller, *Divine Will and Human Choice* (Grand Rapids, MI: Baker Academic, 2017).

[68] For instance, see William J. Abraham, *Divine Agency and Divine Action* (New York: Oxford University Press, 2021).

[69] Garry Friesen speaks of the will of God but wants to affirm God's detailed sovereignty and foreknowledge but also creaturely free will. See *Decision Making and the Will of God* (New York: Penguin Random House, 2004).

[70] Farhan Shah addresses "self-death" and amipotence in "Amipotence: The Risk of Love and its Existential Response to the Possibility of Self-Death," in *Amipotence, vol. 2*, Brandon Brown, et. al., eds. (Grasmere, ID: SacraSage, 2025).

Intellectual conundrums that arose from affirming divine foreordination and foreknowledge led John Calvin and others to appeal to something they called God's "secret" or "hidden" will. In some mysterious way, they say, God can both command creatures to do good and yet cause them to do evil. "We make a distinction between God's will as it is made known to us in His Word," says Calvin, "and His will as it is hidden in Himself. For God's will is not always made manifest to us, and often He decrees what He forbids us to do."[71]

Note this last line: according to Calvin, God sometimes decrees what God forbids us to do. Here we have convoluted reasoning that is also morally problematic. This statement means God decrees the very sin we're forbidden to do. It also raises the epistemological problem that whatever truths God makes known in "His Word" (be that through the Bible or Jesus) are actually contrary to what God *really* wants.

We make better sense of the idea of God's will if we embrace amipotence. As we've seen, amipotence puts love first and understands divine action in light of it. This means we best understand God's will in the light of love. An amipotent Spirit calls all creatures—small and large—to do what's best, given their abilities, circumstances, histories, and possibilities.[72] The uncontrolling Lover neither predetermines nor foreknows, which means our choices matter as we respond to what we believe to be God's will.

The amipotence approach to providence suggests three ways of talking about God's will.[73] The first way points to God's general will; the second identifies God's specific wills; and the third explores the middle path of seasonal vocations.

---

[71] John Calvin, *Institutes of the Christian Religion*, 2 vols., John T. McNeill, ed., Ford Lewis Battles, trans. (Louisville: Westminster John Knox, 1960), 1.18.3.

[72] Melissa Owens Stewart explores problems with traditional views of God's will and the promise of amipotence in her concise essay, "Good Lord Willing," in *Amipotence, vol. 1*, Chris S. Baker, et. al., eds. (Grasmere, ID: SacraSage, 2025).

[73] Leslie Weatherhead's best-selling book, *The Will of God*, divides God's will into three categories: intentional, circumstantial, and ultimate. My approach has similarities to his, but my denial of omnipotence allows me to avoid the pitfalls of his scheme. See Leslie D. Weatherhead, *The Will of God* (Nashville, TN: Abingdon, 2016 [1944]).

## God's General Will

The oft-repeated phrase in scripture, "love one another," identifies the general will of God.[74] According to Jesus, the first and second greatest commands—to love God and others as ourselves—are also examples of God's general will. We find other references to God's general will in passages that point to the Spirit's general desire for flourishing, justice, compassion, unity, and worship. And it's also God's general will that all shall be saved and come to truth (1 Tim. 2:4).

God's general will is unchanging and applies broadly. The Spirit always wants the common good, in the sense of what's good for each creature and all creation. Deity similarly wants abundant life, blessedness, beauty, healing, and a host of other positive values. Love will always be the Spirit's general will, as God calls us to act intentionally, in relational response, to promote overall well-being.[75]

Some theologians say God's general will is "the good." At first, this seems benign or obvious. Thomas Aquinas, for instance, says God's aim is goodness. But Aquinas then also says that "nothing apart from God is His end," or *telos*, and "He Himself is the end [*telos*] with respect to all things made by Him." By "end," Aquinas means that God's will is the good, which is Godself. According to Aquinas, only deity is immutably good. Consequently, God's general will is, for Aquinas, God's enjoyment of God's own good.[76] Creation's left out.

Those who constructed the Westminster Confession understood God's will similarly. The short version of the Confession says, "The decrees of God are his eternal purpose, according to the counsel of

---

[74] See, for instance, Jn. 13:34–35; 15:12, 17; Rom. 12:10; 13:8; 1 Thess. 3:12; 4:9; 1 Pet. 1:22; 4:8; 1 Jn. 3:11, 23; 4:7, 11–12; 2 Jn. 1:5.

[75] Aimee Allison Hein addresses this in terms of love for the earth. See "Power, Control, and our Failure to Love the Earth," in *Amipotence, vol. 2,* Brandon Brown, et. al., eds. (Grasmere, ID: SacraSage, 2025). E. A. Drew Hensley addresses it in terms of loving nonhuman animals in "Amipotence and Animal Rights," in *Amipotence, vol. 2,* Brandon Brown, et. al., eds. (Grasmere, ID: SacraSage, 2025).

[76] Thomas Aquinas, *Summa Theologiae,* vol. 7, *The Existence and Nature of God,* Timothy McDermott, trans. (Cambridge: Cambridge University Press, 2006), I, q. 44, a. 4, ad 1. Aquinas deals with related questions about God's will in this section of his systematic theology.

his will, whereby, for his own glory, he hath foreordained whatsoever comes to pass."[77] The key phrase is "for his own glory." In this view, God's will is God's glory. This aligns with another well-known passage in the Confession that says, "[Humanity's] chief end is to glorify God, and to enjoy him forever."[78] The point: God's will is God's own glory, and following it means glorifying God. This view allows little to no room for creatures to have agency, dignity, or value in themselves.

Many traditional theologians believe following God's general will means acting for God's glory, because they believe deity must be impassible, immutable, simple, and timeless. But this view ends up portraying God as self-centered rather than others-focused; deity sounds egoistic rather than altruistic. Rather than defining God's will as creatures and God promoting well-being for all, the deity described by many traditional theologians sounds like a self-absorbed narcissist. After all, this God's aim is solely Godself, and God's will is only God's own good.

This systematic theology of love understands God's will much differently. It says God's general will is love, and love always aims to promote *overall* well-being. Rather than a human's "chief end" primarily being God's glory, amipotence-based theology says God's will is what's good for humans, other creatures, creation, and God. God's will is the well-being of all, and our following it means acting for the common good.

God's general will is that we aim to promote overall well-being.

## God's Specific Wills

The second way to talk about the divine will addresses God's specific "wills" for creatures. Notice the plural "wills." In addition to having a general will that never changes, the Spirit has particular wills for creatures in every situation. Those wills change, as the Spirit responds to what occurs and what's possible. Using the language of God's various

---

[77] *Westminster Shorter Catechism*, Q. 7, in *The Westminster Confession of Faith and Catechisms*, rev. ed. (Glasgow: Free Presbyterian, 2003).

[78] Ibid., Q. 1.

specific wills means that the Spirit calls creatures to what's best situation by situation, moment by moment.

God's specific wills arise from the Spirit's care for each entity, creature, person, and community. What deity wants will be tailor made for each. Jesus' words about the Father caring for sparrows illustrate divine care even for the smallest and least. While God never micromanages, in the sense of controlling creatures, God invites and even micro-invites, in the sense of caring for and calling even the smallest entities to flourish.

The open and relational theology of this systematic theology of love provides the crucial framework to make sense of God's specific wills. It portrays a relational and responsive Spirit moving through time into an open future. This deity has specific wills for specific creatures in specific situations, but those wills can change as the situations and creatures themselves change. An amipotent God always loves but also adjusts and recalibrates.

Let's take a classic passage often used to address God's will: "'I know the plans I have for you,' declares the Lord, 'plans to prosper you and not to harm you, plans to give you hope and a future'" (Jer. 29:11). This passage nicely points to God's general will, which, according to the passage, includes prosperity, hope, and a future. But when it mentions "plans" in the plural, it also refers to God's specific wills. The Spirit offers specific plans to fulfill the Spirit's general will.

God's specific wills are the many "plans" the Spirit presents for creaturely consideration. We have a choice how to respond. Depending on how creatures respond to each invitation, deity adapts. When adapting, God continually offers new options, each of which reflects other specific wills. Affirming the dynamism underlying these various wills proves especially crucial when discerning what God wants after we've sinned or been the victim of harm committed by others. God offers a course correction, because the Spirit's specific will adapts as history moves into an open future.[79]

---

[79] John Sanders addresses divine providence well in terms of an open future in *The God Who Risks*, rev. ed. (Downers Grove, IL: InterVarsity, 2007 [1998]). Wayne Grudem offers an example of the incoherent traditional view of God's will *Guidance and the Voice of God* (Grand Rapids: Zondervan, 2003).

This view of the Spirit's will differs drastically from the views of those who say God sovereignly controls creation. Kevin DeYoung describes the controlling view well when he says, "God micromanages our lives. He doesn't just plan out a few of the big ticket items." And this means, says DeYoung, "the most heinous act of evil and injustice ever perpetrated on the earth . . . took place according to God's gracious and predetermined will."[80]

By contrast, amipotence says sin and evil are never God's will or decree. Creatures and creation sin and do evil despite the Spirit calling them to love, beauty, and justice. But when harm happens, God meets us wherever we are and offers a new specific will, given our circumstances. No matter how painful, messy, or tragic, the Spirit calls us to the best, given what's possible in that moment.[81]

When something beautiful emerges from evil, we don't have to say that evil formed some part of a "hidden" divine will (also contrary to Calvin). We can say evil and sin aren't ever God's general will or specific wills for us. But God works in all circumstances to wring something right from what was wrong.

God's specific wills for creatures can, in some moments, be opportunities to do co-creative amazing things and have amazing experiences. Sometimes, the Spirit's specific wills may include the miraculous, the radically life-changing, or major turning points. In other moments, God's specific wills may be simply for us to survive a rotten relationship or horrific situation. The Spirit sometimes invites us to endure suffering that can't be stopped or pain that's relentless. Most often, the Spirit's specific wills are fairly mundane, as we do the best we can in the trenches of everyday living. God's specific wills for creatures vary widely, because life varies widely.[82]

Because life changes, the Spirit's specific wills change, as God calls us to do what's best, given what's possible.

---

[80] Kevin DeYoung, *Just Do Something* (Chicago: Moody, 2009), 18. In DeYoung's view, Jesus' crucifixion is the worst evil and injustice. But his view entails that all other sins, evils, and injustices are part of God's sovereign will.

[81] Brandon Ambrosino addresses this well in *Is It God's Will?* (New York: Morehouse, 2025).

[82] Richard Rice offers one of the earlier open theists explanations of this in Richard Rice, *God's Foreknowledge and Man's Free Will* (Eugene, OR: Wipf & Stock Publishers, 2004 [1985]).

## Vocations

Between the general will of God, which remains unchangeable, and God's specific wills, which change moment to moment, we find particular vocations. "Vocation" is another word for "calling," but I'm using it specifically to describe ongoing but not everlasting roles the Spirit might invite us to embrace for ourselves. The vocations God might call us to embrace will align with the Spirit's general will, and they emerge as creatures respond well or poorly to God's specific wills. Vocations can be defined as particular roles we take on, then, for shorter or longer periods of time.

Take marriage as an example. God's general will that we love takes various forms, and those forms may or may not include marriage. The Spirit has specific wills for us in each moment, including the moment we might stand before a potential marriage partner pondering whether to say "yes" to a proposal or affirm "I do" as a wedding vow. But seeing marriage as a vocation asks whether we should be wed at all. And wise ones will explore a host of factors when discerning whether this vocation might be something to which the Spirit might call them.

Or take the question of whether to stay in a job or find a new employment. Or the question of whether to become a resident of another community or stay where we're at. Or maybe there's the question of whether we should adopt a child and, thereby, become a parent (or a parent of more children). Or whether we should considering taking up a position in an organization, a new sport, or hobby. And so on.

We take on vocations like the ones I've mentioned for a season. The season may be short or last nearly a lifetime. For instance, helping an aging parent can be seen as a vocation that may last days, months, or years. Professional careers usually last for a season, whether short-term or long. Even allegiance to groups, organizations, and nation-states are temporary.

When considering possible vocations, it helps to believe the Spirit doesn't control us. God hasn't predestined and doesn't even foreknow what roles we will choose. God doesn't have what Calvinists call a "decretive will," which R. C. Sproul defines as "that will by which God decrees things to come to pass according to His supreme sovereignty."[83] By this, Sproul and others mean God alone sometimes decides what will "come to pass," without any creaturely input. According to this view, vocations would be determined by a deity's decretive will, which logically entails that anything sinister we encounter in that vocation must also be from God.

An open and relational view of God's will takes into account the Spirit's urging, the current situation, and what's possible. This means creatures assess what God may want by drawing from the past, evaluating the present, and speculating about possible futures.[84] Discerning God's will for our vocations typically involves exploring our interests and gifts, our resources and what brings us joy.

In this, we can be oriented by God's general will—which remains that we live lives of love—and by the Spirit's specific wills, which can vary moment by moment. We have genuine choices even in vocational roles.[85] No matter what we decide, the Spirit continues to call us to what's best in each moment, in light of what we've decided and what's best overall.

A key question remains, of course: How can we ever *know* God's will? This might mean wondering what the Spirit wants in this particular moment. Or wondering, What vocation might God be drawing me to take on? Or how can we know God's general aim remains the well-being of all—others, us, creation, and God alike? Answering these questions directs us to consider divine revelation and human interpretation. The second volume of this systematic theology of love begins with those important questions.

In sum, the Spirit inspires us to embrace vocations that, while temporary, express love. And we have freedom within those vocations

---

[83] R. C. Sproul, *Can I Know God's Will?* (Orlando, FL: Reformation Trust, 2012), 9.

[84] Bruce Epperly offers an accessible open and relational exploration of God's will and alternative to Rick Warren's *Purpose-Driven Life* book in *Holy Adventure* (Nashville, TN: Upper Room, 2008).

[85] Robert D. Cornwall explores spiritual gifts in the church in *Unfettered Spirit* (Gonzalez, FL: Energion, 2021).

## Conclusion

The problem of good arises because it's difficult, if not impossible, to account well for the good we witness without appealing to a transcendent Source of goodness. Attempts to reduce goodness to evolutionary advantage or personal preference fail to account for how we actually live every day. We all presuppose a transcendent Measure by which we make value judgments, because we all think some events better or worse than others.

A theistic metaphysics serves as the best explanation for transcendent goodness. Among theistic metaphysical options, the best will claim a universal Spirit of love both prompts creatures to do good and has an immutable nature as the Source of goodness. Rejecting both nihilism and divine omnipotence, but embracing an amipotent God, solves both the problem of good and the problem of evil

Many have understood miracles as events an omnipotent deity caused singlehandedly by intervening or interrupting natural processes. But this view generates serious theological and philosophical problems, especially the problem of selective miracles. The traditional view of miracles also intensifies the problem of evil and stands at odds with scientific explanations. Those who respond to these problems by either saying "everything is miraculous" or claiming all miracles must be fake *both* fail to account for life in all its diversity.

Miracles are better defined as extraordinary, good events that involve both divine and creaturely causation. Miracles aren't ever evil, they're not mundane, and they don't occur through God's action alone. This view accounts for biblical miracles, but avoids blaming victims, as well as preserving scientific integrity by affirming natural causation alongside divine influence.

Traditional accounts of God's will typically portray deity as omnipotent, foreknowing, impassible, and self-oriented. But upholding these traditional accounts while saying tragedies and sin "must be God's will" undermines divine love and creaturely moral responsibility. Instead, we should understand God's will in light of an amipotent and relational Spirit who never controls and isn't primarily interested in receiving glory.

With an uncontrolling love framework in place, we can understand God's will in three interrelated ways: the Spirit has a general will, specific wills, and calls us to vocations. God's general will is always that we promote overall well-being for others, ourselves, creation, and God. God's specific wills, however, vary moment by moment as the Spirit responds creatively to changing situations, always calling creatures to what's best, given what's possible. Vocations are ongoing but seasonal callings, such as marriage, caregiving, or employment. When we understand God's will in one or all of these ways, we become empowered to affirm the Spirit's consistent love, emphasize creaturely action, and see the divine will as involving dynamic, relational invitations to promote flourishing.

An adequate systematic theology prioritizes love in all facets of providence.

# Conclusion to Volume One

At various points in this book, I've admitted to being uncertain God exists. This includes being unsure of the particular ideas or doctrines I have proposed throughout. I could be mostly or entirely wrong about God; but I also could be right . . . at least closer to right than alternative theologies. I'm not certain.

In this volume, I've worked hard to be rationally consistent and coherent. I've drawn repeatedly from experience, both my own and the experiences of others, including voices quite different from me. Sometimes, I've criticized both traditional theologians and atheists for *failing* to align their claims with widespread experience. I've argued that my proposals—even the novel ones—match the broad themes of Christian scripture, although I admit to affirming some biblical ideas over others when discrepancies arise. I also believe my ideas can inspire readers to be more loving, although I'll offer stronger arguments for this claim in the third volume.

The next volume of this systematic theology of love begins with questions of epistemology and how we might know God. I address questions about divine revelation in general and the particular revelation in Jesus of Nazareth. I address both the widespread propensity to sin and individual sins. The second volume also explores salvation and sanctification in light of love.

At the heart of all these endeavors is my conviction that an adequate systematic theology prioritizes love above *all* and integrates love in every doctrine.

# About the Author

Thomas Jay Oord, Ph.D., is a theologian, philosopher, and scholar of multidisciplinary studies. Oord directs the Center for Open and Relational Theology and doctoral students at Northwind Theological Seminary. He is an award-winning and bestselling author who has written or edited more than forty books. A gifted speaker, Oord lectures at universities, conferences, churches, seminaries, and institutions. A world-renown theologian, Oord is also known for his research in science and religion, open and relational theology, the problem of suffering, advocating for queer people, and the implications of freedom for transformational relationships.

For more information, see Dr. Oord's website:
**thomasjayoord.com**

For more on the doctoral programs Dr. Oord directs, see
**northwindseminary.org/center-for-open-relational-theology**

For the Center for Open and Relational Theology Dr. Oord directs, see
**c4ort.com**

For more writing from Thomas Jay Oord, see his Amazon account and Substack
**thomasjayoord759927.substack.com**

# Acknowledgements

*I* have so many to thank for their help with this project. I especially appreciate the following people . . .

Bob Abbey, Rebecca Adams, Art Alexander, Don Allen, Joshua Andrews, Archedon, Maria Arroyave, Jay Atkinson, Philip Averay, John Augustine,

Trevor Bachofner, Chad Bahl, Rob Bailey, Chris Baker, Karen Baker-Fletcher, Colin Barnes, Tom Baynham, Karen Bellamy, Ezrica Bennett, Jonathan Bentley, Craig Bergland, Jennifer Bertoni, Alan Besherse, Charles Bledsoe, Don Boehm, Bill Bond, Steve Boorsma, Donna Bowman, Tim Bowman, Vince Brackett, Alan Bradley, Mike Branch, Michael Brennan, Rod Bristol, Brandon Brown, Gayle Hansen Browne, Steven Bruening, Tim Burnette,

Cliff Cain, Ronald Caldwell, Gary Campbell, Kevin Campbell, Peter Campbell, Anna Case-Winters, Joe Cash, J. Randolph Clark, Timothy Clifford, Monica Coleman, Sean Coleman, Karson Collins, Colin Connor, Gary Corbett, Bob Cornwall, Teila Creekmore, Alan Crews, Simon Cross,

John Dally, Ulrick Dam, Lance David, Andrew M. Davis, Russ Dean, Rod Deaton, Ilia Delio, Steven Denler, Nancy DeStefano, Laura Dion, Teri Ditslear, Tom Donaldson, Pauline Doty, Terry Doyle, Don Drew, Adis Duderija, Charley Earp, Mike Edwards, Garret Ellison, Brendan Engen, Jacob Erickson, Julia Enxing, Thomas Estes,

Brian Felushko, Paul Fiddes, Chris Fisher, Missy Greenleaf Flinn, Allen Fletcher, Alex Forrester, Jonathan Foster, Christi Franklin, Margaret Frantz, Jenny Fujita, Tripp Fuller,

Shane Gabbert, George Gaffga, James Galloway, Tom Gates, Benjamin Geeding, Buddy Gharring, Janna Gonwa, Ricardo Gouvea, Rex Gray, Chelsea Gregoire, Cathi and Dan Gross, Johannes Grossl, Daniel Guy,

Lance Hand, Caden Handran, Chris Hanson, Judy Haralson, Patrick Harmon, Doug Hardy, Patrick Harmon, Rick Harrell, Britt Hartley, Stephen Hasper, Doral Hayes, Dan Held, Alan Helmstetter, Drew Hensley, Thomas Hermans-Webster, Dana Hicks, Jody Hill, Wm. Curtis Holtzen, Gary Hoover, Scott Duncan Hopkins, Nancy Howell, Tim Hudson, Josh Hughes, Greg Hughson, Libby and Jeremy Hugus, Tore Hummelvoll, Charles Hunter, Rob Hutchinson, MaryBeth Ingram,

Greg Janese, Winston Janusz, Chip Johnson, Marshall Johnson, Lisa Jones, Tomasz Józefowicz, Michael Jung, Catherine Keller, Robert Bruce Kelsey, Shaleen Kendrick, Brad Kent, Dan Kidder, Joel Kienkentveld, Sheri Kling, Neil Koppy, Martha Korienek, Alfred Kracher, Andrew Kramer,

Molly LaCroix, Michael Lambros, Sarah Lancaster, Sarah LaRose, Carlton Larsen, Lina Langby, Scott Lederman, Elizabeth Lee, Darl Leman, Jon Carl Lewis, Chris Lilley, Michael Lodahl, Allan Love, Greg Love, Robert Luhn, Dale Lykins,

Richard Mallory, David Margiotta, Lucas Martins, Joel Mathew, Jay McDaniel, Alexandra McGee, Jim McLachlan, Brian McLaren, Tomi McLellan, Sharon McQueary, Mark Meeks, Mason Mennenga, L. Michaels, Alex Middleton-Laing, Tim Miller, Shannon Mimbs, Connie Miroslaw, Bev Mitchell, Roger Haydon Mitchell, Guy Moore, Mary Elizabeth Moore, TC Moore, Jean Mornard, David Morris, Mochel Morris, Hilde Marie Movafagh, RT Mullins,

Tamara Newell, Caleb Norris, Eleanor O'Donnell, Alexa Oord, Amanda Oster, Steve Otteson, Barrett Owen, Tori Owens, Elaine Padilla, Michael Page, Jim Palmer, Josh Patterson, Larry Payne, Ken Pepin, Donn Peters, Izzy Phoenix, Kris Pierson, John Pohl, Nick Polk, Darrell Poeppelmeyer, Jerry Pollard, Robert & Linda Pritchett, John Pruitt, Jory Pryor, Elizabeth Quellette,

Andre Rabe, Janel Apps Ramsey, Amy Rasmussen, Karen Reaume, Clint Redwood, Cody Reeder, Richard Edward Reich, Tom Reinehr, Bruce Reisdorph, Barbara A. Renton, Rick Reynolds, Min Yong Ro, Rob Robayna, A. K. Roberts, Austin Roberts, Michael Rose, Robert Rotz, Richard Routledge, Rodger Rushing, Kyle Russell, Shawn Ryan,

*Acknowledgements*

John Sanders, Clinton Sanford, Manuel Schmid, Wilbert Schremp, Andrew Schwartz, Connie Seifert, Eric Sentell, Peter Shaw, Jennifer Secki Shields, Aaron Shileny, Eleanor Siebert, Eric Siebert, John Sinkey, Karen Sites, Anne Smith, Christian Smith, Bethany Sollereder, Michele Snyder, Stephen Spence, Stuart Sprague, Andy Stanton-Henry, Fran Stedman, Heidemarie Steltz, Charles E Stephan, Phillip T Stephens, Paul Stevens, Melissa Owens Stewart, David Surbaugh, Jon Paul Sydnor,

Tim Tahtinen, Taz, Brad Thibodeaux, Betsy T. Thigpen, Bob Timmer, Ian Todd, Sally Todd, Steve Tollefson, Johan Tredoux, Jason Tripp, Bill Trueblood, Tracy Tucker, Mark Umstot, Charles Varner, Don Viney, Laura Virginia,

Greg Wack, Stewart Walker, Bryson Wallace, Donna Fiser Ward, Keith Ward, Shane Watson, Steve Watson, Bill Watts, Gil Webster, Jeff Wells, Tara Wernsing, Clarence White, Merrill Williams, Stephen Williamson, Deirdre Willis, Barbara A.T. Wilson, Anthony Windau, Karen Winslow, Gilbert Yow Onn Wong, Carolyn McCarter Wood, Randy Woodley, Bill Yarchin, Bethanie Young, Deanna Young, Travis Young, Julie Zdenek, Marisha Zeffer, Anita Zurbrugg

I'm especially grateful to Rebecca Adams, Chuck Stephan, and Bill Watts for their detailed editing of the chapters.

Finally, I'm most grateful for my best friend and life-partner, Cheryl.

# Index

Abraham, William, 416
Adams, Graham, 69
Adams, Robert, 252, 320
Adiprasetya, Joas, 352
African theology, 20-21, 219-20
agape, 7, 71-72, 192, 305
aggregate organisms, 340-42
Al-Ghazali, 44
Albes, Rubem, 249
Albright, William, 141
Alexander, Paul, 407
Alexander, Richard, 391
almighty, 70, 141
Alter, Robert, 141
Althaus-Reid, Marcella, 13
Altizer, Thomas, 245
Alvis, Jason, 122
Ambrosino, Brandon, 12, 47, 421
amipotence, 163-83, 396-97
   definition, 164-66
   divine ability, 172-73
   divine influence, 173-75
   maximal power, 166-68
   puts love first, 168-70
   relational power, 166
analogy of being, 92, 112-13, 171, 196, 251-52, 269, 312-13, 351-52
Anderson, Laura, 57
Andrews, Dave, 201
animate organisms, 340-42
annihilation, 327
Anselm of Canterbury, 45, 167, 187-89

anthropomorphism, 116, 244-45
anthropophobism, 244
antitheodicy, 360
Anzalone, David, 16
apophatic theology, 240-46, 249-51
Applegate, Kathryn, 258
Aquino, Maria, 12
Archer, Kenneth, 90
Arendt, Hannah, 8
arguments against the existence of God, 46-50, 55-57
   ambiguous revelation, 48-49
   problem of evil, 46-48
   theological inconsistencies, 49-50
arguments for the existence of God, 35-57
   abduction, 51-52
   beauty, 43-44
   biblical witness, 36-38
   design and order, 42-43
   first cause, 44
   general revelation, 41-42
   meaning and love, 51-52
   ontological, 45-46
   personal experience, 39-40
   tradition, 38-39
   values, 44-45, 57, 394-96
Aristotle, 117, 127, 189, 198, 346

Arminian theology, 322-23
Arminius, Jacob, 78, 80, 167, 322
arts, 54
Artson, Bradley, 90, 130
Atkins, Charles, 75
Augustine, 7-9, 27, 71, 96, 112, 121, 127-28, 138-40, 154, 167, 212-18, 232-33, 235, 238, 260, 281, 342, 361-63, 365, 377, 403
Aulen, Gustaf, 166
Avis, Paul, 72
Axelrod, Robert, 390

Baggini, Julian, 325
Bahai, 4
Bahl, Chad, 30, 38, 40, 147, 159, 230, 329, 353, 361, 401
Baker-Fletcher, Karen, 14, 188
Baker, Chris, 19, 371
Baker, Matthew, 57
Baker, Vaughn, 235
Baldwin, Jennifer, 23
Barbour, Ian, 96
Barr, Beth Allison, 197
Barrett, Justin, 38
Barrigar, Christian, 153, 325
Barrow, John, 285, 306-07
Barth, Karl, 10, 64, 67, 112-13, 134, 181-83, 239, 280-81, 303, 343
Bartholomew, David, 343
Basilides, 268-69

Basinger, David, 30, 137, 150, 401, 408
Basinger, Randall, 401
Bauckham, Richard, 264
Bauman, Whitney, 273
Bavinck, Herman, 324
Bayman, Henry, 4
Beardslee, William, 121, 247
Becker, John, 239
Bediako, Kwame, 89
being-itself, 116-22
Bennett, Ezrica, 179
Benton, Matthew, 337
Berdyaev, Nikolai, 113
Bergson, Henri, 129, 350
Berkouwer, G. C., 406
Berkowitz, Aaron, 130
Berra, Michael, 188
Betcher, Sharon, 89, 173
Bevere, Allan, 246
Bhakti, 221
Biale, David, 142
Bible,
    diversity, 80-82
    errors, 37-38
Big Bang, 259, 283-85, 306-08, 309
biology, 328, 343, 390-93
Blenkinsopp, Joseph, 262
Boff, Leonardo, 166
Bonhoeffer, Dietrich, 189
Bonting, Sjoerd, 273
Borg, Marcus, 89
Bowler, Kate, 375
Bowman, Donna, 130, 181, 183
Bowne, Borden, 128-29
Boyd, Craig, 72, 397
Boyd, Gregory, 19, 37, 75
Bradley, F. H., 129
Bradley, James, 343
Brady, Bernard, 5
Bray, Gerald, 4-6
Brennan, Michael, 159
Brierley, Michael, 347, 351

Brightman, Edgar, 178, 193, 195
Brock, Rita Nakashima, 15, 72
Brooke, John Hedley, 321, 343, 365
Brown, Brandon, 69
Brown, Candy Gunther, 399, 407
Brown, Joshua, 399
Brown, Willliam, 101, 261-62, 299
Brueggeman, Walter, 149, 190, 302
Bruening, Steven, 124, 264
Brummer, Vincent, 26, 66
Brüntrup, Godehard, 338-40, 350-51
Buber, Martin, 120
Buch-Hansen, Gitte, 100
Buchanan, John, 70
Bulgakov, Sergei, 113
Bultmann, Rudolf, 405
Burnette, Timothy, 130
Burns, Charlene, 131
Burridge, Richard, 18
Burrow, Rufus, 133
Burrus, Virginia, 72

Cahoone, Lawrence, 286
Cain, Clifford, 361
Callen, Barry, 16, 69, 250
Calvin, John, 217, 239, 322-23, 342, 415, 417, 421
Camp, Michael, 22
Cannon, Katie, 197
Caputo, John, 63, 134, 149, 220, 248
Carmichael, Liz, 73
Case-Winters, Anna, 137, 145, 156-57, 202, 324
Case, Brendan, 215
certainty, 243
chance and randomness, 342-44

Charnock, Stephen, 139, 199
Chartier, Gary, 22, 252, 334
Cherry, Natalia, 19
Chicka, Benjamin, 118
Chilcote, Paul, 322
Childs, Brevard, 124, 261
Chilton, Bruce, 20
Christ, Carol, 200
Clark, Kelly James, 167, 189
Clarke, Adam, 400, 403
Clarke, Randolf, 325
classical theism, 118, 154, 232, 269, 283
Clayton, Philip, 25, 94, 121, 177, 195, 216, 258, 271, 324, 332, 334, 347, 349-51, 392
climate change, 12, 32, 274, 334, 402
Cobb, John, v, 19, 28, 67, 69, 106, 131, 176, 189, 206, 250, 281-82
coercion, 70-71
coeternal universe, 309
Coleman, Monica, 49, 131, 197, 375
Collins, Francis, 328
Collins, John, 411
Collins, Kenneth, 16, 69
Collins, Robin, 285
combination problem, 339
compatibilism, 139, 145, 223, 323-34, 326
concursus, 326
Cone, James, 13, 204, 373
Conradie, Ernst, 274
Cooper, John, 348
Copan, Paul, 262, 306
Cornwall, Robert, 423
Cottrell, Jack, 167, 359
covenant, 191, 301-02
Crabtree, J. A., 139
Craig, William Lane, 44, 220, 262, 273, 306

# Index

Crawford, Edwin, 35
creatio ex amore, 282-83
creatio ex christi, 279-81
creatio ex creatione sempiternalis en amore, 292-306, 308, 314-15, 377-79
   biblical support, 297-306
   six "m" words for the Ever Creator, 295-97
creatio ex dei, 279-81
creatio ex materia, 277-78, 310
creatio ex nihilo, 259-74
   alternatives, 275-83
   problems, 271-74
creatio ex potentia, 280-81
creation myths, 276-77
creation through emanation, 278-79
creation through violence, 275-76
creaturely co-creators, 326-27
Cremer, Hermann, 182
Crofford, Gregory, 69
Cross, Frank Moore, 141-42
Cross, Simon, 51
Cullmann, Oscar, 217
Culp, John, 274, 332, 347, 373
cyclic universe, 307-08

Dally, John Wesley, 149
Daly, Mary, 197
Davies, Oliver, 125, 201
Davies, Paul, 285, 308
Davis, Andrew, 84, 129, 334, 350, 394-95
Davison, Andrew, 348
Dawkins, Richard, 35, 391-92
Dean, Russ, 47, 174, 412
Deane-Drummond, Celia, 397

death of God, 245
deconstruction, 22-23, 48
deep incarnation, 103
Delio, Ilia, 78, 94, 153, 166, 328, 332
Deloria, Vine, 88
demiurge, 277
den op Bouw, Rik, 47
DeRolf, Annie, 71
Derrida, Jacques, 63, 125, 134, 242
determinism, 323
Deutsch, Eliot, 88
DeWaal, Franz, 392
deWeese, Garry, 372
deYoung, Kevin, 421
dipolar theism, 206
disability, 12, 173
Distefano, Matthew, 22
divine causation, 189
divine control, 55
divine empathy, 373-74
divine hiddenness, 48-49, 56 58, 104, 138, 151, 158-59, 161, 167, 177, 358
divine punishment, 382-84
divine risk model, 227
Dodds, Michael, 324
Dolezal, James, 167, 233
Dombrowski, Daniel, 39, 65, 107, 165, 206
Dorner, Isaak, 189
Downey, Martha, 22
Drees, Willem, 242
dualism, 336
Duderija, Adis, 4, 75
Dufourmantelle, Anne, 227
Dugatkin, Lee, 390
Dunn, James, 74, 101
Dunning, Ray, 16, 188
Durant, Will, 107

Eastern church, 133, 263-64
Eastman, Timothy, 216, 338

ecology concerns, 334
Edwards, Jonathan, 22, 152, 359
Edwards, Rem, 80
Ehrman, Bart, 366-68
Eichrodt, Walther, 142
Eiesland, Nancy, 173
Einstein, Albert, 404
Ekstrom, Laura, 325
Eldridge, Niles, 328
Ellis, George, 284-85, 287, 307-08
emergence, 331-32, 339, 343
enchantment, 341
Engberg-Pedersen, Troels, 100
Enns, Peter, 22
Enuma Elish, 275-76
Enxing, Julia, 129, 131, 176
Epperly, Bruce, 106, 130, 163, 194, 374, 423
Erickson, Millard, 15, 74, 76-77, 99, 244, 267-68, 282
eros, 72-73, 192, 304
eternal objects, 130-31, 223, 346, 394
eternal vs. everlasting, 220
Evans, James, 13, 158
evil, 46-47, 106, 138, 157-58, 271-72, 344, 358, 363-65, 375, 377, 385
   natural evil, 332, 333, 372, 373
   (see also "problem of evil")
evolution, 57, 153, 159, 259, 328-30, 343, 378
evolutionary psychology, 391
experiential nonnegotiable, 213, 216, 221, 323, 339, 364-65, 391
Eze, Michael Onyebuchi, 21

Faber, Roland, 49, 130-31, 248
Fackenthal, Jeremy, 248
faith healers, 402
Farley, Edward, 202
Farmer, Patricia Adams, 43
Farrer, Austin, 166
Farris, Joshua, 335
Fee, Gordon, 101, 400
Feldman, Liane, 261
Feldmeir, Mark, 102
Felushko, Brian, 4
Fergusson, David, 49, 320
Ferre, Frederick, 334
Ferre, Nels, 166
Feuerbach, Ludwig, 248
Fiddes, Paul, 68, 79, 149, 188, 202, 283
fine-tuning, 285-86
finite and infinite, 246-47
First Nations people, 341-42
Fisher, Christopher, 222
Fitch, David, 160
Fleischer, Matthew, 75
Flescher, Andrew, 392
Flew, Antony, 285
Florensky, Pavel, 113
Ford, Lewis, 247
foreknowledge, 225
forgiveness, 73, 370-71
Forrester, Alex, 13
Foster, Jonathan, 20, 22, 157, 159
Frame, John, 55
Fredrickson, Barbara, 27
freedom, 68, 322-26
  origin of, 328-32
  genuine but limited freedom, 26, 221-26, 322-26
Fretheim, Terence, 17, 80, 101, 104, 146, 148, 190, 192, 199, 217, 261, 263, 299, 300, 350, 385

friendship, 54
Friesen, Garry, 416
Frohm, Erich, 26
Fuller, Tripp, 19, 22, 48, 77, 292
Fung, JoJo, 88
Funkhowser, Eric, 165
Furnish, Victor Paul, 18

Gale, Herbert, 252
Garte, Sy, 285, 328
general revelation, 41-42
Genesis 1, 260-63, 267-68
genetic determinism, 390-91
Ghiselin, Michael, 391-92
Giberson, Karl, 285, 320, 328
gino-theology, 132-34
Givens, Terryl and Fiona, 202
Glueck, Nelson, 301
gnosticism, 268-70
Gnuse, Robert, 231
Göcke, Benedikt, 119, 121, 156, 160, 165, 246
God,
  all-knowing, 221-24
  amipotent, 163-83
  anger, 202-04
  as future, 130
  as nonrelational, 186-88
  as relational, 188-92
  aseity, 233, 311
  becoming, 111-35
  being, 111-35
  beyond being, 122-25
  compassion, 75-76, 191, 201, 219
  covenants, 228
  creator, 263-68, 291-317, 312-14, 326-27
  divine will, 415-23
  empathy, 203-04
  entangled, 349-50

essence-experience binate, 205-08, 373
essential and contingent, 82-83, 127-28, 151, 233-34
essential relations, 208-09, 350
essentially loves, 22
Ever Creator, 291-317
everlasting, 218-21
experiencing, 348
feels, 225-26
feels emotions, 200-04
foreknowledge, 222-24, 416, 417
freedom, 78-80, 119-20, 181-83, 228-30, 270, 313-14
gives freedom and agency, 329-32
glory, 15-16, 260, 418-19
grace, 16, 74-75
healer, 374-75, 410-11
holiness, 21-22, 245-46
I am, 124
immaterial, 96-102, 195-96
immutable, 198-200, 205
incomprehensible, 121, 124
incorporeal, 105-08, 151, 179-81, 195-98, 266-67
independent, 83, 311-12
infinite, 121, 246-47
intervening, 353, 403-04
justice, 76-78
knowledge, 203-04, 225-28
language about, 63-64, 125-26
light, 224-25
love, 61-85

# Index

love isn't God, 67-68
loves the least of these, 332-34
mercy, 74-76, 205
mighty deeds, 147-50
nonbinary, 196-98
omnipotent, 137-84
passible, 188-90
personal, 79-80, 112-16, 120, 126-27, 129-31, 193-96
power, 396-97
punishing, 76, 203-04
rational, 194-95, 201
repenting, 199
requires cooperation, 148-49, 376-77, 409-12
right-sized, 251-53
risk-taking, 226-27
self-limited, 140, 175-79
self-love, 182-83
simplicity, 230-34
soul of the universe, 352
sovereignty, 14-16
speaking, 265-67
spirit, 111-136
suffering, 375
time, 213-221
transcendence, 121, 244-46, 314-15, 350-51
transcendent standard for goodness, 390-96
trusts, 227-28
uncontrolling love, 371-73
uncreated, 315-16
union with, 353
unity, 230-34
universal mind, 395
universal, omnipresent, 102-105, 180-81, 193-94
unloving, 80-81
vagueness, 249-51

wholly other, 245
wisdom, 224-25
worship, 84-85, 90-91, 207-08
God is love, 64-68
God of the philosophers, 128
God's will, 415-23
    decretive will, 422-23
    general will, 418-19
    hidden, 417, 421
    plans, 420-21
    specific wills, 419-21
    vocations, 422-23
Goff, Philip, 98, 285, 337
Goldingay, John, 190, 217, 302
Goldstein, Jonathan, 264-65
Gonwa, Janna, 72
Good, Edwin, 262
Gordon, Gabriel, 37
Goroncy, Jason, 320
Gould, Stephen Jay, 328
Gouvea, Ricardo, 69
Greenberg, Irving, 104
Greene, Paul Joseph, 75
Gregersen, Niels, 103
Grenz, Stanley, 16, 244
Griffin, David Ray, 31, 38, 46, 65, 84, 98, 129, 131, 137, 176, 179, 204, 216, 221, 249, 282, 323, 329, 331, 336-37, 341, 353, 358, 363, 378, 394, 401
Grim, Patrick, 223
Grudem, Wayne, 37, 145, 148, 171, 238, 258, 260, 400, 411, 420
Gunter, Christy, 71
Gupta, Nijay, 6
Gushee, David, 159
Gutiérrez, Gustavo, 12, 65

Habermas, Jürgen, 221
Hafer, Abby, 43

Hamilton, Adam, 373
Hamilton, Heather, 22
Hammond, Geordan, 322
han, 373
Hanson, Chris, 16, 72
Harper, Steve, 69, 159
Harris, Mark, 258
Harris, Tambry, 364
Harrison, Peter, 36
Hart, David Bentley, 118, 167, 311
Hartley, Brittney, 278, 391
Hartshorne, Charles, 45, 84, 107, 129, 131, 152, 176, 179, 180, 199-200, 206, 216, 347, 351
Hasker, William, 30, 42, 152, 165, 233, 325, 361
Hauerwas, Stanley, 11-12
Haught, John, 153, 328, 336
Hayes, Doral, 85
Hayward, Beth, 158
healing, 148
Hector, Kevin, 24
Hefner, Philip, 297, 326, 365
Hegel, G. W. F., 129
Heidegger, Martin, 112, 115, 125, 128
Heidelberg Catechism, 342, 352
Hein, Aimee, 418
Held, Shai, 4, 17, 185, 302
hell, 5
Helm, Paul, 167
Helseth, Paul, 139
Helwa, A. , 4
Henning, Brian, 397
henotheism, 231
Henry, Carl, 199
Hensley, Drew, 418
Heraclitus, 129
Heschel, Abraham, 104, 185, 190, 198
hesed, 17, 300-03
Hewitt, Simon, 194

Hick, John, 151, 153, 359
Hicks, Dana, 22
Hill, Matthew, 153
Hill, Preston, 173
Hoard, Billie, 21
Hoard, Paul, 21
Hocking, W. E., 129
Hodge, Charles, 96, 399-400
Holland, Richard, 219
Hollingsworth, Andrea, 89
Holtzen, Wm. Curtis, 93, 225, 227-28
Hoover, Jon, 292
Howell, Nancy, 49, 107, 161, 197, 339
Hronich, Andrew, 402
Hubler, James, 268
Hugus, Libby Tedder, 140
Hume, David, 403
Hunt, Mary, 73
Hyers, Conrad, 276

Iammarino, Darren, 109, 208
idealism, 335
imago dei, 114
Inbody, Tyron, 326
indeterminacy, 331
indigenous people, 341-342
infinite, 116, 121, 135, 160, 165, 239, 246-48, 286-87, 289, 293, 298, 310-11, 315
infinite universe, 310-12
intrinsic value, 73
Irenaeus, 269
Isasi-Díaz, Ada Maria, 89
Islam, 4, 29, 44, 75, 88, 186, 221, 259

Jackson, Olivia, 22
Jackson, Timothy, 64
Jacober, Amy, 173
Jacobson, Rolf, 302

Jaglom, Henry, 305
James, William, 52, 55, 139
Jantzen, Grace, 107
Janzen, Gerald, 142
Jeanrond, Werner, 6-7, 27, 72
Jersak, Brad, 19, 191
Jesus, 6, 11, 18-19, 23-24, 27, 32, 51, 62, 67, 70, 73, 75-77, 90-93, 99, 105, 112-13, 124, 142, 146-51, 160, 182, 191-92, 201, 219, 224, 227, 231, 253, 327, 333, 365-67, 370, 376, 389, 405, 411, 413, 417-18, 420-21
Johns, Cheryl Bridges, 400
Johnson, Elizabeth, 13, 89, 131
Johnston, Kenny, 97
Jonas, Hans, 338
Jones, Caleb, 51
Jones, Major, 195
Jones, Serene, 23
Jüngel, Eberhard, 62, 113, 134, 168-69, 182, 234, 244, 280
justice, 28, 76-78

Kagame, Alexis, 21
kalam argument, 44, 306
Kamsler, Harold, 301
Kane, Robert, 325
Kant, Immanuel, 45-46
Kärkkäinen, Veli-Matti, 13
Karris, Mark, 48
Kassa, Augustin, 20
Kaur, Valerie, 4
Kearney, Richard, 124, 248
Keefe-Perry, Callid, 248
Keener, Craig, 407
Kelle, Brad, 17

Keller, Catherine, 13, 26, 72, 111, 130, 188, 240, 248, 274-75, 281, 299
Kendrick, Shaleen, 31
kenosis, 46, 146, 149, 151, 153, 160, 283
Kent, Brad, 61
Keuss, Jeffery, 153, 325
Kilner, John, 114
Kim, Grace Ji-Sun, 47, 49, 88
Kim, Jaegwon, 339
King Jr., Martin Luther, 133, 170, 178, 195, 397
Kittle, Simon, 133, 152-53, 324
Kling, Sheri, 94, 106
Knapp, Steven, 195, 271
Knierim, Rolf, 262
Koenig, Harold, 407
Koperski, Jeffrey, 344
Korpman, Matthew, 81
Krainer, Franz, 121
Krause, Karl Christian Friedrich, 347
Krawelitzki, Judith, 148-49
Krenshaw, James, 366
Küng, Hans, 36
Kushner, Harold, 84, 368
Kyung, Chung Hyun, 89

Ladd, Elden, 217
Lambros, Ryan, 374
Lancaster, Sarah, 178, 197
Langby, Lina, 84, 108, 311
Laplace, 381
Larue, Gerald, 301
Latter-Day Saints, 231, 278
law-like regularities, 344-47
laws of nature, 344-47
Lee, Jung, 189
Lee, Matthew, 28
Leidenhag, Joanna, 331, 337, 352

*Index* 441

Lepojärvi, Jason, 7
Levenson, Jon, 17, 191, 260-62, 270, 301
Levinas, Emmanuel, 122, 125
Levison, Jack, 92
Lewis, C. S., 7
liberation theology, 322, 375, 376, 402
libertarian free will, 25, 324-26
Liesendahl, Jason, 47
Lightsey, Pamela, 159
Lilley, Chris, 138, 154
Lindbeck, George, 122
Lindberg, Carter, 5
Linde, Andrei, 284
Lobel, Diana, 395
Lockhart-Rusch, Lakisha, 249
Lodahl, Michael, v, vi, 69, 90, 92, 221, 246, 270, 274, 282-83, 390
Long, Stephen, 401
Loomer, Bernard, 166
Loppnow, John, 71
love,
    biblical, 6-7
    definition, 7-9, 24-28
    emotions, 26-27
    flourishing, 23-24
    freedom, 25, 78-80
    intellectually rigorous, 10-11
    intentional action, 24-25
    Jesus, 18-20
    liberation, 12
    love and systems, 9-10
    meanings, 5-7
    motives, 25
    necessary, 78-80
    overall well-being, 27-28
    permissive, 11-12
    pluriform, 71-73
    relationships, 20-22, 25-26
    religious institutions, 22-24
    scripture, 17-20
    self-giving, others-empowering, 68-69
    sentimental, 10-11
    uncontrolling, 69-71
Love, Gregory Anderson, 75
Lubarsky, Sandra, 84
Lucas, George, 216
Lucretius, 277
Luhn, Robert, 75, 87
Luther, Martin, 149, 399
Lyell, Charles, 331

Maccabees, 263
Macallan, Brian, 353
Mack, Burton, 224
Macquarrie, John, 95, 115, 117, 128
Maddox, Randy, 16, 64, 69
Maimonides, Moses, 188, 260
Manchester, Eric, 130
Manichaeism, 380
Marcion, 269
Margulis, Lynn, 340
Marion, Jean-Luc, 122-25
Markham, Ian, 36, 335
Marshall, Lon, 71
Mary, mother of Jesus, 146
material-mental monism, 98-102, 195-96, 203-04, 335-42, 351-52, 354, 380-81
materialism, 335-36
Matthews, Stephanie, 17
Mawson, T.J., 62, 230, 327
May, Gerhard, 265, 268
Mbiti, John, 220
McCall, Bradford, 94, 165, 328
McCall, Thomas, 170, 322
McClindon, James, 23
McConnaughey, Janyne, 23
McCormick, Steve, 201, 239
McDaniel, Jay, 88, 94, 129-30, 238
McDonald, Lee Martin, 4
McDougall, Joy, 280
McFague, Sallie, 90, 107
McFarland, Ian, 270
McGrath, Alister, 41, 149, 321
McGrath, James, 23
McKnight, Scot, 18
McLachlan, James, 56
McLaren, Brian, 23, 48
McLaughlin, Ryan, 79, 230
McLellan, Dan, 260
Meilander, Gilbert, 73
Mele, Alfred, 25
Mercadante, Linda, 23
Merkle, John, 302
Mesle, Robert, 129, 359
metaphysical assumptions, 115
metaphysics, 125, 127-29, 135, 209, 268, 287-88, 393-94, 414
Michaels, L. , 71
Middleton, Richard, 17, 81, 147, 207, 283, 299-300, 366
Midson, Scott, 341, 409
Migliore, Daniel, 149, 166
Milbank, John, 127
Miller, Patrick, 142
Miller, Tim, 48, 159
Mimbs, Shannon, 374
miracles, 148, 397-415
    agent miracles, 409-10
    blaming the victim, 413-14
    conceptual confidence, 414-15

miracles (*continued*)
    definition, 399-400, 407-10
    everything miraculous, 404
    false miracles, 412
    in our heads, 405-06
    nature miracles, 410
    nothing miraculous, 405
    problem of evil, 402
    problem of scientific explanation, 403-04
    problem of selective miracles, 401
    special divine causation, 412-13
Mirsadri, Saida, 221, 259
Mitchel, Patrick, 17
Mitchell, Bev, 328
Mitchell, Roger Haydon, 159
Moberly, R. W. L., 199
Moltmann, Jürgen, 46, 71, 89, 130-31, 189, 202, 279-81, 283, 304, 352
monotheism, 231
Montgomery, Brint, 188-89
Moore, Mary Elizabeth, 322, 334
moral arc of the universe, 397
moral responsibility, 323-24
Morison, John, 214
Morowitz, Harold, 331
Morriston, Wes, 151, 157, 165
Moser, Paul, 159, 191
Most Moved Mover, 198
Muller, Richard, 416
Mullins, R. T., 20, 27, 82, 154, 156, 189, 200, 204, 213, 215, 217, 220, 224, 232-34, 273, 292, 348

multiverse, 286-88
Mumford, Stephen, 278
Murdoch, Iris, 393
Murphy, Nancey, 285
Murphy, Roland, 224
music, 53-54
mystery, 160, 237-52
    defensive mystery, 238-40
    humble mystery, 242-44
    utter mystery, 240-42
mysticism, 23, 39, 51, 100, 241

Nancarrow, Paul, 106
Nash, Ronald, 152
natural theology, 41-44, 57
Nelson, Susan, 373
Neusner, Jacob, 20
Neville, Robert, 129
Newlands, George, 22, 166, 252-53
Nietzsche, Friedrich, 47, 308, 391
nihilism, 391
Nikkel, David, 331
Noble, Thomas, 113
nonhumans, 193
Nussbaum, Martha, 26, 201
Nygren, Anders, 67, 71

O'Connor, Timothy, 233-34, 325
O'Donnell, Eleanor, 175, 252
occasionalism, 406
Ogden, Schubert, 220
olam, 302-03
Olson, Roger, 152, 244, 322
Olthuis, James, 283
omnipotence, 270
    creaturely freedom, 153
    definition, 139-40, 155-56, 360-61

divine ability, 172-73
divine influence, 173-75
impossibilities for God, 145
maximal power, 156
not in scripture, 141-47
power units and pies, 170-72
qualified, 139-40, 150-55
the harm of, 157-61
zero sum, 170-71
onto-theology, 112-22, 126-28
ontology, 334-42
Oomen, Palmyre, 70
open future, 30-31, 229
open and relational theology, 28-31, 420, 421, 423
open theism, 30, 42, 95, 176, 180, 222-23, 225, 361, 377, 421
Oredein, Oluwatomisin Olayinka, 249
Origen, 4, 268, 298
Osborne, Catherine, 72
Ostler, Blake, 264, 268
Ottati, Douglas, 24, 40, 54, 242, 266
Otto, Rudolf, 245
Overall, Christine, 401

Padgett, Alan, 220
Padilla, Elaine, 72, 193
Padmanabha, Swami, 4, 88, 221
Page, Ben, 193
Page, Ruth, 294
Paige, Terence, 101
Palmer, Jim, 23
panentheism, 103, 107, 340, 347-51
panexperientialism, 336
Panikkar, Raimon, 350
panpsychism, 337

Index 443

pantheism, 67, 102, 107, 117, 194, 245, 247, 270, 279-80, 288, 311, 347, 349
pantokrator, 142-44
Park, Andrew Sung, 373
Park, Song-Mi, 17
Park, Theodore, 397
Parker, Rebecca, 15
participation in God, 117, 132, 148, 348
Pascal, 11-12
Patterson, Joshua, 134
Pattison, George, 125
Peacocke, Arthur, 131, 347, 349
Pearce, Kenneth, 160
Peckham, John, 79, 177
Pederson, Ann, 228
Peirce, C. S., 129
Penprase, Bryan, 277
Penrose, Roger, 307
people of color, 12-14
perfect being theology, 45-46, 199-200
Perrin, David, 122
personal idealism, 195
personalism, 133-34
Perzsyk, Ken, 119
Peters, Ted, 171
Peterson, Brent, 207
Peterson, Gregory, 348
Peterson, Michael, 42, 46
Pharaoh's hardened heart, 146
philia, 73, 192, 305
Phillips, J. V., 250
photography, 54
Pink, Arthur, 139
Pinnock, Clark, 30, 90, 167, 171, 189, 198, 250, 259-60
Plantinga, Alvin, 45, 130, 150-53, 233-34, 359-60
Platinus, 125, 278-79
Plato, 96, 265, 277, 394-95
Platonic metaphysics, 393

pneumatology, 87-109
Pohl, John, 339
political theology, 159
Polk, David, 5, 166
Polkinghorne, John, 42, 46, 96, 176-77, 283, 321, 337, 343-44, 372
polytheism, 231
Pool, Jeff, 189, 202
possibilities, 325
Post, Stephen G., 4, 12, 20, 72
postcolonial, 13-14, 375
Potts, Matthew, 73
Pounds, Austin, 154, 272
Powell, Samuel, 27
predestination, 5, 221, 415–417
Pregeant, Russell, 18, 242
presentism, 220
prevenient grace, 69
primary and secondary causes, 259, 324, 352
problem of evil, 138, 157-58, 270, 271-72, 357-85
    apocalypticism, 367-68
    crucifixion of Jesus, 369-70
    defining evil, 361-65
    divine punishment, 366
    empathetic dimension, 373-74
    events, 363-64
    evidential, 361
    genuine evil, 364-65, 367, 384, 385
    greater good, 361, 367, 369
    lament, 382-85
    logical, 359-60
    natural consequence, 366-67
    origin, 377-79
    pedagogy, 359, 375-76
    privation, 361-63, 365

scripture, 365-71
    synergistic dimension, 376-77
    therapeutic dimension, 374-75
    uncontrolling dimension, 371-73
problem of good, 389-97
progressive Christianity, 51
providence, 319-422
public knowledge, 223
Pugh, Jeffrey, 326
Pugliese, Marc, 239
punctuated equilibria, 328
Putt, Sharon Baker, 31, 75

quantum physics, 343
queer, 12-13, 159, 196-98

Rabe, Andre, 129, 299, 412
racism, 158
Radhakrishnan, Sarvepalli, 88
radical theology, 104, 112, 134
Rahner, Karl, 238
Rambo, Shelly, 23
Ramose, Mogobe, 21
Ramsey, Janelle Apps, 197, 203
Randall, Rory, 95
Randall, Vikki, 179-80
Rasmussen, Joshua, 46
Rauser, Randall, 51
Ray, Janet Kellogg, 328
Rea, Michael, 159
Reddish, Tim, 47, 193
Reformed evangelical tradition, 13-14
Reich, Robert Edward, 107
Reichard, Joshua, 90, 166, 413
Reichel, Hanna, 14
Reid, Thomas, 323
relational, 29-30

Remenyi, Matthias, 47
Remington, Ryan, 342
Rescher, Nicholas, 216
Reynolds, Blair, 90
Rhoda, Alan, 176, 223, 377
Rice, Richard, 30, 180, 311, 421
Richardson, Ian, 143
Ricoeur, Paul, 252
Ritchie, Sarah Lane, 337-38
Robertson, Paul, 101
Robinette, Brian, 270
Rose, Michael, 349
Rowe, William, 229, 313
Royce, Josiah, 129
Rubenstein, Mary-Jane, 102, 279, 286-87, 292, 298, 349
Rubenstein, Richard, 104
Ruether, Rosemary, 13, 197
Rundel, Tom, 399
Runehov, Anne, 201
Russell, Helene, 49, 197, 203
Russell, Robert John, 119
Ruther, Rosemary, 197

Saarinen, Risto, 69
sabaoth, 142-44
Sakenfeld, Katherine, 301
salvation, 27-28
Sanders, John, 16, 30, 189, 212, 221, 226-27, 364, 378, 420
Sandlin, Mark, 51
Sandoval, Lemuel, 69
Sarna, Nahum, 141
Sartre, Jean-Paul, 128
Schafer, Lothar, 335
Schellenberg, J. L. , 159
Schillebeeckx, Edward, 406
Schleiermacher, Friedrich, 24, 40, 55, 406
Schmid, Manuel, 225
Schmidt, Brent, 74

Schnekloth, Clint, 51
Schutz, Paul, 66
Schwartz, Wm. Andrew, 334, 340, 350
science of creation, 283-88, 306-08
Segall, Matthew, 108, 294
Seibert, Eric, 6, 75, 81
Seneca, 75
Sentell, Eric, 164, 223
sex, 53, 268
shaddai, 141-44
Shah, Farhan, 186, 416
*shalom*, 342
Shaw, Pete, 359
Shaw, Susan, 47, 49
Shields, George, 131, 206
Shults, LaRon, 33, 89, 166
Siepert, Glenn, 23
Sikh, 4
Simmons, Aaron, 51
Sina, Ibn, 279
Sirvent, Roberto, 93
skeptical theism, 160, 241, 360, 396-97
Smart, Ninian, 88
Smith, Dustin, 224
Smith, James K. A., 27
Smith, Joseph, 278
Smith, Mark, 231
Smith, Olav Bryant, 139
Smollin, Lee, 345
smooth emergence, 331-32
Sober, Elliot, 390
Sollereder, Bethany, 159, 332
Solovyov, Vladimir, 113
Sonderegger, Katherine, 13, 234, 238
Sorokin, Pitirim, 12
Soughers, Tara, 198
Southgate, Christopher, 332
Sovik, Atle, 158
special revelation, 41-42
Spencer, Scott, 191

Spinoza, Baruch, 107
spirit,
 biblical references, 91-92
 gravity, 94
 living, 95
 mental-material, 98-102
 mind, 93-94
 wind or breath, 92-93
spiritual senses, 97
Spitzer, Toba, 221
Spohn, William, 19
Spong, John Shelby, 17
Sponheim, Paul, 18, 70, 166, 169
sports, 53
Sproul, R. C. , 342, 422-23
Stanglin, Keith, 322
Steinhardt, Paul, 284, 287, 307-08
Stenger, Victor, 306-07
Stewart, Melissa Owens, 417
Stone, Bryan, 67
Strawn, Brent, 17, 190, 192, 199
Strong, Douglas, 329
Stump, James, 258
Suchocki, Marjorie, 13, 31, 90
supernatural, 353
Swanson, Dwight, 143
Swinburne, Richard, 153, 156, 220, 222, 233, 344
Swinton, John, 173
Sydnor, Jon Paul, 31, 79, 198, 298, 387
synergy, 148, 304, 376
systematic theology, 5, 62
systemic evil, 381

Taliaferro, Charles, 151, 335
Tammeus, Bill, 248
Tanner, Kathryn, 166
Tapp, Christian, 119, 121, 156, 160, 165, 246

*Index* 445

Taylor, Charles, 36
Taymiyya, Ibn, 292
Tegmark, Max, 284
Teilhard de Chardin, Pierre, 94, 129, 337, 350
Teresa of Avila, 107
Thandeka, 26
Thatamanil, John, 207
the Devil and demons, 379-81
the Given, 178
theistic evolution, 258
theodicy, 366
theoenpanism, 103, 351-53
theological method, 31-32
Theophilus, 143
theopoetics, 248-49
Thiemann, Ronald, 36
Thiessen, Matthew, 100
Thistleton, Anthony, 101
Thomas a Kempis, 97, 217
Thompson, Richard, 37
Thompson, Samantha, 362
Thorsen, Don, 322
Tillich, Paul, 26, 115-122, 131-33, 167, 193, 238, 404
time, 213-221
Timpe, Kevin, 173, 325
Tipler, Frank, 285
Todd, Patrick, 153
Toner, Jules, 7
Torbitzky, Nichole, 77, 179
Torrance, Alan, 352
Torry, Malcolm, 66
Tracy, David, 242
Trakakis, Nick, 151
transcendence and immanence, 244-46
Tredoux, Johann, 69
Trelstad, Marit, 281
Trenkel, Michael, 69
Trible, Phyllis, 197
trinity, 21, 64, 67, 71, 83, 90, 127, 169, 193, 198, 208-09, 231, 260, 280, 302-03

Tripp, Jason, 6
Trivers, Robert, 390
Tsumura, David, 261
Tucker, Tracy, 158
Tupemahu, Ekaputra, 158, 375
Turney, Nat, 23
Turok, Neil, 284, 287, 307-08
Tutu, Desmond, 21

ultimate concern, 117-18
Umstot, Mark, 180, 296
Unger, Roberto, 345
uniformitarianism, 331

Vacek, Edward, 7
Vail, Eric, 261
van Beveren, David, 47
van den Brink, Gijsbert, 137, 141, 145, 147, 155
van Inwagen, Peter, 324
van Till, Howard, 403
VanderWeele, Tyler, 20
Vanhooser, Kevin, 253, 303
Vicens, Leigh, 153
Vick, Todd, 23
Vickers, Jason, 322
Viney, Donald Wayne, 131, 137, 176, 206
Von Balthasar, Hans, 166

Walker, Theodore, 105
Wallace, Mark, 63, 252
Wallace, Paul, 328
Walters, James, 25, 216, 324
Waltke, Bruce, 262
Walton, John, 101, 262, 276
Ward, Keith, 85, 93, 120, 133, 185, 191, 195, 245-46, 250, 285, 311, 334-35, 389-90, 393
Ward, Thomas, 223
Warren, Janet, 146
Warren, Rick, 423

Waters, Mark, 360
Watson, Steve, 13-14, 327
Wattles, Jeffrey, 12
Watts, Isaac, 74
wave function collapse, 343
Weatherhead, Leslie, 417
Webb, Stephen, 279
Wegter-McNelly, Kirk, 349
Weil, Simone, 94
Weippert, Manfred, 143
Welker, Michael, 90
Welles, Orson, 305
Wells, Jeff, 71, 179, 353
Wesley, John, v, 16, 64-65, 69, 80, 84, 97, 104, 152, 226, 245-46, 322, 329, 352
Wesleyan quadrilateral, 149
Wessling, Jordan, 252, 283, 295, 305
Westermann, Claus, 261
Westminster Confession, 15, 418-19
Wheeler, Demian, 53
White, Clarence, 25, 271
Whitehead, Alfred North, 10, 39, 65, 70, 85, 98, 117, 129-30, 176-79, 183, 194, 204, 206, 216, 249, 287-88, 315-16, 330, 336, 338, 345-46, 394-97
wild mare analogy, 312-13
Wildman, Wesley, 40, 177
Wiles, Maurice, 402
Willems, Curt, 191
Williams, Andrew, 250
Williams, Daniel Day, v, 25, 189, 252
Williams, Dolores, 13
Wilson, Brittany, 196
Wilson, David, 390
Wilson, Douglas, 228
Wilson, E. O., 390
Winslow, Karen, 144, 189, 197
Wirzba, Norman, 283

Wolsey, Roger, 165
Wolterstorff, Nicholas, 189, 220, 233
womanist, 14, 89, 375
Woodley, Randy, 88, 158, 342, 375
world as God's body, 107-108, 179-81
worship, 54, 314-15
Worthen, Daniel, 392
Wreen, Michael, 150
Wright, Jacob, 4
Wright, N. T., 19, 352, 358, 368-371, 376, 379
Wright, Robert, 392
Wykstra, Stephen, 160
Wynkoop, Mildred Bangs, v, 4, 69, 246, 408-09

Yang, Eric, 97
Yong, Amos, v, 13, 28, 88-90, 349, 403, 408-09
Young Earth creationism, 258
Young, Deanna, 70, 75, 180
Young, Frances, 262
Young, James Travis, 147
Youngs, Samuel, 280

Zahnd, Brian, 19, 70, 169
Zbaraschuk, Michael, 105, 245, 274
Zimmerman, Dean, 42, 220
Zoroastrianism, 380

**OTHER BOOKS FROM**
Thomas Jay Oord...

# THOMAS JAY OORD

# Pluriform Love

AN OPEN AND RELATIONAL
THEOLOGY OF WELL-BEING

# The Death of Omnipotence and Birth of Amipotence

Thomas Jay Oord

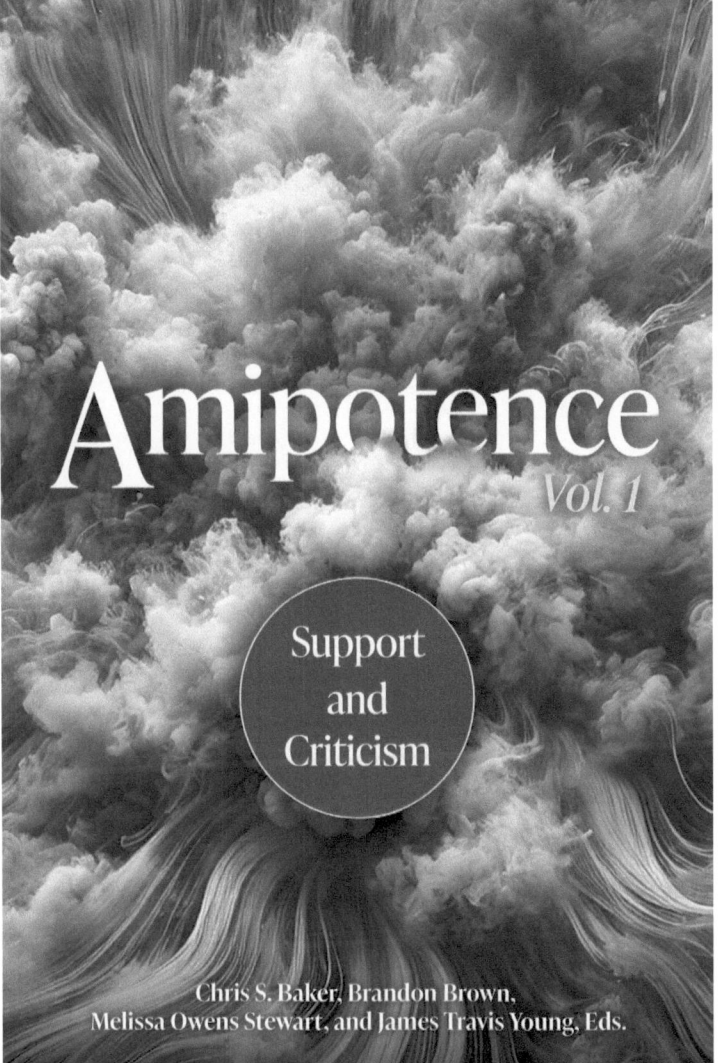

# OPEN AND RELATIONAL THEOLOGY

## AN INTRODUCTION TO LIFE-CHANGING IDEAS

### THOMAS JAY OORD

Best Seller

# GOD CAN'T

HOW TO BELIEVE IN GOD
AND LOVE
AFTER TRAGEDY,
ABUSE, AND OTHER EVILS

## THOMAS JAY OORD

Author of the Award-Winning Book, *The Uncontrolling Love of God*

www.ingramcontent.com/pod-product-compliance
Ingram Content Group UK Ltd.
Pitfield, Milton Keynes, MK11 3LW, UK
UKHW041903230426
12049UKWH00002B/27